Masculine Landscapes

*Walt Whitman
and the
Homoerotic
Text*

Byrne R. S. Fone

*Southern Illinois University Press
Carbondale and Edwardsville*

Copyright © 1992 by the Board of Trustees,
Southern Illinois University
All rights reserved
Printed in the United States of America
Edited by Jill Butler
Designed by Christopher Bucci
Production supervised by Natalia Nadraga

95 94 93 92   4 3 2 1

Library of Congress Cataloging-in-Publication Data

Fone, Byrne R. S.
Masculine landscapes: Walt Whitman and the
homoerotic text / Byrne R. S. Fone.
p.   cm.
Includes bibliographical references and index.
1. Whitman, Walt, 1819–1892—Criticism and interpretation.
2. Homosexuality and literature—United States—History—19th
century. 3. Erotic literature, American—History and criticism.
4. Masculinity (Psychology) in literature. 5. Desire in literature.
6. Men in literature. I. Title.
PS3242.H56F66   1992
811'.3—dc20   91-31153
ISBN 0-8093-1761-3   CIP

This book is for all my students
from whom I learn so much.

And as always it is for Alain.

Contents

Preface   ix
Primary References   xiii

1. Introduction: Before Homosexuality   1
2. Words Unsaid   10
3. Man's Words   20
4. The Fountains of Love: Poetry and
      Fiction, 1838–1850   36
5. Fierce Wrestler: Notebooks, 1845–1854   63
6. Masculine Landscapes: "The Sleepers" and
      "Song of Myself," 1855   115
7. Brethren and Lovers   205
8. Epilogue: The Path Ahead   261

Notes   267
Works Cited   295
Index   301

Preface

Among the voices in Whitman's lines, there is a hidden voice that I have tried to hear and on which I report in this book. I take that image of hidden voices from a text on the super-title screen at the Paris Opera, during a performance of Luciano Berio's *Un Re In Ascolto,* with a libretto by Berio and Italo Calvino. I was reminded then of Foucault's comments about the silence of texts and also of Whitman's observation that writing may be powerfully understood "by what you leave unsaid more than by what you say." I had that day completed this book and that night, listening to Berio's opera, which in time and space and effect seemed to have little to do with what I had been devoting nearly two years of my life to finishing, there was given as a gift that perfect text with which to begin this book, perfect because it so precisely described my purpose, which was to listen to and translate the erotic voices, both hidden and evident, in Whitman's texts and to try to discern also the message of the silences that so enhance that remarkable voice, those remarkable voices.

In this book there are also hidden voices, and it is the purpose of this note to acknowledge them. Professor Floyd Stovall and Professor Gay Wilson Allen quickened in the first instance and supported in the other my early interest in Whitman. My colleague Professor Arthur Golden of the City College of the City University of New York exemplified the standard of admirable and elegant scholarship to which all who write about Whitman are indebted. Professor Saul Brody, also of the City College of New York, has been an unfailing friend and a wise counselor in so many things beyond the scope of scholarship. When we talked about this book, he was generous and helpful in his response and, as always, provided fascinating insights about that more distant time in which we both delight, he as an erudite and discriminating scholar, I as an amateur. He supported me when my doubts were grave, perhaps even when he did not know that I doubted. I value him. Professor Cecilia Macheski, that best of all friends, listened and sustained, sharing her discoveries in the landscape of women's studies, which she is so richly charting, and often guiding me along those paths when I did not know the way. Our conversations and our silences are rich and among my most valued treasures.

Professor Valden Madsen of Brooklyn College, whose own researches in American Studies have enriched my perceptions, and William Rose, who gave me quiet times to talk or not, occupy a special place founded on affection and long friendship, which I want to tell them here if I have not before. Tomm Eaton, Jennifer Kermath, Robert Winge, and Frank Faulkner, dear friends, have all provided safe havens and much laughter and intimacy. Though they have all heard probably quite enough about this book, I hope they will enjoy it more when they know how much they helped me with it. There is a special place in this company for George Jurgsatis and Robert Barnes. George knew how to listen and knew even better when to talk and make me listen. I can never say how much his support, patience, and friendship means to me. Jeremiah Rusconi helped me to escape from the web of voices and turn instead to rich prospects of pure and exciting seeing. Our wanderings together in worlds of which he is so superbly master and which he so wonderfully invokes were the tonic I needed to be able to return to words when I thought I had had enough of them. My esteem for Thomas Hall, though of a different order, is just as strong. He may not think I know it, but he too is very much a part of this book, and often when I talked to him, I could better hear myself. Richard Hall already knows that I value and love him. His calm voice has in many ways changed my life. I also admire him for what he is: an insightful critic, a superb writer, a dear friend. To Gabriel de la Portilla, student, poet, earnest scholar, friend, I will say that this book is filled with the result of his thoughtful reading, incisive questions, and very special and wise conversations in which much was revealed. At the begining of his great career, I am delighted to warmly greet him. My students, to whom I dedicate this book, are the source of it all, since their illuminating response to Whitman provided the fertile soil in which my ideas could grow.

To Curtis Clark, acquisitions editor at the press, whose comments and encouragement have been of immeasurable aid, to Carol Burns, the project editor, with whom I have had many valuable conversations and whose guiding hand has led this book into production, and to Jill Butler, whose sharp-eyed copyediting caught, and whose careful hand corrected, my errors, I can only offer the thanks any author gives to those who save him from disaster.

At the last, ever first, there is Alain Pioton, who without complaint shared me with Whitman, but who must now be as glad to see Walt go as he is glad to have me return, as glad as I am to return to him. His patience, forebearance, and strength sustained me then as they do now. My secret words to him he already knows, and that is sufficient.

Primary References

All references to "Song of Myself" (1855) are from Malcolm Cowley, ed., *"Leaves of Grass": The First (1855) Edition,* New York: Viking, 1959. In all cases references to "Song of Myself" are to the untitled first poem of the first edition. Line citations in the text are indicated when necessary by the abbreviation *SM* and the line number.

Citations from *Calamus* drawn from Fredson Bowers, ed., *Whitman's Manuscripts: Leaves of Grass (1860),* Chicago: Chicago University Press, 1955, are cited in text as Bowers. All other citations from *Calamus* are identified by the numbering of the 1860 edition.

All other citations of Whitman's work are included in the text under the following abbreviations.

Citations from Gay Wilson Allen et al., eds., *The Collected Writings of Walt Whitman,* New York: New York University Press, 1961–84:

Corr   Edwin Haviland Miller, ed. *The Correspondence.* 6 vols. 1961–77.

DBN   William White, ed. *Daybooks and Notebooks.* 3 vols. 1978.

EPF   Thomas L. Brasher, ed. *The Early Poems and Fiction.* 1963.

LG Var   Sculley Bradley, Harold W. Blodgett, Arthur Golden, William White, eds. *Leaves of Grass: A Textual Variorum of the Printed Poems, 3 vols. 1980.*

NUPM   Edward F. Grier, ed. *Notebooks and Unpublished Manuscripts.* 6 vols. 1984.

PW   Floyd Stovall, ed. *Prose Works 1892.* 2 vols. 1963–64.

Citations from sources other than Allen et al.:

Bradley   Sculley Bradley and Harold W. Blodgett, eds. *Leaves of Grass.* New York: W. W. Norton, 1973.

Cowley   Malcolm Cowley, ed. *"Leaves of Grass": The First (1855) Edition.* New York: Viking, 1959.

Trigg   Oscar Lovell Trigg. "Variorum Readings of Leaves of Grass," in *Leaves of Grass,* ed. Emory Holloway, Inclusive Edition. New York: Doubleday, Doran, 1928.

1

Introduction

Before Homosexuality

Listener up there! . . . what have you to confide to me?
                                    — "Song of Myself," 1855

Walt Whitman had written most of his "homosexual" text well before the coinage of the word in 1869 and before the arrival of the moment in 1870 at which Foucault so famously sites the birth of the homosexual species—a species that Whitman had by then spent nearly three decades identifying, locating their habitations within the masculine landscapes he had been so passionately constructing.[1] Before homosexuality and before homosexuals, Whitman had insistently, inquisitively, and persistently asked questions about a love that did not speak its name only because it had none. In 1841 he wondered about "young beings, strangers, who seem to touch the fountains of our love, and draw forth their swelling waters" (EPF 74 n. 23). In 1856 he more pointedly and passionately asked: "Why be there men I meet . . . that while they are with me, the sunlight of Paradise . . . expands my blood . . . that when they leave me the pennants of joy sink flat and lank. . . . and though we may never meet . . . again, we know . . . that we two have . . . exchanged the . . . mysterious unspoken password . . . and . . . are thence free . . . comers to . . . each other's . . . most interior love?" (*DBN* 3:764–65). By 1860, in *Calamus* 1, he asked no more questions but instead decided to tell the "secret of my nights and days." Not many now doubt what secret was concealed within the "substantial life" that Whitman determined to reveal when he proceeded to write, for "all who are or have been young men," the greatest of America's homoerotic texts.

Few readers now are unwilling to affirm the presence of some sort of homoeroticism in the text, not only in the *Calamus* poems of 1860, but in *Leaves of Grass* (1855). Nor is there any longer much debate about the question of Whitman's homosexuality. If it has not yet been proved by the location of a biographical fact that might substantiate what he may have "done," and with what man, at least few would argue about the appropriate association of "Whitman" and "homosexual." In this essay I have no interest in nor do I intend to search for that as yet undiscovered biographical fact, to ask what and who, in an attempt to document Whitman's homosexuality or to demonstrate in the general (and unexamined) sense that he was homosexual. This does not seem to me to be a useful question. Questions more interesting than those that try to prove or disprove Whitman's homosexuality are those that speak to the specific nature and the larger resonances of those textual elements Jacob Stockinger so suggestively described as "homotextual."[2] More intriguing questions concern the paths—and the obstacles thereupon—that Whitman took to the site where he could celebrate this substantial life and sing his manly songs. By 1860 his journey had led him to the banks of the Calamus pond. I will try to identify and map the untrodden paths he took to get to that sacred place and to show what masculine landscapes he discovered, traversed, and recorded, in order to be born into the new life that, as he so profoundly observed, contains all the rest.

Whitman urged that literature ought to be "the courageous wrestle with live subjects—the strong gymnasia of the mind" and asserted that "poems are to arouse the reason, suggest, give freedom, strength, muscle, candor to the person who reads them—and assist that person to see the realities for himself in his own way, with his own individuality and after his own fashion" (*NUPM* 4:1561, 1563). Whitman recognized that poems have many "realities." The particular reality with which I would like to wrestle is that of the consequences that homosexual desire had for Whitman's text. I am not interested in looking between the sheets so that, finding them stained, I might shout "Eureka!" I will ask instead, to use David Halperin's general phrase in my own specific context, "how the significance of same-sex sexual contact has been variously constructed over time by members of human living groups."[3] The member of a human living group I am most concerned about is obviously Whitman, who was, after all, a member of an American nineteenth-century social living group. The time primarily under discussion is brief, the twenty or so years between Whitman's first published poetry in 1838 and the appearance of *Leaves of Grass* (1855). The texts I will approach include nearly everything that Whitman wrote between 1838 and 1855. Usefully for this discussion, Whitman is situated, as are the texts I will discuss, at the chronological threshold of radical changes in the definition of homosexuals not only externally (legally and medically, politically and historically) by society, but internally (spiritually, philosophically, and sexually) by themselves. I will primarily center my remarks on a reading of a discourse of homosexual desire and identity within the confines of that text we call Whitman. In focusing uniquely on the textual conventions that speak to questions of identity and desire as well as an aesthetics of that desire, I will associate the Whitman text with some others inscribed within a ninteenth-century, largely American, homoerotic discourse. My remarks will also address specifically the presence of certain conventions of homoeroticism as they evolve within the Whitman text, especially the early poetry and fiction, the manuscripts and notebooks, and *Leaves of Grass* (1855).

One of Whitman's most powerful icons in his homoerotic texts is the powerful Fierce Wrestler, whose presence dominates his texts and obsesses the poet. That Fierce Wrestler inhabits Whitman's comments about literature and creates a confrontational context with texts. Whitman suggested that "the reader will always have his or her part to do, just as much as I have had mine. I seek . . . to bring you, reader, into the atmosphere of the theme or thought—there to pursue your own flight" (*PW* 2:725). J. Hillis Miller has suggested that "the critic adds his weaving to the Penelope's web of the text, or unravels it so that its structuring threads may be laid bare, or re-weaves it, or traces out one thread in the text to reveal the design it inscribes."[4]

I hope to add some useful weaving, perhaps even some modest reweaving. I do not intend a wholesale unraveling, but I do intend to trace one thread with care, the one thread that I believe—to add figure to figure—primarily colors the pattern in the carpet. In this book, by paying closest attention to Whitman's writing prior to the 1855 edition and to the major poems of *Leaves of Grass* (1855), I intend to show that his awareness of his role as the bard of comrades, together with the homosexual text it implies, has a long foreground in his work, that it can be found even in his earliest writing, and that in this early writing and in *Leaves of Grass* (1855) as much as in *Leaves of Grass* (1860), it is a dominating metaphor and the primary subject of the text. Despite his assertion in a letter to Emerson in 1856 (Bradley 729) that there is "not the first breath" of manly love in print, he was nevertheless a participant in, as well as a creator of, certain nineteenth-century discourses of homosexual desire.

Those discourses not only addressed "manly love" but implied a great deal, most often by exclusion, about women and their inscription within these homoerotic discourses. This topic, though often alluded to, explosively by D. H. Lawrence and often, by later critics, in the contexts of Whitman's post-1855 work, still needs attention in the context of early Whitman texts as well as in the first version of "Song of Myself." Though I find that Whitman is no feminist, a finding already ratified by some other readers, I hope my close attention to this context will enlarge and more precisely document this still problematized portion of the Whitman discourse.

Foucault observed that "there is no binary division to be made between what one says and what one does not say; we must try to determine the different ways of not saying such things. . . . There is not one but many silences, and they are an integral part of the strategies that underlie and permeate discourses."[5] In Whitman's writing it is possible to clearly discern the conversion of homosexual desire into an informing aesthetic governed as much by what he does not say as by what he says. It is my intention to listen for the messages of this silence as intently as I listen to his words so as to show that the fully realized ability to create homoerotic fantasy and to "drench" his texts in sex—that is to engage not only in intertextual and intratextual dialogues but to penetrate or, perhaps more precisely, interpenetrate textuality with erotic subtextuality—coincides precisely with and explains the development of his mature style.

By the time *homosexual* entered the legal, medical, and sexual discourse in 1869, Whitman had nearly completed his exploration of what he called "adhesiveness," "manly love," and "comradeship."[6] What *homosexual* has come to represent for us, however, may well not be at all what "manly love" meant for Whitman, and it is certain that what *homosexual* meant at its creation is only distantly connected to what it has come to mean here and now.[7] At our precise moment in the polylogue—to borrow from Kristeva—concerning sexuality and its literary dissonances and consonances, those early speculations that attempted to fix a specific homosexuality—or identify the homosexual—have come to seem not only antique, but descriptive, some insist, of nothing at all.[8] Two questions are most often asked. Has homosexuality and have gay people—in the sense of sexually self-identified persons responding in any number of ways to their sexuality within a given social and historical context—always existed as a sexual and social community that reflects certain unchanging attitudes and that can be identified historically, culturally, and socially within identifiable categories? Or, can homosexuals at any given historical moment be adequately defined by an anachronistic term that is culturally specific and even static, and that only speaks—and then problematically—to homosexuality as we understand it today? Many insist that it is impossible to firmly situate or adequately describe homosexuality and the homosexual as unchanging sexual categories within differing historical or cultural contexts.[9] Others would assert that homosexuality is not primarily a sexual category at all, but a social, cultural, or even anthropological one, and so it may be fraught with peril to presume that Whitman's homosexuality is the same homosexuality as our own. In this context Halperin's useful warning ought to be heeded that it is quite as dangerous to presume other homosexualities are in fact necessarily other, that is different in degree, kind, and response vis à vis the homoerotic stimuli familiar to us.[10]

Having included what is now a nearly obligatory summary for those who may not read gay theory, I want to register appreciation not only for Sedgwick's observation that such a summary has become "the compulsory setpiece" of "any gay oriented book written in the late 1980s" but also for her hope that the "meditation on and attempted ajudication of constructivist versus essentialist views of homosexuality" might well become a task against which one needs to "vigourously demur" as well as for her cogent argument for that demurral.[11] Sedgwick argues that questions about the meaning of "homo/heterosexual definition" in a life are more central and valuable than either speculations about the causes of homosexuality or attempted definitions of homosexuality within any given social, cultural, or historical frame. In fact, Whitman raised all those questions, ranging freely across the boundaries of theories not yet theorized, at once an essentialist and constructivist, pursuing both essence and accident.

However, in this book I will not debate, though I am certainly aware of, the questions raised as to whether "homosexuality" and "homosexual"—separated for the moment here from homosexual desire in something of the same way that Foucault separates sex from sexuality—are definitive and historically identifiable categories or fluctuating social constructions.[12] Perhaps the real thrust of an argument in a "gay oriented book" written in the 1990s should not be about terms but should demonstrate what Sedgwick so often directly and tacitly advances—an antihomophobic narrative.[13]

I hope this book is that. Since *homosexual* is the most available word we have, I have decided to follow Havelock Ellis' example concerning its use. As he says, "it is a barbarously hybrid word; however it is convenient and now widely used."[14] It is for convenience also that I use it despite its heavy historical freight. I use it here to define genital activity between men. I will use *homoerotic* to describe expressed or hidden desire for and fantasy about such genital activity, and to indicate the presence of homosexuality as a textual manifestation, whether it is depicted overtly as a physical event or covertly as the coded subject of metaphor.[15]

In one of his earliest fictions, "The Child's Champion" (1841), Whitman invoked the muse who would be a constant and increasingly eroticized presence in his texts. This muse is embodied in "young beings, strangers who seem to touch the fountains of our love, and draw forth their swelling waters" (EPF 74 n. 23). This stranger appears throughout Whitman's texts but most powerfully as the Fierce Wrestler, who is identified in a notebook written shortly before "Song of Myself" as he who struggles "at the threshold with spasms more delicious than all before," whose passion so fills the speaker with wonder that he exclaims: "I did not think I was big enough for so much ecstasy" (*NUPM* 1:77). The Fierce Wrestler is the fully eroticized muse, who in Section 29 of "Song of Myself" becomes "blind loving wrestling touch," and who has in the notebooks filled Whitman with a "library of instant knowledge" (*NUPM* 1:75). The knowledge "Whitman" was granted at that erotic threshold is sexual and homoerotic, and when he came to write *Calamus,* he called that knowledge the "secret of my nights and days."[16]

The intent readers who first read Whitman as a homosexual text may well have guessed the secret and therefore eagerly participated in the intentional fallacy—if indeed it is a fallacy (though in Whitman's case they certainly hoped it was intentional phallacy)— taking Whitman at what seemed to be his word that the "Walt Whitman" who spoke in the poem was the same Walt Whitman who wrote it. But Whitman had pondered the questions of intent and authorial voice, and though at times he might have insisted that he intended his poetry to speak what he thought, and may have intended, believed, or imagined that the "Whitman" who inhabited his texts was the same Whitman who was writing them, and though he even said so in his poems, it seems clear that he was not sure, belatedly confiding to Traubel that maybe he did not know after all what he meant, and earlier and more dramatically, erasing himself at the end of "Song of Myself." The Whitman I talk about therefore is the one who speaks in the poetry, but who is at once created and undone by the text. He wrote himself into it and out of it; it makes and unmakes him. Certainly the fictional construction appears from time to time in the textures he allowed us to see of his life, just as the historical Whitman may from time to time without warning enter into the text. Whether this is Whitman or "Whitman" almost seems unimportant. Whether "writing" or "speaking," both participate in the creation of the text; they are both fictions, each creating the other, both (re)created by their readers. That Whitman knew this is shown not only by that frontispiece picture in the first edition of *Leaves of Grass,* which anonymously glosses so many of his words and suggests some others that can be found between the lines, but also by the insertion of his newly named self at the point in that text when he has at last learned what his name is. For certainly the author of this book was not left unnamed for anonymity's sake merely, but instead to unsettle text, reader, and poet. The text at that moment surely creates him, and how much more unsettling it is that when he is named at last, the name is almost immediately lost in a cosmos of definition—of renaming. Whitman knew what we mean when he equated that book and that man.

It is clear on every page of "Song of Myself" that speech constantly defers and can never define—to borrow without appropriating it (or making much of it) Derridean *différance.* The catalogs, for example, do not add to definition; they destabilize and even destroy it, constantly admitting dubiety about the possibilities of defining what they list. The tense objectifications of sexual experience are also deconstructions of that experience. His language does not allow mere definition, but instead provokes a constantly revised and certainly deferred comprehension of the implications of the text. Whitman by any name—and he uses a thousand names to name himself in that passage toward invisibility

and (homo)sexual essence that is the most useful defining outline of
"Song of Myself"—is our greatest poet of language as an ever-
revising trope.

I hope that the preceding does not suggest that I intend to
promiscuously lie with Whitman in one or another critical embrace. Prompted by his words in section 1 of "Song of Myself," I
keep special "creeds and schools in abeyance," though at further
prompting I also recall that he recognized they should be "never
forgotten." I would most like to heed Bloom when he so provocatively urges that "we must learn to see rhetoric as transcending the
epistemology of tropes and re-entering the space of the will-to-
persuasion."[17] I cannot help it, and there may be, perhaps should
be, no help for it, that when I read Whitman, I feel, despite theory
that powerful will, and I am aroused in every sense by the presence
of the Fierce Wrestler and by the erotic pleasures of the text. One of
those pleasures, and one that insistently empowers my reading, is
that "shock of recognition" that Melville recognized as the defining element of the erotics of texts. That electricity—to use Whitman's own image for textual eroticism—leaps between that text
and my reading when I encounter and am provoked by that
demanding homoerotic muse who Whitman so startlingly introduces in his notebooks at that moment when his mere and derivative works suddenly become his possessed and original poetry.

Whitman warns in section 2 of "Song of Myself" that though
we may "possess the origin of all poems" we may never "get at the
meaning of poems," and he reminds us in section 17 of an intertextuality when he says that his "thoughts are really the thoughts of all
men in all ages. . . . they are not original [read "originary"] with
me." Whitman is also our most accomplished poet of the written
text in the fullest sense of our present conceptions of writing, and
"Song of Myself" is the most completely written of any American
text, if for no other reason than it so completely and insistently
pretends to be speech and yet so constantly unsettles every definition of speech. Whitman's fascination with words led him to
constantly revise them and indeed to constantly re(de)construct
them. The notebooks are a stunning project in the construction of
such fluid texts; "Song of Myself" is the most fluid of all his texts.
In "Song of Myself," most powerfully and most poignantly, the
case for the anxieties of definition (as well as for the anxieties of
influence) is made, remade, and revised, each revision foreground-
ing writing and its processes, distancing speech and its inade-

quacies from the text. Even as he insists on the original energy of his voice in section 25 of "Song of Myself," he is forced to say: "speech . . . is unequal to measure itself."

But just as Whitman allows "Whitman" to dissolve in lacy jags at the end of "Song of Myself," so any attempt to pin down either intentionality or voice, or to untangle the superbly tangled skein of fact, fiction, and fantasy—of difference and deferral—is probably doomed to be as evanescent as Whitman/"Whitman's" dissolving self. In the end, reading Whitman always brings me to where we took one another, every time a different place, and, in section 52, to his most exhilarating warning: "You will hardly know who I am or what I mean." Therefore, it is not a doctrinal statement but a necessary one when I say I can do nothing but give my reader as much leave and freedom to decide which Whitman, where, and how as Whitman has given his readers to make the same demanding choice. For he has not so much given us leave as made us honor bound to read skeptically, dangerously: "He most honors my style who learns under it to destroy the teacher" (*SM* 1233). The final lines of "Song of Myself," in section 51, are his ultimate poetics and his most penetrating, because the most elusive, commentary on the theory of texts. When I attend to his most difficult question— "Listener up there! . . . what have you to confide to me?"—I recognize the task that he has set for every reader.[18] I also know the impossibility of that task and the trap he sets when I read with sometimes sinking though determined heart the saddest and most demanding admonition he makes: "Talk honestly, for no one else hears you."

2

Words Unsaid

It is without name . . . it is a word unsaid. . . .
— "Song of Myself," 1855

Among the multitude of identities Walt Whitman claimed to contain, one, his "homosexual identity," has been the continued subject of a vexed questioning raised during his lifetime and pursued ever since. Presumptions were made: that he was homosexual, that he was heterosexual, that he was not sexual at all, that he transcended sexuality entirely, that he was bisexual. Of course, when he wrote *Leaves of Grass* (1855) and during most of his lifetime, these particular terms were specifically unavailable to him, even though the medical models that lie behind them were rapidly coalescing. During the late eighteenth and early nineteenth centuries, old, largely religious proscriptions concerned with sexual object choice—increasingly problematized, laden with anxiety, and historically unstable at best—coexisted in a state of considerable speculative dissonance with new theories—mostly legal and medical. These last posited very different ways of classification, identification, interpretation, and judgment of the social/historical (and hence political) as well as textual/aesthetic consequences of sexual desire and act. These discourses, so furiously intent on self-revelation, as Foucault has observed and Smith-Rosenberg elaborated, were equally at odds with one another. As Smith-Rosenberg has said, "sexual discourse was just that, a discourse, at times a babel, but never a monologue." These discourses "created disparate fantasies, debated one another, condemned one another—all in the language of sexuality." Running as an obbligato beneath, around, and interpenetratingly through this general sexual discourse—was a hesitant, though incipiently pow-

erful companion discourse engaged with both the theories about
and the political actualities of the existence and experiences—in
both the generally social and specifically sexual sense—of a discrete
sexual minority whose constitution—self-defined not imposed—
derived not from act but from the implications and imperatives of
homoerotic desire. It is to this last discourse that Whitman most
powerfully contributes. He was a major participant in this debate
in his journalism, early verse, fiction, and notebooks, and *Leaves of
Grass* appeared and was revised and enlarged at the time when that
discourse became a monologue, dominated as Smith-Rosenberg
says by "the voice of the bourgeois male."[1]

When the giddy formation and reformation of these radical
speculations about sexuality (as opposed to sex to borrow Foucault's distinction) began to interpenetrate not only general texts
but specific critical discussions, especially Whitman criticism, that
dominant male voice was there most often heard. But the substance of these discourses was only hazily appreciated and sometimes even more vaguely appropriated by those writers who
addressed what most saw as the "problem" of Whitman's sexuality. More damaging, the discourse was often deliberately misread, especially by those who chose to definitively situate Whitman within one or another spectrum of sexuality. In section 52 of
"Song of Myself," Whitman foretold the coming fluctuating
ambiguity of critical language when he said about himself *as text*:
"I effuse my flesh in eddies and drift it in lacy jags." To most early
readers Whitman's sexuality seemed more important than textuality. At one obsessed juncture even Symonds—Whitman's earliest and in many ways still most provocative critic—was more
interested in what the text revealed about Whitman's extra-textual
activities than what the text revealed about itself.

Many critics who addressed the subject after Whitman's death
vehemently denied what many of them clearly felt was a blot on the
purity of the legend or attempted to dehomosexualize the undeniable celebrations of the text by forceful denial, by ingenious misreading, or as in the celebrated instance of Emory Holloway's
pronomial blindness, by textual tampering.[2] Even if the homoeroticism of the texts was grudgingly admitted, critics recoiled at
the possibility that what art implied life might ratify. But just as
Foucault said in the larger context, it was through this continued
process of constant verbal denial that the discourse was begun.
Even if the physical manifestation was doubted, dismissed, or

trivialized, the homosexuality thus defused, diffused, or purified as a "psychical" predilection (to use a term from Eduard Bertz, an early commentator who did presume that Whitman was homosexual), the question about Whitman's sexuality rather than about the sexual resonance of the texts became inevitably the paramount subject.[3] For example, in 1906 Bliss Perry, Whitman's earliest scholarly biographer insisted that "as far as I know there has never been the slightest evidence that Whitman practised homo-sexuality." He asserted that in his conversations with those who knew Whitman well—Burroughs, Traubel, and Bucke—"I have never heard the slightest hint of the charge" that Whitman was homosexual.[4] As Robert K. Martin in *The Homosexual Tradition in American Poetry* has shown, such denial and fear of criminalization (note "charge") has dominated Whitman biography until very recently. Martin describes this general "distortion of meaning and the willful misreading" of the poet as a powerful example of the maintenance of "social and moral prejudice." It should be noted, he adds, that "the very few critics who spoke against this tradition of distortion were Europeans, who perhaps did not share American society's total and relentless hostility to the homosexual."[5]

Since Martin wrote, some of the blunt instruments used to threaten the academic homosexual discourse concerned with Whitman's homosexual discourse have been tactfully retired, but much of the hostility is still present, and subtler weapons with sharper edges are still wielded.[6] In 1955, for example, G. W. Allen could assert that the early Calamus emotions were "not yet pathological" and doubted that "actual perversion" was likely between Peter Doyle and Whitman.[7] While three decades later such language is rarely used, and indeed—except in political or religious homophobic discourse—is no longer acceptable, nevertheless, some recent critics have suggested that Whitman's homosexual discourse is not an issue worth talking about. Writing in 1985 about "Whitman in the Eighties," William White—to whom Whitman scholars are so much in debt—mentions that in the 1980s a few scholars have written an "article or two, or a chapter in a book, on the subject of Whitman's homosexuality." Most critics nowadays, he says, are not "sidestepping the issue." But he continues, "for some of us it is simply not an issue since there is no real evidence that Whitman was a practicing homosexual." White seems to feel that without practice there is no homosexuality. Hence it is not a subject worth discussing, since, as he says, even though "writers in gay magazines" feel that Whitman was one of them, most "contributors to the periodicals prefer dealing with other subjects."8

Writing in 1988, David S. Reynolds is not willing to come "to a firm conclusion about Whitman's sexual preferences" and instead does seem to sidestep the "issue" by asserting that Whitman "wanted to avoid the deceit and artificiality, the amorality, that he associated with the heterosexual love plot." Reynolds argues that a way of "avoiding the love plot was to emphasize adhesive love," which "in the phrenological terms of the day was not associated with homosexuality." Thus Reynolds seems to imply that Whitman didn't really mean it.9 It is true that Whitman drew his term *adhesive* from phrenology; it is true that he was appalled by sentimental plots about heterosexual love. But that did not stop him from writing sentimental stories about veiled homoerotic relationships between men and boys, and most of his poems in *Calamus* are, after all, love plots dealing with relationships between men. Furthermore, in *Democratic Vistas* (1871) Whitman noted that he looked for the presence of "adhesive love" to offset the long reign of "amative love hitherto possessing imaginative literature," making a clear distinction between the two and for good measure adding "love" to phrenology's non-specific terms (*PW* 414). He insisted in "Song of the Open Road" (1856) that his use of the term was new: it was "not previously fashioned." He specifically equates it with the emotions and the acts of homosexual desire.10 Both White and Reynolds seem eager to disassociate "Whitman" from homosexuality, and despite their evenhandedness their narrative is in that sense homophobic. What White overlooks is that gay scholars — until recently — have been as threatened by the subtle as by the blunt instruments of academic power and that such comments trivialize and affect the viability and visibility of an exchange between scholars — gay or not — about gay writers. The possibility that Reynolds overlooks, more simply, is that it may not have been only the deceit and amorality of the "heterosexual love plot" that Whitman disliked; it may have been the heterosexuality.

Both early and recent discussions of Whitman's sexuality tend to deny the possibility of homosexual acts or the validity of homosexual feelings, employ a language powerfully charged with disapprobation, and dismiss the question as relatively unimportant, as Bliss Perry's early and David Reynolds' and William White's later examples demonstrate. To some writers, homosexual feelings are so repugnant that their presence in a text seems almost

to invalidate the text itself. For example, this position, documented by Martin in his observations on the work of several
critics, was taken by Mark van Doren in 1942 when he described
Whitman's "manly love" as "deficient and abnormal love," and by
Edwin Miller (1968), who suggested that Whitman's "deviancy"
and "absence of [heterosexual] experience" are barriers to a mature
art. This position admits the homosexuality but insists, as Martin
observes, that homosexuality contributed to his art in no way
"except to flaw it."[11] So John Snyder (1975) speculates that the
"lover in *Calamus* . . . fails because failure is the given end of
homosexuality" and thus implies that because of that double failure
the text fails too. David Leverenz (1989) bluntly announces that
Whitman's homosexuality and homoeroticism "make me, as a
heterosexual male, recoil."[12] Leverenz' comment is only the most
recent example of an attitude engaged by the earliest reviewer of
Leaves of Grass, Rufus Griswold, whose angry review in *The New
York Criterion* of 10 November 1855 concluded with the warning
that these texts dealt with the unspeakable, so unspeakable that he
could not name "it" in English. In one of the earliest recognitions
of the homoerotic textuality of Whitman's poetry, Griswold asserted his own speechlessness concerning the presumed subject of
the text: "In our allusion to this book, we have found it impossible
to convey . . . even the most faint idea of its style and contents,
and of our disgust and detestation of them, without employing
language that cannot be pleasing to ears polite." He relies on Latin
to make his point: "Peccatum illud horribile, inter Christianos non
nominandum."[13] This same classic description of sodomy was
given by a Maryland court in 1810 that described it as the most "horrid and detestable crime, (among Christians not to be named)."[14]
The formula has been—and seems occasionally still to be—constantly written: homosexuality is a sin not to be named, repugnant
not only to Christians but also to critics.

The Whitman discourse, when centered on homosexuality,
has had to carry a heavy baggage of externalized and (surely)
internalized homophobia, which freight has encumbered textual
and biographical study. But of course, this homophobia is also a
useful part of the discourse, since it sets in train fecund speculation
about the place of such prohibitive discourses in current thought
about Whitman and within the nexus, not only of his own self-
evaluation, but of the aesthetic, historical, and political siting of his
texts as counterdiscourses. The deep questions are thus implied in

Leverenz's word "recoil" or raised by asking why it is, as White says, that critics "prefer dealing with other subjects" than Whitman's homosexuality, with other subjects than that which Whitman himself described as the "pulse" of his life. Indeed, even so careful and intuitive a critic as M. Jimmie Killingsworth, who does deal with the subject in *Whitman's Poetry of the Body* (1989), can speak of "indulging homosexual experiences" as opposed to "engaging" in them, can perhaps unintentionally refer to Whitman's "indirect denial of his perversion," and can also say, somewhat astoundingly given his otherwise careful language throughout the book, that "to charge Whitman with homosexuality, we need to have Whitman in our historical background." The theory is unexceptionable, the diction—that unhappy "charge"—distressing.[15]

It was Whitman himself who first recognized that these are attitudes shared by both the critic and the culture. His recognition is implicit in the very formulations of his text. When he speaks in "Vigil Strange I Kept on the Field One Night" about a "boy of responding kisses" for example, implicit therein is the presumption that most boys do not respond to the kisses of men and that boys who do are "men like me," who, like those in *Calamus* 4, love "as I am capable of loving." The qualifications of his texts are significant, not the presumed subjects or actions. Here *responding, like,* and *as*—not *kisses* or *loving* or *men*—are the key signs that show the nature of the discourse. Just so the key elements in his statement "Or may-be a stranger will read this who has secretly loved me" (Bowers 94), are *stranger* and *loved.* The specific "stranger" who could be loved in the specifically anonymous though significantly public locale *stranger* suggests, spotlights and defines the nature of the "love", the kind of love that deliberately transgresses against public codes of privacy, intimacy, and decency and has a specific, encoded speech that can be read by those who can understand it, a speech created not through logic but by signified desire, a desire ratified through sexual contact. Whitman was well aware that most people (Smith-Rosenberg's "bourgeois males") would answer no to his questions since a yes answer might well invoke those dangerous concerns Sedgwick has described as "homosexual panic."[16] Those who could say yes to the question would be eligible for admittance into what these few—at least if our own current research is on the right track—were beginning to suspect was most surely a fraternity.

It was also clear to Whitman how both culture and the common reader might respond to his writing, and a good deal of the

critical heritage has proved him right. He enunciates the insight
hesitantly in one of his earliest stories, "The Child's Champion"
(1841), when he observes that "the forms of custom . . . so generally smother" the "wish to love and be loved" (*NUPM* 1:74 n. 23).
Whitman emphasises "wish" here, not act. In the rather narrow
area of act, Allen is right when he says that unless positive proof of
homosexual acts can be obtained, then no biographer can make an
assertion that a homosexual act—he calls it "sodomy"—actually
took place.[17] As Justin Kaplan also observes, "coherent, honest,
and sensitive biographical narrative relies on intimate evidence
and . . . evidence of this sort is hard to find when you're dealing
with Whitman." Kaplan goes on to suggest that "maybe it doesn't
matter" what "Whitman actually 'did' with Peter Doyle and the
others." Of course it does matter, and saying that it doesn't is
another example of the critical trivialization of homosexual sex and
desire. Kaplan is precisely correct, however, when he says that
"what does matter is the way Whitman defines himself as homosexual in his poetry, in his letters and journals, in his daily conduct,
in his frequently tormented relations with younger men and his
evasive relations with women." He further says that it is important
how Whitman defines himself as homosexual "in the way he uses
democratic political models as a way of emancipating sexuality, in
the way he invokes androgyny as a liberating imaginative mode."
Kaplan insists that "we have to acknowledge the gulf that exists
between the life Whitman lived, to the extent that we can learn it,
and the imagined life that appears in his poems."[18]

Kaplan believes that the "cycle of discussion, as far as the
sexuality issue is concerned, seems to have completed and maybe
exhausted itself."[19] I am not at all sure that this is so, and I am
supported by a good deal of the most recent criticism. Indeed the
sexuality question—though perhaps in a very different sense than
Kaplan means—is still provocatively being explored. The tradition
of such current explorations begins of course with J. A. Symonds.
Symonds' letters to Whitman (despite the gossipy subtext concerned with who, what, and when) and his *Walt Whitman, A Study*
(1893) mark the precise moments wherein the study of the sexual
interpenetrations of Whitman's textuality begins. And that process
is ratified, perhaps inadvertently and in a prohibitive context (note
"diagnosis"), by Eduard Bertz in a letter (1914) to W.C. Rivers,
wherein he observes that "for the diagnosis of homosexuality, such
deeds are of secondary importance only, it is true; the manner of

feeling unveiled in Whitman's works, is primarily evidential."[20] Continued by Edward Carpenter in *Days With Walt Whitman* (1906) and *Some Friends of Walt Whitman: A Study of Sex Psychology (1924)*, the gradual process of disentangling Whitman's texts, at least from the rigors of critical homophobia, were best assisted by Frederik Schyberg (1933), Malcolm Cowley (1946), Newton Arvin (1938), and Roger Asselineau (1960/1962), among earlier studies, while the work of Robert K. Martin, *The Homosexual Tradition in American Poetry* (1979), stands as an original bridge between them and recent books by Betsy Erkkila (1989), M. Jimmie Killingsworth (1989), and Michael Moon (1991), which reflect the new and richly provocative paths that gay and feminist gender studies have begun to open.[21] Martin's book, now a classic study, first fully opened up the possibilities of considering Whitman's texts as homosexual texts rather than as poems by a writer who may have been homosexual. His book is a landmark in gay studies, and though he has been criticized for his unitary articulation of "the" Homosexual Tradition, his conclusions about the homosexual text have anticipated most later studies, and are the foundation upon which they rightfully rest.

Erkkila, in *Whitman: The Political Poet,* is most interested in the structures of Whitman's texts as they are produced by and affect questions of power, race, class, and gender, that is, questions of politics and history. Erkkila's argument that Whitman conflated his own eroticized body and the political body of America is unexceptionable; the book is a carefully and excitingly documented study. Her reading of the homosexual textuality of "Song of Myself," though, is not as extensive, and of *Calamus* not as profound, as Martin's or as Killingsworth's in *Whitman's Poetry of the Body: Sexuality, Politics, and the Text.* Killingsworth considers many of the same questions that Erkkila poses but confronts more conclusively and provocatively the question of sexuality and the homosexual text. Erkkila's study derives its force from the dense texture of political text and context, deals with the homosexual textuality largely as a surface manifestation, and is, it seems to me, limited in its observations about the generalized "(homo)sexuality," as she describes it, of the texts. Killingsworth, while solidly attending to the political context, also derives his illuminating conclusions by situating his readings of Whitman within a context that includes sexual advice and health literature and early feminist texts contemporaneous with Whitman. Killingsworth's book addresses the deep homosexual texture of the poetry more extensively and originally than any study since Martin, explores Whitman's sexual politics, and maps, as he says using Sedgwick's word's, "an 'anxious, sharply dichotomised landscape' of social, political, and poetic relationships" within which Whitman "lived and wrote."[22] Michael Moon's *Disseminating Whitman: Revision and Corporeality in "Leaves of Grass"* explores the fascinating and largely unexplored matter of Whitman's revisions of *Leaves of Grass* and foregrounds Whitman's project of representing sexuality and especially sexuality between men. Moon's readings not only firmly situate Whitman within the context of nineteenth-century sexual discourse but also link Whitman's revisionary practice in the text to the poet's own unsettled and increasingly revised position after 1860 concerning the social implications of a politics of male-male sexual desire. These books as well as other works by Gilbert, Martin, Moon, and Sedgwick, have well begun the siting of Whitman within a fluid — not static — history of sexual and political relations, within what appears to be a destabilized pattern of concepts of male-bonding and gender, and within a cultural frame in which those challenges Foucault has made to received theories of nineteenth-century sexuality can be fully elaborated.

The sexuality issue then, far from being exhausted, will have to be raised in order to explore the matrix of intertextuality that combines to form the textual and imaginative fabric of what has been described (though perhaps with just as much anxiety) as the homosexual imagination, an "imaginative mode," a "sensibility," which — if it exists — is quite different from that which defines itself as heterosexual.[23] I do not think at all that the sexuality issue is exhausted because neither sex nor sexual acts are the precise issue — sexual desire is. Thus, the important homosexual question is not whether Whitman was homosexual. Instead we must ask what homosexuality — whatever its construction — meant to Whitman and what his construction of it was? To what extent if at all did he construct and identify himself and his texts as situated within a homosexual context and as participating in a discourse of desire? And what are the defining textual characteristics — those Bloomian tropes — that he invoked to explain to his readers and to himself why these desires were so powerful that he was impelled to utter them? Actions after all, are the consummation of desire; it is desire that fuels the imagination; it is desire that defines the meaning of an act, especially when that act becomes text.

In 1877, in "A Backward Glance O'er Travel'd Roads," Whitman touched on the sexuality issue in precisely this way:

It has become in my opinion, imperative to achieve a shifted attitude from superior men and women towards the thought and fact of sexuality, as an element of character, personality, the emotions, and a theme in literature. I am not going to argue the question by itself; it does not stand by itself. The vitality of it is altogether in its relations, bearings, significance. . . . *Leaves of Grass* . . . has mainly been the outcropping of my own emotional and other personal nature—an attempt, from the first to the last, to put a Person, a human being (myself, in the latter half of the Nineteenth Century, in America,) freely, fully, and truly on record." (*PW* 2:728)

In what might be construed to be a breathtaking anticipation of Foucault, Whitman seems pointedly to choose "sexuality" instead of sex, though at other textual crises he habitually "drenched" his songs specifically in sex. The point is that sexuality "does not stand by itself" and it cannot be argued uniquely. Therefore, in these terms—his terms—I am not at all sure that the sexuality issue has been exhausted because I am not sure that it has really been fully explored.[24]

Kaplan asks why "after more than a century of biographical inquiry we still have only the most approximate notion of how and why Walter Whitman, printer, schoolteacher, editor, fiction writer, and building contractor, a shadowy figure in most accounts, untamed, untranslateable, projected his barbaric yawp over the roofs of the world. This of course is the heart of his mystery."[25] The shadowy figure who also inhabits this list is that other Walter Whitman who so early on not only asked why the forms of custom smother the wish to be loved but also observed that the need to be loved "will sometimes burst forth in spite of all obstacles." In Whitman's typical invocation of ejaculative power—"burst forth"—there is inscribed all those tropes he would later engage in "Song of Myself" to answer that same, so often repeated question, tropes that would radically transgress all obstacles, (those social, political, and aesthetic forms of custom), tropes that would confront "creeds and schools" and the "grammar of the old cartouches" with "a new identity" and "a new tongue," the translated tongue and mastered writing of the homoerotic text. That is the real heart of his mystery.

3

Man's Words

Man's words, for the Young men of these states, are all words . . . to identify an erect . . . athletic . . . hardy . . . upright boyhood . . . an sweet erect . . . lusty body.

—"The Primer of Words," c. 1855–56

The letter Whitman wrote to Emerson and included with the poems of the second edition of *Leaves of Grass* (1856) provides a terminus for my study, and with that ending I would like to begin. In it he complained that "as to manly friendship, everywhere observed in The States, there is not the first breath of it to be observed in print" (Bradley 729). When he wrote this, Whitman was standing at the beginning of the discourse in which, as Foucault affirms, the "homosexual became a personage, a past . . . in addition to being a type of life, a life form . . . with an indiscreet anatomy and possibly a mysterious physiology. Nothing that went into his total composition was unaffected by his sexuality. It was everywhere present in him . . . at the root of all his actions . . . written immodestly in his face and body . . . a secret that always gave itself away. . . . it was consubstantial with him . . . a singular nature. . . . a sexual sensibility." Foucault dates this categorization from 1870.[1] Whitman forecast this sensibility and contributed to the identifying discourse as early as 1840 and definitively described it in *Calamus* 1 (1860), as the "substantial life" that does not "exhibit itself yet contains all the rest," positing that "men like me" whose eyes offer love identified themselves to one another, as he says in *Calamus* 42, as those who had "blood like mine" circling in their veins.

In a notebook (*DBN* 3:739–40) written in the early fifties, shortly before the appearance of *Leaves of Grass* (1855), Whitman says that there are no "man's words" to express manly friendship.[2] Emerson had demanded these words as well in a journal entry written in 1841: "Give me initiative, spermatic, prophesying, man-making words." Emerson's spermatic man-making words and the muscular words Whitman wants are the language that will give to American literature that special character Whitman defines as "strong, limber . . . full of ease, of passionate friendliness" (Bradley 741). The masculine and assertively sexual characteristics of this language contrast with Whitman's definitions in the letter to Emerson of what man's words are not and what his new tongue will oppose. He characterizes the literature he hopes to displace as one "without manhood or power" in which only "geldings" are depicted. Like the unaroused penis, "its flesh is soft; it shows less and less of the indefinable hard something that is Nature." The young men who will be his subject are "savage and luxuriant" in contrast with the "helpless dandies" who "can neither fight, work, shoot, ride, run, command" but who are instead "devout, some quite insane, castrated," who can be seen "smirking and skipping along . . . no one behaving . . . out of any natural and manly tastes of his own." These dandies espouse and produce a literature in which the "men and women . . . appear to have been . . . of the neuter gender. . . . if the dresses were changed the men might easily pass for women, and the women for men." This literature makes "unmentionable" the "manhood of a man . . . sex, womanhood, maternity, desires, lusty animations, organs, acts" (Bradley 736–39). Whitman poses against his manly young men whose language he hopes to infuse with terms descriptive of passionate friendship a detailed rendering of the cliché of the effeminate homosexual. This cliché is exemplified in a parody of Whitman's poetry written around 1860 in which a "Counter-jumper," the dry goods salesman who had become associated with effeminacy and homosexuality, is described as "weak and effeminate," depraved and "feeble," all terms that accord with the developing medical and legal model of the homosexual as sexually enervated, aberrant, and mentally damaged.

Whitman insists that he likes words that are not "delicate lady words" and observes that there is a language that can apply to "men not fond of women, women not fond of men" (*DBN* 3:746). This oblique definition of same-sex affection is unique in his texts. Whitman rarely uses any specific formulae to describe homosexuals, but this may well be one, just as his mention of "foo-foos," "fancy men," "neuters and geldings," and "onanists" is directed at effeminate or secretive homosexuals. Whitman's use of "insane" and "castrated" forecasts the medical model, while "smirking and skipping" reflects at one and the same time a self-identification by some homosexuals and homophobic clichés of effeminacy. Sedgwick suggests that in England, at least, one model for a "homosexual role seems to have been available to aristocratic Englishmen . . . for at least two centuries and probably much longer." Its "strongest associations are with . . . effeminacy, transvestitism, promiscuity, prostitution, continental culture and the arts."[3] That there was a homosexual subculture in England reflecting these associations and in which effeminacy was a sign of homosexual genital activity has been more fully demonstrated than that there was a similar subculture in early nineteenth-century America. The existence of both subcultures is reasonably certain, however, and Whitman's helpless dandies as well as the Counter-jumper indicate that the cliché may represent an early version of a reality that has been substantially documented for the last decades of the century.[4] Of course, the associations Sedgwick identifies have to do not only with genital activity but even more importantly with the style and substance of what Foucault described as an "aesthetics of existence" that defined areas of homosexual social, sexual, and imaginative life.[5] Whitman wants to recover for American literature a masculinized, virilized, anti-aristocratic, democratic style that he defines within an aesthetics of homoeroticized male existence. As he observed in another notebook, "what is lacking in literature can . . . only be generated from the seminal freshness and propulsion of new masculine persons."(DBN 1:223). His mission is to save American literature not from homosexuality but from the "effeminate" anti-democratic misuse and denial of "manly" sexuality. The effect of an effeminate homosexual model was to "reduce perceived masculinity, rather than to redouble it."[6] Whitman's intention is to reverse that perception and erase effeminacy, but not homosexual desire, from American literature.

Whitman's eroticized language identifies effeminate sexuality as the cause of the "non-personality and indistinctness of modern . . . books." That identification calls for a redoubled attention to manly friendship in literature, but it also implies that homophobia itself is a cause of literary weakness, since identification with effeminacy denies the real "organic equality" of men "among themselves" (Bradley 739). If he rejects both effeminate models of homosexuality and the homophobia they imply, he also then equally resists a discourse that valorizes homophobia and the anti-feminism and racism that attend upon it—a discourse illustrated, for example, by the Davy Crockett Almanacs, written in the 1830s and 1840s, which Smith-Rosenberg has recovered and about which I will have more to say.[7]

I would caution in addition that Whitman's advocacy of women's sexuality in the letter to Emerson needs to be read against an incipient anti-feminism in his own earlier texts. Friedlander has provocatively identified homosexuality "as the "highest most perfect evolutionary stage of gender identification." This model expressed, as Showalter comments, "heightened forms of masculinity and femininity" that "were the most purely 'manly' or 'womanly' representatives of their sex" and asserted that "sexual preference for their own sex was . . . determined by their sexual disgust for the opposite sex rather than by sharing its desires."[8] My borrowing from Showalter's comments on European discourse is not meant to be, of course, an accurate description of Whitman's American program, but it may be a subtext that Sedgwick recognizes when she speaks about "our developing understanding of the centrality of homosocial bonds to patriarchal heterosexist culture."[9] What is an element of Whitman's program is that his aims for that female sexuality he emphasizes are primarily reproductive. As Gagnier points out, the perception of women as "the means of reproduction was . . . the source of the anti-feminist thread running through the homosexual literature of the period."[10]

Whitman's call for a literature that repeals the "filthy law" silencing the sexual discourse in which "the body is to be expressed, and sex is" and that rejects the neutered and helpless dandies who write the law, echoes and eroticizes Emerson's rejection of the courtly muses of Europe and also valorizes women and female sexuality. But the context in which it does so indicates that for Whitman the realization of women's free sexuality is only a necessary prelude to what appears to be for him the more important realization of male-male genital activity. He insists that if sex is admitted to literature women will "approach the day of organic equality with men "(Bradley 739). He does not mean "organic" in any Transcendental sense. It is "organs and acts" of which he speaks—the "indefinable hard something" of nature—and which he makes specific in section 21 of "Proto-Leaf" (1860) as "sexual organs and acts" (Bowers 13). The great achievement of that organic equality will be the ability of men to celebrate their own "organic" liberation from exclusive heterosexuality, for without organic equality between men and women, "men cannot have organic equality among themselves." That exclusive and exclud-ing "among" makes clear that his context includes sexual as well as affectional — "passionate friendliness" — relations among men, cer-tainly not excluding the equally organic relations between men and women, but certainly excluding the effeminacy and the sexual passivity — though not the sexuality itself — of the unmanly homo-sexual. He more precisely enunciates the idea in the famous foot-note to *Democratic Vistas* (1871), in which he argues that:

It is to the development, identification, and general prevalence of that fervid comradeship, (the adhesive love, at least rivaling the amative love hitherto possessing imaginative literature, if not going beyond it,) that I look for the counterbalance and offset of our materialistic and vulgar American democracy, and for the spiritualization thereof. . . . I confidently expect a time when there will be seen running, like a half-hid warp through all the myriad audible and visible worldly interests of America, threads of manly friendship, fond and loving, pure and sweet, strong and life-long, carried to degrees hitherto unknown — not only giving tone to individual character, and making it unpreceden-tedly emotional, muscular, heroic, and refined, but having the deepest relation to general politics. I say democracy infers such loving comradeship, as its most inevitable twin or counterpart, without which it would be incomplete, in vain, and incapable of perpetuating itself. (*PW* 2:414–15)

In his 1876 preface to *Two Rivulets,* Whitman again affirmed that the importance of *Calamus* "resides in its Political signifi-cance," for it is by the "fervent, accepted development of Com-radeship, the beautiful and sane affection of man for man, latent in all young fellows . . . and what goes indirectly and directly along with it, that the United States of the future, (I cannot too often repeat,) are to be most effectually welded together, intercalated, anneal'd into a Living Union" (Bradley 753). Unfortunately, he did not repeat it too often, canceling the passage in later editions. But the "sane" affection of man for man is surely the antidote for what Whitman sees as the "insane" and castrated weakness of effem-inacy. This sane affection will translate that inactive, flawed, and unmanly love into a manly sexual expression, which is, as by indirection he implies, what "goes directly and indirectly along with it."

Whitman's presumption that manly affection did not appear in print was most fully enunciated in "The Primer of Words," upon which he had been working in the early fifties, and which was later published as "An American Primer" (1904). In the manuscript version of this entry, which I here transcribe exactly so as to include his deletions (in brackets), his changes indicate a suggestive pursuit and experimentation with the possibilities of a sex-laden—sex-drenched—language. Again, the "young men of these states" appear, young men who need "man's words." Man's words are "all words that have arisen out of the qualities of mastership, [freedom go] going first, brunting danger first, — words to identify [an erect a ma an athletic] a hardy [upright] boyhood—[an unstained] knowledge—an [sweet] erect, sweet lusty, body, without taint—[those where whence all] choice and clear of its [love life] pure power" (DBN 3:739–40).

It takes no deep psychology to see the other content of this passage. Men's words—*freedom, mastership, erect, upright, sweet, lusty*—are words of power, sexual words, phallic words. They are words of desire applied to the young men of these states, words that Whitman had already used in the notebooks and in "Song of Myself" to describe the mastership of his Fierce Wrestler. They are placed in opposition to words that suggest more shamefaced perceptions of desire, *taint* and *unstained,* as if the seminal wet he would later invoke could, if expended in the usual and expected channels of heterosexual intercourse, corrupt the sweet erect lusty body, a body not only phallically erect but also "athletic," the charged word that in *Calamus* always signifies the presence of homoerotic desire. Though an unstained and untainted boyhood implies sexual innocence, Whitman will not allow innocence to negate the power of the sexual text. His deletions spell out caution, but they also indicate desire. A "hardy boyhood" was—wishful fantasy—also an "erect" and "upright" boyhood. The unblemished and unstained text says that young men's love equals pure erect phallic power. Just as sodomy was linked to debauchery and "unnatural vice," so by the mid-eighteenth century "unnatural vice" was linked with effeminacy. It was a short trip between those linkages and the transformation of sodomy/homosexuality into "gross indecency," which was "defined against a normative stan-

dard which deified the 'purity' of the middle-class 'household.'"[11]
In this text Whitman reclaims manly love for purity and rejects its
associations with debauchery and effeminacy.

In another entry Whitman wishes for men's words and makes
the same complaint he had made to Emerson. Indeed, here is the
more elaborate source of that complaint (Whitman's deletions are
in brackets):

This is to be said among the young men of these states, that
with a wonderful tenacity of friendship, and [a manliness] of
passionate fondness for their friends, and always a manly readiness to make friends, yet they have remarkably few words [to]
of names for the friendly sentiments. — They seem to be words
that do not thrive here among the muscular classes, where the
real quality of friendship is always freely found. Also they are
words which the muscular classes,[and] the young men of these
states, [are] rarely use, and have an aversion for; — they never
give words to their most ardent friendships. (*DBN* 3:740–41)

The deleted "manliness" that precedes "passionate fondness,"
briefly links passion and manliness, just as "erect" links "boyhood" with phallic potency. Here is the repeated assertion of "Song
of Myself" that the muscular classes, those working men and
roughs — made identical to "young men" by the deletion of "and"
and "are" — are somehow, as Foucault had suggested about the
nineteenth-century "working classes," more open to friendship,
and had, as Foucault put it, escaped the "deployment of 'sexuality'."[12] Indeed, these muscular men — *athlete* and *comrade* surely
consort with *muscular* in a subtext — are those in whose relationships the "real quality" of friendship can be found. "Real" hints at
the presence of the unreal and of the unrealized in friendships. In
the landscape of the unexplored "real" there is a country most men
have never found — the landscape of sexual desire. Whitman wants
to loosen the tongues of the lusty, muscular, young men — tongues
he has already envisioned in "Song of Myself" as penetratingly
plunging to his barestripped and naked heart, giving him there also
access to words of "mastership" and "pure power." Later he says "I
like a limber, lashing tongue — fierce words" (*DBN* 3:746). He is
convinced, however, that the words, the naming, and the definition will one day come: "When the time comes for them to
represent any thing or any state of things, the words will surely

follow . . . As for me, I feel a hundred realities . . . clearly determined in me, that words are not yet formed to represent. Men like
me . . . will gradually get to be more and more numerous . . .
then the words will follow" (*DBN* 3:745). Again that refrain
appears, "Men like me," but now it is coupled with the notion that
such men will grow into a community that possesses these special
words. The certainty of "determined" precisely implies that his
conflation of sex with friendship encompasses essence not accident. Yet the imprecise indirection of "hundred realities," which
avoids naming the most significant of all the determined facets of
the self "in" him, conflates with the assertive invocation of "men
like me" and inevitably evokes that later, pointed definition in
Calamus 4: "only . . . them that love as I myself am capable of
loving." Indeed he embraced his words like he wanted to embrace
his lovers. When he talks of one, the other is a passionate real
presence: "Words . . . are showing themselves, with . . . foreheads
muscular necks and breasts. — These gladden me! — I put my arms
around them — touch my lips to them" (*DBN* 3:739). These are
words made flesh.

In the letter to Emerson, Whitman hopes that if the "United
States are founding a literature," then "in poems, the young men of
these States shall be represented, for they outrival the rest of the
earth." That "shall" very nearly has the weight of "must." This is
prophetic of the similar assertion in *Democratic Vistas* that places the
effectiveness of American politics and spiritual health firmly upon
the same foundation of manly friendship and suggests that an
American literature will not be complete until its young men and
their friendship is adequately and specifically represented in its
poetry. Whitman continues that, in order to make that representation, "everyday I go . . . among the young men, to discover the
spirit of them and to refresh myself." His mission is very nearly
apostolic, going "among" men to discover the "spirit," just as the
apostles went out among men to preach another gospel. These
daily wanderings among his masculine muses are more powerful
pilgrimages than any that contemporary literature had yet offered
him: "I am myself more drawn here than to those authors, pub-
lishers, importations, reprints" that now comprise what America
reads. Just as Bloom had said, strong poets read only themselves,
and Whitman reads these young men to find the materials of
writing as he would read himself. It may also be that homosexual
poets especially read only themselves, and read that self most

persuasively when it is absent in texts. Certainly, Whitman continues, these imports and reprints do "indispensable service . . . outside of men like me." There ought to be no doubt that the tense
opposition he creates between men like him and the implied others
who are not men like him is also reflected in those many texts in
which men like him do not appear, not only texts "outside of" men
like him but texts he is also "outside of." His insistence on the
absence of manly friendship in literature is invisibly paralleled in a
companion and unwritten text; there is no "breath" because writers have not dared to breathe a word of it, and without that breath
of masculine life, much contemporary literature is painfully "outside of"—irrelevant to—the lives of "men like me."

Whitman wrote against a background in which sodomy and
buggery, the two terms usually applied to homosexual activity,
were sins and crimes too heinous to be named among Christians.
The pejorative and indeed vituperative language associated with
any mention of same-sex practices and found not only in popular
texts but in legal documents as well must stand as a background to
Whitman's comments about the invisibility of manly love in
literature, as must, obviously, the social disapprobation and legal
prohibitions raised against such practices, which were, of course,
criminalized. Crompton has written eloquently about Georgian
homophobia in England and provides substantial documentation
for British homophobia and the vituperation that described it in
late eighteenth- and early nineteenth-century England.[13] In America sodomy is described in 1810 as "a horrid and detestable crime"
and an "abominable sin" and in 1824 as "dreadful degradation." In
1866 Horatio Alger is accused of the "abominable and revolting
crime of unnatural familiarity with boys."[14] In an 1885 diary
recovered by Duberman, a young man discovers that his friend is
"a C——sucker & that he loves and enjoys that d——d custom so
revolting to every right minded person." Yet in another entry he
denies that his own practice of hugging and kissing a loving
bedfellow—"I loved to hug & kiss him"—was the "least demonstration of unmanly and abnormal passion," asserting that such a
thing would be as "revolting" to his friend "as it is & ever has been
to me."[15] Despite this, Whitman describes his own loving bedfellow in "Song of Myself," summoning the image of the lover-
poet who blows the breath of life into his disciple. The literature he
imagines and intends to create will also breathe life into men,
celebrate manly friendship, and chart those masculine landscapes

not yet adequately recorded in print, providing an alternate language for the description of manly love. These new texts will be not only drenched in sex but informed by the metaphors of manly friendship that will site friendship within the specific terrain of homosexual love and sex and reclaim it from the terrain of criminality and vituperation.

Whitman was aware that the construction of sexualities depends as much on language as on sexual activities; sexuality can be derived as potently from the text as from an embrace. His excursions had convinced him that there was no literature because there was no useful language in which to express it. What is "important in poems" is the ability to name "in specific words" what he calls "the main matter." That main matter "is so far quite unexpressed in poems; but . . . the body is to be expressed and sex is." Sex, "avowed, empowered, unabashed," is that on which "all existence, all souls, all realization, all decency, all health, all that is worth being here for, all of women and of men, all beauty, all purity, all sweetness, all friendship, all strength, all life, all immortality depend" (Bradley 739–40). In that torrent of words, the subtle even sly inclusion of "friendship" should not be ignored, nor the more daringly though invisibly inserted correlative assertion that friendship too depends on sex. To find the "specific words" to describe this special dependency is the task Whitman set for himself.

His recognition of the need to create these words indicates Whitman's awareness of the difficulties accompanying such invention, derivation, and definition. His insistence on their present absence (as well as their absent presence) and on the powerful subtext that their absence implies suggests his awareness also of a climate hostile to what these absent words potently suggested and of the linguistic horror that the possibility of their coinage inspired in readers. Michael Moon speaks about the "increasing predominance of homophobia in American society from the 1830's forward."[16] In the face of that, such texts as might have existed, among them those texts Whitman had already written and those he proposed to write, necessarily existed in a state of considerable, though perhaps not clearly understood, tension with the presumptions of a society in which homosexual acts were linguistically eradicated so as "not to be named among Christians." They were, indeed, not named until that intense discourse Foucault has identified began to transform sin into sickness, act into desire. Whitman stands precisely at that point when it first began to appear that the sodomite who had been a "temporary aberration" might well become a homosexual "species."[17]

Whitman stands at the beginning of this changing discourse and is an initial and powerful participant in it, clearly seeing what Foucault describes—namely, that language could translate a solitary or a shared act of physical release into a community, even a communion, of desire, changing sex into sexuality. Whitman seems to be well aware that such possible and provocative texts— specifically privileged, embodying discourse at once secret, forbidden, and necessarily indirect—were also potent agents for calling into life not only the discourse but the very society they hopefully and effectually prophesied. Therefore Whitman's formulae—"manly friendship," "the young men" of the states, and "men like me" recognize that there were men who might be conceived of as citizens in this shared community of desire, a community that shared not only sexual but certain social and psychological responses and perhaps even a specific historical consciousness. Standing "outside of" the world of the common reader, Whitman's brief suggestive phrases and his coded formulae can be deciphered to read: uniqueness, difference, separateness, perhaps even awareness of oppression. Here is the conviction that such desire dominatingly defined even the minor acts of daily life, and here in that stated "shall" and that implied but imperative *must* is the urgent exposition of the necessity for the translation of that same breath, described in the beginning of "Song of Myself" as "respiration and inspiration," into the active weapons of words.[18] In *Calamus* 1 (1860), when Whitman described manly love as "the life that does not exhibit itself yet contains all the rest," he had formulated the first modern definition of a homosexuality, perhaps even the first definition of a homosexual sensibility, which he succinctly named in "Song of the Open Road" and defined in *Calamus* 6: "O adhesiveness! O pulse of my life!"

Whitman's meditations—perhaps more accurately his passionate engagements—with men's words, always seem to suppose a repeated question, a homosexual question. He asks it in these notes that may have been written prior to "Song of Myself:"

Why be there men I meet, and [many] others I know, that while they are with me, the sunlight of Paradise [warms] expands my blood—that [if] I walk with an arm of theirs around my neck, my soul leaps and laughs . . . that when they leave me

the pennants of my joy sink flat and lank in the deadest
calm? . . . Some fisherman . . . some carpenter . . . some driver . . . men, rough, not handsome, not accomplished, why do I
know that the subtle chloroform of our spirits is affecting each
other, and though we may [never meet] encounter not again,[we
know feel that] we two have [pass] exchanged the right [myste-
rious] [unspoken] password [of the night], and [have] are thence
free [entrance] comers to [each] the guarded tents of each other's
[love] most interior love? (What is the [cause] meaning, any
how, of my [love attachment] adhesiveness for toward others?—
What is the cause of theirs [love for] toward [for] me?)—(Am I
loved by them boundlessly because my love for them is more
boundless? (*DBN* 3:764–65).[19]

What a remarkable passage this is. The speaker assumes both
Whitman's reported and fictive persona. Here detailed are the
specific effects of his excursions among the young men of these
states, which he had reported to Emerson, and indeed there is also
an echo of Emerson's own warm rejoicing in those he saw in the
street, whose language of turning eye-balls spoke to him. Here
Whitman conflates flesh and spirit in his best manner; the expanded phallic pennants and pulsing blood recall and foretell
poetry past and to come. The leaping and laughing poet conjures
the voice that describes the twenty-ninth bather and the sleeping
dreamer. Both are made more comprehensible by the certain
homoerotic context of this note. The "breath of manly love"
becomes more potently defined when read in conjunction with the
"subtle chloroform," an aphrodisiac that he intoxicatingly shares
with fishermen, carpenters, drivers, and other "rough" men, all of
them muscular young men of these states, all of whom he embraces, like his words, with the gesture so typical of his descriptions of the need for the touch of comrades: "I walk with an arm of
theirs around my neck." The encounters with these men are
precisely those detailed when he asks in other lines about the love
of strangers, for here too the adventures are not conducted within
the realms of conventional social proprieties, but are contained
instead in the erotic universe of a single glance, an "encounter" on
a city street. This encounter becomes a testament to the existence
of a special language nonverbally employed by special men in a
special world—the "mysterious unspoken password of the night."

This word not only intoxicates; it fascinates. It opens worlds into which only "men like me" can pass. The military metaphor governing the entire passage hearkens forward to the armies of lovers who will march in *Calamus* and to those soldier boys whose elegies will be chanted in *Drum-Taps*. It enlarges perceptions of the sentries who guard and then "desert" him, or perhaps more accurately free him by desertion, in section 28 of "Song of Myself." The closed indirection of the language—*mysterious, guarded, interior*—expands the obsessive secrecy of the passage. This love is surrounded by mystery, protected from the potentially hostile onslaughts of the "other" world, and is in fact so closed that it has no exterior manifestation at all. By those who "know" it, it is known as an interior response to the coded signals of desire. This realm is jealously guarded by those who inhabit it. They are indeed a beleaguered army and a sacred band of lovers, an encampment of soldier comrades whose interior love cannot reveal itself or even speak its name.

As the speaker moves intimately and inwardly through the battle lines, toward the guards, uttering the password that gives him access to his rendezvous with lovers, he is determined to find the "specific words" that define what he feels and what he does. How fascinating is his initial homosexual question about the "cause" of adhesiveness, which he quickly changes to the far more profound query about its "meaning," thus transferring "adhesiveness" from the realm of sex to that of sexuality, from the realm of sin and pathology to the erotic discourse that embraces all others— social, political, and spiritual. How moving also is the repeatedly deleted though progressive struggle toward definition—"love" to "attachment" to "adhesiveness"—making clear that the feeling is special and unique enough to need a new word, since none yet coined, not "love" nor "attachment" will suffice. The entire passage floats on the intoxication of the subtle chloroform and dilates on manly breath and breathlessness. Indeed, it is almost breathless in its onrushing attempt to question and define. Here is the world of the sudden and indrawn breath of the recognition of sexual comrades and the breathless "inspiration," as well as the slow "respiration," of sexual desire fulfilled. In this world no breath of manly love can be uttered save in the guarded tents. Indeed, in this circumscribed and guarded world, love is paradoxically "more boundless" because it is between men, for only men know the password.

There is another dimension to this passage also. Numerous commentators have mentioned the mixture of masculine and feminine imagery Whitman appropriates in his sexual descriptions. Gilbert and Gubar have suggested that one of the central symbolic concerns of women's literature is the enclosed vagina-like cave they describe as, among other things, "female space."[20] Their point, also applied to Whitman by Killingsworth, is that much of Whitman's sexual imagery involves just this enclosed enfolding, which links it to vaginal imagery and sexuality and sets it against assertively displayed masculine sexuality. In this kind of imagery, as Killingsworth says, "male creative power is thus thoroughly infused with femininity. Moreover masculinity, as a model for creative power, is not as comprehensive as femininity, with its deep enfolding."[21] That Whitman's lines above display deep enfolding seems clear; and Whitman as phallologocentric poet penetrates into the guarded tents, here no longer feminine but masculine secret havens of desire. But just as Whitman urges a homosexual rejection of vaginal imagery, while employing it, when he demands "*Do not fold* yourself so in your pink tinged roots timid leaves" (*Calamus* 2; my italics), so in these lines his use of enfolding and enclosed imagery does not empower but immasculates— masculinizes—its feminine parallels, for the sole occupants of the tents are men whose availability for adhesiveness not only excludes women but indicates that women can never have access to the passwords of the night. As Lawrence Lipking has noted about women in male texts in another context, in this male text women do not have the ability to speak. Here the words of power have transformed the vaginal cave—now penetrated by that long phallic line—"love affection adhesiveness"—into a masculine space, no longer feminine and enclosed, but masculine, homosexual, and therefore, "more boundless."[22] This passage is a central and passionate lexicon that foretells and recalls. It is an intense exercise in the poetic transgression and inversion of gender-oriented imagery and a definitive locale of the primary and dominant homoerotic metaphors that inform Whitman's text.

I conclude with a diversion, though one not without a serious intent. Though Whitman had determined when laying down rules for composition to "take no illustrations" from other texts (*NUPM* 1:101), he did illustrate his own with that erotically arrogant picture that invitingly prefaces the first edition of *Leaves of Grass*. In the notebooks, Whitman passingly glanced at the work of Jean Paul

Richter, naming him as "the originator of much of the soft and
sentimental ways of the swarm of tale writers of the last thirty
years." About Richter, Whitman includes one pointedly chosen
detail, commenting that he "stood out in costume, wore his shirt
open at the neck, &c—horrified all the Magisters—held out in
costume seven years then returned to orthodoxy" (*NUPM* 1835).
By the time he wrote this entry in 1856, Whitman had certainly
renounced orthodoxy, rejected the stylistic textures of his own soft
and sentimental tales, though not their deeper structures, and as his
portrait in *Leaves of Grass* (1855) shows, also stood out in costume
and wore his shirt open at the neck. I weave Richter and Whitman
within the fabric of a companion discourse when I note that in a late
edition of *Sexual Inversion* Havelock Ellis observes:

Certain peculiarities of taste as regards costume have rightly or
wrongly been attributed to inverts . . . and may here be mentioned. Tardieu many years ago [1857] referred to the taste for
keeping the neck uncovered. This peculiarity may certainly be
observed among a considerable proportion of inverts, especially
the more artistic among them. The cause does not appear to be
precisely vanity so much as that physical consciousness
which . . . induces the more feminine . . . to cultivate feminine
grace of form, and the more masculine to emphasize the masculine athletic habit.[23]

From Whitman's casual picture, if Ellis is right, insightful readers
could construct a revealing text, one that might also invoke in them
curiosity about an equally and provokingly ambiguous use of the
word "habit." Ellis' late choice of "athletic" constructs another
text as well, for it resonates against these notebooks wherein
Whitman also employs and eroticizes that telling sign of the
masculine and homoerotic habit and converts the flesh to words:
"Man's words . . . are all words to identify an . . . athletic . . .
erect . . . lusty body." Whitman will use it again in *Calamus* 38
when he comes to raise sex to metaphysics, describing manly love
as "the last athletic reality," where "I ascend, I float in the regions
of your love O Man." This erotic and athletic ascent, the specific
homoerotic recreation of the great dissolution and rebirth at the
end of "Song of Myself," returns us to those regions where the
"sunlight of paradise" illuminates and the "subtle chloroform" of

desire intoxicatingly perfumes the guarded tents of a specifically masculine love.

Perhaps his insistence in 1856 that there were no literary ancestors to challenge his claim of primacy in a task he would soon announce is evidence of that anxiety of influence that is said to beset our writers. Perhaps it was also an attempt to pre-empt for himself a subject he already felt was in the air and to appropriate to himself the originating responsibility for the invention of the manly discourses he claimed not to find. But though he was, in fact, a relative latecomer to some aspects of the American homo-erotic discourse, because of what he had already written by 1856 in his early poetry, fiction, notebooks, and in *Leaves of Grass,* he had, more profoundly, originally, and extensively than any other American writer, early and militantly joined battle against the production of those discourses that as Foucault says through "an *incorporation of perversions* and a new *specification of individuals*" sought to engage in a "new persecution of peripheral sexualities."[24] Perhaps he did not know what he had done; perhaps he was not satisfied with it and, as he would say in "Starting From Paumanok," sought to clear a path ahead for a more sufficient manifesto. The path, of course, will lead from his problematized assertion that there is no manly friendship in print to the solution, which is to sing no songs but those of manly attachment. It will come to sacred groves and the holy waters of *Calamus* shores. But it begins in the "hurried walks of life," where, impelled by the glance of "young beings, strangers" (*NUPM* 1:74), the swelling fountains of love start to flow.

4

The Fountains of Love

Poetry and Fiction, 1838–1850

Why was it that from the first moment of seeing him, the young man's heart had moved with a strange feeling of kindness toward the boy? He felt anxious to know more of him—he felt that he should love him. O, it is passing wondrous, how in the hurried walks of life and business, we meet with young beings, strangers, who seem to touch the fountains of our love, and draw forth their swelling waters.

— "The Child's Champion," 1841

If certain nineteenth-century readers of Whitman had been given access to notebooks written around 1847, men who loved men might have found the force of erotic scripture in the unmistakable mythology that vibrated about the image of that Fierce Wrestler, in whose powerful masculine embrace that unnamed lover deliriously struggled, and to whose sexual power he so willingly surrendered in these lines:

> Fierce Wrestler! do you keep your heaviest grip for the last?
> Will you sting me most even at parting?
> Will you struggle even at the threshold with spasms more
>   delicious than all before?
> Does it make you ache so to leave me?
> . . . .
> Pass as you will; take drops of my life if that is what you are
>   after. . . . . . .
> I held more than I thought
> I did not think I was big enough for so much ecstasy. . . .
> (*NUPM*: 77)

But those same special readers, had they read some of the poetry or short fiction one Walter Whitman wrote and published a few years earlier than the notebooks, would have had to be especially sympathetic and penetrating searchers for intimations of homosexuality or for disguised hints of homoerotic longing to readily and obviously find what they hoped to discover. Yet textuality does intimate, nuances call out to those who need to hear, and in the early poetry and prose, the coming of the Fierce Wrestler is subtly prophesied, and masculine landscapes can be dimly perceived.

Whitman published his first poem in 1838, his first fiction in 1841. He had had five years of formal schooling and had done odd jobs and trained as printer, a trade he entered in 1835. His work was cut short by the great fire of August 1835, and in the summer of 1836, at the age of seventeen, he began teaching in Long Island. Over the next three years until the end of 1838, he held several teaching posts, all of them in one room schools, and if he was noticed at all, it was as a minor eccentric who kept to himself. He was well liked by his pupils, as one of them, Charles Roe, recalls: "We were all deeply attached to him, and were sorry when he went away." When he went away, he went home and spent the summers with his large family—his silent and difficult father, his brothers, George, Jeff, Andrew, and Eddy, and his sisters Hannah and Mary. His mother, who had once described him as "a very good, but very strange boy," was his adored icon. To her he attributed his genius, to her he unquestioningly gave his love. Out of the materials his teaching and family provided, he began to build his fiction, and out of the isolation he seemed to impose upon himself came muted hints about perhaps as yet undefined desires. Charles Roe, however, had not failed to note that "the girls did not seem to attract him. He did not specially go anywhere with them or show any extra fondness for their society," in fact he "seemed indeed to shun it." He did not shun the society of his students, however, and the fondness they felt for him was strongly reciprocated. He told a story about this sort of fondness to a friend in later years, revealing how the "grown up son of a farmer" with whom he had been boarding while he was teaching school became very fond of him, and Walt of the boy, but "the father quite reproved him for making such a pet of the boy."[1] Another story more darkly and vaguely suggests that Whitman was forced to leave Southold where he had been teaching in 1841, denounced from the pulpit as a "sodomite," and tarred, feathered, and run out of town because of his attentions to a boy.[2] There is no evidence for this; it is legend — or perhaps just gossip. It is surely true that after 1841 he never taught again and that he also left Long Island in May 1841, to work in New York. But perhaps this is one of those legends that, even though, or precisely because, it may not be true, hints at a substantial version of reality. His first story, published in May 1841 is called "Death in The Schoolroom" and is about a schoolmaster who beats an innocent boy for an alleged infraction only to discover that he is already dead — terrified to death by the threat of the schoolmaster's sadistic punishment. If Whitman were to be inscribed in this story, he might be there as a reflection of the "childhood" that Foucault says the species homosexual was now claimed to possess — an innocent victim of the punishment of a reproving parent, the object of social condemnation and perhaps of sexual desire — or as the schoolboy pet whose own submerged desires lead to death at the hands of fierce authority. Fictions are legends too, though perhaps also muted testimony to a life beneath the life.

Between 1838 and 1850 Whitman worked as a printer, as a free-lance writer, and as editor for a number of newspapers in New York and Brooklyn. In some of these papers he also began to publish his poetry and fiction, alongside the numerous reviews and editorials he was rapidly turning out. He lived and worked in New York from 1841–45, listing his address at a succession of boarding houses, and with his parents on Prince Street in Brooklyn from August 1846. It was during his busy tenure as a journalist, and after his departure from teaching and from living at home, that he produced most of his poems and fiction. Between 1838 and 1840 he wrote eleven poems. Between May 1841 and July 1846, however, he wrote, or at least published, only two poems, revising and publishing some of the earlier pieces. But during this time he produced almost all of his fiction, over twenty stories including the temperance novel *Franklin Evans.* When he moved to Brooklyn in 1846 he took up poetry again and wrote eight more poems and two more stories. Between 1846 and 1848 he edited the Brooklyn *Eagle,* spent two months working for a paper in New Orleans, and returned to Brooklyn in June 1848. He became editor of the Brooklyn *Freeman* in September 1848, but a fire destroyed the building and brought an end to his career as an editor and journalist. He published no more poetry until 1855.

As Thomas Brasher observes, Whitman's earliest published poetry and prose occasionally reflect the ambiguity of the *Calamus*

poems.³ The reflection is faint, and no strong case for their
profundity or their quality should be made. They are hack work,
the range of emotion narrow and conventional, the subjects clichéd. The fruitless search for affection, the death of fair maidens,
hymns to freedom, the dubious rewards of fame, the solace of
death, warnings against the effects of pride and vanity, and laments
for lost love inform them with the stock sentiments of minor verse
and of the fledgling poet. But a handful of images are worth
examination.

Whitman had been teaching in Babylon in the winter of
1836/37, then at Long Swamp in the spring of 1837, and finally at
Smithtown in fall and winter 1837/38, when he wrote "Our Future
Lot." The poem was published in the *Long Island Democrat* on 31
October 1838, making it Whitman's earliest published poem. It is a
threnody on the inevitability of death, but it introduces one of his
major themes, that is, the inchoate need and anguished longing of
the human heart. He speaks of "this breast" that "alternate burns /
With flashing hope, and gloomy fear," and of the "heart that knows
the hue/Which aching bosoms wear." Man is a theater where
"craving wants unceasing play," his heart "troubled" and "sorrow-
ing" (EPF 28). These opening lines were slightly revised in a reworking Whitman gave the poem when he published it in the
Aurora on 9 April 1842. Therein, the first two stanzas speak of "the
brain which now alternate throbs / with swelling hope and gloomy
fear," and the cravings are no longer "unceasing," but have become
"unrequited." Though death is the ostensible subject, the language of the poem — unrequited cravings, aching bosoms, burning
breasts, troubled hearts — reflects the conventional language of lost
love, and in tone it is the same language that he will employ in
several of the *Calamus* poems wherein he laments unrequited
homosexual passion. It is in this early poem that he first introduces
the image of the longing heart. Here the longing is unspecified, the
object of desire as yet unnamed, perhaps as yet unknown.

It is interesting that Whitman later remembered from this
same period the incident of the "grown up son of a farmer with
whom he was boarding," and of whom he made a "pet," and the
parental reproval of his affection for that son. When he revised the
poem, he changed the unceasing and unspecified cravings into a
fantasy of unrequited love. He published the revised version in
April 1842, a year after he had taken up residence in New York.
Whether as a result of memory, current reality, or just a considered

choice of a stock cliché to render his poem more accessible to readers for whom "unrequited" might seem less sinister than "unceasing" cravings, Whitman was impelled to publish the poem again and change the introspective "unceasing" to the more out- wardly directed "unrequited." Cravings that are unceasing can be vague and dangerous, suggestive of lonely pathology, and need have no specific object; unrequited cravings however suggest there is an object craved that, or who, may not be reciprocating in the way the craving soul desires and that can unthreateningly exist within a sentimental literature of unrequited love. He published the revised poem in the *Aurora,* the paper on which he was working, and the young printer of that paper, William Cauldwell, records that Whitman became "quite chummy" with him: "Fre- quently while I was engaged in sticking type, he would ask me to let him take my case for a little while, and he seemed to enjoy the recreation."[4] Cauldwell's place in this text may be as incidental as that of the farmer's boy. But nevertheless, the poem is a complaint about unrequited cravings, suggesting not only unsatisfied love but unsatisfied desire.

That boys—not girls—were more likely to attract Whitman's eye and affection can be inferred from the comment of his younger brother George, his assistant in 1838 on the *Long Islander,* of which Whitman was founder/editor: "I am confident I never knew Walt to fall in love with young girls or even to show them marked attention."[5] In a poem he wrote in 1840, "Young Grimes," Whit- man approvingly creates a character who did not show the girls marked attention:

> Young Grimes ne'er went to see the girls
> Before he was fourteen;
> Nor smoked, nor swore, for that he knew
> Gave Mrs. Grimes much pain.
>
> (*EPF* 3)

This archetypal good lad will appear often in the early work, always willing to spare his mother the pain of vice or the prospect of her virginal son's association with other women. When Horace Traubel and Daniel Brinton interviewed friends of Whitman years later and asked whether Whitman had been a "gay lad among the lasses" the answer was that "he seemed to hate women." Charles

A. Roe, Whitman's pupil, had also observed that "he did not care for women's society. . . . Young as I was, I was aware of the fact."

Traubel and Brinton, commenting on the assertion that Whitman hated women, suggest ambiguously, naively—or guardedly—that his assessment was one "which forcibly shows how alien even to his hot blood of twenty summers were all effeminate longings."[6] "Effeminate" was a word in flux, moving away from Traubel's apparent association of it with a longing for contact with women and toward its eventual association with stereotypes about homosexual behavior. In number 7 of his "Sun-Down Papers," written in 1840/41, Whitman comments that he "would carefully avoid saying anything of women; because it behooves a modest personage like myself not to speak upon a class of beings whose nature, habits, notions, and ways he has not been able to gather any knowledge about by experience or observation."[7] This jocular—and distancing—comment does not seem to hint at much serious craving for feminine mystery. Was the ache about which Whitman writes a manifestation of the as yet uncomprehended need of comrades, his alleged hatred of women—and his own admitted inexperience—the inexplicable opposite of what to him may have been his equally inexplicable need to make pets of young men? Were the unrequited longings and the mysteries prompted by the response of his "hot blood" to "grown sons" and "chummy" printers? Though he may have had no knowledge of "effeminate" ways, he had gathered some knowledge of the ways of young men already. He had been making pets and chums of them. These men will be translated from the fragmentary reality of autobiographical confession or the suggestive precincts of gossip and legend into the far more sharply defined regions of fiction. Years later, these unceasing cravings will be sharply rendered as the "sick sick dread" of the *Calamus* poems, and the hot blood that Traubel intuited, though perhaps wrongly interpreted, will boil up and fertilize masculine landscapes.

Certain of the other poems offer equally allusive clues that add other features to the geography I am trying to chart. "The Love That is Hereafter" (1840) asserts Whitman's desire to find "one heart to love," a desire not limited to any sexual persuasion surely, but nevertheless a particularly potent theme in the literature of homosexual desire—the theme of the quest to find that archetypal figure the ideal friend. The poem invokes the "mighty powers of destiny," and the poet asks these powers to help him find "one heart to love,/as I would wish to love." The verbal foreshadowing of "them that love as I am capable of loving" is striking. The phrase "I would wish to love" hints at the fear that the wish might be denied and suggests that the "way" of this love is not the way in which most men love. In this world "we seek affection" but rarely find it. Here the heart doomed to loneliness must "die in dull despair," if it does not have "a single breast,/Where this tired soul its hope may rest" to cure the "sickness of the heart" (*EPF* 8). This need for affection is echoed in the apostrophe to the passing stranger in *Calamus* 22, "Passing Stranger! you do not know how longingly I look upon you,/you must be he I was seeking," and in the assertion in "I Saw in Louisiana a Live-Oak Growing" that he could not live "without a friend, a lover, near." So too the sickness and the fear will become the painful assertion of that "sick, sick dread" of indifference and the subject of that most powerful of the *Calamus* poems, so powerful that Whitman excluded it from his final text, which begins "Hours continuing long, sore and heavy hearted." As Allen observes about the early poem, "already this young man felt a premonition of his destiny to be a solitary singer. Despite the friendly faces around him he was beginning to wonder if he would ever find the one person capable of responding as he himself 'would wish to love.'"[8]

There is more than a premonition of destiny however; there is also a similarity of language and sentiment between these early poems that are not specifically homoerotic and those later poems that are that suggests that there is far more than just an ambiguous hint of adhesiveness in them. Allen calls Whitman "this young man," and an unnamed young man is the central subject and the speaker in the early poems and fiction. Certainly "this young man" may well be the same who appears in "Each Has His Grief" (1841), where "luckless love pines on unknown." There "the young man's ills are pride, desire,/And heart sickness; and in his breast/The heat of passion's fire" (*EPF* 16). These same ills—desire, heart sickness, the heat of passion—the "hot blood of twenty summers"—beset the "hero" who figures unnamed in many of these early verses, verses about young men written by one of their own. Would Traubel consider such ills as "heart sickness" and the need to "find one heart to love" unforgivable "effeminate longings? Would the parodist whose lines fix more firmly the usage of that term and who mocked Whitman in March 1860 as "the Counter-jumper, weak and effeminate . . . the creature of weak depravities" take these utterances as a proof for his mockery?[9] By asserting Whitman's manly hot blood, Traubel may well have been trying to distance Whitman from associations with one sort of effeminate longing, but the parodist irrevocably associates him with another.

The early poetry shows young men indulging in the very longings the parodist mocks and by which Traubel may well have been troubled. It is only young men who figure in other poems of this period. In "Death of the Nature-Lover" (1843), a later version of "My Departure" (1839), the youth has come to die. However he does not want to die in "a gorgeous hall of pride/Where tears fall thick, and loved ones sigh," but instead in "the fresh free air" (EPF 30). In the earlier version, the youth had envisioned "the tears of grief and friendship's sigh" in the gorgeous hall. The fantasized death of young men and an attendant weeping friend will become potent and dominate images in *Drum-Taps,* and in *Calamus* 17 the poet will tell us that "Of him I love day and night, I dreamed I heard he was dead." Death seems to be the inevitable and melancholy destiny of those whose hearts must suffer unrequited cravings. Though the poems Whitman wrote and revised from 1840–43 suggest that loneliness, if no other emotion, was affecting him, there are other stirrings—"cravings"—that hint at more insistent desires.

In "Ambition" (first published as "Fame's Vanity" in 1839, revised and published in January 1842), an "obscure youth" lies musing on his desire for fame, dreaming a "youthful dream/of grandeur, love, and power." The 1839 version is a cautionary meditation in the first person, in which he warns himself, the "foolish soul," against the pursuit of fame. The revised version changes the "I" to "thou" and adds an interesting portrait of the young man. He is capable of conjuring up "from out of the depths of air" answers "wild and mystical." He is solitary, a "wanderer," who is "sick at heart" to "have his airy castle thus dashed down" (*EPF* 21–23). The association of "love and power" is first made here, an association that will culminate in the sexual triumph of the Fierce Wrestler in the notebooks and "Song of Myself." So too the nascent persona of the solitary singer of 1855 is more sharply delineated, and the conjurer poet here makes his first appearance and first acquaintance with the wild and mystical ecstasy that will become very nearly the dominant mood of the notebooks and "Song of Myself"—an ecstasy that will be directly equated with homoerotic desire. If this young man's airy castles are dashed down here, he will build them again in air, allowing them to become triumphantly vaporous at the end of "Song of Myself," and rebuilding them in *Calamus* as cities of lovers.

Whitman published little poetry between 1846 and 1848. In "The Play Ground" (*EPF* 33) he again displays a penchant toward melancholy:

> When painfully athwart my brain
> Dark thoughts come crowding on,
> And, sick of worldly hollowness,
> My heart feels sad or lone—

then, like Ishmael who in the same situation went to sea, the poet goes to the playground to see "lovely, happy children" and lose himself in childhood memories. In 1848, "The Mississippi at Midnight" also complains of the difficulties of life. Here the "gazer" looks deep into the "kindred darkness" that envelopes him on the allegorical river. He is surrounded by "river fiends," and the journey down the river seems to him to bury life beneath the "chill drops" of the "tireless waters." Here, again like Ishmael, the speaker is a water gazer searching for his ungraspable phantom of life, a phantom that could be grasped more easily if he could only discover "one heart to love, / As I would wish to love." In a revision of the poem years later in *Collect* (1892), Melvillian echoes are again invoked in a warning to the young pilot of life:

> But when there comes a voluptuous languor,
> Soft the sunshine, silent the air,
> Bewitching your craft with safety and sweetness,
> Then, young pilot of life, beware
>
> (*EPF* 43).

Ishmael too had discovered this danger and warned that such voluptuous "vacant unconscious reveries" can lull the "absent minded youth" into an "enchanted mood." Then, one false move and, "in the fairest weather, with one half-throttled shriek you drop through the transparent air into the summer sea, no more to rise for ever. Heed it well, ye Pantheists!"[10] Pantheistic Whitman had perhaps no less cause to heed this warning than did the young pilot of life who looked back nostalgically and sadly upon his Mississippi voyaging. When Whitman later wrote another poem about that Mississippi voyage, he remembered another phantom lover, "only the man who wandered with me, there, for love of me" (Bowers 64).

During the years between 1841 and 1847, Whitman wrote all of his fiction. By 1850 he had finished writing his early verse. In the last poems he becomes more specific about friendship, a subject that he had been exploring in some depth in the fiction. In the two poems written in 1850, "The House of Friends" and "Resurgemus" (*EPF* 38–39), the images of friendship that begin to appear in embryo are those he will develop in *Calamus*. In the first a "band braver than warriors" is urged to fight on, a band of friends who are "faithful and few as Spartans." The incomplete comparison "braver than warriors" implies the unspoken equation "warriors are brave, lovers are braver," because the "warriors" emulate the Theban Sacred Band, who to death defended liberty and their special love. Whitman's faithful Spartans echo this legend from the homoerotic mythology of Greece and foreshadow the armies of lovers who will be summoned to battle in *Calamus*. "Resurgemus" dwells upon the "bloody corpses of young men," corpses Whitman will enfold in his arms in *Drum-Taps*. These dead boys "live in other young men, O, Kings, / They live in brothers, again ready to defy you." "Again" conjures warrior lovers who, like the Sacred Band, will again defy tyranny, just as lovers like Harmodios and Aristogeiton defied the tyranny of kings, and dying for their cause, were memorialized as heroes for their bravery and elevated as exemplars of manly love before whose images lovers plighted their fidelity. If the death of a beautiful woman was for Poe the most poetic subject, the death of a handsome youth was for Whitman as highly charged. Dead young men and young men pining for love and heated with passion and desire have a tentative habitation in this early verse. In *Drum-Taps* and *Calamus* they will be powerfully realized, their lives and their deaths fully celebrated.

While these poems certainly exhibit conventions of homoerotic texts, they also inhabit another sort of discourse perhaps closer to Whitman and to home, namely a literature of reform texts that composed a significant portion of the current sexual debate, which was becoming more heated even as Whitman participated in it. Such texts as William Alcott's *The Young Man's Guide* (1833) or Sylvester Graham's *Lecture to Young Men on Chastity* (1834) prescribed a system of conduct in which dietary and sexual abstinence countered the temptations to excess in every sensual sphere. The chief actor in these texts was the adolescent male, conceived of as beset on every side by the lures of rich food, masturbation, and women. Young Peter Grimes inhabits these texts, just as he does Whitman's earliest poem. The young men of these texts are, as Smith-Rosenberg says, "frail and endangered male" adolescents, the same pale and solitary young men who are Whitman's subjects.[11] These young men are cautioned against excess and offered the safe haven of the bourgeois home and a late and largely sexless marriage as the antidote to practices that will lead to death. The most dangerous of these pernicious practices is masturbation, which leads to insanity and death. Sex outside of marital bounds — especially if touched by the deeper hue of the unnatural — is the sure path to the same dread destination. Longing for unnamed lovers in an environment in which no woman ever appears and the hovering spectre of death are master themes in Whitman's early poetic narratives as well as in much of his fiction. The anxiety surrounding forbidden sexual contexts and their consequences is as equally inscribed in the "desire and heart-sickness" that are "young men's ills" as it is in the young men's ills that the cautioning pages of *The Young Man's Guide* detail. The forbidden sexual contexts that the reform texts construct are suggestively present in Whitman's texts as well.

Nothing in these early poems directly suggests that Whitman was specifically writing about homosexual feelings or even that he was aware of them in himself. Yet the essential materials are there in his allusive images and tantalizing suggestions. The aching needs of the human heart, lost or unrequited love, the undefined nature of the passion, the need for an ideal friend, armies of devoted warriors, dying youths, the power of comradeship, all are subtextual contexts recalling homoerotic mythologies. These contexts, so much a part of the fabric of his later verse as well as staple subjects of homosexual literature, are here strong threads in an unfinished tapestry.

If Whitman's early poetry is suggestive, the prose he wrote between 1841 and 1848 reveals rather more distinct landmarks in this geography, so that the masculine landscape of his mature poetry can already be sighted. These stories show increasing preoccupation with the death of young men, with the fond delineation of male beauty, and with the grand and central fantasy of so many of these stories — the protection of a young and vulnerable boy by an older and handsome man. The subjects of these tales are almost always young men who are often weak, sickly, vaguely effeminate, and generally misunderstood and oppressed by authority, usually social or parental. In "Song of Myself," Whitman's iconography of desire erotically displays young men. He dwells on their rippling muscles, on the "sheer lithe" of their waists (section 12), on the sexuality of their movement. It is not surprising then that in the early stories a similar iconography can be discerned. The young men, for women are never so fully described, are always handsome, the boys usually slight, pale, finely featured, often ethereal, and tending toward death. The boy Tim Barker in "Death in the Schoolroom" (1841) is a "slight fair looking boy of about thirteen," whose countenance, "however, was too unearthly fair for health . . . a singular cast as if some inward disease, and that a fearful one, were seated within" (EPF 55). The unnamed nephew in "The Last Loyalist" (1842) was "always delicate" (EPF 105), while Reuben in "Reuben's Last Wish"(1842) is an invalid and "naturally delicate" (*EPF* 111). All three suffer from the horrors of punishment at the hands of their elders: Tim is whipped by the vile Lugar; the nephew dies because of the "cruelty and punishment and whipping and starvation inflicted by the new master on his nephew"(*EPF* 104); and Reuben's invalidism comes about because of his father's "wretched sensuality" and drunkenness (*EPF* 111). A beautiful dead boy epitomizes them all in "My Boys and Girls" (1844):

For him there is no fear of the future. The clouds shall not darken over his young head—nor the taint of wickedness corrupt his heart—nor poignant remorse knaw him inwardly for wrongs done. No weary bane of body or soul—no disappointed hope— no unrequited love—no feverish ambition—no revenge, nor hate, nor pride, no struggling poverty, nor temptation, nor death—may ever trouble him more. He lies now in the graveyard on the hill. Very beautiful was he, and the promise of an honorable manhood shone brightly in him. (*EPF* 249)

There is a curious and dreadful beauty about these beautiful dying youths: "There is something very solemn in the sickness of children. The ashiness, and the moisture on the brow, and the film over the eyeballs—what man can look upon the sight, and not feel his heart awed within him? Children, I have noticed too, increase in beauty as their illness deepens" (*EPF* 111). Though this is said of young Rueben, we can hear muffled drum taps. These children are, of course, Whitman's own avatars. He once observed that "the time of my boyhood was a very restless and unhappy one; I did not know what to do."[12] Tim Barker, when accused by Lugar, "seem'd hardly to know what to do with himself" (*EPF* 57). Most of these boys are aimless and unsure, looking for affection from fathers but denied it, punished rather than rewarded for loving. Whitman wrote this story after he came to New York, after he was "reproved"—punished—by a father who rebuked him for making a pet of his grown-up son, after—if the gossip is true—he was punished for attentions to an unknown young man. In this tale the schoolmaster—a job Whitman had just left and perhaps under a cloud—whips with sadistic delight a boy who because he is dead is no longer available to him. Lugar's sadism is not far from the sexual; his desire to hurt not far from the desire to possess. Later Whitman will be brutally possessed by his Fierce Wrestler; sexual ecstasy and pain are never far apart in his best lines. But he will also powerfully possess at least one young man, and perhaps in an attempt at regenerative expiation for Tim, he will order: "Clutch fast to me, my ungrown brother, / That I may infuse you with the grit and jets of life" (*NUPM* 1:74).

Not only boys are pictured in Whitman's early tales. Young men also appear, handsome possessors of mythic and classic beauty. These young men, unlike the wan children, are high blooded and lively, a sacred band of American comrades. Frank, the unhappy hero of "Wild Frank's Return" (1841), is sensuous, virile, insolent, much like those coarse "roughs" idealized in many notebooks and in "Song of Myself": "Dust covered the clothes of the wayfarer, and his brow was moist with sweat. . . . Sitting down on a rude bench, he told a female who made her appearance behind the bar that he would have a glass of brandy and sugar. He took off the liquor at a draught: after which he lit and began to smoke a cigar, with which he supplied himself from his pocket—stretching out one leg, and leaning his elbow down on the bench, in the attitude of a man who takes an insolent lounge" (*EPF* 61). Frank is one of the loving loungers who Whitman encounters in his fantasy, a loafer like himself lounging on summer grass. This exotic and sensuous male is in rich contrast to the dismissively noted "female who made her appearance." She is undescribed by the author—and unnoticed not only by Frank but perhaps even by the reader as well, who may be far more taken by Frank's luxuriant allure. Frank is, as all such men are in Whitman's myths, his mother's favorite; a "capricious, high-temper'd lad" of nineteen, his "kisses seemed sweetest to her lips." The other parental ingredient in this tale is the unjust father. He is an unsavory companion to the wicked Lugar or the cruel last loyalist and a brother to the drunken father of the unfortunate Rueben. He is the unjust father who will drive his son to die. Die indeed Frank must, for it is the fate of handsome men to die in these stories, just as beautiful women died in other, equally sentimental, fiction. Frank dies horribly, dragged to death by his coal black horse, his body brought home to mother, who is thus also punished, perhaps for loving too much.

Not death but madness destroys Luke, the handsome martyr of "Bervance" (1841). Like Frank, Luke is "bold, eccentric, and high temper'd," and like Frank—and like Whitman—he is a second son, whose father denies him love and finally commits him, against all reason, to an asylum where he descends into true madness. Once again, beauty, promise, and a passionate heart are destroyed by the paternal beast. The story offers one wan gleam of hope, one faint intimation of the power of friendship, extinguished before it can save Luke, and that is in the person of Alban, whose perseverance in searching for Luke after he disappears, whose faithfulness in visiting him while incarcerated, and whose eloquent pleading for him before Luke is sent away suggest the dedication of a friend and the fidelity of a lover. Alban is a "mild gentlemanly man, with nothing remarkable about his personal appearance, unless his eyes might be called so. They were grey—large, deep, and having a softly beautiful expression, that I have never seen in any others; and which, while they at times produced an extraordinary influence upon me, and yet dwell so vividly in my memory, no words that I can use could exactly describe" (*EPF* 81). Alban's devotion to Luke and the fact that he is Luke's tutor—a teacher like Whitman had been—place him squarely as a figure within a homoerotic literary tradition, for he is the dedicated *erastes* of Greek life and legend, an inspirer who taught his young *eromenos* the power of love and democracy. He is the devoted lover who sacrifices everything for his friend. He is the Jamesian tutor whose love for his charge informs "The Pupil" or the schoolmaster who inhabits the genre of the British school story, who loves his lads more than a man can say. Like Socrates to Phaedrus, Maurice to Alec, Housman to his Shropshire lad, he loves and instructs the younger man. Those deep set eyes and the softly beautiful expression that speaks volumes when it looked upon his favorite can only become in *Calamus* 18 the side-curved look Whitman casts upon a passing boy in a Manhattan street as he responds to "eyes offering me love."

All of these young men are depicted as sexually desirable. Luke and Frank are presented in brief swift strokes, their good looks hinted at but not fully defined. However Nathan in "A Legend of Life and Love" (1842) is the most fully described of Whitman's fictional young men. Nathan "had hardly seen his twentieth summer. He was a beautiful youth. Glossy hair clustered upon his head, and his cheeks were very brown from sunshine and air. Though the eyes of Nathan were soft and liquid, like a girl's, and his lips curled with a voluptuous swell, exercise and labor had developed his limbs into noble and manly proportions" (*EPF* 115). Nathan combines every detail; he is almost feminine with his girlish eyes, appealingly exotic with his voluptuous lips, excitingly sexual with his manly proportions. He is an ancestor of the beautiful wrestlers who struggle in section 2 of "I Sing The Body Electric," "hair rumpled over and blinding the eyes." His eyes too, also soft like Alban's, are those of a passing stranger. In these stories he is another sensual icon; later he will be the muse.

If Nathan offers in full measure the combination of androgynous beauty and firm manhood that defines the men of the later poetry, Windfoot, the Indian lad who appears in the tale within a tale in *Franklin Evans* (1842), is equally alluring. He is "of the age of fourteen or fifteen years. He was a noble youth! His limbs never had been distorted by the ligatures of fashion; his figure was graceful as the slender ash, and symmetrical and springily as the bounding stag. It was the chief's son—the last and loveliest of his offspring—the soft-lipped nimble Windfoot" (*EPF* 135). Here are more entries in a catalog of desire: Nathan's voluptuous eyes, Frank's sweet kisses, and Windfoot's soft lips. Lips like these will give "a few light kisses in section 2 of "Song of Myself," and Frank's sweet kisses will be tenderly returned on the lips of soldier boys.

These handsome boys are joined in the fiction by handsome men who respond freely and warmly to other handsome men. Franklin Evans, himself a "robust youth" of twenty, befriends Colby, a young man with a "lively good- tempered face" and the two of them become instantly on "quite sociable terms."(*EPF* 128, 131). So too in the fragment "The Madman," Richard Arden, the impoverished dandy, encounters Barcoure, who is as Arden describes him "a man of rather pleasant countenance" and who he later describes as "a strange and dreamy creature" (*EPF* 243). (The dandy and the dreamer will appear again in Whitman's work, often walking hand in hand. It may be interjected also that at the time Whitman wrote these tales he could be seen, as early photographs show, nattily dressed and playing that dandified role. The other persona—dreamer and poet—would also be often photographed, and appears in many disguises in the poetry.) Barcoure and Arden develop a friendship; indeed they "become near and dear to one another," though Whitman cautiously adds that "their friendship was not of the grosser kind which is riveted by intimacy in scenes of dissipation" (*EPF* 243). This is a curious disclaimer, that harsh, active, and penetrative verb "riveted" a curious choice to couple with "intimacy." There is no hint of what sort of "dissipation" they avoided, but the subtext to this disclaimer, colored by the assertion of their intimacy, is the one that in other such contexts— for example, Bayard Taylor's *Joseph and His Friend* (1870)—also asserts the Platonic purity of the passion and describes it, as Taylor does, as passing the love of woman. Whitman backs away from the dangers of implication and leaves the tale a fragment. What sort of story this prospective tale of manly friendship might have become cannot be known, but most of Whitman's early tales are tales of manly friendship only.

A later and more fully realized manifestation of these fragmentary and embryonic comrades appears in "The Half-Breed: A Tale of the Western Frontier" (1846). The hero is a combination of Alban, the sickly youth, and the dreamy Barcoure. His name is Caleb, and "he was a pale young man, from the East—and, because his strength did not allow him to engage in the heavy labors of his comrades (for in the West, all men are comrades) he gladly accepted an offer . . . to take charge of the education of the small people" (*EPF* 257). This is Whitman's first use of "comrades," and he is mythmaking even here, offering a fragmentary image—"in the west all men are comrades"—that will eventually expand into those western cities of loving comrades, the best habitations of democracy. As Martin points out in his discussion of some later American fictions in which manly friendship is a subject, the American West was "a recaptured Arcadia." In the fictions Martin describes, the West is often compared to Greece, "a place where personal liberty, political liberty, and erotic attraction were joined." Whitman conflates the homoerotic valence of the Arcadian image with the West and with "comrades," his definitive verbal sign for manly love.[13]

If Caleb is a pale and sickly figure, Peter Brown the blacksmith is noble and manly: "He was a stout, well-made, strongly jointed young man, with light hair, and clear grey eyes. — Though not what is called handsome, he was far from being ill-looking. His lips were beautifully cut, and his neck might have been taken by the most fastidious sculptor as a model of that part of the human form in some fine work of art." Here again are the lips, here again the admiration of the manly form. We very nearly hear later poetry: "The carriage of his neck, the flex of his waist and / knees. . . . you linger to see his back, and the back of his neck and shoul- / der-side." Whitman lingers here too, entranced by the man he is making. The trinity of masculinity is completed by Quincy Thorne, Caleb's favorite: "Of all the rest, Quincy Thorne, the tall gentle boy, was the one he loved, and whose company he preferred." The tale in which these three figure is a kind of Hardy Boys romance of death, vengeance, and justice thwarted. Throughout it all, Caleb and Quincy, the "teacher and his young intimate," do their best to save those whom fate has decreed should die. They fail in their task, yet at the end the two men — both unmarried — become so riveted in closest intimacy that they forever maintain a "communion of friendship" (EPF 261–91).

These tales of a western frontier in which all men are comrades, in which Arden and Barcoure, or Caleb and Quincey, or Alban and Luke display the faithful intimacies of comradeship, are the prefiguring fictional counterparts of the rough and tumble, sexually charged world of "We Two Boys Clinging Together" or of that most tender dream "When I Heard At The Close of Day." In those poems these characters from the fiction are elevated to potent symbol and finally find a home and a friend. Most of these stories are suggestive only; they are not "about" homosexual or homoerotic encounters. Though of course it is not, and never is, the text seems innocent. However innocence here is freighted with the same knowing subtexts found in Whitman's suggestive definition of man's words, which identified that "erect . . . athletic" boyhood and those "sweet erect lusty" bodies.

Smith-Rosenberg's discussion of the Davy Crockett Almanacs provides a useful companion discourse to Whitman's fiction and to one of his central icons — the wild young man, that nascent rough of the Manhatten streets.[14] In these almanacs, Crockett is an "autonomous, free-roaming adolescent" who spends his life in "a boundless wilderness, daily battling with wild animals and a wilder nature." This figure will also resonate powerfully in "Song of Myself," but he can be invoked here to provide another context for the fiction, since Davy Crockett and Wild Frank inhabit that same western wilderness where "all men are comrades." Smith-Rosenberg demonstrates that in these almanacs "masturbation, the anathema of the male reformers, was frequently if covertly referred to." She points out that "along the Crockett frontier, male sexuality was violent, non-reproductive, usually nongenital, and frequently homosexual."[15] Whitman's stories are violent, and there can be no opportunity for reproduction since there are no women. The stories focus on male beauty and male lives, often invoke a preliminary version of the genital textuality that will similarly figure in "Song of Myself," and display a strong context of fluid and ejaculative imagery—in short a generalized and powerful atmosphere of homoeroticism. Not only that, but the early poems and fiction construct an image of a lover as that archetype, the ideal friend. This ideal is given one set of characteristics in one story or poem, others in another. But retrospectively there are common details attributable to all of these young men and a common plot that they enact. Some are hot-blooded and sexually desirable, others weak, sickly, effeminate and in need of protection. Their protector/saviour/lover is noble and manly, older than they, and as handsome as they are androgynously sensual. They are all beset by a cruel parent, employer, or the wicked world itself, whose authoritarian anger seems directed as much at their beauty as at any real or imagined misdeed. Many of them rebel against the father in the same way as those sons who Smith-Rosenberg has identified as symbolically attempting the destruction of the patriarchal family and the Jacksonian social order.[16] They are inevitably described in terms that emphasize not so much their character as their physical attraction. All of them, whether protector or protected, look out of the pages with inviting eyes, offering lips too voluptuous to ignore.

Of all these stories, "The Child and The Profligate" is the most suggestive and the most fully realized example of what should clearly be seen as an homoerotic genre. The publishing history is interesting; the revisions fascinating. The story was first published in the *New World* on 20 November 1841 and was called "The Child's Champion." It was reprinted under its present title "The Child and The Profligate" in the *Columbian Magazine* in October 1844 and again in the Brooklyn *Eagle* in January 1847. There are variations among these texts. But the significant variations occur when Whitman came to publish the story in the *Complete Prose Works* in 1892. There he radically revised, and at that late date the revisions serve to nullify and conceal the implied homoerotic text of the original tale. This anxious revision of one of the most revelatory of his earliest works is also one of the most complete of his exercises in what might be called "dehomosexualization." As Grier says, under its original title "its theme was then the regenerative power of love, specifically the love of a young man for a boy. Under its present title . . . it became a blatant temperance tale."[17]

The story is simple. Young Charles is saved by a handsome youth from the brutal attentions of a sailor in a barroom. The youth is a jaded sophisticate, but the innocence of Charles leads to his reform, and their friendship blossoms into love. However the story is far more remarkable in its fullness than in outline, and more remarkable in its original than revised form. The characters, other than the sailor and the child's mother, are Charles and the handsome reprobate John Langton. The former is aged twelve in the first and second version (*NW* and *C*), fourteen in the third (*E*), and thirteen in *Collect*.[18] When Charles first appears, he is described as "languid." His dead, hence absent, father, and adoring mother ally him to other young men in Whitman's stories, as does his apprenticeship to a wicked father surrogate, farmer Ellis, who is an "unyielding taskmaster." His kinship with some of Whitman's other boys is sealed when, as he and his mother parted, "each pressed a long kiss on the lips of the other." Though he is languid, he is also attractive, "fresh and manly looking, and large for his age" (*EPF* 70).

On the way from his mother's house to his master's, he peers into the windows of a tavern where men are drinking: "In the middle of the room were five or six sailors, some of them quite drunk. . . . The men in the middle of the room were dancing. . . . in short the whole party was engaged in drunken frolic." But what draws the eye of Charles is not the dancing sailors. Instead "what excited the boy's attention more than any other object was an individual. . . . His appearance was youthful. He might have been twenty-one or two years old. His countenance was intelligent, and had the air of city life and society. He was dress'd not gaudily, but in every respect fashionably . . . and his whole aspect that of one whose counterpart may now and then be seen upon the

pave in Broadway of a fine afternoon" (EPF 71). In the earliest
(NW) version, Langton—there Lankton—is instead described as
"a counterpart to those who might be nightly seen in the dress
circles of our most respectable theatres." Whether there is greater
iniquity in being a boulevardier or a theater-goer is hard to decide,
but whichever place he haunts, he lives in different realms than the
provincial and cheerless world Charles inhabits.

The boy, staring at Langton, is sighted by one of the drunken
sailors, who literally pulls him through the window into the bar,
and upon taking a "fair view of the boy, who though not what is
called pretty"—this is an oddly apologetic comment—"was fresh
and manly looking, and large for his age," exclaims, "There my
lads . . . there's a new recruit for you. Not so coarse a one either."
The sailor's eye for youthful good looks is a curious touch, perhaps
even a sinister one, especially since he seems intent on recruiting
Charles into their dissipated ranks. Charles, however, is apparently not unfamiliar with such attention or with such places.
Indeed, he is a habitué of male establishments. *Collect* says that
"Charles was not exactly frightn'd, for he was a lively fellow, and
had often been at the country merry makings, and at the parties of
the place." But *NW* is rather more precise: he had been at "the
country merry makings, and with the young men of the place who
were very fond of him" (*EPF* 72–73).

The sailor offers Charles brandy, which he refuses. In *Collect* he
says "I've no occasion. Besides, my mother has often pray'd me not
to drink, and I've promised to obey." In *NW*, though, there is no
temperance sentiment. There Charles says brandy "makes my
headache and I have promised my mother not to drink any," for
medicinal rather than doctrinal reasons presumably. Irritated, the
sailor forces the lad to drink, but Charles smartly rebuffs him, and
the sailor, angrier still, strikes him. This passage is remarkable in
that just as its text involves force, so its subtext implies rape. The
sailor's pederastic eye for young male beauty leads him to his
violent act, an act that in the very details of the violence, suggests
forcible sexuality, for the sailor placed "one of his tremendous paws
on the back of the boy's head, with the other he thrust the edge of
the glass to his lips." Charles resists, the liquor is spilled over
Charles, and the furious sailor—in the earliest, later deleted,
version—"seized the child with a grip of iron; he bent Charles half
way over, and with the side of his heavy foot" gave him a "sharp
and solid kick." The scene need hardly be glossed to reveal the

erotic text beneath the violent one, or to elaborate the encoded homosexual rape. Enraged by the sailor's cruel act, Langton comes to the boy's rescue, and "assuming, unconciously, however, the attitude of a boxer," beats the sailor, and takes protection of Charles who "now thoroughly terrified, clung round his legs" (*EPF* 73). It ought to be observed that it is the violence that not only impels Langton to the boy's rescue but also convinces him, as we will shortly see, that "he should love him" and sets flowing the fountains of love and the swelling waters. It is this torrent of desire that carries the two of them eventually to bed, Charles the dreamy boy and Langton, a dandy already transformed into a boxer, transformed indeed into a Fierce Wrestler, by love.

This sentimental situation, like the sentimental plots of his other stories, parallels similar clichés in domestic fiction. But here there is no fair maid protected against the depredations of the villain by a handsome hero who will shortly become her husband. Here there are no women at all. Instead the hero is himself invested with the appealing sexual allure that the street and theater implies. If the hero is attracted to modest maids in those other fictions, here the boy is as active as those maids are shy, for what "excited the boy's attention" is Langton's good looks. Indeed the choice of a sailor as the villain attacker draws upon sexual and homoerotic conventions long associated with sailors, conventions that Melville had already introduced into both *Redburn* and *Whitejacket*. This is not to say that the story is to be read as an incident in a gay bar wherein a lustful sailor attacks a handsome boy and forces him to commit an act against his will and inclination. That is not what obviously happens, but it is what subtextually and subliminally occurs, for the consequences of this event will lead to an irreducible moment of homosexual eros—Langton and the boy will go to bed together. This event is inscribed in the tender and erotic invitation of section 46 of "Song of Myself": "shoulder your duds, dear son. . . . if you tire, give me both burdens, and rest the chuff of your hand on my hip." In "The Child's Champion," one of Whitman's earliest attempts at homoerotic fantasy, are tentative phrases in the discourse of desire. Moon suggests that "the most persuasive evidence that Whitman was aware of the strong homoerotic quality" of the story "is that when he came to revise it for republication . . . he did so by censoring it of a number of . . . pronounced and recurrent homoerotic references."[19] But even the censoring retained a substantial homoerotic subtext, while adding a temperance text, and Langton in all versions remains, as Whitman remains in all revisions of "Song of Myself," a lover and protector.

But why should Langton protect the boy, since most of the other denizens of the place "were content to let the matter go as chance would have it" (*EPF* 73)? *Collect* gives one reason, the earlier version another. In *NW* Charles declined the drink because he did not want it, because it made his head ache, and because he had promised not to drink, while in the later version the temperance motif is strengthened by his promise to his mother. Hence, for Langton in *Collect*, "the mists of months roll'd aside, and presented to his soul's eye the picture of his mother, and a prayer of exactly similar import." He also asks another question: "Why was it, too, that the young man's heart moved with a feeling of kindness toward the harshly treated child?" (*EPF* 74). *Collect* does not answer the question. *NW*, however, does, and makes no reference to drink or temperance, or indeed to mother. Here is the earlier version:

> Why was it that from the first moment of seeing him, the young man's heart had moved with a strange feeling of kindness toward the boy? He felt anxious to know more of him—he felt that he should love him. O, it is passing wondrous, how in the hurried walks of life and business, we meet with young beings, strangers, who seem to touch the fountains of our love, and draw forth their swelling waters. The wish to be loved, which the forms of custom, and the engrossing anxiety for gain, so generally smother, will sometimes burst forth in spite of all obstacles; and kindled by one, who, till the hour was unknown to us, will burn with a lovely and pure brightness. (*EPF* 74 n. 23)

Langton is attracted to Charles, not because of any temperance sentiment, but instead by the power of love. Charles becomes an icon, a "young being" and a "stranger" whose eye is caught in passing on the street and whose bright attraction looses the swelling waters of love. Langton might almost have asked "do you know how longingly I look upon / you?" The deeply felt needs of love and longing establish as their object this young being, this unknown youth, muse and center of desire. Years later Whitman cancelled this passage, cancelling thus a small revelation as well. Here, the language of desire is oblique yet sexual. The imagery of

the swelling and jetting fountains is phallic and ejaculatory. "Unclench your floodgates, you are too much for me," he would soon
say in section 28 of "Song of Myself." The description of the love
that can "burst forth in spite of all obstacles" when it is "kindled"
by a boy such as Charles originates imagery yet to be written:
"Come, I am determined to unbare this broad breast of mine—I
have long enough stifled and choked." (*Calamus* 2). In the story the
love will "burn with a lovely and pure brightness." Whitman had
yet to write, in *Calamus* 14, "not heat flames up and consumes
. . . consuming, burning for his love whom I love." In Calamus 36
he warns of "something fierce in me eligible to burst forth." What
was eligible to burst forth was his love for the athlete who is
"enamour'd of me." The athlete Langton is enamored of Charles,
who simply waits to be taken in his powerful lover's arms, just as
Whitman waited for his Fierce Wrestler and his loving athlete. In a
later story Whitman asks disingenuously, "Who can help loving a
wild, thoughtless heedless, joyous boy?" (*EPF* 255). For Langton,
there is only one answer: "He felt that he should love him." The fire
is kindled, what is eligible to burst forth revealed, and the tale now
moves more deeply into allegory and into a realm of oblique
homoeroticism and sexual mysticism, Whitman's later, mastered,
metier. The too sit side by side now. The party drunkenly returns
to its revels. In *Collect* "they conversed together." In *NW*, however,
"they held communion together." In the former they shared mere
talk, in the latter, sacrament. In both versions midnight comes, and
Langton proposes that they spend the night together at the inn. In
Collect all is separate innocence:

> It was now past midnight. The young man told Charles that
> on the morrow he would take steps to relieve him from his ser-
> vitude—that for the present night the landlord would probably
> give him lodging at the inn—and little persuading did the host
> need for that.
>   As he retired to sleep, very pleasant thoughts filled the mind
> of the young man—thoughts of a worthy action perform'd—
> thoughts too, newly awakened ones, of walking in a steadier and
> wiser path than formerly.
>   That roof, then, sheltered two beings that night—one of
> them innocent and sinless of wrong—the other—oh, to that other
> what evil had not been present, either in action, or to his desires.
> (*EPF* 76)

But in the earlier version the hint of forbidden desires is present. Present too are fictional desires that Whitman censored decades later, but that are far more than merely suggestive here:

It was now past midnight. The young man told Charles that on the morrow he would take steps to have him liberated from his servitude; for the present night, he said, it would be best for the boy to stay and share his bed at the inn; and little persuading did the child need to do so. As they retired to sleep, very pleasant thoughts filled the mind of the young man; thoughts of a worthy action performed; of unsullied affection; thoughts, too — newly awakened ones — of walking in a steadier and wiser path than formerly. All his imaginings seemed to be interwoven with the youth who lay by his side; he folded his arms around him, and while they slept, the boy's cheek rested on his bosom. Fair were those two creatures in their unconscious beauty — glorious, but yet how differently glorious! One of them was innocent and sinless of all wrong: the other — O to that other, what evil had not been present, either in action or to his desires! (*EPF* 76 n. 38)

In this passage, the boy will be "liberated," a far more romantic and thrilling notion than the release of mere "relief." So too, the host's willingness to let them spend the night is a pale revision of the boy's eagerness to share Langton's bed. And once in bed, Langton is awash in amorous speculation. "All his imaginings seemed to be interwoven with the youth who lay by his side!" Surely this is a scene from the mythology of redemptive love, but it is also a scene from the iconography of the homosexual imagination. The ideal friend has been found, in whose arms all ills will be cured, all fears assuaged. Thus this "glorious" pair, whose beauty is so remarkable, become Jonathon and David, Damon and Pythias, Orestes and Pylades, mythic figures from the pantheon of homosexual lovers.

They are blessed by goodness, which is as it should be in allegory, but which Whitman apparently felt in 1892 could not be so in fiction, for he drastically revised this scene. In the early versions the two sleep lovingly side by side, and in the morning an angel visits them, smiling down on "those who slumbered there in each other's arms." The angel kisses Charles and after a "bright ray of sunlight," presumably from heaven, gives him leave. He kisses Langton also, giving the two his blessing. In the *C* and *E* versions

Charles only dreams the incident, and they seem to have become separated during the night. *Collect* cancels the passage entirely; there the two sleep soundly and separately, undisturbed by angelic visitation. Without the matrimonial blessing of angels, the friendship of Charles and Langton is only friendship. But in the earliest version as they lie in one another's arms they are dangerously proximate, and it cannot fail to be noticed that they begin the night side by side, but end it entwined, just as other lovers yet to come would do in section 8 of "The Sleepers": "The breath of the boy goes with the breath of the man....friend is inarmed with friend." A scene from *Calamus* 11 completes the parallels: "In the stillness of the autumn moonbeams his face was inclined / toward me, / And his arm lay lightly around my breast—and that night I was happy." Langton too is happy, his thoughts of the youth engendering powerful emotions of "unsullied affection," his passions burning, like Wilde's hard gem-like flame, with a "lovely and pure brightness." Langton surely and Whitman presumably were happy then, the former with his new friend, the latter with his fictional embodiment of homoerotic passion.

This image of two so passionately intertwined undergoes a dozen repetitions throughout Whitman's poetry and appears in its most specific and marginally provocative form in "Bunch Poem" (1856-afterwards, "Spontaneous Me") where he fully realizes and most transgressively presents the fantasy. There, the "two sleepers at night lying close together as they sleep, / one with an arm slanting down across and below the waist of the other," are the "boy" and the "young man" now come to engage in a dreamy half-waking masturbatory and homosexual encounter. The boy "arouses" the young man by confiding his erotic dream. In response, "privileged feelers" are now given leave to be "intimate" with the penis and testicles—"the hubbed sting . . . the sensitive, orbic, under-lapp'd brothers"—which await the "curious roamer the hand" as it grasps and arouses. The pulsing and steady metrical beat—pangs, visions, sweats—the pulse pounding through palms"—leads to that moment of sexual *jouissance* when the young man, at once "ashamed and angry," is also blissfully purified by the seminal souse and concludes the vison "willing and naked" and at peace. The boy, whose longings introduced the sexual activity of the piece, is also the active agent of the sexual adventure. He arouses the young man with "pressure" and the exciting recital of his erotic dreams and brings him to climax with his privileged roaming hand, releasing in him, as Charles had in Langton, the "swelling waters" of the "fountains of love." The business begun in "The Child's Champion" is finished here. The forms of custom that story metaphorically transgresses are specifically shattered in this poem, not only in the general homoerotic context and the specific homosexual activity, but in the reversal of expectations when the boy, not the young man, initiates the forbidden. But the final line, the "moral" as it were in parallel texts of heterosexual romantic discourse, is most transgressive of all. The young man, like Langton, is "willing" to acquiesce in this complicitous seduction, and after the young man's orgasm, though "ashamed and angry," his shame is washed away by the "souse upon me of my lover the sea." He and the boy are translated into the realms of that oceanic and homosexual mythology to which Whitman will also willingly resign in "Song of Myself." The boy, of course, like Charles, is liberated too, for as Killingsworth points out, "by accepting libidinal desires, the adolescent is freed to love not only himself but others as well."[20]

The ending of the story is a pure expression of a homoerotic utopian dream. Charles and Langton are to be forever together. Langton reforms. In *Collect,* their friendship "grew not slack with time," but in the first version, even though Langton marries, "the close knit love of the boy and him grew not slack with time" (*EPF* 79.) Surely Charles and Langton live forever in one another's arms, graven on their own Grecian urn. As Whitman sees them slumbering "in each others arms," he offers us an early form of one of those many vignettes that appear so memorably in *Calamus* 29 — glimpses caught through an interstice "of a youth who loves me and whom I love." Whitman and Langton each sit in the corner of their respective barrooms. Langton finds there his ideal friend and saves him from the "forms of custom and the engrossing anxiety" of the "hurried walks of life," what Whitman will later call in *Calamus* 1 "the pleasures, profits, conformities . . . the clank of the world." Langton and Charles, at least the implied fantasy hopes, will spend the rest of their days in a very nearly mystical and certainly spiritually uplifting union.

In 1841 Whitman was perhaps still "unremark'd seated in a / corner," waiting for his ideal friend to gloriously appear. But in his earliest poetry and short stories, Whitman cautiously, though deliberately, explores some of the landscapes of homoerotic desire, and engages in homoerotic fantasies. While it is certainly true that specific genital homosexuality does not occur in these works, there is a distinct attempt to explore questions of same-sex attraction and even of sexual identity and object choices. Martin feels that "in the 1840's" homosexuality was "indistinguishable" in literature "from other forms of male friendship."[21] This is largely true, but in the deeper structures of his texts, Whitman is, I think, clearly attempting to make that distinction. The clues are faint and indirect indeed and the signs, "secret and divine," are often opaque. But we should heed him when he reminds us in *Calamus* that texts are never innocent: "I meant that you should discover me so by faint indirections."

Whitman published no further fiction after 1850; there was to be no further publication until 1855. He spent his time on Myrtle Avenue, in a building which he built for himself and his family. He ran a printing office and stationary store, and hoping to profit from the Brooklyn real estate boom, built houses to sell for speculation. He also read voluminously, and following his usual practice, annotated and clipped out things that intrigued him. Sometime in 1846 he had begun to jot down his thoughts in little notebooks, and these notes increasingly engaged his attention. Between then and 1855 he filled page after page, book after book, and as we read through them we can exclaim, like Yeats did in the face of marvels, surely some revelation is at hand.

5

Fierce Wrestler

Notebooks, 1845–1854

Fierce Wrestler! do you keep your heaviest grip for the last?
                                            —Notebooks, c. 1854

Whitman told Edward Carpenter that "the *Democratic Review* . . . tales came from the surface of the mind, and had no connection with what lay below—a great deal of which was below consciousness. At last came the time when that concealed growth had to come to light, and the first edition of *Leaves of Grass* was written and published."[1] Though Whitman insists that they do not, the poems and short stories offer some faint clues and indirect insinuations indicating "what lay below" and hint at fantasies about the sexually roving life. The notebooks however are the best source for that underground sensibility. Their contents—poetic catalogs, lists of names, fragments of poems yet to be written—pre-figure new technique, style, and strategy. These texts reveal a far more interestingly explicit concern with sexuality and with the specifically autoerotic and homoerotic nature of that sexuality. Here is the level "below consciousness," where flourish those roots of concealed growth the "sweet" and "timid leaves" that in *Calamus* 2 are "the blossoms of my breast"—live-oak, calamus, leaves of grass. These notebooks might well be called the unwritten private diaries of the young men whose veiled and allusory desires inform both plot and story in Whitman's fiction and the early poems. In these notebooks the young man who seeks the protection of an older man, the yearning youth who longs for a friend, or the troubled and dissolute hero who in saving a handsome boy saves himself, is engaged by more than indirection: the discourse of desire is enhanced by specifically described and richly imagined sex. Vague wishes become specific fantasies; incoherent longing becomes the coherent need for male love. The young man who in an early poem had vaguely hoped to find a friend to love, in the notebooks creates a powerful partner to master, subdue, and indeed, to rape him. The singular becomes double; desire creates; the Fierce Wrestler, muse and master, is born.

These notebooks, written during 1845–50, begin with a series of autobiographical sketches, "Family Notes and Autobiography," offering facts and dates, context, and the "surface of the mind." The second group, "Brooklyn and New York," begins to dive deeply beneath that surface. Two of the earliest entries, "Of a Summer Evening" and "This Singular Young Man," present the figure who had become the central presence of the fiction and poems—the lonely, yearning, sensitive youth. In the first selection, the youth mourns his mother's death (surely the worst of Whitman's fears—perhaps the most potent of his desires?). But no matter whether poet or persona, character or construct, or figment of the reader's interpretation, the text follows hard upon mortal brooding with inward turning:

This singular young man was unnoted for any strong qualities; and he certainly had no bad qualities . . . possessed very little of what is called education. —He remained much by himself; though he had many brothers, sisters, and relations and acquaintances. —He did no work like the rest. —By far the most of the time he remained silent. —He was not eccentric, nor did any one suspect him insane: —He loved in summer, to sit or lean on the rails of the fence, apparently in pleasant thought. —He was rather less than the good size of a man: his figure and face were full, his complexion without much color, his eyes, large, clear, and black. —He never drank rum, never went after women, and took no part in the country frolics. (*NUPM* 1:50)

Though this young lounger, leaning on the rails of the fence, solitary, isolated, idle, prefigures the more robust figure who will greet us on the frontispiece of *Leaves of Grass* a decade later, there he has acquired voice, power, and potency, and introspection becomes bold invitation and utterance. He is the loving lounger in the poet's path and the loafing poet. But here he is the same singular young man who figures in the stories and poems. Like them he is slight, rather "less than the good size of a man," lacking, therefore in those attributes of rough manhood that Wild Frank possesses, but sharing in the sensitivity of Alban, Charles, and all the unnamed young men in the poetry who only wish but do not act. Like Young Grimes, another singular young man who

> ne'er went to see the girls
> Before he was fourteen:
> Nor smoked, nor swore, for that he knew
> Gave Mrs Grimes much pain,

and like the Whitman that Traubel describes, who "the girls never seemed to attract," this young man has abstained from all the vices. And of course there are those eyes, penetrating and remarkable, like Alban's. Eyes always express the undefinable in the stories and early poems just as they specifically indicate in all the later texts, offering passionate unspeakable love to passing strangers, becoming the means and medium for sexual invitation and seduction in the homoerotic imagery of *Calamus*.

The singular young man described here is, most importantly, "singular"—unique, alone, different, as the dark eyes contrasting with his pale complexion physically picture him to be, and sexually different too. Indeed that same pale complexion may well indicate that difference if Melville's Claggart signifies, just as the host of pale and sensitive men who figure in the cautionary literature of masturbation—practitioners of the solitary vice— become the usually isolated and "different" men who populate English and American homoerotic poetry and fiction in the later nineteenth and early twentieth centuries, an implication that can be drawn from Michael Moon's comments situating anti-onanist literature within a homophobic discourse.[2] Difference and isolation is the essential quality of all the young men in Whitman's stories and poems: Luke, eventually isolated by madness and by lack of paternal love; Wild Frank, yearning for a father's love that he can never have; and young Charles, daringly seeking it in a barroom and finding it in the arms of Langton. Though not all the singular young men discover comfort and fulfillment of desire as Charles and Langton do, this notebook entry is inscribed within but expands the same discourse that "The Child's Champion" had begun to fully explore and provocatively realize in fantasized consummation.

What is most important about the young man is his health and cultural context: he is neither "eccentric" nor "insane." He is neither educated nor informed by fixed values. He is a blank slate, with neither "strong" nor "bad" qualities, on which can be written new words. He escapes the interior isolations of the stories and poems, which occur in closed and claustrophobic venues—the interior monologues of the poems, Luke's punishing parentally created incarceration, Frank's obsessive paternally created isolation, the narrow and painful authoritarian schoolroom, and the closed economy that exploits young Charles and drives him to the equally closed and sexually dangerous barroom of "The Child's Champion" (though once there Charles is able to enter unfettered regions of love in the upstairs bedroom of the inn, where Divinity destroys enclosure and angels watch).

This uneducated, and hence unspoiled, young man stands upon the threshold of the summer world of "Song of Myself" and *Calamus*, where he is not obliged to go "after women" or to participate in the "country frolics," which denote intimate social, and potential sexual, association with women. This is a masculine landscape in which the texts of the inscribing world remain unread or can be ignored and in which even eccentricity and insanity—dangers contextually associated with the sexually excessive and the perverse by the paternal Others of the closed world—are transformed into good health.

This entry and "Of a Summer Evening" (*NUPM* 1:46), written at about the same time, also confront death. Both the singular young man and the boy in "Of A Summer Evening" see visions of death, each being granted "the power of a foreseer." Curiously, the boy who foresees his sister's death in "Of a Summer Evening" is given his dream of his mother's death after he fell asleep "with the tears of a foolish passion yet undried upon his cheeks." Passion in the poems and stories is inevitably directed towards men and boys, and if tears are shed, they are for the loss or absence of lovers. That mothers should die in dreams fertilized by unhappy and anxious love affairs is an obvious enough commentary on the locations of judgment and punishment. Indeed, in the poems, stories, and the notebook entries I have discussed, the one constant female is the mother, and she is often hurt, punished, or displaced in her son's affections. Langton steals Charles from his mother, while Frank's mother is faced with, and punished by, the horrible spectacle of her dead son. In "Of a Summer Evening," with tears of guilty passion on his cheeks — passion unnamed but, since he is one with all Whitman's young men who "have nothing to do with women," he too surely dreams of his Langton — the foolish boy dreams his mother to death, disposing of her while loving her. The singular young man who never went after women turns his back on them entirely, leaving his mother alone at dinner, and in his vision he sees his sister dead as well.

While sisters and mothers die in dreams, handsome men are saved to live again in the fragment "Distinctness every syllable" (*NUPM* 1:48). Pete, like Frank, "coarse, wild, sensual, and strong" saves his "tipsy friend" from the "wildest storm he had ever known." Pete brings his friend back and "had a good time fighting the death in him the whole night." But he "saved him." In both the notebooks (*NUPM* 1:74) and section 40 of "Song of Myself," Whitman will be a saviour again. He will urge his "ungrown brother" to "clutch fast to me" as "I infuse you with jets of life." And of course Whitman the wound dresser will fulfill in life these messianic desires to save young men. In this notebook entry, Pete is both wild Frank and Langton. Like Langton, "coarse, wild and strong had been his life," and like Langton, he saves his young friend from death. Like Langton, he has rejected the priggish manners and morals of society, for "the castrated goodness of schools and churches he knew nothing of." Indeed, like the poet of *Calamus* 1, he rejects "the standards hitherto published." These young men, so unlike the dreamy and sensitive boys with whom they seem inevitably to become paired, are the fictional and prefiguring counterparts of those lists of roughs Whitman so delighted to compile, the brothers of the "dear friends" who flock around him in *Calamus*, the fictional recreations of those same roughs Whitman so admired and with whom he eagerly consorted on the streets of Manhattan.

These tales of young men protected by older men, these stories of inevitably handsome, uneducated, and rebellious youths — all of whom are described in one way or another as coarse, wild, and sensual — hark to the conventions of homosexual texts in which older men teach, protect, or love their younger lover/pupils, or more directly, simply desire them. In these texts, handsome, uneducated youths — those "erect . . . athletic . . . upright . . . unstained . . . lusty" bodies, uneducated and thus uncorrupted by

the moral strictures of a castrated society—become icons of sexual
desire. These texts engage fantasized sexuality couched in obscure, and obscured, sexual descriptions—a protective older lover
and an exotic and eroticized young man who must be trained or
tamed, civilized or taught, and who will become an ideal friend
with, as Wilde said, "all the hope and glamor of life before him."
And a subtle but suggestive homoerotic subtext plays as a powerful
obbligato beneath the more conventional and even moral purpose
of the texts. Remember that "A Legend of Life and Love," for
example, is a tale of sentimental morality. But Nathan, its hero, is
described with a passion so loving that it could almost be described
as pornographically desirous. He is the beautiful youth with hair
"clustered upon his head," with lips that "curled with a voluptuous swell," "soft and liquid eyes," and a body of "noble and
manly proportions." No matter how evident the intent to draw a
moral may be, Nathan is as much the object of desire as the *Calamus*
athlete, and this brief description is a love song. The consciousness
of male attraction and the consciousness of attraction to males, two
states of quite differing anxiety, enclose these texts. The growing
realization that sexual fulfillment might be found with what was
desired and not with what was expected, men not women, is the
obbligato theme that sounds in these pages, a theme developing and
experimental, which waits now for its triumphant announcement
and exploration in *Leaves of Grass*.

In the most remarkable entry in the early notebooks, the
startling fragment "albot Wilson" (*NUPM* 1:53–82), written as the
editor convincingly suggests around 1847, the cautious indirections of the earlier texts are suddenly and dramatically displaced,
replaced in fact by the appearance of the mature Whitman style.
The judicious and derivative voice of the early poetry and fiction is
displaced by a very radical swerve, indeed nearly a right angle
turn, into the strong style and voice of *Leaves of Grass* itself.
Whitman rewrites his early works out of existence, and in the
process he saves himself and makes it impossible for American
poetry or his own ever to be the same again. Following lines that
are a recognizable try-out for *Leaves of Grass*, there begins a great
sexual trope:

> Where is one abortive, mangy cold—
> Starved of his masculine lustiness
> Without core

Loose in the knees,
Clutch fast to me, my ungrown brother,
That I infuse you with grit and jets of life
I am not to be denied—I compel;
It is quite indifferent to me who you are.
And of whatsoever I have I bestow upon you
and first I bestow my love.

                                        (*NUPM* 1:73–74)

In this passage Langton or Wild Frank or Pete—that coarse, wild, sensual dream boy—speaks in the first person and lends a voice to the sexual stance of the dominating male thus far silent. No longer the passive though highly vocal admirer of male beauty, whether rough or refined, the poet is now himself the object of desire—and of his own desire too. He is a muscular savior, the powerful embodiment of sheer regenerative sexuality. Just as Langton saved Charles, or Alban tried to save Luke, so this new hero will save his ungrown brother, who is kin to the voluptuous Nathan, to Tim, and to the other dreamy youths. But the emphasis is now not only on protection; it is on domination. Langton may have tenderly slept with Charles in his arms, and Pete, for all his coarse, wild, sensual nature, still labors tenderly to save his friend. But now something far more potent is offered—sexual rejuvenation. The anonymous ungrown brother has been starved of his "masculine lustiness." He will be fed and his lustiness restored. The ungrown brother is—in the original notebook version— "weakened, / Loose in the knees, without core." The young man's weakness arises from sexual deprivation and is both physical— "loose in the knees"—and spiritual—"without core." The boy is "ungrown," unformed, younger, innocent, on the brink of sexual awakening, and he will be awakened. He has fallen to his knees— the presumed effect of weakness and loose knees—and the potent poet commands him to "clutch fast to me," a perfect recollection and recreation of the image of the passive Charles clutching fast to the knees of Langton. The image is sexually charged; yet it is sacred and moving as well. The youth kneels before the poet, adores, and awaits.

In response to the diagnostic question that needs no answer, "where is one abortive, mangy cold," the poet offers credo and intent: "I am not to be denied—I compel." There is no choice now for the ungrown brother but to grow into sexual awareness by a sacramental rape, forced to accept the rejuvenating "jet." This penetration will be the violent cure for the boy's malaise. The promise that he will "infuse" the youth with "grit and jets of life" is made even more potently suggestive by an earlier cancelled text: "I will infuse you with grit and jets of new life." These infusing jets can be nothing but seminal, infusing not only life in the most literal sense but courage and manliness as well, feeding the starved masculine lustiness with new sustenance. The act is violent, sexual, and homosexual. It is the earliest realized appearance in Whitman's poetry of fellatio as a great symbolic act, a precise and phallic analogue to the fountains of love. I describe this passage as a sexual encounter, but I insist on its sacred text as well. It is also the first instance of another great trope of the texts—one hinted at in the earlier poems and fiction but made explicit and profound here. What Whitman did not write in "The Child's Champion" he entrusted to this notebook. What happened to Charles is what happens to the ungrown brother. Dominated before the dominator, communicant before the priest, he takes into his mouth the phallic host and is compelled to accept the jets of life. The act is sexual and sacramental, a homoerotic fantasy that results not only in sexual rejuvenation but in spiritual regeneration.

These lines from "albot Wilson" are also made the more remarkable by their conclusion, wherein Whitman announces, also for the first time, though implicitly, the assertion he will make in "Starting from Paumanok" and *Calamus*—that he will be the poet of comrades and of homosexual love. Though he asserts that "it is quite indifferent to me who you are" (suggesting, at least to contemporary gay readings, one of the presumed aspects of homosexual encounter—namely, anonymous sex—and suggesting a later textual participation in midnight orgies), it may not be such a matter of indifference. Whitman's "indifference" to the object of sexual satisfaction should not be ignored any more than "difference" should be forgotten as the point upon which his texts anxiously balance. Indifference is another dimension of power and an indicator of the possibility of sexual transgression since indifference does not comfortably consort with the "love" that is to be bestowed first, at least not in the common sense inscribed in the worlds of country frolics. Rather, the fantasies derived from the desire for careless and anonymous sexual possession transgress and destroy any of the usual codes of accepted social congress in which sexual forms and expectations are encoded, and they belong strictly to the differing and indifferent codes and locales of forbidden and hidden sexualities, rape, prostitution, masturbation, and homosexuality. And yet the last line, ending the text where it should begin, valorizing homosexuality and empowering sexual weakness, offers the cleansing medicine for all sexual illegalities: "I have stores plenty and to spare . . . first I bestow of my love." He had written in an earlier version: "And of whatsoever I have I share fully with you." It is unlikely that "sharing" was used to mean having sex as Forster uses it in *Maurice*. But that is not so important as is the change to the more dignified "bestow," which adds a generous dignity but does not change the erotic power of the lines. Indeed, the final version of the lines, appearing in "Song of Myself," while much less suggestive sexually, adds one hint as to the nature of the act: "You there, impotent, loose in the knees, / Open your scarfed chops till I blow grit within you." The scarf that ties up the jaws of the dead tells us that Whitman poses here as resurrecting savior, raising his impotent lover from the dead and revivifying him sexually. The open chops provide an opportunity for oral sex but also the chance for the return of speech. Though impotence—lack of grit—is now clearly the illness that he intends to cure, the silence of the grave is banished too.

It may be unfortunate but finally of no matter that Whitman rejected the seminal jets and left only blown grit, perhaps reconstituting the dust to which we return, substituting the breath of life for the seminal waters of life. It is no matter because, whether breath or semen, both imperatively deduce orality and hence voice. Just as Langton liberated Charles from his bonds and his participation in the silent world of economic dependence, and as in turn, through love and comradeship, Charles liberated Langton from the chains of profligacy and allowed him to enter into the contemplation of, and to formulate questions about, love, so this voice—Whitman's voice—is dramatically liberated also. I insistently must urge that the sudden appearance of Whitman's mature style coincides precisely with the clear manifestation of his fully realized ability to create homoerotic fantasy. The exercise of this violent fellatio and the admission of an indifference that defines "difference," together with the achieved ability to conflate this with "love," allows that voice that has been so silent yet so powerfully and suggestively present in all the early verse and fiction to speak at last in authentic tones. It is here at this precise moment that what had in those early works before been merely speech—at the best a repressed writing—now becomes a text: a writing with all the implications of difference and deferral. These seminal jets not only infuse and strengthen that ungrown brother and lover (who is of course but another textual dimension of Whitman) but empower Whitman now to write—and grow—as a reborn poet must.

Whitman's notebook entries, illuminating brief explorations of the metaphors of sexual discourse, explore one of the central questions of sexuality—the locus of power. The imagery is often violent and physically homoerotic, yet the satisfactions of sexual reciprocity and the processes of sexual and aesthetic rejuvenation are the primary subjects of the discourse, a discourse asserting that the ultimate power of sexuality—and here clearly, homosexuality—is as an instrument of spiritual power, as an avenue through mystical ecstasy to a new life. Rejection of the physical and material and denial of the sexual urge are requisite for embarkation upon a spiritual path. Homosexuality, of course, has always been excluded from that journey. Whitman reverses the proposition; through the transforming power of sexuality/homosexuality, the ecstasy of mystical experience can be attained, and spiritual rebirth can be achieved.

The notebook entry discussed above appears on page 73 of "albot Wilson", a notebook of 106 pages. The manuscript shows considerable and interesting revision. Page 74 is largely unrevised. Pages 75–78 have apparently been cut out, and 79, after considerable revision, is entirely cancelled by a vertical line. The missing 75–78 will always speculatively fascinate, but the remarkable power of 79, the earliest form of section 28 of "Song of Myself," and as Bloom speculates perhaps the kernel of the entire poem, offers ample material for examination, for here Whitman abdicates the role of rapist to become, quite paradoxically yet quite accurately, raped.[3] He introduces the figure that shadows him throughout all the poetry, that icon of desire whose presence informs every line and every act, every recreation of himself with which Whitman fills his text. This figure could well have named the poem— indeed "Song of the Wrestler" is a notebook entry—had not the poet finally conquered him and at the end dissolved into him so that he could begin again to read and celebrate himself first and at last.

The Fierce Wrestler is the most terrifying figure in Whitman's myth of sheer phallic power and untamed original energy. His is that Dionysiac poetic voice so sacred that it cannot be yet must be heard, that same "Destroyer and Preserver" that Shelley invokes. His presence is nearly kinetic, reaching out beyond poet and text and painfully, erotically touching the reader, touching his person to ours, which is about as much as we can stand.[4] If there is a signifier of sheer energy—as shifting and shifted as energy itself— which impels this poem into an existence far beyond its orginary voice or greater than any single reading, it is this Fierce Wrestler. His appearance in the text occurs at an extraordinary moment of transition in Whitman's works. It is the moment when the closed formalities and the pretense of a writing presumptively anterior to speech that characterize the early works, in which as Derrida suggests "all free reflection on the origin and status of writing" is suspended, dissolve not only into the substitution of "strong" writing for speech, but into the "merge" to use Whitman's word, the (in)differentiation, of writing and speech. It is the great process of this text that, though it pretends to be spontaneous mere speech, it engages on every front those tensions that only writing can generate.[5] For the Walter Whitman whose fictions we read and for the Walt Whitman who so thrillingly pretends to speech, inhabitant and author of that text, the Fierce Wrestler is the inspiring and alluring homoerotic—and autoerotic—preserving and destroying muse. I quote the notebook passage of his epiphany entire:

> One touch of a tug of me has unhaltered all my senses but
>   feeling
> That pleases the rest so, they have given up to it in
>   submission
> They are all emulous to swap themselves off for what it can
>   do to them,
> Every one must be a touch. —
> Or else she will abdicate and nibble only at the edges of
>   feeling.
> They move caressingly up and down my body
> [80] They leave themselves and come with bribes to
>   whatever part of me touches. —
> To my lips, to the palms of my hands, and whatever my
>   hands hold.
> Each brings the best she has,
> For each is in love with touch.
> [85; 81–84 cut out] I do not wonder that one feeling now,
>   does so much for me,

He is free of all the rest, — and swiftly begets offspring of
   them, better than dams.

A touch now reads me a library of knowledge in an instant,
It smells for me the fragrance cf wine and lemon-blows,
It tastes for me ripe strawberries and melons.
[86] It talks for me with a tongue of its own,
It finds an ear wherever it rests or taps,
It brings the rest around it, and enjoy them[?] meanwhile
   and then they all stand on a headland and mock me
The sentries have deserted every other part of me
They have all come to the headland to witness and assist
   against me. —
They have left me helpless to the torrent of touch
[87] I am given up by traitors,
I talk wildly I [?] am surely out of my head,
I am myself the greatest traitor
I went myself first to the headland

Unloose me touch you are taking the breath from my throat
Unbar your gates — you are too much for me. —
[88] Fierce Wrestler! do you keep your heaviest grip for the
   last?
Will you sting me most even at parting?
Will you struggle even at the threshold with spasms more
   delicious than all before?
Does it make you ache so to leave me?
Do you wish to show me that even what you did before was
   nothing to what you can do
Or have you and all the rest combined to see how much I
   can endure
[89] Pass as you will; take drops of my life if that is what
   you are after
Only pass to someone else, for I can contain you no longer.
I held more than I thought
I did not think I was big enough for so much exstasy
Or that touch could take it all out of me.

                                         (*NUPM* 1:74–77)

"Touch" is the immediate indicator of the direction of these
lines, and "tug," here a noun — the trace or chain of a harness — not
a verb, nevertheless also allows its active sense to lure us toward the
moment of freedom when this chain is pulled and all of the senses

are "unhaltered," all of the senses "but feeling," that is, touch. The implied freed horses of desire, and an earlier version, make it clear: "One touch of a tug of me has made all my other senses run / but feeling." He means tactile "feeling"—now a verb—specifically the act of feeling his own body, touching himself autoerotically. The pulled tug is as phallic as the act of pulling is masturbatory. All of the other senses, in "submission" to the primacy of the imperative sexual touch, abdicate their own sensual roles to allow "touch" to dominate. Indeed all the senses become touch; they "must be a touch." The earlier version reads, "or if that cannot be they will abdicate and nibble only at the edges of feeling."

The introduction of the feeding image—"nibble"—adds another dimension of orality to the sexuality, and his revision of "they" to "she" is startling though sexually more orthodox. Perhaps the cautious Whitman, who, still not sure of his ground, destroyed four possibly fascinating pages at this point in the notebook, was exercising the same kind of caution he would later exercise when he altered the pronouns in "Once I Pass'd through a Populous City" from the masculine to the feminine. Nevertheless, even though touch is for the moment denominated as "she," the sexual exploration continues "caressingly up and down my body," and the feelings offer bribes—sensations—to his lips, to his palms, and to "whatever my hands hold." What his hand holds is surely his erect penis. What his "hands" hold may be what he desires, the fantasized Fierce Wrestler.

What happened in the deleted four pages is a mystery. Possibly the pages were another version of what follows. Or they may have been entirely unconnected to the material, as the stubs of two of the leaves suggest with their hint at a list of accounts. But perhaps they were more specific than Whitman felt he could entrust even to his notebook. Whatever may have been there, the next two lines are clearly a continuation of the argument, except that now "touch" dramatically changes gender. On page 85 "touch" now becomes "he" rather than "she": "I do not wonder that one feeling now, does so much for me, / He is free of all the rest." Whether in the missing pages or in a moment of inspiration, clarity has been achieved; he no longer "wonders". What is clear is that only "one" powerful feeling does so much for him—a feeling "free of all the rest" and now masculine. This one, single, unitary masculine feeling "begets offspring" on all the rest of the feelings, usurping and banishing the matriarchal role and power, doing it better than mothers ever can — "better than dams." We have moved here into a Platonic realm — as the *Symposium* also suggests — where those male devotees of the heavenly love produce children far superior to those produced by the earthly Venus. The union of homosexual lovers produce children of the imagination, while the union of heterosexual lovers produces merely mortal flesh. These lines are Whitman's first realized exploration of the landscape of homoerotic discourse, a country wherein the love of comrades creates passionate words, "man's words," poems of homosexual love.

Now that touch has become masculine, it not only offers physical ecstasy but provides access to the grammar of a new language — "a library of knowledge." Around him now arise sensual fragrances, and he experiences Edenic tastes — for these images consort with those that surrounded Adam when he first encountered knowledge. He smells "wine and lemon-blows," tastes "strawberries and melons." Similar sensual manifestations will accompany those moments of intense homoeroticism when, next to the sacred *Calamus* pond, he plucks tokens for lovers, the lilac, pinks, laurel, maple, wild orange, chestnut, and plum-blows. These essences perfume his erotic garden, where he gives the calamus leaf only to "them that love as I myself am capable of loving." Just as in *Calamus* the love of comrades is the "base of all metaphysics" and offers him untold and untellable wisdom, so here touch also offers a "library" from which he can cull the instant knowledge that will transform the old tongue to the new. Only masculine touch teaches this knowledge and "talks for me with a tongue of its own," the special tongue of homoerotic desire. Here is introduced and identified the tongue that will plunge to his naked heart, the same "aromatic" tongue that will speak to him next to the *Calamus* pond, that "ocean of incarnation" that Plato identifies.[6] But the force of that "for" should not be ignored here any more than should its similar use in the lines in *Calamus* 1 where he creates the intricate trinity of the "soul of the man I speak for." This tongue possesses and inspires and is the tongue of prophecy as well as power. It talks for him, not to him. The touching and transforming tongue is the pivot (quite literally because of its central site in the lines) upon which this passage turns in its movement from an ostensible meditation on the effects of homoerotic touch toward its central purpose as an essay on the necessity for a homoerotics of language.

The offspring that touch "swiftly begets" await section 28 of "Song of Myself" to be fully described. Though unwritten here, the masculine offspring of a masculine touch, children better than children of the flesh, will be described ecstatically in 1855 as the "sprouts" that "stand by the curb prolific and vital." Soon these sprouts—like those men's words that will also accumulate—will phallically populate the "projected" masculine landscapes of art and desire. There ejaculated semen rains down and fertilizes the landscape of the imagination, and out of that richly dispersed potency come masculine poems, their lustiness no longer starved. Here in the notebook at this crucial juncture, touch can no longer have any significant meaning if it is imagined as "she." There is only "one" feeling and only "one" meaningful masculine touch, which section 28 will identify as that which "thrills me to a new identity." This notebook will shortly identify that touch as the embrace of the potent Fierce Wrestler. But it has already conflated "touch" and "tongue," and in pages 85–86 it further identifies these with the aroused phallus and with the speaker himself, for that shifting and unstable "it" embraces all three positions and quickly shades into "me."

The pleasures of touch lead to loss of control. All the senses, now yoked together, "stand on a headland and mock me." Indeed the vigilant sentries—repression, moral voices, the guards at the doors of the guarded tents, and the smothering forms of custom patrolling the busy walks of life—are silent as the roaming hand reaches the "headland," which Bloom sees as the "threshold stage between self-excitation and orgasm,"[7] and which is also surely the erect penis, its ecstatically tender and probably uncircumcised "head" certainly one of the things that "my hands hold." He focuses all thought, feeling, desire, and control on the straining phallus/tongue, which is now the captive of all the senses: "they have all come to the headland to witness against me." The presence of the phallic totem induces loss of control, ecstasy, and the Dionysiac voice of prophecy, for he is "helpless to a torrent of touch. . . . I talk wildly I am surely out of my head." He nods briefly to his guilt—"I was the greatest traitor"—but he is soon mastered by desire: "Unloose me touch you are taking the breath from my throat / Unbar you gates—you are too much for me." This is the moment of ejaculation. The homoerotic imagination now fully takes control and casts aside any pretense to orthodox sexuality. Even autoeroticism is banished, and full-scale fantasy takes command. "Touch" is personified, and the homoerotic muse appears now as a dominating sexual partner who powerfully takes command and who is named "Fierce Wrestler!"

The speaker is the passive youth of the fiction—one to whom time and experience have begun to give a new language—at last held in the "grip" of the embodiment of all those coarse and powerful figures who were so incompletely realized but who now come at last to grapple with him in the person of the potent and long desired Wrestler. He is mastered by this embodied myth, held in its heaviest grip, and subdued by an act of forcible penetration: "Fierce Wrestler! do keep your heaviest grip for the last? / Will you sting me most even at parting? / Will you struggle even at the threshold with spasms more delicious than all before?" Tellingly, "heaviest grip" was revised from the original "heaviest strike," that "strike" a blow identifying the penetrating penis, just as "sting" implies the pain of entry.

The speaker, exhausted, the rapist/lover is urged to leave: "pass as you will; take drops of life." The fantasy shifts, and anal seems to become oral sex. The seminal "drops" are the same seminal jets of life from the earlier lines and the same "confession drops" that trickle from "where I was conceal'd" in the *Calamus* poem "Trickle Drops." Yet he also expresses wonder that "I held more than I thought / I did not think I was big enough for so much ecstasy / Or that a touch could take it all out of me." The delicious ambiguity of these lines—the shifting play of oral and anal activity—is inscribed within the erotic play between the activities and the phallic personification of the two lovers: wonder at the ability to receive and contain the gigantic thrusting penis of his lover, pleasure that his own penis was so richly stocked with the seminal jets of life. The violence of Whitman's text will be the prelude to aesthetic revelation in "Song of Myself." But in the notebooks it is primarily sex that drenches the text.

The violence of these lines echoes too the sexual violence of the nation, which Smith-Rosenberg recognizes in her recovery of the Davy Crockett Almanacs, fascinating popular records of the not too deeply submerged urge to violence that Smith-Rosenberg describes as the "natural characteristic of the young white American male." Smith-Rosenberg identifies this violence as "directed toward women," and demonstrates also that "racism is central to the Crockett myth" as is a virulent jingoistic nationalism.[8] In one of the Crockett almanacs (1836), Crockett engages in erotic and violent wrestling with one of Whitman's own roughs, a stagecoach driver. Here there is no aesthetic subtext but there is an ironic political one. Crockett, one of the wilder young men of these States, rapes the driver into adoring submission: "Says I, take care how I lite on you, upon that I jumped right down on the driver and he tore my trowsers right off me. I was driven almost distracted and should have been used up, but luckily there was a poker in the fire which I thrust down his throat, and by that means mastered him. Says he, stranger you are the yellow flower of the forest. If you are ever up for Congress I'll come all the way to Duck river . . . for you."[9]

The sly suggestion that a rapist might well be a useful member of Congress and that the voter is the passive even willing victim of homosexual rape is as witty as Whitman's eventual assertion that homosexual rape can be the source of poetry is daring. Though this text suggests that the parameters of American manhood and manly braggadocio permit a homosexual context, its apparent valorizing of homosexual sex is inscribed within another context also, for the stagecoach driver initiates the homosexual act—"he tore my trowsers off"—and Crockett brutally punishes him for his transgression against the "yellow flower" of American manhood.

Another manuscript version of Whitman's text should be read with this one and conflated with Crockett's homosexual panic, evidenced by his distraction at the loss of his trousers, his fear that he might be "used up," and his use of the phallic poker as the weapon of enforced and punitive fellatio.

Grip'd Wrestler! do you keep the hardest
pull for the last?
Must you bite with your teeth with the worst spasms at
parting?
Will you struggle worst when I plunge you from the
threshold?
Does it make you ache so leaving me?
Take what you like, I can resist you no longer.
I think I shall sink.
Take drops of my life, if that is what you are after.
Only pass to someone else, for I will contain you no
longer.
Pass to someone else; leap to the nearest landing.

Little as your mouth is, it has drained me dry of my
    strength.
I am faintish.[10]

Whitman's text enhances not only the rape but the orality of
the scene, adding another dimension of passivity, for here the
wrestler not only penetrates the poet anally but satisfies him orally
as well. But the difference is that in Whitman's text the speaker
inhabits the very un-American position of passive recipient of
sexual power, and there is no hint of punishment. Like Crockett, he
fears that he might be used up, but unlike Crockett, he accepts that
exhaustion, even welcomes it, and does not resist the transformation of homosexual experience. Whitman's text speaks to the very
different assumptions he makes about the inscription of male
sexual roles within the received clichés of American manhood. In
the Crockett text, the only acceptable form of homosexual sex—
punitive rape directed against a dispoiler of manly ideals—is
transformed in Whitman's text into the willing celebration of
homosexual desire and homosexual pleasure within the context of
a passive and hence "unmanly" sexual event. The resultant disap-
pearance of homosexual panic within the economy of homosexual
pleasure might allow homoerotic desire to be inscribed as a "natural characteristic of the young white American male." This version
of Whitman's text connects ecstasy, powerlessness, and sex. In
other deleted verses he says, "I roam about drunk and stagger."
Indeed in these verses he fears that it will "kill me." But he
cancelled this close brush with death and insisted instead that,
though "faintish" (that fainting which accompanies pregnancy?),
he was now impregnated by the jets of a new life and that the breath
that had been taken from his throat has been replenished now by
the sweeter air of his newly learned homoerotic tongue.

Another notebook text that also found its way into "Song of
Myself" (as section 26) is "You Know How the One," (*NUPM*
1:124–27). Though much different in its subject than the lines from
"albot Wilson," it is very similar in its invocation of the effects of
overwhelming ecstasy. Here, however, music is the active force
rendering the poet powerless in the same way that sexual ecstasy
had done. If the "albot Wilson" lines directly appeal to homoerotic
fantasy, these lines sexualize music. Here, as in "albot Wilson," the
poet is powerless. But now he is powerless against the ecstatic

delight of music, and in similar imagery, he is mastered by it. That he invokes the tenor and the soprano lends an interesting dual sexuality to the lines, especially since he confesses to having been convulsed by the "love-grip" of the soprano, a grip similar to the "heaviest grip" in his invocation to the Fierce Wrestler. Nor is it accidental, I think, that the "orbed parting" of the tenor's mouth releases the "sluices" of delight. The liquid image with its seminal subtext also recalls the Fierce Wrestler passage, though here the sexual context functions subtextually. We should recall that in one notebook entry Whitman had told the wrestler, that "little as your mouth is, it has drained me dry of my strength." The orbed mouth of the tenor pours out that lost seminal strength, now potent music.

The soprano also convulses him and grips him just as the wrestler had done, indeed actively masters him just as the wrestler had done. The result of the outpouring of the sluices of delight—an image consonant with the "spasms more delicious than the rest"— is an ecstatic and orgasmic experience entirely similar to the "albot Wilson" lines. In its eventual appearance in "Song of Myself," Whitman marvels that the music "wrenches such ardors from me I did not know I possessed," the same ardors translated from the sexually ecstatic to the aesthetically ecstatic, which caused him to observe in "albot Wilson," "I did not think I was big enough for so much exstasy." The "albot Wilson" passage speaks of his "capacity to receive kisses"—receive, not give—and in the passage from "You Know How the One," he wants the music to be "filling his capacities to receive," again a passive image. Music, like sex, enlarges him, "dilating me beyond time and space," and like the striking penis, "stabbing me with myriads of forked distractions," or as he has it a few lines later, "stabbing my heart with myriads of forked distractions." In "Song of Myself" he will consolidate all of these images, the aesthetic and the homoerotic, when he describes his soul plunging its tongue to his bare-stripped heart in an act of sexually aesthetic penetration that results in revelation.

Sexual desire appears disjunctively also. Often, suggestive phrases or images will hint at another train of thought. Discussing religion in this same notebook, Whitman begins the passage with an observation about religion but concludes the passage with what in fact is a reverie about a homosexual embrace. The passage is notable not for its doctrine but for the language of allusive homoerotic desire and for its brief but telling descriptions of young men.

You have for instance been warned through your whole life,
week days and Sundays to pay your devoir [?] to God. Religion
the original and main matter. Really there is no such thing. —
What is called such . . . is but one little sum of that boundless
account which a man should always be balancing with his own
soul. I have seen corpses shrunken and shrivelled . . . But no
corpse have I seen . . . that appears more shrunken, from comparison to the fullest muscular health of some fine giant . . .
more awfully a corpse because a perfect shaped and affectionate
youth, in living strength and suppleness, stands ready to take his
room . . . Religion, seems to me in comparison with the devotion . . . loving in a sort worthy that immeasurable love, stronger than the propulsion of this globe, ecstatic as the closest
embraces of the god that made this globe—fiercer than the fires
of the sun around which it eternally swings—more faithful than
the faith that keeps in its company and place—divergent and vast
as the space that lies beyond—which belongs to any well-developed man which is the great law whence springs the lesser laws
we call Nature's. (*NUPM* 1:124)

Though ostensibly about religion, the focus here is on the "fullest
muscular health of some young giant." The "perfect shaped and
affectionate youth, in living strength and suppleness," is as much an
object of desire as he is an exemplar of virtue. In his peroration,
Whitman becomes nearly incoherent in his attempt to suggest that
love—"that immeasurable love"—is far more valuable than religion.
The love he champions is the love of "any well developed man,"
presumably a "young giant" or an "affectionate youth." Like the
heaviest grip of his Fierce Wrestler, this love creates a passion "ecstatic
as the closest embraces of the god that made this globe," and is in fact
the "great law" from which even the laws of nature are derived. As he
will describe it in "Song of Myself," "a kelson of the creation is love."
    These notebooks are extended meditations on the possibilities
of ecstasy and the sources of ecstatic experience. In "albot Wilson,"
ecstasy is sexual; in "You Know How the One" it is aesthetic. But
in the latter, the aesthetic experience is described in the same terms
as the sexual experience of the first notebook. And the sexual
power of the Fierce Wrestler sequence—clearly homoerotic—will
be transformed in "Song of Myself" into a seminal doctrine
emphasizing the unity of sexual and aesthetic experience. The
image that stands dominantly and dramatically above all of these

entries is surely archetypal—the muscular fine giant, the affectionate youth, the Fierce Wrestler, the homoerotic muse of Whitman's art.

These passages all conflate erotic homosexuality and a homoerotic aesthetic. Perhaps Whitman found them too powerful, for in
the manuscript the entire passage above is cancelled, just as is much
of the sequence concerning the tenor. Indeed, several pages of the
Fierce Wrestler sequence have been cut out entirely—81–84—and
80 and 85–89 of that sequence have been cancelled with sharp
vertical strokes, a stroke as sharp and heavy as the wrestler's
"strike." Whitman confessed, even while giving in to the overpowering ecstasy of "touch," that he was the greatest traitor. He
knew that the moral sentries had deserted him. Were these cross-
ings out and strikings through a half-hearted attempt to return the
sentries to their posts? If so, it was an attempt that happily did not
fully succeed, since he did not in fact destroy these early and
potently homoerotic lines. Cancellations indicate a desire to undo,
yet the artist saw that the work was good; the man saw that it was
true, an honest indicator of desire. Finally, however, he did conceal
his Fierce Wrestler for all that remains of him in the final reduction
of these notebook texts in section 29 of "Song of Myself" is the
personified "blind loving wrestling touch, sheath'd hooded sharptoothed touch." Michael Moon, asserting Whitman's "political
opposition to the cultural construction" of the body as an entity
"subject . . . to regulation by the state," suggests that Whitman
"repudiates the fantasy of the self-instantiated, self-instantiating
phallus as center and ground of meaning which has been used to
underwrite . . . ideas of sexuality, and of power and politics in
general."[11] Here however there is no repudiation; the Fierce Wrestler has surely been epitomized into what to the eagerly receptive
poet was his most elemental, powerful, and desirable facet—a
center and ground of aesthetic and sexual meaning—his creating,
driving, potent phallus, the symbol of power, the muse itself.

In two other notebook entries written about this same time,
certainly no later than early 1855, Whitman begins his interesting labors as a maker of lists, lists that by banishing grammatical
or syntactic connection at once reduce to the essential and expand to the infinite the discourse of homoerotic sexuality. These
passages that make up the entries "Loveblows. Loveblossoms"
(*NUPM* 1:181) and "Sweet Flag" (194) are among the earliest of
Whitman's lists, certainly the earliest in the notebooks, and their
content and concern is sexual and homoerotic: "Loveblows. Love-

blossoms. Loveapples. Loveleaves. Loveclimbers. Loveverdure. Love Vines. Lovebranches. Loveroot. Climber-blossom. Verdure, branch, fruit and vine. Loveroot. Juice Climber. Silk crotch. Crotch bulb and bine [sic]. juicy, climbering mine. Bulb, silk-thread crotch and . . . ".

The hypnotic rhythm of the list enhances the sexually allusive imagery, and that unclosed "and" leads back to the "loveblows" again. As Bucke pointed out, the first entry may be the embryo for section 2 of "Song of Myself" wherein the poet invokes the loveroot, silkthread and vine, selecting from this notebook list the most specifically phallic images, the root, the vine, and the silken threads of semen. But the entry itself is primarily concerned with phallic imagery: phallic leaves, climbers, vines, branches, roots, testicular apples, fruit, bulbs, seminal juice and silkthread, and intriguing crotches. There are pictorial and suggestive phrases, "verdure, branch, fruit and vine," which are themselves phallic spells. Even the last phrase offers suggestive hints of desire, for the juicy crotch bulb and [v?]bine are described as "climbering mine." Perhaps his own juicy crotch bulb and vine have become inter-twined with another's equally phallic vegetation.

The second entry is rich with allusion to both "Song of Myself" and *Calamus*. (I conflate pertinent and interesting dele-tions in brackets.)

Sweet flag Sweet fern illuminated face clarified unpolluted
    flour-corn aromatic
Calamus sweet-green bulb and melons with bulbs [sure]
    grateful to the hand
I am a mystic in a trance exaltation
something wild and untamed—half savage
       Coarse[?] things
[The sweet] Trickling Sap [drops] flows from the end of the
    manly [pole, little] maple tooth of delight tooth-
prong—tine spend spend
bulbous
Living bulbs, melons with polished rinds [the soothing] [the
    hand to touch] that smooth to the reached hand
Bulbs of life-lilies, polished melons flavored for the mildest
    [gentlest] hand that shall
reach

                        (*NUPM* 1:194)

The plot of the entry is this: homoerotic desire is aroused by the sweet flag. The hand reaches to caress the erect phallus: "flour-corn . . . and melons with bulbs grateful to the hand." The poet, who equates the sexual urge with mystical experience, enters a trance of exaltation. To him is revealed the elemental and primal nature of his homosexual desire. This is followed by ejaculation, the trickling seminal drops of the phallic tooth. Out of this sexual moment comes spiritual revelation. He enters the Arcadian *Calamus* garden, where miracles occur. The phallic lilies and the testicular melons are no longer rough and threatening but smooth and indeed grateful—available—to the hand. The taste is no longer bitter but flavored, and the hands that reach do not overpower or inflict pain but are the mildest and the gentlest hands. In contrast to the previous experiences he has described, wherein homosexual sex is at once desired and yet fraught with fear and pain, this moment is celebratory and free from fear.

This entry offers one very important line that informs and makes coherent the sexual imagery of the notebook entries that I have thus far discussed: "I am a mystic in a trance exaltation." This assertion, which is also a confession, elaborates, intensifies, and subtly changes the dimension of a similar line in "albot Wilson." There he said: "I talk wildly I am surely out of my head." But here, the loss of control is qualitatively different and has been elevated—exalted—to a far different plane. For here he is no longer "drunk" or staggering; here he has achieved new and wonderful knowledge. In this trance he experiences spiritual exaltation, a sexual revelation. The text offers clear assertions of his new condition; the phallic sweet flag is "illuminated", "clarified", "unpolluted." The phallicism that surrounds his announcement of a new identity—both an awareness of the power of phallic identity and an increasing certainty about his homosexual identity—is rendered in a breathless, sexually rhythmic stream of free-associative language, tapping deep roots of unconscious desire. His words and his emotions here have the same force and the same impelling rhythms, the same onrushing power, as do the ecstasies he described when possessed emotionally by music or physically by the Fierce Wrestler.

There is, however, a vital difference between the submissive surrender to the Fierce Wrestler and this celebratory paean, and that difference is that force and coercion are not present here, nor are resistance or pain. The phallic and testicular calamus root is grasped no longer in an enforced tight grip but is now "grateful to the hand," falling like Marvell's melons into the poet's eager palm. The imagery, still autoerotic and masturbatory, is no longer fraught with the subtextual threat of rape and violence found in "albot Wilson." Here in this ecstatic Arcadia, as opposed to the suffocating restriction of the Fierce Wrestler's bower, where the atmosphere is so intoxicating that the poet staggers and loses his wits and his rational grip on reality, everything is clear and illuminated, there are no shadows and no doubts, and as is so often part of the description of mystic experiences, the air is "aromatic." The phallic images of sweet flag, sweet fern, flour-corn, and manly maple tooth rise erect and inviting. Action precedes knowledge. The reaching hand touches and then caresses the roots and bulbs. Ecstasy, ejaculation, exaltation follow, indeed explode, and the trance induced at first by sexual desire, concentration, and obsessiveness expands into mystic knowledge and into contact with the vital and the primal, with "something wild and untamed—half savage."

Now the "trickling sap" flows from the end of the manly maple tooth of delight in a moment of delirious orgasm. Sex is illuminated and unpolluted at last, and the phallic lilies of life and the testicular polished melons are now "flavored for the mildest hand that shall reach," that is, no constraint is raised, and touch is now gentle and fulfilling. There are no more sentries. And rising, both metaphorically and literally, at the center of the passage is the manly maple tooth of delight, its function, without impediment, censure, or restriction, to deliriously "spend spend." Awash in semen, baptized in it and regenerated by it, he has entered the phallic garden, and his hand reaches for the sacrament offered there. Here is the source and the embryo of those symbolic moments of sexual revelation that will inform "Song of Myself." This is the first of many repetitions of the central symbolic act of his homoerotic poetry. The trickling tooth spends its semen, and the hand is thus made free at last to reach the "living bulb" and the "life-lilies," to grasp without fear the potent phallic icon. Through acceptance of homosexual desire, by participation in homosexual sex, fear is banished, and revelation is achieved through sexual ecstasy.

Despite the celebratory mode of these lines, Whitman nevertheless does not neglect to retain a hint of that more threatening and powerful wrestling phallus, for even here the maple tooth, which orally bites, is also a "tooth-prong—tine," which like a fork, sharply penetrates, reminding us of the passive Whitman, supine beneath the "sting" of and grippingly embraced by the penetrating wrestler. We should recall the intensities of "albot Wilson" and the caress of that Fierce Wrestler, for he too is "wild and untamed—half savage." The wrestler has introduced the poet to a moment of primal knowledge, the moment of surrender to overwhelming sexual power. It is a moment never understood unless experienced when one man is mastered by another, receiving from him the liquid jetting of seminal life, surrendering to the insistent thrusting of the conquering phallic god. Even in the trance of exaltation, Whitman does not forget that potent drama powerfully played out on the emotional and psychic stage of sexual power. Thus, "Sweet Flag," so obviously phallic, is also allusively homoerotic, celebrating and rejoicing in the freedom found in the grip of that masculine passion when the moral censors are at last overcome.

One last notebook entry remains to be considered. Sometime before he began to write and then publish *Leaves of Grass,* Whitman set down in his notebook his first long and recognizably Whitmanic poem, "Pictures." Here Whitman engages in his first catalog, a list of the pictures "hanging suspended" in the gallery of his mind. The totality of these pictures portrays the "phallic choice of America." But curiously, the content of the poem is not especially "phallic" in the sense that we have seen in the other notebook entries. Missing is the phallic ecstasy, the mysticism of the phallic trance, the joy of the phallic dance, and the ascension to new knowledge. The undeniable sexuality of the notebook sequences in "albot Wilson," and the rushing ejaculatory movement of "Sweet Flag" are absent also. The phallic and homoerotic ambience is heard only in a subdued and minor key. In short, the power that unbridled homosexual experience gave to the poet, which is reflected in the brilliance of the homoerotic poetry, is absent. What we do find in "Pictures," however, is an allusive but still informative subtext. Though it celebrates the "phallic choice of America," which is "to enjoy the/breeding of full-sized men, or one full-sized man or woman," the phallic choice of America—and certainly of the poet—seems to fall primarily on men not women. The men in these lines appear in groups or couples: "There five men, a group of sworn friends, stalwart bearded, determined, / work their way together through all the troubles and impediments of the world," while "here and there couples or trios ["of men"—later del.] young and old, clear faced, and of perfect/physique, walk with twined arms." Like the unconquerable friends in *Calamus* 34, the "divine friendship" they share certainly recalls legends of Greek homosexual eros. Whitman enriches his text with these allusions and they describe not only the beauty—"perfect physique"—of these heroes but the exemplary devotion of their union as they "work their way together" through the troubles of the world. The men here are all comrades. (*NUPM* 4:1296, 1298).

These men celebrate a friendship they have found in the halls of Socratic philosophy. In Frances Wright's *A Few Days in Athens* (1822), just such a scene of philosophic friendship appears. Whitman was powerfully influenced by this book, which aside from its Epicurean message also celebrates that same divine friendship Whitman himself praises. Indeed, Wright's portrait of Zeno's disciples seems to reappear, with some very telling additions, in "Pictures." In Wright's description "a crowd of disciples was assembled, waiting the arrival of their master. Some, crowded into groups, listened to the harangues of an elder or more able scholar: others, walking in parties of six or a dozen, reasoning, debating, and disputing; while innumerable single figures, undisturbed by the buzz around them, leaned against the pillars, studying each from a manuscript, or stood with arms folded, and heads dropped on their bosoms in silent meditation."[12] "Pictures" similarly describes how "Young men, pupils, collect in gardens of a favorite master, waiting for him / Some, crowded in groups, listen to the harangues or arguments of the elder ones, / Elsewhere, single figures, undisturbed by the buzz around them, lean against pillars, or within recesses, meditating, or studying from manuscripts." (*NUPM* 4:1297–98).

Wright's young men are scholars; Whitman pictures lovers too. What Whitman significantly adds to this nearly verbatim lifting from Wright is the line in which the breath of manly love is as evident as what also may well be a passing reference to Plato's heavenly love: "here and there, couples . . . walk . . . in divine friendship." (*NUPM* 4:1298). Men are loving philosophers, heroes, and "unconquerable" comrades. Men are the supreme image of the poem. Indeed, in a moment of nearly incoherent passion, a minor essay in barely controlled auto-eroticism, the poet ejaculates:

> But for all that, nigh, at hand, see, a wonder beyond any of them,
> Namely yourself—the form and thoughts of a man,
> A man! because all the world, and all the inventions of the world, are but food
> for the body and Soul of one man."

(NUPM 4:1302)

Whitman has his own divine friends. Their pictures hang side by side. They are in fact called "close comrades": "And there hang, side by side, certain close comrades of mine—a Broadway / stage driver, a lumberman of Maine, and a deck hand of a Mississippi / steamboat." But chief among them is "the young man of Mannahatta, the celebrated rough, / (The one I love well—let others sing whom they may—him I sing, for a / thousand years!) (*NUPM* 4:1305–7). Whitman here is lucidly clear about his subject, and he has only one. He is the archetypical, mythic, even mystical figure who has been dimly advancing toward Whitman and toward us in these early works. All the unnamed young men of the earliest poetry, all the roughs and handsome lads of the fiction, and the Fierce Wrestler himself are conflated and personified in this young man of Mannahatta. He is the ideal friend. He will be the central icon of Whitman's sexual imagination as well as the chief object of his desire. I resist the temptation to speculate about some conjunction of life and art, some real young man inscribed in these lines, though at least one critic has proposed a candidate.[13] But such reality is of no matter. Myth is more powerful than physical reality. But whether or not he gave Whitman real kisses in life, here he awaits on the doorstep of poetry, ready for Whitman to give him the kiss of life, incarnate him into "Song of Myself," and conduct him to the shores of the *Calamus* pond, that equally incarnating ocean, where he will receive the sweet flag token.

In her *Views of Society and Manners in America* (1821), Frances Wright observes that "the American woman might with advantage, be taught early in youth to excel in the race, to hit a mark, to swim and in short, to use every exercise which would impart vigor to their frames and independence to their minds."[14] In "Poem of Procreation," Whitman recasts these lines but adds some telling activities: "They know how to swim, row, ride, wrestle, shoot, run, strike, retreat, advance, resist, defend themselves, / They are ultimate in their own right—they are calm, clear, well possessed of themselves."(*LG Var.* 1:239).

Wright's passage is a manifesto calling for the admission of women into the active and liberated world of men. But it could also be argued that Whitman's lines make women into men, indeed for the moment displace women entirely.[15] Wrestling and resisting, those sexual codes, dominate the lines and radically contrast with the sexual position toward women that the rest of the poem promotes, a position defined by Elizabeth Stanton in a commentary on this poem written in 1883: "He speaks as if the female must be forced to the creative act, apparently ignorant of the great natural fact that a healthy woman has as much passion as a man." Stanton's position reflects a large body of radical opinion affirming the presence and the extent of women's sexuality, some of which Whitman may have known, but much of which was also informed by male misconceptions and attitudes about women, especially in relation to sexual desire and the presumed obligations of pregnancy.[16] As Erkilla, who also quotes this observation, remarks: "The male is subject, the female object; he is active, she is passive."[17] Smith-Rosenberg points out that the acceptance of this "passion" as a natural fact was common to late eighteenth- and early nineteenth century medical and popular literature, but that as the middle of the nineteenth-century approached (and as Whitman neared publication of *Leaves of Grass*), these works increasingly "presented a context devoid of sexuality," just as Whitman's text, as I argue, also largely presents such a context in relation to heterosexuality. Smith-Rosenberg also insists, echoing Stanton's devastating word, that feminist scholarship is bound to defensively address "theories formed in ignorance of women's experience," an ignorance that Stanton acutely observed in Whitman's text.[18]

Stanton's assertion of Whitman's "ignorance" of that great natural fact resonates against every rhetorical utterance Whitman makes concerning the rights and role of women. Erkilla's suggestion that his "undoing of traditional male and female spheres" is only "apparent" also resonates strongly at these rhetorical junctures. Killingsworth's discussion of this problem—he describes the poems of the 1856 edition as "self-subversive"—suggests that "beginning in 1856 we come to associate women with a sense of unfulfilled potential," and that "Whitman seems to fall prey to the male jealousy of female power that leads to the definition of femaleness as a lack of maleness."[19] This definition obtains well before 1856, though Whitman attempts to add that missing maleness, at least in "Poem of Procreation." But it is also a missing femaleness that is the dominant absent trope of the work to 1855. Though Aspiz suggests that Whitman's rhetoric "harmonizes with the avant-garde feminist opinion of his era," I would argue that all his work up to and including *Leaves of Grass* (1855) shows, as Erkilla says, that "Whitman participated in the sexual ideology of his age even as he sought to challenge and transform it."[20] My comments below speak to the apparent nature of that challenge and transformation as it can be read in the early poems, fiction, and notebooks. My comments do not mean to imply that Whitman did not speak about women's sexuality or argue for women's sexual equality. Erkilla has convincingly argued that case, just as Killingsworth has persuasively demonstrated the ambiguity of Whitman's position toward women's sexuality. My observations here, though, may add other dimensions to that discourse by a consideration of the notebooks—and the early fiction and poetry—which suggest that Whitman's rhetorical and doctrinal position concerning women's sexuality needs to be read not only in conjunction with his post-1855 texts as is generally done, but more specifically against the tense and contradictory assertions of this early work and of *Leaves of Grass* (1855). These textual contradictions—Killingsworth's self-subversions—have been best defined by Gilbert's formulation of Whitman as a poet whose work is unalterably inscribed despite its rhetoric in "male defined genres."[21]

Men and boys, phallic sexuality, homoerotic fantasy, visions of ideal friendships, and dreams of devoted comrades are incorporated into the early poetry, fiction, and notebooks as symbols within sexual contexts. But do women ascend to symbolic status and inhabit sexual contexts? As Killingsworth has observed, women in popular novels were presented as the "idealized and essentially sexless image of womanliness. . . . male writers in particular consigned women to the safe haven of home," though women themselves were often equally willing to accept "these ideological restraints."[22] Killingsworth implies that in 1856, "Whitman's initiation of women into the world of power involves raising their sexual awareness," in order to escape these restraints.[23] Obviously, such culture-bound concepts of sexual roles rigidly linked women, passivity, and sexuality. To the extent that it was discussed at all, such concepts also linked homosexuality and passivity. The "weak and effeminate" Counter-jumper, whose anonymous creator parodied Whitman in 1860, was a creature of "weak depravity," who sounded his "feeble yelp over the woofs of the world."[24] Whitman's attack on sexual passivity may be intended not only to disentangle women from the web of domestic gentility but also to liberate homosexuality itself from its associations with passivity and femininity. He might have said, to paraphrase, "The comrade is not the same as the woman." Indeed, in a notebook he does say just that.

Whitman's hint in number 7 (1840) of the "Sun-Down Papers" that he has had no experience of women may indeed be worth considering with Stanton's comment about his ignorance of women's sexuality.[25] He sets up a textual distance between himself and women, just as he creates barriers between men and women in his verse and prose. These barriers can be as complex as the suggestive imagery in which he describes women—imagery which firmly places them in certain rigid social or sexual roles—or as simple as the fact that he often ignores them entirely. These texts establish a prescriptive and restrictive status for women, binding them in clichés of sexuality from which Whitman was not especially free, and centering around a deified icon of the maternal. While in the early poetry women rarely appear at all, the poems populated by young men who are either narcissistically self-absorbed or pining for a lost or unrequited—and always gender unspecified—love, in the fiction women are equally absent or, if present, are supporting players. The most powerful woman is always the mother. Widowed mothers inhabit the first three stories. In "Bervance," the narrator's wife is dead. In "Tomb Blossoms," an aged widow's sole reason for existence is to perpetuate the memory of her dead husband. There are no significant women in "The Last of the Sacred Army," and none at all in "The Last Loyalist." "Reuben's Last Wish" primarily displays a drunken father and a battered wife who remains on the sidelines to watch her son die. In "The Angel of Tears," the "soul of a dead girl" is the only presence. None of the women in these stories have either depth or fictional reality. They are not so much realized characters as they are moral exemplars or victims. They are, as in *Franklin Evans,* "modest, delicate, sweet." Franklin Evans marries Mary, a "most industrious, prudent, and affectionate" young woman, herself the daughter of a widow who has died in pain. Mary is a paragon of virtue, but the dissolute Evans causes her death, for Mary, "stricken to the heart" and unable to bear up longer against the accumulated weight of shame and misery, sank into the grave—the innocent victim of another's drunkenness. Obviously, the presentation of women as victim's of male insensitivity or sexual desire or of social irresponsibility argues that Whitman is aware of their victimized status. But it is not so much the victimization that he inscribes but their fortitude in bearing it, not unlike the advice given to women in contemporary marriage manuals, which insist that though sex and childbirth might be painful it was their duty as women to bear the pain.

When women are not victims, they are often either perceived to be or are the actual perpetrators of sexual duplicity. In *Franklin*

Evans (*EPF* 124), the dark Creole Margaret, and the temptress—and widow—Conway exemplify two of them. Margaret is the exotic female of "luscious and fascinating appearance," with "large soft voluptuous eyes and beautifully cut lips, set off in a form of faultless proportions," who often appears as a very nearly pornographic image in American fiction. See, for example, Isabel in Melville's *Pierre*. Margaret is not dissimilar in appearance, by the way, to some of Whitman's exotic young men. For example, in "A Legend of Life and Love," Nathan has eyes that are "soft and liquid like a girl's" and "lips curled with a voluptuous swell." Evans treats Margaret badly, but she is, after all, only a Creole, "not of my own race," and, as well, a slave. And, she is also a woman, who, Evans soon convinces himself, had entrapped him into marriage. Evans deserts her. But he is soon entrapped by another woman, the widow Conway, she a "woman of the world," who "had but one aim, the conquest of hearts." For her promiscuity she too must be punished, and she dies of a southern "epidemical disease." The melodrama of the story is not unusual in an age of melodrama, and one must not fault Whitman for practicing rather than overthrowing the conventions of sentimental literature, in which, after all, women are mostly widows, and wherein, as in Poe, they are more glorious dead than alive. Fiction remains fiction after all, in part in control of its maker, and in a fiction wherein women are either widows, entrapping females, prudent mothers, or chaste wives, and wherein they inevitably die, leaving alive only the vibrant and morally unexceptionable or sexually attractive young men, then that fiction surely writes another text of its own, reflecting desire.

In the remaining stories, women exist as marginally as in the others, exhibit their same virtues, and suffer their same fate. In "My Boys and Girls" and "The Little Sleighers," there are no women, only children, and "Dumb Kate," who is "gentle, timid, and affectionate," is betrayed and dies. Peter Brown's bride in "The Half-Breed" is a model wife, while the sister of Father Luke in that story, betrayed by a man, dies deranged, and Father Luke's Indian mistress dies in childbirth. In "Shirval," the women lose their sons and are widowed. The stories begin and end with widows. Throughout them, women are, if not the victims of male cruelty, the survivors who must continue after their men are gone. Save for Peter Brown's wife, who is presumably "happy" and fulfilled because she bears "quite a little family" of children, there are no women in the fiction for whom life offers—or to whom Whitman offered—anything more than the

miserable life of a "kitchen drudge." Abused by thoughtless men,
their only occasional happiness is found perhaps in the distant
contemplation of one of Whitman's golden lads—one of their sons
perhaps, for whom a life of manly comradeship is understandably far
more attractive than the domestic perils of a life spent with a drunken
father or a fading and widowed mother. In these early poems and
stories, women are hedged in by reverential sentiment, indeed by
sentimentality. Though they are widows and mothers, they are
hardly ever mistresses. They are admired but never desired; they are
symbolic, not sexual. Whereas every young man in these poems and
stories is inescapably sexual and desirable, homoerotic icons all, the
women, save for the "luscious" Margaret, have no sexual dimension.
Sexuality is denied them. Widows, mothers, and wives do not exist in
the realm of the sensual, and those women who do hint at sexuality
are punished for it fatally.

But in the notebooks, where so much is confided and wherein
we have encountered Whitman's confidences concerning his tentative exploration into the expression and acceptance of homoerotic
passion, women occupy a truly problematic position. In "albot
Wilson," he announces, "I am the poet of women as well as men. /
The woman is not less than the man / but she is never the same."
But when these lines are developed in "Song of Myself," he deletes
"and she is never the same" and adds "and I say there is nothing
greater than the mother of men." The notebook offered equality to
women. Indeed in asserting that they are "not less" than men, the
lines deny traditional sexual stereotypes and assert an important
feminist position—that women are not inferior to men and that
they are also vitally different. Most importantly, the notebook
lines assign no clichéd roles. But in "Song of Myself," women have
been denied their separate equality and have been reverentially
returned to the traditional and secure—and sexually unthreaten-
ing—role of mothers, though not the lovers, of men.

Another notebook meditation on difference is not so comfortably feminist. In an entry written perhaps in the late 1850s, "Lect[ure]
To Women" (*NUPM* 1:341), Whitman asserts that "the love and
comradeship of a woman . . . does not and cannot satisfy the
grandest requirements of a manly soul for love and comradeship. —
The man he loves, he often loves with more passionate attachment
than ever he bestows on any woman. . . . is it that the growth of
love needs free air—the seasons, perhaps more wildness, more
rudeness?" Why, he asks "is the love of women so invalid? so

transient?" It seems clear in this passage that the woman is hardly "as great as the man," and indeed it could fairly be said that women are "never the same" because their love is lacking, "invalid," and "transient." His implication is clear: passion is what is missing between men and women—or at least between women and those men with a "manly soul." "Comradeship" here is as potent and complex a homoerotic term as it is in *Calamus,* and it represents an emotion—this notebook surely implies—of which women are incapable. The "free air" is reserved for men only, and it is the same "atmosphere" that he will breath in "Song of Myself," just as the "wildness" and "rudeness" is that "something wild and untamed" that possessed him during the exotic phallic trance and that will possess him in "Song of Myself" when he becomes undisguised and naked. Of course Whitman's text, whatever else it may express, also registers participation in a more general convention of texts, a convention derived from the Biblical story of David and Jonathon, namely, that in which the love of men is described in one way or another as "passing the love of women." Bayard Taylor's invocation of the convention in *Joseph and His Friend* (1870)— "manly love, rarer, alas! but as tender and true as the love of woman," intensified later in the book as "a man's perfect friendship is rarer than a woman's love,"—specifically identifies a sentiment present in texts as widely separated as Strato, Tennyson, the pseudo-Byronic *Don Leon,* Emerson, Thoreau, Melville, and numerous examples of nineteenth-century English and American Uranian verse, which are either specifically homoerotic or more generally inscribed within the less sexually specific though still male-male friendship tradition. In Taylor's novel, Joseph marries his friend's twin sister, thus satisfying a heterosexual propriety while in a sense having his friend as well, but it is clear that it is a choice of last resort. In Theodore Winthrop's novel *Cecil Dreeme* (c. 1860), the hero, Cecil Dreeme, turns out at the end of the novel to be a woman in disguise. Byng, who marries her, ambivalently comments: "Every moment it came to me that Cecil Dreeme and I could never be Damon and Pythias again. Ignorantly I had loved my friend as one loves a woman only. This was love—unforced, self-created, undoubting, complete. And now that friend proved a woman, a great gulf opened between us."[26] Whitman, too, perceives a great gulf as well, a frightening abyss that symbolism easily construes, which only the complete, valid, and self-creating love of man for man can bridge.

In the notebook pages women most often appear in glimpses only. Single lines mention them in such phrases fraught with sentimental cliché as "gallantry toward females" (*NUPM* 1:85) or depict them as domestic servants: "Females of the [domestic] class are Irish women and girls" (89). There are suffering women — suffering the preferred lot that Whitman assigns to women. A "worthy woman . . . inveigled into marriage" with a pickpocket is mentioned in a hint for a story written about 1852, and in another an "elderly woman" comes to save her "arrested son" (97). The notebook "Poem Incarnating the Mind," which with "albot Wilson" is among the earliest surviving notebooks, is filled with jottings that would later take shape in "Song of Myself." The women who appear therein all share a single association, tragedy or death. There is the proposed "Story of Julia Scudder whose husband left her"(103). Or he plans to tell "how the lank white faced women looked when ferried safely at last as from the sides [of] their prepared graves" (108). Or he describes "the old woman that was chained and burnt" (109) or "the great queens that walked serenely to the block"(108). Or he fantasizes about "the creek on Long Island when the boating party were returning and capsized, and the young man saved his sweetheart and lost his sister" (112). The focus of the piece is on the "young man"; all of the women described above are about to die.

The soprano in whose "love-grip" he lay (126) is the only one with sexual life, while the longest description of a woman in the notebooks written prior to 1855 is of another archetypical mother: "a fullsized woman of calm and voluptuous beauty . . . the unspeakable charm of the face of the mother of many children is the charm of her face . . . she is clean and sweet and simple with immortal health." (141). In this same notebook, "Memorials," he repeats his program of equality — "If I become a devotee it shall be to men and women" — but then offers a woman at auction who is "not only herself, she is the bearer of other women, who shall be mothers, / She is the bearer of men who shall be fathers." In another entry he imagines a "poem descriptive of a good wife (housekeeper, cook, Mother of many children.)" (167). If he offers us a woman as fully drawn as the "perfect man," whose "flex of waist and hips" he so pointedly observed, it is the fullsized mother of many children, whose sisters in these pages have usually died, lived in lonely widowhood, or been relegated to the symbolic position of the woman standing on the block at auction — her sole function to breed. These women, indeed all women in his work discussed so far, are thus enshrined. In his imagination and in his poems, the greatest accolade that he bestows upon any woman is that she is a "good wife (housekeeper, cook, Mother of many children.)."

In his hot-blooded thirties, Whitman was well aware of the power of sexual passion and of the demands and resonances of homosexual desire as well. In a curious entry, "The Analogy," he apparently attempts to make a metaphysical comment about this sexual passion. It is illuminating: "The analogy holds in this way — that the soul of the universe is the genital master, the impregnating and animating spirit. — Physical matter is female and Mother, and waits barren and bloomless, the jets of life from the masculine vigor, the undermost first cause of all that is not what Death is" (*NUPM* 1:176). He might well have called the "genital master" the phallic impulse. If the soul of the universe is male, then presumably human souls, which are not physical, are male also, offering the curious conclusion that women either have male souls or, being female and hence physical, none at all.

Whitman again discusses the nature of the soul in "Do you Know What Music Does," asserting that "the soul of a man has within itself all the vitality of all that is harmonious" (*NUPM* 1:191). The inclusive "all" should be noted, for the masculine soul, vital and harmonious, shares with the soul of the universe the animating power. "Only the soul burns," while the rest "is impotent." While it may well be necessary in his analogy for the animating spirit to impregnate female matter in order to create life, it is not necessary — if his analogy is pursued — for the "soul of a man," which in harmony and vitality is complete, to seek out that barren and bloomless female body in order to create that complete harmony that he surely believes to be poetry. He has already inscribed poetry within strictly masculine parameters in an earlier notebook, "Memorials," when he observes that the sight of a handsome man "conveys the impression of hearing a beautiful poem,"(*NUPM* 1:151). In this notebook he observes: "the reason that anything pleases the soul, is that it finds its relations there, and awakes it — and the twain kiss each other" (*NUPM* 1:192). Abstract and vague as his theorizing may be — though Whitman need not be tried for illogicality — yet the rudimentary Platonism is obvious, for just as the two halves of Plato's separated lovers seek each other, so Whitman's soul seeks out corresponding passions where its "relations" are. The masculine soul seeks its "twain" and "awakes" it in the same way that, as we will see, the friend awakes the lover in one of the most significant and climactic passages of "Song of Myself." In the "Preface" to *Leaves of Grass* (1855), he observes that the soul "has sympathy as measureless as its pride and the one balances the other. . . . The innermost secrets of art sleep with the twain" (Cowley 12). This assertion that the secrets of art are enclosed within the boundaries of the passionate soul, when considered within the terms of his analogy and within his speculations about the masculine nature of the soul, suggest a companion asertion about the essentially masculine landscape of art.

Though Whitman mentions women in "Pictures," that last and closest notebook to "Song of Myself," there seems to be no advance there toward the later public doctrine. The few women mentioned are mothers or are either conquered or dead. The women whose pictures appear in the poem are "my dear mother," "my . . . sisters," "Eve . . . side by side" with Adam, a "queen on her way to the scaffold," a "beloved daughter . . . carried in her coffin," an unsexed but presumably feminine "drudge in the kitchen," "countless . . . women, after death, wandering," and some laboring slaves, who he describes as "clumsy, hideous, black, pouting, grinning, sly, besotted, sensual, shameless." The women in "Pictures" are a numerical and moral minority in comparison to the heroic and exemplary men. These women are mothers, sisters, or domestic clichés. Though the poem celebrates well-formed and well-trained women, their training seems largely to enable them to fulfill the expected roles of faceless femininity. Thomas Wentworth Higginson, in what was at once a suggestion about Whitman's sexuality as well as a pointed observation about his texts, observed in the *Nation* in 1892 that "there is the same curious deficiency shown in him, almost alone among poets, of anything like personal and romantic love. Whenever we come upon anything that suggests a glimpse of it, the object always turns out to be a man and not a woman."[27]

Though Whitman claims that he lay in the love grip of the passionate soprano, he heard other music, for he also lay in the similar love grip of the wrestler. Both lovers gripped him; both mastered him sexually. The similarity is in the mastering. If Whitman considers woman sexually at all, he generally sees them as passive. The soprano is in fact the only woman in the notebooks who is actively and sexually dominant, and the language used to describe her domination echoes the language used to described the much more fully imagined wrestler. Sex is always masculine and active. But in every description of a sexual event thus far discussed, with the exception of the "ungrown brother" sequence, the narrator is the passive recipient of sexual attention. Thus, as the recipient of sexual attention, he responds to masculine sexuality conceived of as active sexuality only, and describes even ostensible heterosexual experience in terms of homoerotic active masculinity. In one of his editorials, Whitman had insisted that "if goodness, charity, faith and love, reside not in the breasts of females, they reside not on earth. . . . In their souls is preserved the ark of the covenant of purity." In a review of one of the many domestic novels of the day, he praised the book for "depicting in especial the character of a good, gentle mother" and for cautioning that "indulgence in stormy passion leads inevitably to sorrow."[28] In each of these comments he substantially distances women from stormy passion, suggesting that maternal love is woman's best and only true emotion. Whitman would surely engage in stormy passion, for which see his anguish over Peter Doyle, but we do not need to look that far to find the stormy passion of his homoerotic texts, where real love is wild and untamed and male.

It is surely true, as both Killingsworth and Erkilla have pointed out, that Whitman expresses profound public sympathy with the plight of women as they existed in the "close atmosphere of the guarded castle" of nineteeth-century male-dominated sexual theory and practice.[29] His journalism clearly suggests his own empathy with women's sexual oppression and repression, just as his parallel image of the "guarded tents of interior love" shows that his sympathy clearly—and more profoundly—extended to the problem of the expression of homosexual love as well. The pictures of sexually oppressed women that he often draws in his prose writings stand as a conflicted commentary, as Killingsworth says, against the enfolding of "a number of Victorian male attitudes" in that same journalism and in his fiction and notebooks.[30] In "The Child's Champion," as indeed in all the fiction, the oppressed mother—no longer whole because she is a widow—is noted yet gets no respite from her situation. But the child finds love in another man's arms and leaves his mother behind. As Michael Moon has suggested, in a story like "The Child's Champion," which Moon describes as a "male-sentimental master narrative" of homoeroticism that serves as a "counterdiscourse" to the "culture

of self-reliant male rectitude," the "abject boy is . . . recovered for
a scene of male domesticity and affluence from which the equally
abject mother—and, along with her, the femininity which she
metonymically represents—is excluded."[31] Perhaps also playing
against this picture of women whose oppression is a function of
their perceived incompleteness without a man, and who are therefore doubly excluded, there is also the fear, suggested by Foucault,
that beneath the folds of covering chastity and maternal poise lurks
the voracious sexual monster of the "hysteric" woman.[32] Killingsworth suggests that this may well be the impulse that lies behind
the twenty-eight bathers sequence in "Song of Myself," and many
readers have suggested that fear of women's sexuality—Stanton's
"ignorance"—lies at the heart of Whitman's own enclosure of them
in the guarded castles of his poetry, castles that only seem to be
defended bastions of women's liberation.[33] Erkilla sees the twenty-
ninth bather, for example, as "a mask for Whitman himself anonymously fondling the bodies of young men in solitary fantasy." This
returns to my earlier point; if this woman is only a mask, then she
is not there at all. Whitman would be the poet of women the same
as men if there were women in his poetry. But there are no women,
only versions of Whitman himself. His interest is not so much in
women as it is in his own myth of what women, in the masculine
and homoerotic terms of that myth, ought to be. The women he
does describe are not, by his description, validated or liberated in
any feminist sense at all. Rather their institutionalized symbolic
presence only enforces the obsessive masculinity of his own self-
creation and in a very profound sense renders women unnecessary
to it.

It may have been a cautionary note that he inscribed in the
notebook "Understand That You can Have," written about 1855/56,
in which he warned: "Understand that you can have in your
writing no qualities which you do not honestly entertain in yourself . . . if you possess a vile opinion of women . . . these will
appear by what you leave unsaid more than by what you say"
(*NUPM* 1:226). Martin has pointed out that in certain male friendship texts of the nineteenth-century misogyny and "elevation of
the feminine" seem to be paradoxically joined. However, as he
says, this is "an apparent paradox: for both the hatred of women
and the elevation of women act as a means of prohibiting relations
between men and women other than those of property."[34] I do not
think that Whitman hated women, though he may well have, if

Stanton's intuition is right, feared them. He does, however, inscribe them within a conventional nexus of property and possession. Gilbert has drawn a comparison between the work of Fanny
Fern and Whitman in which she shows that Fern interestingly
prefigures section 15 of "Song of Myself."[35] Fern writes: "the
bride standing at the altar . . . sisters, in linsey woolsey, toil in the
garrets. . . . the unpaid sempstress begems with tears the fairy
festal robe." Whitman's bride "unrumples her white dress, the
minute hand of the clock moves slowly," and "the spinning-girl
retreats and advances to the hum of the big wheel." In Fern's lines
Gilbert correctly sees models that Whitman may have used. However what is also there is what is left unsaid by Whitman, for Fern is
acutely aware of the social and economic oppression of these
women, an awareness that remains unspoken, perhaps even unob-
served, in Whitman's transmutations. In Whitman's lines the bride
does not await a husband who may never come but only a husband
who is delayed, and the "spinning-girl," rather than being a living
actor in a tragedy of economic exploitation, seems to have become
an approved part of what is in fact the dehumanized functioning of
her machine, reduced to the same role, but not imagined, I would
argue, within the same consciousness of the injustice of that role
that Fern displays.

Surely, in his journalism and in the poetry of *Leaves of Grass*
1856 and 1860, Whitman said a great deal about women. But what
he left unsaid resonates against what he did say in his intimate
notebook, that private guarded tent pitched so far from the public
grounds of his journalism, which was that the love of women is "so
invalid, so transient." The "grandest requirements . . . for love
and comradeship" can be filled only by the "passionate attachment" of one man for another "manly soul." He exercised the same
trope in 1889, when he told Traubel: "Comradeship—yes, that's
the thing; getting one and one together to make two—getting two
together everywhere to make all; that's the only bond we should
accept and that's the only freedom we should desire; comradeship,
comradeship."[36]

This is not to say, however, that the eroticized woman is
completely absent from the notebooks, especially in the remarkable lines that were translated into the fifth poem of *Leaves of Grass*
(1855), which would become "I Sing the Body Electric." This
poem is nearly as powerfully present in the notebooks as it is in the
text of the 1855 edition. It is an erotic bridge between the sugges-

tive notebooks and the realized text of the first edition, and I will cross it here as I pass from my discussion of the notebooks to that of the two major poems of *Leaves of Grass* (1855). The intention of the fifth poem is to celebrate the bodies of men and women, the perfect male and the perfect female. In the notebooks, however, it is the perfect male whose body most fascinates. In "Memorials," certainly written before 1855, though probably no earlier than 1854, there is a full description of a "perfect made man":

The expression of a perfect made man appears not only in his face—but in his limbs—the motion of his hands and arms and all his joints—his walk—the carriage of his neck—and the flex of waist and hips[.] Dress does not hide him. The quality he has and the strong sweet supple nature he has strike through cotton and woolen.—To see him walk conveys the impression of hearing a beautiful poem.—To see his back and the back of his neck and shoulderside is a spectacle. Great is the body!—There is something in the touch of an candid clean person,—what it is I do not know. . . . but it fills me with wonderful and exquisite sensations. It is enough to be with him or her. (*NUPM* 1:151)

In the notebook the "flex of his waist and hips" attracts and impels the speaker to look beneath "the cotton and woolen" to the naked man underneath. The 1855 text however, shows some small but telling revisions of the notebook passage—minor alterations that predict some of the later desexualizing revisions and that not only suggest textual caution but also show that the homoerotic implications of the notebook text were neither innocent nor accidental. In the poem "the flex of his waist and knees" replaces the the sexually suggestive "hips" that become the neutral "knees." In this 1855 text he also looks beneath the cotton and broadcloth, but enthusiasm is more controlled than in the notebook, for the "beautiful" poem of the notebook becomes the less powerful "best" poem. He further contains his enthusiasm for he no longer describes male beauty as a "spectacle." However now he does "linger" to see "his back and the back of his neck and shouderside." In the fifth poem he also equates the power of masculine attraction with poetry: "to see him pass conveys as much as the best poem. . perhaps more" (Cowley 116,2.7-12). Though he cancels the aural aspect of the image—"hearing"—he enlarges "convey" by "as much" so that the passing man carries the weight of the more complex implications of meaning and becomes the poem itself. He also adds the speculative observation "perhaps more." What "more" does this passing convey? He answers that question in the "Preface" to *Leaves of Grass*: "your very flesh shall be a great poem and have the richest fluency not only in its words but in the silent lines of its lips and face and between the lashes of your eyes and in every motion and joint of your body." (Cowley 11). The detailed accounting of "every motion" of this gender unspecific body echoes the sharp delineation of the specifically masculine body in the notebook and tells that the "more" is not only the physical attraction of the body but the cancelled intimations of homoerotic desire that inform the notebook passage. His lingering eye begins here the process of sexual appraisal that will culminate in the response to eyes that offer him love. The pleasure derived from viewing the perfect man produces passionate ecstasy, so even the "touch" of such a person, like the grip of his wrestler, leaves the poet nearly speechless: "What it is I do not know." The "wonderful and exquisite sensations" are a foreshadowing formulation of the homoerotic longings he cannot define—"I do not know what it is"—which are satisfied by the embrace of a friend in "Song of Myself." Like the eroticized young giant, the perfect man is "supple"; his nature shines forth through his clothes, beneath which is the naked god. Seeing such divinity once again arouses the ecstasies of sexual desire, and while Whitman nods at the last minute to evenhandedness—"him or her"—his focus is on the perfect made man whose touch has so often before thrilled him to new identity.

In the fifth poem, however, the meditation on the perfect man is in effect interrupted by a few lines that seem intended to provide what the parallelism of "the male is perfect, and the female is perfect" suggests and what the description of the well-made man promises. However the passage is brief and brings neither passion nor original diction to the text: "The sprawl and fulness of babes. . . . the bosoms and heads of women. . . . the folds of their dress. . . . their style as we pass in the street. . . . the contour of their shape downwards" (2.13). These lines, unlike the fluent description of men, are halting, unsure, and awkward. The section quite remarkably avoids the precise physical enumerations of the previous lines and instead initially asserts women's maternal function. When he looks at these woman he sees only faceless "heads," and he mentions but does not describe "bosoms," which, unlike the naked and accessible masculine "joints of hips" and the "flex

of . . . waist and knees," are covered by the "folds of their dress."
When he looks at men, he is clear about what he sees: "dress does
not hide him." But in women he sees fashion not flesh, style not
sexuality. Instead of the finely articulated musculature of men,
women are dressmaker's models, displaying only the outlined
"contour of their shape downwards," their bodies and their sexuality hidden by bell-shaped crinolines, safely shielded from desirous eyes. When men pass he turns to enjoy the spectacle. When
women "pass in the street" he neither lingers nor looks.

When he mentions women in the catalog that follows (2.13–
28), he continues to avoid mentioning their bodies; women's roles,
not women, are the subject. He mentions "girls and mothers and
housekeepers in all their exquisite tasks," or a "female soothing a
child. . . . the farmer's daughter in the garden or cowyard," engaged in woman's work. The penultimate line of the catalog finds
him "at the mother's breast with the little child," in a minor
regressive fantasy wherein women are desired as mothers but not
as lovers. Though his announced theme is the sexual body electric
and the "expression of the body of man or woman," he does not
describe women's bodies at all, only the institution not the flesh.
Of the fifteen lines of the catalog, only four are devoted to women,
and in none of them do women become poems or even poetic.

Whereas the women were caught in static iconographic poses—
vignettes that display roles and enforce their inscription within
rigid social and sexual conventions—the men are all action. With
the appearance of the naked swimmer, the imagery quite suddenly
recovers its power. Downward contours and "bosoms" will not do
here. Instead the swimmer "swims through the salt transparent
greenshine." Passion is translated unto impressionism, captured
by a desirous eye. The active catalog continues with rowers who
are "bending forward and backward," the horseman who is "in his
saddle," the woodman "rapidly swinging his ax in the woods,"
and the young fellow "hoeing corn." When women do appear
again, they are wives "waiting" for their men, a group of laborers
eating together—without women—at noontime (2.14–20).

As it was with the well-made man, Whitman's eye is ever on
rippling muscles, backs and shoulders. So erotic is the effect that
his descriptions enter the realm of sexual metaphor, and he calls
upon his most potent metaphor, wrestling, embracing men. He
introduces the wrestling apprentice boys—who are not only "quite
grown" but "lusty"—his version of the sexual wrestlers who

figure in the conventions of homosexual literature, archetypical
icons from the legendary of homoerotic desire—Dionysos wrestling with Amphelos, Maurice with Durham, and Vidal's lovers
wrestling on the shores of their sacred pond in *The City and the
Pillar*. Their lusty wrestling becomes the "embrace of love and
resistance," as he describes the "upperhold and underhold—the
hair rumpled over and blinding the eyes" (2.21–23). These young
wrestlers are the devoted male couples who appear in the fiction
now allowed passionate physical contact. They will become metaphor in "Song of Myself," where the rumpled hair of these boys
becomes "mixed tussled hay of head and beard and brawn," and
where their thrown down clothes becomes the "unbuttoning" of
section 28, when he is wrestled into homoerotic awareness. These
wrestlers, soon also to be boys who will cling together in *Calamus*
26, "elbows stretching, fingers clutching," derive their life from
the ur-text of wrestling rape in the notebook, younger versions of
his own Fierce Wrestler.

The firemen who now march into the text of the fifth poem are
no longer workmen doing their job but objects of erotic desire
(2.24–26). When women appeared in costumes, Whitman saw only
the contour of their shape, but when the firemen appear "in their
own costumes," he sees "the play of the masculine muscle through
the cleansetting trowsers and waistbands." The specificity of that
article is definite and should not go unnoticed; it is not the "play of
masculine muscle" (the form of a later revision), but the play of
"the" masculine muscle that shows "through cleansetting trousers" and that powerfully attracts him. It is not the simple and
general play of masculine muscle that attracts his eye but the
specific allure of an outlined display of genital proportion and
promise, which is the object of his interest and his desire. He will
celebrate this "rude" and plunging "semitic" muscle in later
poetry, most prodigally in "Song of Myself," and become one in
"The Sleepers." This is the first time, however, that he specifically
indicates that another's penis attracts him. Among the items in this
catalog, "the" masculine muscle is one of those things about which
he says "such-like I love." The sight of this object he loves, striking
through and outlined against the fabric of those clinging trousers,
so loosens and arouses him that oral gratification is suddenly and
apparently his most obsessive need, and he finds himself "at the
mother's breast" nursing at her nipple, a safe substitute for the
masculine muscle that is the real object of his oral desire. Though

he may momentarily suckle at "the mothers breast," his most powerful fantasy is quickly activated—to "swim with the swimmer, wrestle with the wrestlers" and march in line with the firemen, not only joining their democratic company, but participating in their sexual power as well. He chooses the world of masculine action against the womanly world of babes, fashion, and housewifely chores. In that world there may be maternal love and even comfort, but there is no passion and there is no penis. The embrace is maternal and he is a little child; his response is passive, the image static. With men there is active desire and there is power, the "embrace of love and resistance." In this man's world, rather than suckle at the mother's breast, he can perform upon those swimmers, as he will do in fantasy in section 11 of "Song of Myself," and upon those wrestlers, as he had done in the notebooks, and upon those firemen, red marauding roughs, an act of worshipful fellatio. Both Erkilla and Killingsworth are certainly correct when they indicate that the eroticized body creates, as Killingsworth puts it, a "common denominator among all classes."[37] But to stress the political contexts of the poem over the sexual, as Erkilla tends to do, perhaps too strongly obscures the real genesis of the fifth poem in the eroticized contexts of the notebooks.

In section 3, though the text appropriates working class men, they are not presented as examples of political but of sexual power and innocence. Though the text includes working class women, their roles are supplementary to those of their men, and they are, in terms of the sheer volume of the text, nearly erased by the more powerful depictions of masculine desire. Though the maternal may slip from view, the image of the father, both idealized and eroticized, is created in a man of "wonderful vigor and calmness and beauty of person." Surrounded on his forays by his sons and grandsons, he is a man of such magnetism and wisdom that "you would wish long and long to be with him" and whose attraction is so powerful, a mixture of paternal love and masculine allure, that "you would wish to sit by him in the boat that you and he might touch each other." His description is freighted with filial respect and with longing that is not satisfied. He "used to go and visit," but he must be content with hope only: "you would wish," he says, to be with him, you would wish to sit by him, and you would wish that he might "touch" you. In section 4, he finds some relief from that longing, for he can find comfort in being "with those I like." Those he likes are "men and women," and he is happy when he

rests his "arm ever so lightly around his or her neck for a moment."
This touch "is enough" to take the place of that fatherly touch. He
insists that his soul is pleased by "staying close to men and women"
and "in the contact and odor of them." The delight that he obtains
from this touch is such that "I swim in it as in a sea." The oceanic
touch, however, and his immersion in it, has primarily homoerotic
associations not only in this poem but in "The Sleepers" and "Song
of Myself." The twenty-eight bathers, his lover the sea who dashes
him with "amorous wet" in "Song of Myself," and the naked
swimmer in the swimming bath are all images of that desire, the
pleasure he obtains from their touch conjuring there like here the
seascape of homoerotic fantasy.

The fifth poem continues with an elaboration of the fragment
"Bridalnight" that appears in the notebook "Memorials." He
seems to offer lines that speak directly to the heterosexual experience:

> One quivering jelly of love limpid transparent—
> Limitless jets of love, hot and enormous
> Arms of love strong as attraction reach as wide and large as
>   the air
> Drunken and crazy with love, swing in its in the plumetless
>   sea
> Loveflesh swelling and deliciously aching whiteblood of
>   love.
>
> (*NUPM* 1:149)

However, the bridalnight is described solely in terms of phallic
"jets" and phallic swellings. The language of the piece, despite its
name, is exclusively descriptive of ejaculation and of semen. The
quivering jelly of love, the jets themselves, and the whiteblood of
love are all seminal images. The primary image is of the phallus,
which is "enormous" and swelling, and which deliciously aches
with the pressure of unreleased semen. The lover(s) are described
as having "arms of love strong as attraction." Strength seems to be
a necessary concomitant of a lover for Whitman, and it is a quality
possessed thus far preeminently by the Fierce Wrestler. Like his
experience with "touch" and with the wrestler, here too he loses
his wits and control and is "drunken and crazy with love." In short,
the images of "Bridalnight," despite the ostensible intention of the
text as a hymn to heterosexual intercourse, functionally and
referentially recall other texts wherein these images—ecstasy,

swelling penises, jetting semen, drunken delights, and strong arms—
detail homoerotic rather than heterosexual fantasies. These lines
share imagery—the intense ecstatic tropes, the evocations of wildness—that has been seen to be homoerotically charged in other
textual locations. The distinction between the jelly of love and the
jets of love suggests both vaginal and phallic secretions, but the
embracing arms embrace nothing but the "air" and evoke only the
powerful arms of the Fierce Wrestler. Just as he was ecstatically
uncontrolled and homoerotically aroused in other notebook passages, he is drunk and possessed here as he plunges into the sea, a
definitive homoerotic locale. The passage ends in ejaculation, the
jelly, if it is vaginal, disappears, and the image is now solely that of
the swelling and then ejaculating phallic loveflesh that jets the
whiteblood of love, the familiar seminal "milky stream pale
strippings" of his life. If there is a bride in this passage, she has
disappeared into the surrounding air, again present only in her
absence, and the speaker, ignoring his partner, focuses solely on the
achievement of his own orgasm.

This material was re-worked for "I Sing the Body Electric,"
and new lines were added, (5.46-57). The "female form," seen
through exhaling mists and surrounded from "head to foot" by a
"divine nimbus," is elevated to icon, around it an impenetrable
wall of divinity. The exhalations are not unlike the "subtle chloroform" that intoxicated him when in the presence of men he loved,
and they parallel the "strong sweet quality" that strikes through
men's clothes. The "fierce undeniable attraction" causes him to
lose control and become a "helpless vapor." He becomes the subtle
chloroform and predicts the same erotic dematerialization he will
undergo at the end of "Song of Myself." The helplessness that
paralyzed him in the arms of the Fierce Wrestler and in the "Sweet
Flag" garden overwhelms him here, allowing him to reject the
artificiality of cultural constructions and presumptions. The universe itself disappears, as he ascends into a sexual ecstasy as intense
as that in the Fierce Wrestler sequence. The female form projects
"mad filaments" and "ungovernable shoots," which elicit an equally
ungovernable response, entangling him in an erotic web. The
notebook lines are introduced here, but the "bridalnight" has now
become a "bridegroom night." The speaker in the notebook was
possessed by the strong arms of desire and occupied that airy space
vacated by the dominated bride. Even as the speaker identifies with
the bridegroom, the powerful female form, dominant in the

beginning of the sequence, also diffuses and merges with the "working" bridegroom. The filaments and shoots that play out of the divine nimbus phallically complement rather than contrast with the phallic loveflesh that swells and limitlessly shoots limpid jets of semen into the "cleave of the clasping," vaginal, "sweet-fleshed day." Killingsworth suggests that the description "represents the male principle encountering the ideal 'female form'" and that the description "engulfs physical and metaphysical."[38] In fact, both the male and female form are engulfed; they disappear, are "diffused," and all that is left is the depersonalized aching loveflesh and quivering jelly. In a sense also, what is left is not human sexuality but the great currents of nature itself—the night ebbing and flowing into the day, neither heterosexual nor homosexual. As H. C. Wright, a radical sex reformer urged in 1855, the union between man and woman should create "one existence, one life, one eternity," in which the "ecstatic expression of the soul" is the ultimate achievement.[39]

However to be lost in the "cleave of the clasping" sweetflesh is a text freighted as much with fear as pleasure. The generalized desexualization of women that the notebooks have presented, the dubiety about the validity of women's love, and the images of rape that Whitman inevitably associates with those rare and few descriptions of himself engaged in heterosexual activity suggest that to lose himself to a woman's power is a projected activity invested with considerable anxiety. To avoid losing control he must be the genital master. In this passage he fantasizes that mastery, and he cancels the momentary ascription of sexual power to women when he asserts that the female form is the "prostrate dawn," "willing and yielding." When he found himself overpowered by the Fierce Wrestler, he too yielded willingly and allowed himself to enter into that "trance exaltation" of ecstasy wherein he could succumb to the "embrace of love and resistance." When he allows the archetype of male sexual power to "turn over upon him" in "Song of Myself," he knows full well that he is not in danger of being lost in, or injured by, the cleave of the clasping vagina. Just as the phallic text pivots on that subtle "the," so this text—a vaginal text—pivots on that ambiguous verb "lost" and that dangerous verb *clasp*. Although it might be theorized that this text shares a considerable texture of homoeroticism with other such texts, invested as it is with daring vaginal imagery, it resonates against the lines that so sharply focus our attention upon the masculine muscle as a balancing document to the discourse of homoerotic desire. The alluring display of the genitals of marching men calls forth fantasies of forbidden acts, acts so forbidden that he must substitute accepted images of maternal nursing for the desired fellatio. As they pass through the scrutinizing consciousness of the reader, the truly transgressive fantasies of fellatio are intercepted, negated, and effaced by the "vaginal" text, which though also daring and transgressive, is also sexually orthodox and metaphoric, while the phallic text is specific and proscribed. As if to definitively effect that effacement, Whitman let the vaginal text stand and in later revisions emasculated the other text by the sharp elimination of that small but potent "the."

The electric qualities of the female form that he has just celebrated—the mad filaments, the ungovernable shoots—lead inevitably to procreation and the "bath of birth" out of which the child is born. Out of this same bath of sexual experience, man—the adult male—is born also, finding a rebirth in heterosexual coitus. Women, both mothers and sexual teachers, are psychic and sexual gates through whom pass body and soul. They contain "all qualities," and they move with "perfect balance." Far more so than men, they are invested with divinity and enveloped in mystery: a woman is "all things duly veiled," seen "through a mist." Like an image of an ancient goddess seen through the smoke of incense and sacrifice, she stands elevated and enshrined like the icons of divine Marian maternity, an immobile object of "inexpressible completeness and beauty, her "bent head and arms folded over the breast." Whereas the firemen, who also stand with bent heads are at active rest, keenly listening for a signal to spring into life, this woman does not move or march. There can be no sight of the play of muscle or the revelation of merely human fleshly allure, for we are in the presence now of the Great Goddess, the "bearer of the great fruit of immortality." Those who are not worthy can not enter into her holy and inviolate shrine. Here, the "good" of this fruit is "not tasted by roues, and never can be" (5.58–65). The sexual ecstasy of the preceding lines, as if it had become too ungovernable, too dangerous, too suggestive of unbridled heterosexual passion, is immersed and finally diffused in the atmosphere of pious adoration of the maternal goddess. He banishes the sexual and celebrates the symbolic. As Showalter says in her discussion of "decadent" literature, such women are ultimately "desexualized through maternity or thoroughly aestheticized, stylized, and turned into icons or fetishes."[40] The nimbus that surrounds the female form not only renders it divine and untouchable but imprisons its dangerous sexuality. The female can be viewed safely through her divine nimbus, worshipped perhaps, but never in fact passionately loved. This woman, untouched by earthly desire—by roues—and indeed unavailable to such desire, is surrounded by a barrier through which profane males cannot and must not pass. If the protecting shield is penetrated by desire, if the divine maternal is blasphemously translated into the secularly passionate, then there can be no other result but punishment, a castrating loss of power and virility. Then men face loss, danger to the phallic life, and unbearable clasping restriction. In the world of men, power and virility are protected and enhanced by the active embrace of love and resistance, a daytime world as far distant from the nighttime purlieus of the clasping female as from the static images of the mother. The atmosphere wherein there is no such restriction is described in that notebook entry I again recall, perhaps more pointedly here: "the growth of love needs free air . . . more wildness, more rudeness. . . . Why is the love of woman so invalid? so transient?" (*NUPM* 1:341).

This realm of wildness and rudeness—the landscape of the rude masculine muscle—is inscribed on the body of the male himself in section 6. Here the god is made manifest as the Fierce Wrestler, the image and the spirit of the masculine universe, whose rites are celebrated not with the soft and crooning hymns of the mother, but with songs of homoerotic ecstasy, the text of which asserts that the male is "action and power. . . . the flush of the known universe is in him." He possesses the "fiercest largest passions." Though the female form may offer ungovernable shoots and mad filaments and, undeniably, sexual pleasure, that act is only incidentally passionate and primarily procreative. Women "conceive daughters as well as sons and sons as well as daughters." Her dangerous passions, momentarily allowed to surface in the procreative act, must finally be harnessed and fully submerged again in the persona of the veiled and perfectly balanced mother, standing submissively "in her place," head bent. Her place is defined by Wright, whose *Marriage and Parentage* (1855) establishes a context for Whitman. His use of such terms as "reverence" and "obedience" firmly indicates where that place is and implies which power has established it: "Maternity is a divinely appointed mission, to be a mother is a sacred trust. To reverence this trust and come into close communion with the heart of all life replaces fear and dread with joy and satisfaction. This is . . . nature's plan, a law of the spirit. Acknowledgement of and obedience to this law lessen . . . the sufferings of pregnancy."[41]

Men have deeper passions, more profound emotions, wider and more potent purposes. Their "fiercest passions," appropriate to the fierce wrestlers that they are, lead them to experience "bliss that is utmost and sorrow that is utmost." "Pride is for him . . . knowledge becomes him . . . he brings everything to the test of himself." These last words specifically echo Whitman's claims for the poet in the "Preface." There, "the one complete lover . . . is the greatest poet" (Cowley 11). This poet, like this man, feels more deeply, and experiences the most exalted and profound passions. If Whitman believes that women can also feel so deeply he does not say it.

The final lines, sections 7–8, offer a picture of two naked human creatures, a man and a woman, who epitomize in their Edenic nakedness the qualities he has assigned to the bodies electric of men and women.[42] The male has "exquisite senses, lifelit eyes, pluck, volition," and in his heart are "all passions and desires. . / all reachings and aspirations." His description, like that of the well-made man, is redolent with desire: "flakes of breast muscle, pliant backbone," as well as other "wonders within." The woman is one thing only: "the teeming mother of mothers, / she is the bearer of them that shall grow and be mates to the mothers. . . . Who knows . . . what heroes may come from" the daughters she produces? The question is startling and the implied answer clear: mothers will produce daughters to bear more children, but their sons — and their sons only — will be heroes, just as men are always given precedence in the text, in the common formulae for mentioning them both: "the bodies of men and women . . . the body of a man or woman . . . to rest my arm ever so lightly round his neck or her neck . . . closer to men and women . . . the man's body is sacred and the woman's body is sacred . . . each has his or her place . . . and he or she has no right to sight . . . and in a man or woman a clean strong firmfibered body . . . the fool that corrupted his own live body . . . or . . . her own live body." He concludes by asking, "Have you ever loved a woman?" The next line, separated from these queries by no metrical pause, not even by a heartbeat, is "Your mother. . . . is she living?. . . . Have you been much with her? and has she been much with you?" (8.110).

The hurried interjection of this parent into what promised to be a continuation of the sexual context quickly dissipates that context. However, anxiety informs the questions about the mother. If there is a woman to love, this hurried response suggests, it is the mother, not the lover or the wife.

There is literally no room for the lover or the wife in these lines; the mother fills them all. Remove, as an experiment only, the intrusive interrogatives, and the lines might read, "Have you ever loved a woman / Your mother?" Did he ever love a woman? There is no space in these lines for such love, and he has told us that love needs space—"love needs the free air . . . more wildness, more rudeness." Women are neither wild nor rude, nor do they inhabit the free air in "I Sing the Body Electric." Instead they dwell in misty temples, their realms claustrophobic. They are veiled, and their privilege "encloses the rest," just as their sexuality frighteningly clasps. When he expressed his sense of oppression in a notebook entry, he described it in terms of being wrapped in a tightly clinging shroud. Depression and spiritual disease are associated with images of restriction and imprisonment, the same images that define the female form. In the world created in this poem and in the meditative and ecstatic texts of the notebooks, just as much as in the fiction, he undeniably offers a program that, as Killingsworth says, represents "a threat to the established institutions of American society" and sought to "return physical love to its proper place" celebrating women's sexuality as well as men's.[43] Yet the real nature of his threat does not lie in his proclamation of women's sexual equality, for despite the assertions of the text, the deeper grain reveals a view of women's sexual "place" that is as profoundly heterosexist in its attitudes about the proper application of masculine power as that of any bourgeois male. As Killingsworth says, the fifth poem is "in one sense . . . a critique of bourgeois ideology, in another a profound application of it." D. H. Lawrence asked, "What is woman to Whitman?" His answer was "not much . . . she is a great function. . . . she must bend her head and submit to her functioning capacity."[44] Killingsworth warns that we should not accept an "oversimplified reading of Whitman as the prototype of male assertiveness" and insists that Whitman's "sexual poetics introduce the far more complex concept of interpenetration" of sexual poetics and sexual politics.[45] This is surely so and becomes clearer as Whitman reevaluates his position concerning women's sexuality after 1856. However, neither his actual or subtextual confrontation with women's sexuality nor his often uncertain and anxious forays into the acceptance or rejection of heterosexual male sexual stereotyping are in fact the truly most subversive and transgressive features of his early texts. His most subversive and exciting activity, I argue, is his inscription within the sentimental and clichéd forms of his own early poetry and fiction of a deeply felt but undefined homosexual desire, and the exploration, elaboration, and initial definition of that desire in the notebooks. Here Whitman began to map and create the textual landscape in which men only, his company of Fierce Wrestlers, become the true charged conduits of electrical homoerotic desire.

6

Masculine Landscapes

"The Sleepers" and "Song of Myself," 1855

Landscapes . . . masculine full-sized and golden . . .

— "Song of Myself," 1855

I would sound out the shadowy shore . . .

— "The Sleepers," 1855

I will go to the bank by the wood. . . .

— "Song of Myself," 1855

In 1855 Whitman produced a book, the result as he said of tremendous pressure, that explosively and beyond expectation fulfilled the promise and stunningly realized the implications of what he had been daily recording in the little books he constantly carried with him. In *Calamus,* just a few years later, he would also write about an almost unbearable pressure and explicitly say that the "aching and throbbing," the "hungering desires" that he had "stifled and choked too long," had to be released so that he could "sound myself and comrades only." In "Song of Myself" and "The Sleepers," the pressure to enunciate his new poetry and broadcast his language experiment was equally fueled by the need to "escape from the costume, the play which was proposed to me" (Bowers 72) and to use his new tongue to announce what he had begun to see was a new — and homosexual — identity.

In these poems, far more than in any of the others in the first edition, Whitman pursues the implications of what until then had

been the fragmentary and even furtive, privately inscribed, examination of that unexhibited life. He was now ready to examine
publicly, in depth, and completely the spiritual and personal
implications of homosexuality, exploring the inner landscapes of
homoerotic desire, which he had only begun to dimly perceive in
the notebooks and early work. His was to be a profound analysis of
the homosexual desires that he had discovered in himself, desires
that so insistently demanded explanation and identification. But
his task was even more formidable than that. Not only did he need
to understand the nature of these imperious demands, but he
needed a vocabulary with which to describe and celebrate that
desire. He was daily possessed by a new language, and he had to
turn that new tongue to the service and description of a desire that
was insistent, unknown, forbidden, and potentially filled with
peril. Consciousness of homosexual desire and the need to understand and explain that desire are the emotional facts that create the
controlling and central metaphors of the first and fourth poems,
eventually called "Song of Myself" and "The Sleepers." Other
than "Song of Myself" and "The Sleepers," ten poems completed
the 1855 edition. The fifth, eventually titled "I Sing the Body
Electric," though uneven, stands as the additional and revealingly
important document in the discussion of the homoerotic text, in
which the hand of the poet turned cartographer finely descends
from temples to ribs to thighs, tracing the route of desire upon the
homoerotic map of the word made flesh. "The Sleepers" and
"Song of Myself" massively elaborate and continue the explora-
tory pilgrimage across the masculine landscapes of the homosexual
imagination, identifying new scenery and charting new landmarks
in this geography, expanding the already fluid boundaries of this
sexual kingdom. Together, "Song of Myself" and "The Sleepers,"
as has often been observed, explore daylight and midnight realms.
Indeed most critics have derived metaphors dealing with dark and
light, sleep and waking, from the obvious distinction between the
two poems as polar opposites in the realms of day and night,
habitations of joyous waking consciousness or nightmare mysteries.[1] "Song of Myself" and "The Sleepers" chart the furthest
boundaries and the most distant and unknown lands. There is little
ground that they do not cover, mapping both the firm terrain of
physical geography and the shadowy shores of spiritual, emotional, and sexual continents.

The Shadowy Shore

"The Sleepers" deals with Whitman's most deeply felt themes: death, sex, and ecstasy. The poem is a dream vision and details a story of death and resurrection, of revelation and growth into sexual awareness. Like "Song of Myself," "The Sleepers" pursues the vexed question of identity, which Erkilla sees as "a dream consciousness that is at once public and private, personal and political," a dream world "where the bounds between male and female disappear" and in which "Whitman releases his homosexual yearnings in ambiguous but sexually nuanced images."[2] "Song of Myself" conducts this exploration in the daylight landscapes of consciousness and alert sensual experience. The action occurs in the bright sunlight of physical and spiritual revelation. Even his explorations into the effects of touch and the mechanics of homoerotic response are conducted in the light of day. The masculine landscapes are golden, and the sprouts take and accumulate in the illuminating and clarifying sunlight of his new found awareness and realized passion. "The Sleepers" however, penetrates into regions not explored in "Song of Myself," the realm of dreams, nightmares, and the fearsome world of unconscious desire. "The Sleepers" profoundly evokes the hidden images of the dream world and "enacts a psychic drama metaphorically relating the cyclic stages of sexual development."[3] I would argue, however, that the theater of sexuality is not so generalized; instead, as the speaker confronts the most primal and irrational facets of his sexuality and engages in rituals of the unconscious, he is initiated into a cult of homosexual desire. It is in the signifying world of dreams that the most secret and potent sacraments of homoerotic life are celebrated; there he will literally eat the phallic flesh and drink the seminal blood of his now fully confirmed homosexual identity.

Whitman succinctly describes his spiritual and emotional state in the opening lines. He is confused, "lost to myself. . . . ill assorted. . . . contradictory." He describes such perilous emotional circumstances in a notebook written in the period shortly before publication of *Leaves of Grass:* "I am not glad to night. Gloom has gathered around me like a mantle, tightly folded." The mantle, folded almost as tightly as a shroud, envelopes him so restrictively that "the oppression of my heart is not fitful and has no pangs; but a torpor like that of a stagnant pool" (*NUPM* 1:211–

12). The paralyzed depression of this passage suggests not only a dream but death itself. In "The Sleepers" at least, he is able to act, "wandering . . . pausing and gazing and bending and stopping." Spiritual confusion is a common state in dream visions, but the dark night of the soul is the inevitable prelude to enlightenment. Whitman cures spiritual ill health through sexual action, as he had done in the notebook when, "helpless" and having "lost his wits," he allowed the Fierce Wrestler to thrill him to a new identity. Here he will seek that same remedy.

Years later Whitman observed, "I think Swedenborg was right when he said that there was a close connection between the state we call religious ecstasy and the desire to copulate."[4] In a manuscript fragment reminiscent of the "Sweet Flag" notebook, he had said "I am a look—mystic—in a trance—exaltation."[5] In "The Sleepers" too, he is a "look," for he resolves his spiritual malaise by looking at the sleepers. Typically, he lists them and finally joins them: "I sleep close with the . . . sleepers, each in turn; / I dream in my dream all the dreams of the other dreamers, / And I become the other dreamers." Sleeping with them suggests not only sexual but psychic union. He inhabits them and their dreams. The shared sleep is transformed into ecstasy, for having "become the other dreamers," the religious ecstasy akin to copulation is provoked; he is suddenly possessed: "The fit is whirling me fast." This is the same fit that had mastered him in the manuscript fragment as well as in the notebook entry "Sweet Flag." The fit is the "trance—exaltation." In this trance he will proceed to dream, passing through successively more complex psychological states, descending more and more deeply into the unconscious self, each dream sequence exploring a portion of his identity.

The first dream begins in a celebratory mood: "I am a dance . . . I am the everlaughing." Joy is the primary emotion, laughing and dancing associated with either the potential for or the aftermath of sexual adventure. In "Song of Myself" section 3, just before the loving bedfellow "comes . . . and sleeps at my side all night," he experiences similar feelings—"I see, dance, laugh, sing"—and in section 11 the twenty-ninth bather goes to the beach "dancing and laughing" to possess the twenty-eight young men. The initial confusion and contradiction of the opening lines is washed away in the wildness of the moment, and Whitman—liberated as he dances from self and even from identity—metonymically becomes the dance. This dance is a phallic ritual, celebrating not only "ancient puberty rites," as E. H. Miller suggests, but more—the wild and untamed potency of homosexual energy.[6] The "mirthshouting music" and the dance recall the rites of midsummer nights, phallic dances performed during the "new moon and twilight." In a notebook, Whitman speculated about "Phallic festivals—Wild mirthful processions in honor of the god Dionysus (Bacchus) in Athens, and in other parts of Greece—unbounded licenses—mocking jibes and irony . . . " (DBN 3:772). Among these festivals was that which celebrated Orpheus, who having descended into Hades in search of lost Eurydice and having returned without her, preached and celebrated homosexual love. Murdered for this by the revengeful Maenads, his head neverthe-less continued to sing. The wild dance is such a procession, and it continues "with mirthshouting music," as Whitman and the "jour-neymen divine," a "gay gang of blackguards" who are foreshadow-ing brothers to the "troop" of spirits of "dear friends" that sur-round him in the *Calamus* 5, raise their "wildflapping pennants of joy," certainly erect banners of desire. In that same notebook, we recall, he had engaged in a meditation on the mystery of attraction wherein he asks, "why as I just catch a look . . . at some work-man's half turned face, do I love that being. . . . Why be there men I meet . . . that while they are with me, the sunlight of paradise expands my blood . . . that when they leave me the pennants of my joy sink flat . . . and lank in the deadest calm?" (DBN 3:764–65). The gay gang of blackguards and the journeymen are now precisely identified with workmen and roughs; the notebook entry clearly indicates who arouses his pennant of joy from its lank state. Killingsworth points out the nineteenth-century usage of black-guard as a "general term for a user of vulgar and obscene lan-guage," and the language of this section, while neither vulgar nor obscene is obsessively erotic.[7] This orgiastic scene rewrites his gambols with gangs of roughs in *Specimen Days* and in the note-books and repeats the moment of resurrected power in "Song of Myself" (section 38) when in the company of "an average unend-ing procession" of "eleves" he announces, I "troop forth re-plenished with supreme power," and gives them the "blossoms we wear in our hats," the same blossoms handed out to "comrades" and "youths" in *Calamus* 5 where they are there the symbols of manly love.

The imagery engendered by his union with the sleepers con-jures "nimble ghosts," the "journeymen divine" who "surround"

and "lead" him. The ambiguity of his utterance hints at both
mastery and submission: "I reckon I am their boss, and they make
me a pet besides." He will shortly use "boss tooth" to describe the
entry of the phallus into the waiting mouth, later becoming the
boss/master/phallus. He sees the "hiding of douceurs,"—sweets,
delights, bribes—in the earth or in the sea or "where it is neither
ground or sea," under the "cunning covers" of the nimble ghosts.
In "Sweet Flag" the calamus root is described not only as "sweet
flag" but as a "sweet green-bulb" and as a "manly maple tooth of
delight." In each case sweetness and delight is associated with the
phallic image. In that fragment too, the sweet bulbs and melons fall
"grateful to the hand . . . that shall reach" (*NUPM* 1:194). Here
the nimble ghosts also reach out to the poet and "signify me with
outstretched arms" as they "lift their cunning covers," revealing
beneath them the sweet phallic douceurs. These douceurs and
covers can be associated with the "bulging" baskets covered with
"white towels" left by the loving bedfellow in "Song of Myself."[8]
In a notebook, the poet and his work is also associated with acts of
concealment and with "cunning covers" that hide revelations
represented by the "most private . . . Delight"—the phallus—
which though intially cancelled is soon recalled and undressed so
that the poet in an act of voyeurism, an exciting pornographic peep
show, can look under the covers and see what is provocatively there
(I omit all of Whitman's cancellations save one in brackets): "I see
them lead him onward . . . Onward he moves with the gay procession and the laughing pioneers, and the wild trilling bugles of
joy. . . . They do their jobs well; those journeymen divine. Only
from the poet they can hide nothing. . . . Him they wait on night
and day and uncover all, that he shall see the naked breast and the
most private . . . [Delight]. . . . they . . . lift their cunning covers, and signify him with pointed stretched arms. They undress
delight"(*DBN* 3: 766).

These journeymen offer the same promises of promiscuous
homosexual love as do the lovers who "suffocate" him in "Song of
Myself" section 45, coming "naked to me at night . . . bussing
my body with kisses," and giving him "handfuls of their hearts."
In the same notebook, Whitman describes the prodigal affection
offered to him by lovers: "Some god walks in noiseless and
resistless, and takes their hearts out of their breasts, and gives them
to me forever" (*DBN* 3:766). The "resistless" god—the Fierce
Wrestler now divine—whose shocking gift of the torn out heart

recalls the bare-stripped heart of "Song of Myself," introduces the presence of a terrible divinity into the text, inferring again the Dionysian and Orphic mysteries that led the initiate from spiritual confusion through sexual abandon and worship of the phallic godhead into spiritual regeneration. The "wandering" and confusion of the first lines have been converted into triumphant and carnival certainty as he has discovered the hiding place of the hidden phallic douceurs — phallus and poem. To signify his victory over the "ill-assorted" and "contradictory" self, he raises the phallic pennants of joy — sweet flags indeed — and gleefully marches with his bodyguard gang of seductive blackguards. In "Native Moments" he boasts about another erotic gang: "I go consort with Nature's darlings . . . / I am for those who believe in loose delights, I share the midnight / orgies of young men" (*LG Var* 2:359). Under the "new moon and the twilight" these are masculine midnight orgies too. In section 21 of "Song of Myself," in its only nighttime scene, he "walks with the tender and growing night," asking it to "press close" so that they can couple in the "mad naked summer night." During that mad midsummer night, he invokes the "prodigal" who has given him love and calls upon the "thruster" to hold him tight and hurt him "as the bride and bridegroom hurt each other." During that night also he is raped by the sea, to whom he willingly "resigns" himself in section 22, accepting the invitation of the "crooked inviting fingers," just as he had accepted the invitation of the "stretched arms" of the nimble ghosts. The mad naked summer night, so rich with homoerotic imagery and passion in "Song of Myself" is the same midsummer night in which these rites of dream time are celebrated.

The moonlight and twilight turn now to darkness. Sleep becomes deeper and more profound as he descends deeper into unconscious realms. The brazen music fades; the phallic procession disappears. Having asserted and celebrated one identity in the dream just past, he now dreams another. He asserts the possibility of various identities, but the most telling are the actor and actress. The choice of "actor and actress" signifies not only the adoption of dual gender but also his awareness that these are roles in a psychic play, in psychic play. Whitman's role is "she who adorn'd herself." He is double-sexed now, just as in "Song of Myself" he is "maternal as well as paternal." Since he is both actor and actress, the duality allows an assumption of more complex roles. Not only does he play an actor playing the part of a woman, he is a male who plays an actress who plays a feminine role. In neither case is he the woman herself. Since he does not tell us which role he plays and indeed asserts that he is both, the gender of the participants is both hidden and deliberately confused. "She" adorns herself in expectation of the arrival of her "truant lover." But even the lover role is doubled. The speaker calls upon the darkness to be a lover and an actor as well: "double yourself and receive me darkness, / Receive me and my lover too. . . . he will not let me go without him." In the resulting confusion of role and voice, desire—the woman who adorns herself—is directed not only toward the truant lover but also toward the masculine darkness, who is "he whom I call" who "takes the place of my lover." By casting himself as a player, Whitman transforms the scene into a drama, a fiction within a fiction. Whether Whitman is the poet/actor playing the actress who plays the role of the adorned woman or the poet/actor playing the actor playing the role of "she who adorn'd herself"—her femininity marked only by her adornment and by no other indication—he is doubly able, beneath the feminine masks, to exercise his rejection of the blackguard truant whose "hot moisture" has forcibly impregnated him and to assert his desire for the gentle masculine lover hidden by darkness whose love will cleanse him. The truant is violent: "He will not let me go. . . . his flesh was sweaty and panting."

Though Whitman may describe himself as "she who adorn'd herself," he has not become a woman in order to create a heterosexual episode. He has not assumed gender; he has displaced it and invalidated it within the multiple depictions and confusions of gender possibilities. The shifting sexual fabric of the dream, uncertain and anxious, can not locate a fixed point upon which a determination of gender or sexual object can be based, for each mask removed displays only another mask. If there is any meaning that can be ascribed to "heterosexuality" here, it is erased under the pressure of constant play, a play that says there is no immutable law that defines sexual roles, sexual objects, or even gender itself.

Levitating from the bed—"he rises silently with me from the bed"—in a version of a floating and falling dream that offers rich implications of sexual desire, they begin an airborne passage toward the "shadowy shore" to which darkness also journeys. Whitman wants to "sound up" that shore, that is, explore its depths by dropping a sounding line into the deep waters. This additional image of penetration plays upon the plunging of the soul's tongue to the poet's heart, though now it is the poet who penetrates—"I would sound"—and who also is the penetrating object, the phallic sounding line. This shadowy shore marks the furthest boundaries of the masculine landscape. Voyaging toward these shores, that are dangerously close to the dim verges of death itself, and which provocatively intimate Platonic shores next to the sea of beauty, the poet would identify the darkness, but the dream begins to fade. However this masculine darkness can in fact be identified. It is the masculine soul of the universe that Whitman has already described in "The Analogy" (*NUPM* 1:176) as the "genital master, the impregnating and animating spirit." In the kaleidoscopic changes of the dream world, nothing is certain long, and in an echo of the confusion and contradiction of the beginning of the poem, Whitman is still unsure: "What was it touched me? / I thought my lover had gone. . . . else darkness and he are one, / I hear the heart-beat. . . . I follow. .I fade away." He cannot entirely reject the allure of the brutal truant lover, a kind of genital master, nor is he willing to reject the gentle sexual consolation and healing of the darkness, the animating spirit and the dream world parallel to the sweetfleshed day of "I Sing the Body Electric." Hence he presumes—hopes—that they may in fact be one, and follows the sound of the heart beat, fading away as he fades away into nothingness at the end of "Song of Myself." As this dream dissolves, he is no longer actor or actress, his specific masculine and feminine identities dissolve also. What remains dominates the next dream sequence. There he becomes what he has for so long worshipped.

He has warned the darkness to "be careful," and this alarm presages what is to follow, a truly terrifying world wherein all masks and pretenses are stripped away. He asks the most profound question that the psyche dares voice: "Where shall I run?" He describes his new state:

> O hotcheeked and blushing! O foolish hectic!
> O for pity's sake, no one must see me now!. . . . my clothes
>   were stolen while I was abed,
> Now I am thrust forth, where shall I run?"

These lines are remarkable for their evocation of the deepest fear of the dream world—loss of control. The poet is naked, as he is at the beginning of "Song of Myself." Here, however, he is not the naked poet but the naked penis. In "Spontaneous Me," Whitman describes the young man whose "hot hand" sought to "repress what would master him," but who, losing control and surrendering to the imperative of desire, allows his "trembling encircling fingers" to masturbate, and becomes "color'd, ashamed, angry" (*LG Var* 1:257). Here, experiencing the same conflict, he is "hot cheeked and blushing"; he is "thrust forth" like an erect penis. He personifies and addresses the phallic "pier that I saw dimly last night," asking that he be allowed to "catch myself with you and stay." Does he envision a leap from his window, a psychic fall, followed by a landing—a "catch"—on the phallic pier? Is this fall the dream sign for that disturbing mixture of sexual uncertainty and desire? Once he has caught himself—for as thrust forth penis and phallic pier he and the pier are now one merged symbol—he promises that he will not "chafe you." Will he catch the penis/pier with his hand or with his mouth, and in whichever case, will he gently masturbate or fellate it so as not to chafe the tender organ? Like the boy overmastered by the desire to masturbate, who is filled with "vexed corrosion so pensive and painful," and because of the insistent demands of the "limpid liquid within" him, Whitman is "curious to know . . . what is this flooding me, childhood or manhood. . . . and the hunger that crosses the bridge between." His vision is obsessively phallocentric, and all his identity is submerged in the symbol. Referring to Whitman's phallic boasting, Sedgwick suggests that the "deeper . . . drama" lay in his "being like a woman, since to have to enact rather than possess a phallus is (in this system) a feminine condition."[9] In other Whitman systems she may have a point, though the actress Whitman enacts could as easily be construed as a role that disguises the possession of a phallus. But here he does not "enact"; he is the phallus, and he embodies its imperious demands for orgasm and the gnawing hunger for sexual experience as manhood enticingly and ominously beckons. In what has gone before Whitman inserts himself not in, but as, the text of the poem. He does not describe, he is and he embodies, the phallus, dance, actor, actress, dream. In a comprehensive and daring substitution of a physical for a linguistic metonymy, he both enlarges and erases himself.

Thrust out, naked, ashamed, curious, hungry, and flooded with desire and withheld semen, in as perilous an emotional state as he was at the beginning of the poem, he then turns for solace to a full scale fantasy of homosexual fellatio.[10] He will not chafe the penis/pier, for he will indulge himself in a "sweet eating and drinking," as he takes the vibrantly erect penis—the penis he himself has become, for the desire for autofellatio is paramount in the sexual vocabulary of homoerotic dreams—into his mouth. The testicular "life-swelling yolks" are sweetly filled with seminal fluid. The lips "lap," that is, cover over as well as lick, the phallic "ear of rose-corn," which is the erect rose-red penis, "ripened" and filled with "milky" semen. The thrusting penis—the "boss-tooth"advances into the "darkness" of the mouth, past the "white teeth" that "stay," and soon the seminal "liquor" is spilled. Liquor can be spilled in a pledge of love on lips and on bosoms, but semen is the "best liquor," and once the pledge of love has been made, semen is spilled "afterward" in the act of love.

The exceptionally explicit and accurate homosexual mechanics and the tight oral context of this scene in which the cloth laps, both in the sense of covering over and licking as only the mouth can do, should certainly suggest the homosexual oral imagery that Martin sees rather than the imagery of vaginal intercourse that James Miller finds.[11] Whitman's revision of these lines in 1856 and final cancellation of them in later editions of *Leaves of Grass,* which seem to be part of a project of dehomosexualization, infers that they should be read as a homoerotic rather than as a heterosexual fantasy.[12] While the white teeth may suggest the *vagina dentata* at the level of unconscious fear, these same teeth do indeed un-threateningly "stay," and the boss tooth advances triumphantly into the strictly oral context represented by the lapping, eating, and drinking mouth. The phallic images are metaphorically de-scribed as food—the swelling yolks and the rose-corn—and the milky semen compared to the liquor drunk in a toast is like that liquor, spilled on lips, or perhaps, in withdrawal from the mouth, on bosoms. Whitman has before described phallic imagery as food—the manly maple tooth, the fibre of manly wheat, the nest of guarded duplicate eggs and the testicular melons of the "Sweet Flag" notebook. In those cases the context was homoerotic; it is so here as well. The boss tooth certainly recalls his characterization of himself as the "boss" of the nimble ghosts. There he was master—and as their pet, mastered. Here he is the mastering boss tooth, whose own mouth—if we remember that in the earlier lines he had become his own penis—brings himself to orgasm in the dream-world of desire. The nimble ghosts petted him into erection and orgasm to the strains of mirthshouting music. Surely the strains of that music can be heard here as Whitman crosses the phallic bridge, itself thrust out across the abyss of desire that leads from uncertain adolescence to full homosexual manhood. His pennants flap joyfully now, for he is indeed, literally and metaphorically, the boss.

As his homoerotic communion with his soul enables him to experience the peace that passes understanding and to possess all the knowledge of the world, and as his homosexual orgy of touch and his sensual battle with the Fierce Wrestler allow him to "jet" the sprouts that would create his masculine landscapes, so his homosexual fantasy in the darkened dreamworld allows him to celebrate a midnight Dionysian festival of sensual revelation, an orgiastic counterpart to the daylight Apollonian rite of aesthetic revelation described in section 5 of "Song of Myself." In section 2 of "The Sleepers" he "descends" from this ecstatic height, for his "sinews are flaccid," surely the aftermath of orgasm. The best liquor that had been spilled after his volcanic orgasm is the seminal liquor of spiritual and poetic power. This scene, of course, is precisely parallel to section 29 of "Song of Myself" wherein orgasm is described as "rich showering rain," that produces "recompense richer afterward." This "best liquor afterward," a magic elixir, also produces a recompense as rich as the projected masculine landscapes, for the sexual awareness that has been granted him in section 1 is the catalyst that, having transformed Whitman from an adolescent dreamer into a mature poet, now allows him to see the visions of the sleepers he proceeds to describe in sections 2–6. Indeed the sexually potent poet is now capable of describing these sleepers. He has drunk the creative liquor—the best liquor, indeed the milk of paradise—imbibing it as the outward and sacramental sign ejaculated by the rose-corn phallus, thus allowing him to possess, and be possessed by, the inward grace and power of the mature poet. In dreams—and hence in desire—just as the Fierce Wrestler penetrated him with the potent phallus, just as his soul plunged his phallic tongue to the waiting heart, so here again the metaphor of aesthetic homosexual fertilization is repeated. The boss tooth advances into the darkness, and the penetration and ejaculation lighten that darkness. He is inspired and reborn, for now "perfume and youth course through me." His new found power, achieved through homoerotic orality, enables him to continue his progress and to embody what he sees: "It is I too. . . . the sleepless widow. . . . A shroud I see—and I am the shroud."

The tone changes and darkens in sections 3 and 4. Here is detailed that barren landscape of dreams where the primary emotion is loss, loss of the living and loss of the loved. He dreams of the death of the giant swimmer, sees the drowned victims of shipwreck, tells of his mother's loss of her Indian friend, a powerful small essay in lesbian homoeroticism, incidentally, and describes the loss of a lover, the "Lucifer" passage later dropped from the poem. These sections invoke the most profound archetypes of separation, to use Killingsworth's phrase.[13] In the dreamscapes that are explored in these sections, the deepest needs and most profound fears of the human heart are explored—the problematic world of sexual desire and the barren world of loss and death. But perhaps the deepest fear is conflated into one image in his nightmare about the death of the beautiful gigantic swimmer. The swimmer, we have seen, is a homoerotic icon. He is the Fierce Wrestler in another disguise. By dreaming him to death, Whitman may see his own death too, for surely the "courageous giant" in the "prime of his middle age" is a picture of himself. The subjective fears expressed here, loss of life, loss of potency, and fear that the great project of art and life will be cut short "in the prime of his middle age" are expressed in tandem with the other fears, namely, that the giant is being "baffled and banged and bruised" by overwhelming forces that conspire to punish him, even destroy him, for the unorthodox sexuality in which he has engaged in the lines preceding and for his willingness to admit his homosexual identity. Punished he is, for he dies, "an icon of male love, smashed on the rocks."[14] The destruction of Whitman himself and of his own sexual desire, as evidenced in his poetry, was in a small part accomplished when, struggling like the swimmer, he twice revised then cancelled the sexually explicit images of the boss tooth in later editions, finally succumbing to that sad death wish.

The scenes in sections 3 through 6 are confused nightmare visions of public and conscious loss, which parallel the intimate and private experiences of sexual confusion and desire in section 1. But dreams can heal as well as terrify. In section 7 he ascends out of the darkness and returns to the opening scene of "summer softness." The images now are infused with love, completion, and well-being. The lost sailors return home; the lost swimmer and the unrequited lover are "restored." Throughout the catalog he repeats a refrain: the barns are "wellfilled," the poor Irishman is surrounded by "wellknown" neighbors, and he is "welloff." "Wellfilled" ships enter the ports. Indeed night and sleep have restored that which was lost and resurrected those who were dead, calmed the deepest fears and banished horror: "The wildest and bloodiest is over and all is peace." He has passed through the dream world of multiple sexual identity, engaged in a dream of homoerotic fantasy, and from there penetrated deeper into the world of nightmare, and deeper still into the unconscious realm of primal fear, coming to the gates of death itself. There, like Christ harrowing hell, he has restored the dead to life, restored himself to life. Having successfully passed through these successive trials of the psyche, ritual moments of psychic initiation, he can now begin to move upward from the unconscious realm into the clear light of day and renewal.

In the notebooks and in "Song of Myself" sexual experience is accompanied both by fear—the uncertain terrors of section 28 and its notebook sources—and by ecstasy, the end of section 3, section 5, and section 11, and the revelation of section 29. In every case, the poet is granted a new vision, a new life, an expanded consciousness. Here, too, the paradigm is repeated, and he is now certain that "the soul is always beautiful," the genitals are "perfect and clean," and "the universe is duly in order. . . . everything is in its place." Night and sleep have healed the universe, and as each of the participants in the dream—and Whitman is one of them and all of them—awake, they awake to new life. The poet awakes to new life also; he has been able to pass unharmed through the dark world of nightmarish fear, pass through the underground and unconscious world of death itself. Carrying his phallic totem and empowered by its magical ejaculated liquor, he has come through these trials and testings into the clean, perfect, and ordered light of day, where at last everything is clear, and where everything is indeed in its place.

In the "Preface," talking of the role of the poet, Whitman observes that "nothing out of its place is good and nothing in its place is bad. He [the poet] bestows on every object or quality its fit proportions neither more nor less" (Cowley 8). The creation of fit proportion and the siting of a perfect proper place fit for the conduct of poetry are the ultimate business of this poem. To achieve that proper place he has had to descend into the deepest recesses of the unconscious dreamworld and uncover there the hidden phallic secrets, unearthing and uncovering the secret of his own sexual identity. "The Sleepers" records a quest and an initiation. Whitman, the hero, the initiate, the savior to be, moves from test to test, passes through the dream world's rigors, and celebrates its rituals. He becomes an initiate into the mysteries of the cult of homoeroticism, passing through the ritual stages of that initiation, recognizing his phallic identity, becoming in fact the phallus itself, and participating finally in an act of homosexual initiation as he takes the sacramental boss tooth into his mouth, drinking from that sacred phallic vessel the best liquor, the seminal milk of power. Thus empowered, he is able to confront the primal fears—loss by death, loss of love, loss of self—and triumph over them. He is finally reborn into a new life, a life made possible by his exploration of the multiple aspects of sexuality. But to take the sacraments of this special cult, he has had to make a choice, and that choice is to reject the "sweaty and panting" embraces of heterosexual love and submit to the risen god, the Fierce Wrestler, muse and lover.

The Bank by the Wood

"Song of Myself" is a chart of the spiritual and sexual pilgrimage begun in the early works and notebooks. It also shows not only how homosexual desire is transformed from the mere promptings of that desire into the base of a metaphysics and of a poetics but how it is inscribed in a text. Like "the Sleepers," "Song of Myself" also records a journey. "The Sleepers" was a personal, introspective, and even intimate pilgrimage. "Song of Myself" is an epic journey, filled with trials and tests and temptations, peopled with nations, ending in new self-knowledge, but like all epic journeys it ends where it began, in this case in a moment of pure, undisguised and naked homoerotic ecstasy. The task of the poem is to define and to utter the "word unsaid." At the end of the poem the word remains unsaid, but it is defined within the new, vast, and fluid landscapes of homoerotic textuality that the poem has created, landscapes that open now into greater vistas of homosexuality and eroticism, the social, the aesthetic, and the spiritual. At the end of "Song of Myself," Whitman affirms that the poem is a map and that he is the object of the quest he has bequeathed to us: "Missing me one *place* search *another*, / I stop *somewhere* waiting for you" (my emphasis). Once we find him, he who has become essence, he who has now become the Fierce Wrestler, we too can be possessed by the inseminating ecstasy of the plunging tongue and learn therefore the secret language of the valved voice, which alone can speak the word unsaid. E. H. Miller, commenting about readings of "Song of Myself," has "reservations as to the adequacy of any single approach, regardless of its breadth or depth, in reflecting the resonances and meanings of one of the most difficult and exciting poems in our literature."[15] Indeed, I am not sure that any reading of the poem, following on what Miller describes as "the thousands of pages and hundreds of thousands of words" devoted "to explicate a poem consisting of 1336 lines," can arrive at any startlingly "new" interpretation. Miller shows, in fact, just how often scholars have repeated one another, or, perhaps more kindly and accurately, confirmed or are indebted to one another, just as it also shows just how often they can be at variance or simply disagree. My reading will also be inevitably indebted to some of those hundreds of pages, and I try to indicate that indebtedness as I proceed. In what follows my project will be to show how the fabric of the poem is interwoven with the homoerotic textures I have traced in the early works and notebooks and to more broadly suggest how the text employs the language and conventions of a homosexual textuality that is either created or evoked in those same texts. Finally I will try to demonstrate in what way Whitman's homoerotic text resonates against, within, and outside of other discourses of homoerotic desire.

Whitman's imperative insistence that what "I assume you shall assume" creates at once the necessity of a continuing relationship between the speaker and reader that must last throughout any reading of the text, but it also establishes the initial though not the final tone of that relationship. At this juncture the relationship is the unequal one between teacher and student. The repeated "you shall," at once promise and command, as well as the imperative "Stop . . . with me" indicate the locus of power and, when read against that same tonality in the Fierce Wrestler and the ungrown brother notebooks, indicate the presence of desire. Thus, just as these notebook entries because of their contexts of sexual possession and mastery were, so "Song of Myself" is immediately identified as a site of erotic tension. Hence the pedagogical relationship is invested with the sexual; teachers become lovers and the beloved becomes the pupil. The paradigm already established in the early poetry, the fiction, and in many of the notebook entries is truly present here. As Martin points out, "the poem is cast as a love poem; it involves a seduction."[16] But it is important to enlarge this so as to see that not only love but mastery is involved, not only passion but learning. Martin further suggests that the entire poem is a "dream-vision based on a [homo]sexual experience." This too is an illuminating reading, and Martin's comments enlarge the general homosexual contexts of the poem, but it is also necessary to recognize in just what way the poem becomes a commentary on far more than the sexual aspect of the homoerotic consciousness.

I want to look at the end of the poem before continuing with its beginning, for the significant question asked at the end colors the project of a rereading: "Listener up there! Here you. . . . what have you to confide in me?" The absolute reversal of roles—the reader now confides instead of the poet—is the significant event of the poem vis-à-vis the reader who can now, upon beginning the poem again—for the poem is always begun again—approach the teacher/lover from a new situation of erotic power. Hence the absolute possession that the poet infers in section 1—"every atom belonging to me as good belongs to you"—also recalls the absolute possession of the Fierce Wrestler and prefigures the power that the rereader will gain over the poet. This power, like all true power, is erotic. Therefore "Song of Myself" directly and immediately addresses the presence of homoerotic power and desire because of this evocation of its intertextual relations with other homoerotic Whitman texts and also because of its position within the conventions of homoerotic intertextuality—in this case the familiar literary convention of pederastic pedagogy, which is invoked deeply in the opening as well as the closing lines and indeed throughout the text.

But in section 1, the "you" after only a moment of anticipated freedom is instantly overpowered by the "I." Indeed the "you" disappears, though soon to be recalled by further lessons and promises, and the nonchalant "I" takes command of the site. "I loafe and invite my soul. / I lean and loafe at my ease." The nonchalant "self" he celebrates is both the loafing singular young man of the notebooks and one of the roughs. And the soul against whom he will lean with equal nonchalance and carelessness of appearance, lounging intimately with him on the grass, is the first of those roughs as well, the essence of the Fierce Wrestler. This loafing establishes a further context that also indicates the homoerotic siting of the text—namely, the presence in the "loafing" text of those other texts that invoke at this moment, as if they were guardian muses, all those roughs who figure in all preceding texts.

Who are these "roughs" to whom he claims kinship, and why are they such potent symbols? Consider them for a moment. He has given us brief living pictures of some of these archetypical roughs in the notebooks. Tellingly described there are Bill Guess, Peter, and George Finch. Bill has "a thoughtless, strong, generous animal nature, fond of direct pleasures, eating, drinking, women, fun." Peter is a "large, strong boned" boy who was "free and candid to me the very first time he saw me." He was "open, coarse, self-willed, strong and free from the sickly desire to be on society's lines and points." George Finch possessed a "fine nature, amiable, of sensitive feelings, a natural gentleman, quite a reflective turn . . . Good looking, tall curly haired." (*NUPM* 1:199–200). These are Whitman's roughs, and his descriptions of them, especially of Peter, curiously echo other lines in the notebooks. In "Lect[ure] To Women," he describes masculine homosexual love as being wild and rude, and in "Sweet Flag," *Calamus* passions appear "wild and untamed—half savage/coarse." Whitman tells us in "Omnibus Jaunts and Drivers" in *Specimen Days* how such men became icons for him:

They had immense qualities, largely animal—eating drinking, women—great personal pride, in their way—perhaps a few slouches here and there, but I should have trusted the general run of them, in their simple good-will and honor, under all circumstances. Not only for comradeship and sometimes affection—great studies I found them also. (I suppose the critics will laugh heartily, but the influence of those Broadway omnibus jaunts and drivers and declamations and escapades undoubtedly entered into the gestation of *Leaves of Grass* (*PW* 19).

Whitman can be so tantalizing, his hint of escapades and the coy "sometimes affection" are precisely the sort of things that so intrigued and irritated Traubel. It is enough, however, to accept his assessment that these roughs did indeed contribute to *Leaves of Grass.* Indeed they are its muses, and Whitman drew strength from them, loved them, and modelled himself upon them, especially when they were "free and candid" with him, qualities that only "manly souls" could fully offer. Freedom and candor, wildness and untamed coarseness, these terms describe not only men but the ecstasy of sexual experience and the language he uses to describe it. It is no accident that Whitman uses the same words to describe what he feels and who he loves. Whether this double vocabulary is also suggestive of actual experience as well as of desire I cannot say. It is enough to say that the spirits of such men, sexually desirable and poetically inspiring, surround Whitman as he opens his great poem with his invitation to loaf with him and observe a "spear of

summer grass." Indeed, they will constantly surround him throughout his poetry and his life, for not only do we encounter them in the
streets of Manhattan, as captured in the notebooks, but they can be
seen again and again in "Song of Myself" as he joins troops of
comrades, becomes part of his "numberless gangs" of eleves, and
wanders the streets of the city with his arm around their shoulders.
He will riot with the "gay gang of blackguards" who accompany
him in "The Sleepers" and gaily head down to the *Calamus* pond
with the troop of dear friends who will surround him awaiting his
tokens of love. He will join in the midnight orgies of young men
and listen to the calls of his lovers when they call him by his nighest
name. He will join them for drinks at Pfaffs and sit by their bedside
in Washington, and at the end of his life they would surround him
still. The constant presence of these young men, these admirers,
these acolytes, these lovers, inspired and vivified him. Though the
ideal friend is the great object of his search—his "great wish"—
these gay gangs of comrades sang him on his way, male muses and,
as he said, poems themselves. In the "Preface" to *Leaves of Grass* he
asserts about America: "Here are the roughs and the beards and
space and ruggedness and nonchalance that the soul loves" (Cowley
5). Here, indeed, are masculine landscapes, where all men are
comrades.

The great invocation of the self-created muse unites Whitman
immediately with those nonchalant roughs. Here is no high and
formal bard, but one who "loafes" and leans" and seductively
"invites." This invitation to the soul/lover/rough, who can be
nothing else but male, to "lean and loafe" and join him as he
lounges on the grass is in itself fraught with suggestive sexuality,
transgressing as it does the usual proprieties of male-male intimacy. In 1892, Julian Hawthorne enunciated the fears such arrogant and sexually inviting display could invoke. Whitman, he says,
"abandons all personal dignity and reserve and sprawls inconti-
nently before us in his own proper person."[17] Whitman's nakedness and his invitation to the reader to join him in that nakedness in
negligent and provocative loafing inspire in Hawthorne just those
fears of homosexual intimacy that might well be inspired in a male
reader of this poem, for after all, Hawthorne, like other readers had
done, might well insist that this poem was suitable to be read only
by men—and that it was therefore addressed only to men.

In the notebooks, Whitman had asserted that the soul of the
world is masculine; it is the genital master (*NUPM* 1:176). Whit-

man's invitation to the soul to join him is an invitation to the genital master to rape him, as this master will soon do. But first Whitman must become intoxicated enough to achieve the ecstasy he had experienced in the Fierce Wrestler notebook. He breathes the special "atmosphere," which intoxicates him in the same way that sex intoxicated him in the notebooks: "I roam about drunk and stagger" (*NUPM* 1:76). Drunken and staggering, he submitted to that other genital master, the Fierce Wrestler. The atmosphere there was exclusively masculine. It is here also. Now Whitman wants to be intoxicated with this same masculine atmosphere: "I am mad for it to be in contact with me" (*SM* 12). He gives in to the madness of intoxication and rejects the perfumes of houses and rooms, the atmosphere of artificial life—what he had called "societies points and lines." He determines to reject the laws of the artificial world and, to use that earlier vocabulary, to go where he can be "wild, untamed, coarse, candid and free." He knows the location of the sacred grove where this epiphany can be achieved and the rituals necessary for its realization: "I will go to the bank by the wood and become undisguised and naked" (11). "Undisguised!" The masks will drop. The sacred pond, that locale so symbolic in so much gay literature, on the banks of which he now stands in the heart of the wood, is the site of intoxicating madness, a madness of sexual and homoerotic desire. He has described this frenzied bower in "Sweet Flag," dwelt there in "albot Wilson," and he will return to it in *Calamus,* when he glorifies the image by raising it to sacramental status: "In paths untrodden, / In the growth by the margins of pond waters." But now the ecstasy is less specifically homosexual. Here there are as yet no actually present comrades, though in fantasy there are lovers waiting to offer a few light kisses. But there is extensive sexual and homoerotic experience nevertheless:

> The smoke of my own breath
> Echoes, ripples, buzzed whispers. . . . loveroot, silkthread,
>   crotch and vine,
> My respiration and inspiration. . . . the beating of my
>   heart. . . . the passing of blood and air through my lungs,
> The sniff of green leaves and dry leaves, and of the shore and
>   darkcolored sea-rocks, and of hay in the barn,
> The sound of the belched words of my voice. . . . words
>   loosed to the eddies of the wind,

A few light kisses. . . . a few embraces. . . . a reaching
   around of arms,
The play of shine and shade on the trees as the supple boughs
   wag,
The delight alone or in the rush of the streets, or along the
   fields and hillsides,
The feeling of health. . . . the full-noon trill. . . . the song
   of me rising from bed and meeting the sun.

                                                          (*SM* 13–21)

This sexual idyll echoes images taken from the notebook
"Sweet-Flag," images I have already shown to be profoundly
homoerotic. He places this experience next to the pond that will
eventually be named in *Calamus* as the site of his homoerotic
communion with "them that love as I myself am capable of
loving." Here the retreat is unnamed, but it is the same sacred
locale, filled with suggestive voices whose buzzed whispers tanta-
lize and invoke inspiring images of the phallic "loveroot" and its
seminal "silkthread," of the crotch and the phallic vine. So exciting
are these images of phallic desire that his breath comes in quick
gasps. He not only respires and inspires, but he is inspired by these
images, intoxicated by them, and thus enters into that familiar
state of visionary ecstasy. In the notebook "Memorials," there is a
specific source for these inspirations and his title reveals a further
inspiration: "Poem of the Wrestlers / My respiration and inspiration . . . the beating of my heart. . . . the passing of blood and air
through my lungs" (*NUPM* 1:152). When he struggled with his
Fierce Wrestler in the transport of homosexual passion, he cried
"you are taking the breath from my throat." Like that other
notebook poem of a wrestler, like his memorial to the sexual
implications of masculine struggle, here too the respiration and
inspiration (in both senses of the word) is surely a breath of manly
love.
   In this passage in "Song of Myself," Whitman is transported
upon the winds, and he exhales a new breath—his newly minted,
belched words. These are prophetic words, for he, like the Sibyl, is
possessed with the power of prophecy, and the Apollonian gift of
poetry. The rites of this untamed and wild sexuality are performed
on the shore, on the hillside, in the barn, and by the pond. In an
orgiastic scene in which kisses and embraces are exchanged,
arms—many of them—reach around to touch, and multiple "sup-

ple," phallic "boughs" wag. Whenever Whitman imagines multiple sexual experience, as he will do later in "Song of Myself" and as he has done in the notebooks, the theater of his imagination seems to present groups of men and men alone: twenty-eight bathers, gay gangs of blackguards, troops of dear friends, firemen, athletes, and swimmers. They are envisioned as lurking loungers awaiting a passionate rendezvous in some pastoral bower. Here too, though the sex is unspecific, the lure of orgiastic homosexuality is immensely powerful, and the locale and the phallic boughs suggest the identity of these promiscuous lovers. He discovers, as he always discovers in the grip of sex or sexual fantasy, a new realization and a new power. He is granted a song, having experienced both autoerotic delight—"alone"—and imagined sexual congress with others, either "in the rush of the streets" where he has always returned the glances offering love or in the sexually charged pastoral retreats—"along the fields and hillsides"—where loving loungers always await.

This is the first of many such sexual experiences that take place in this wilderness retreat, the same metaphoric grove next to the same metaphoric pond to which Whitman will have occasion to so often repair in *Calamus*. This hidden bower of sexual bliss is a central image in the lives and texts of gay people, from its actual manifestation in the groves of Fire Island or Central Park to its literary celebration in Vergil's second "Eclogue," wherein Corydon laments his lost Alexis and invites him to return to his own sacred grove and, like Marlowe's Shepherd, to come live with him and be his love. Just as in his journal Thoreau records being taken by his voyeuristic observation of the erotic spectacle of boys bathing in the river and being led into speculations that can only be described as homoerotic reverie, so Bayard Taylor in his American fable of manly love *Joseph and His Friend* (1870), Melville in *Typee*, and Xavier Mayne (Edward Prime-Stevenson) in the American homoerotic novel *Imre* (1906) each send their male lovers to isolated groves or valleys, there to escape, as Joseph says, the "laws of men" and to love as only they are capable of loving. It is in the secluded pond in Forster's *A Room with a View* where Reverend Beebe, swimming with the handsome young men he so admires, asserts that the experience affirms their comradeship. And in *Maurice*, when Scudder and Maurice promise to meet in the boathouse next to the lake to ratify their love, they plan to live together in the isolated greenwood. So too Hopkins has his swimmer in "Epithalamion" discover his desire for men as he swims in the healing homoerotic waters of his secluded pool.In Gore Vidal's *The City and The Pillar,* the two young heroes make love next to the hidden pond, while in *Death in Venice,* Aschenbach retires to the isolated wood to declare that it is Tadzio he so frighteningly loves. This site—isolated grove and sacred pond—appears as a defining scenic convention in gay texts, and the evocation of this place in this first scene of "Song of Myself" engages archetypes of the homosexual imagination that establish the site of the ritual theater of the text within the purlieu of this specifically homoerotic locale. It is there, safe from all interruption and intervention by hostile forces, from the "forms" of society, and its moral "pulling and hauling," that the poet can achieve the "trance exaltation" and union with the masculine soul. The opening lines of "Song of Myself" are, in this reading, an earlier and less specific, though more mystically intense and erotic, version of the first *Calamus,* which, though not the first, is the most specific and complete evocation of this archetypical locale of homoerotic desire in American literature.[18]

With the bestowal of a "few light kisses" and "a few embraces," the erotic focus is widened. Though he surely is engaged in autoerotic fantasy, what he fantasizes is not solitary pleasure but an orgiastic involvement with many "arms." The love of self has expanded into the love of another, the love of one manly soul is broadened into the love of all men, and the poet is impelled to utter this love and his new knowledge. Thus the sexual experience is transformed into poetry. Just as in "Sweet Flag," where, exalted by the trickling sap of the manly maple tooth, the poet enters into a mystic "trance exaltation," so here, intoxicated by the atmosphere of the masculine universe, brought to orgasm and understanding by many embraces, he arises liberated from his bed, possessing now the power of his song and the power to instruct and to liberate his prospective comrade/student/lover. The new knowledge he has gained and can now impart is the knowledge of freedom, freedom from "creeds and schools," freedom from second hand knowledge, freedom also from the social, moral, and sexual restraints that reject manly love. The freedom he preaches is self-reliance. But this knowledge of the self has come from sexual knowledge, indeed sexual knowledge achieved through homosexual experience. In the notebooks, as well as in other gay texts, freedom and phallic sexuality are inevitably linked—"The growth of [manly] love needs free air,"—and these free locales and these ecstatic reactions are inevitably heavily freighted with homoerotic implications.

Out of this union with the soul/lover there comes a stunning promise: "Stop this day *and* night with me and you shall possess the origin of all poems" (*SM* 25). This is another invitation to spend the day and night with the poet, and thus it is both a sexual and a social offer. Social and sexual intercourse with the poet/teacher is the agency of liberation. The you/soul/lover/reader, having been invited by the poet, inspired by the phallic spear of grass, and intoxicated with the atmosphere in which society and moral repression have no part and in which only true art can flourish, an atmosphere informed by a subtext of homoerotic desire, takes on yet another identity. He becomes the student/lover/reader who will, in following the teacher, be able not only to free himself of all preconception but to free himself of the teacher as well: "You shall no longer take things at second or third hand, nor look through the eyes of the dead, nor feed on the spectres in books, / You shall not look through my eyes either, nor take things from me, / You shall listen to all sides and filter them from yourself." This promise is founded upon the presumption of sex. Stopping the day and night foretells the night spent with the "loving bedfellow" as well as with his "friend" in *Calamus* and recalls most specifically the night spent together by the child and his champion, Charles and Langton—student and teacher, lovers—from which both achieved spiritual and sexual revelation. Marlowe did not promise as much when he invited his lover to share with him the pleasures not only of nature but of the mind. Whitman breathtakingly promises that homosexual love will open the door to the very source of art and reveal the path to spiritual freedom. The literature of homosexual instruction that resonates against this text has its most obvious classical location in Plato, its most thoughtful theorists in J. A. Symonds and Edward Carpenter, and its most powerful example in Whitman's text itself.[19]

These lines from section 2 offer a paradigm of the structure of several similar events within the poem and indeed, in a general way, of the entire poem itself. A sexual adventure—usually an autoerotic fantasy—grows into an uncontrollably orgiastic experience culminating in orgasm. Out of the intoxication of the experience comes revelatory knowledge. This is the same paradigm Whitman will later employ—for example, in "Native Moments" and in several of the *Calamus* poems. It is repeated, indeed, in the first *Calamus* as the dominant symbolic act of that poem. That it is also the general outline of the poem is suggested by the final lines, in which the speaker, having become invisible, becomes a drifting and spermatic cloud evoked by the multiple experiences of erotic contact that are the substance of the text and that have led the speaker/poet and the reader, the you and I, to the edge of the most significant knowledge—"you will hardly know who I am or what I mean"—and to the place where it is now possible to return to the beginning of the poem and begin again with a rereading and thus with a more profound celebration. The "atmosphere" and the "smoke" of his breath, the "respiration and inspiration," which rise here like incense at this masculine shrine, are touched by and touch that first and final "vapor," that effused spermatic flesh, that departed "air."

Inspiring and respiring the air of sexual freedom, Whitman announces in section 3 that he is at ease with the "mystery" of the "procreant urge of the world." Though the "talkers"—the same who urge blind obedience to creeds and schools—talk of the beginning and the end, Whitman rejects that conversation and urges that the present moment is the only moment worth considering. These same talkers stress the procreant urge of the world—this "mystery." But it is pointless "to elaborate," or to intellectualize a mystery that is inexplicable. Whitman is at ease with it: "I and this mystery here we stand." Thus in section 3 he seems to address heterosexual experience as his subject, and most critics assent to this. Killingsworth, for example, says that the repeated "urge" announces that the "sexual activity of the world, the creative force, never ceases" and that it is "not simply creative, it is procreative and thereby depends on the merging of opposites."[20] However some readers suggest, as Duncan has done, that in "Urge and Urge and Urge" can be heard "a homosexuality in distress, not only in its cry for a mate . . . but in its generative loss . . . in the longing for a woman not as a lover but as a mother to his fathering desire." Tuveson believes that the lines celebrate bisexuality, for "the individual is not complete without including in his being the principles of both sexes."[21] I would like to suggest a slightly different reading.

The talkers who talk of the procreant urge "always" talk of it, and while Whitman is at ease with this mystery and accepts the procreative principle, he is also at ease with another and greater mystery, the mystery of independent selfhood. After his definition of the procreant urge, he quite abruptly turns his back on the subject and concentrates not on this inexplicable mystery but upon the "clear and sweet" union of self and soul, the homoerotic subject of the opening lines, the soul and body there bound in an indissoluble homoerotic union. There is no point to showing the best and making distinctions as the talkers try to do; intellectual casuistry is vain. While the talkers talk, discussing not only the beginning and the end but the procreant urge and the best and the worst, Whitman again distances himself from the discussion and goes to "bathe and admire myself."

The procreant urge is rejected as part of the talk of the talkers, who are the same talkers he will shortly call trippers and askers, the same, he will eventually assert, who have promulgated standards hitherto published and have insisted upon conformities to the sexually orthodox world. The procreant urge is a mystery in which he has no interest. More interesting to him is the mystery of the self and soul, but that too is not to be discussed but to be admired. But what is to be most admired is "myself" and "every organ and attribute of me." Though he is comfortable with it, he rejects the procreant urge of the world as being irrelevant to his life and desire. He is "silent" while "they discuss," this silence an admission that he has nothing to say about the procreant urge, which the remainder of the poem will affirm. As Miller points out, the poet "retreats from a society given to what he considers to be the lengthy discussion of irrelevancies" and "caresses his body, verbally and visually, if not tactilely."[22] The solipsistic, even onanistic, "myself" implies the need for no other partner. But if there is to be another partner he is specific about who it should be, as specific, I urge, as when he repeatedly asserts his advocacy of "the woman the same as the man."

Whitman welcomes "every organ and attribute" of "any man hearty and clean, / Not an inch nor a particle of an inch is vile, and none shall be less familiar than the rest" (*SM* 49). No attributes and few organs, save for the penis, are linearly measured in inches, and no organs carry the enforced taboo against familiarity except that enticing organ forbidden to other men. In addition, his attributes are also part of his homoerotic vocabulary. In the notebooks, especially that describing Bill Guess and that listing a phalanx of clean and hearty men (*NUPM* 1:246), a vital concomitant of sexual attractiveness is this same heartiness and cleanliness. Indeed, the unspoken text may well be that women are not as hearty or clean as he would like them to be. Awareness of that subliminal fear may

have prompted Stanton's forceful choice of "ignorant" to describe
Whitman's sexual knowledge of women, and her word might well
provocatively echo here. These lines, then, celebrate not heterosexual but homosexual union, not the "always" discussed procreant urge of the world, but the sexual attraction of the masculine
body and the aesthetically and spiritually procreant urge of the
masculine body and the masculine soul, that same union out of
which, Plato urged in that fecund ur-text of gay textual convention, came the art that is the spiritual offspring of male lovers.[23]

This evocation of masculinity leads him into a ritual dance of
pleasure and a celebration of a specific and startling male lover: "I
am satisfied—I see, dance, laugh, sing" (*SM* 51). He celebrates his
new sight and knowledge and defends it by asking what he should
do when his loving bedfellow withdraws at "the peep of the day."
Here is another scene of homoerotic fantasy, but now, for the first
time in the poem and for the first time since the Fierce Wrestler,
there is another specific partner. The partner, however, is stunning,
for he is, perhaps, divine: "As God comes a loving bedfellow." I say
perhaps since the cunning grammar allows him to be God or to be
like God—like a God perhaps, indeed a possessing Dionysiac God,
the Fierce Wrestler again. The experience has been a happy one, and
the departing bedfellow leaves the poet with "baskets covered with
white towels bulging the house with their plenty" (53). The
bulging baskets, which suggest not only swelling organs but
rising bread, is an image at once phallically evocative and suggestive of pregnancy, as most readers have observed.[24] If the bedfellow is God, his presence has lent divine sanction to their
lovemaking, and the swelling baskets are not only symbols of
phallic potency but of divine impregnation. Then, as Martin says,
Whitman has been "impregnated by the word of God."[25] Whitman adopts the role of passively receptive lover.[26] The procreant
urge of the world is indeed redundant and unnecessary in this
divinely blessed homosexual union, the symbol and fruition of
which is the pregnant and potent symbol of the phallically swelling
baskets containing a very special eucharistic bread. In the notebook "Poem Incarnating the Mind" (*NUPM* 1:102), written prior
to 1855, he dilates in prose on "Myself," and experiments with
concepts that may have entered into "Song of Myself" from this
passage, and shows how the eucharistic bread becomes sexual and
aesthetic sustenance:

All around me I hear how great is Adam or Eve—how significant the illustrious Greeks. . . . Yes Christ was large and
Homer was great . . . and in my soul I know that I am large and
strong as any of them, probably larger. Because all that they did
I feel that I could do, and more and that multiplied; and after
none of them or their achievements does my stomach say enough
and satisfied [?] Except [?] Christ; he alone brings the perfumed
bread ever vivifying and clean, to me, —ever fresh and plenty
ever welcome and to spare. —Not even God is so great to me as
Myself is great to me. . . . Now I stand here, a personality in
the Universe, a personality perfect and sound.

There is no Christ in "Song of Myself" at this point, but the
perfumed bread is there in as much "plenty" in the notebook as in
the poem. His soul is now as vivified and clean as any organ or any
man. The Dionysiac dancing and singing have been the celebratory
rites and rituals that are the prelude to the ecstatic communion
with the divine. In this dance and during that night he is "a mystic
in a trance exaltation," conceiving without procreation, creating
without need of the procreant urge. He is father, mother, lover, and
poet.

Gelpi curiously insists that "the unspecified sex of the bedfellow leaves ambiguous the homosexual feelings" but "results in a
sense of completion which is felt explicitly as androgynous."[27] Just
how unspecified the sex is within a patriarchal tradition of divinity
may be queried, but since no significant bedfellow has been
anything but male in the texts I have considered, the imputation of
androgyny, which Gelpi seems to confuse with homosexuality,
must be erased to make way for the inclusion of homosexuality as
the subject of this specific and masculine text, a text anxious only
in its questioning of the meaning of the act and not of the act itself.
The significant focus of interpretation should not be upon the
reasonably obvious identity of the bedfellow or even the construction of the phallic baskets, containers of inspiration, but upon the
tense questions asked at the end of the sequence.

Once the bedfellow is gone, Whitman possesses the plenty of
the baskets, the gift of bread, the gift of art. Yet the euphoria of the
night is converted to an agonized uncertainty as he watches the
lover depart. He is suddenly overwhelmed by an agony of uncertainty and anxiety. He asks the vital questions that the departure of
the lover inspires: Shall I postpone accepting what I have realized?

Shall I forcibly turn my eyes away from the departing and soon to be lost lover, whose departure has forced the realization? How will I construe—"cipher"—this experience and what it says about "me"?

The surreal and mystical night of divine possession contrasts poignantly with the sudden touch of painful reality that the figure of the lover disappearing "down the road" invokes. God has in a stroke become man, a man whose gift of sexual pleasure may well be negated by his withdrawal. Watching the lover disappear down the road, unable to tear his eyes away from the miraculous and still human figure, what he realizes and what he must now accept is that the well-kept secret of his nights and days is that vital well-spring of his creative power, which is founded upon and defined by his sexual desire for men. This is the moment when he knows, as if by divine intervention, the only true direction of his desire. If he should "scream at my eyes" to turn away from the departing lover, who is, of course, not God at all, but who "as God" has quickened him through homosexual love into a recognition of his homosexual life, then he would deny both lover and the love. If he does turn away, then there can only be more ciphering, more, as he will shortly say in section 4, sweating "through fog with linguists and contenders." The adversaries he confronts in these lines, the talkers, the trippers and askers, the linguists and contenders, and the cipherers of morality all urge postponement and adherence to the standards hitherto published. The loving bedfellow, that fierce and God-like wrestler, has given him a gift that cannot be ciphered and shown him that the "me" cannot be reckoned by the laws of the talkers. Like Hopkins, who in that time of now done darkness wrestled with his homoerotic Lord, so Whitman wrestles with himself, and finally, does not turn from gazing after and down the road but, accepting the pain of loss and the realization of the nature of his desire, looks ahead to where masculine landscapes glitter in the light of a transparent summer morning in June. The concluding lines of section 3 offer the answering homoerotic parallel to the mystery of heterosexual procreation. The single, one, unitary poet of body and soul, the "Me myself," the nascent poet of comrades and homosexual love, is at last satisfied. He has bathed and been baptized in the pond in the woods. He has danced the ecstatic ritual. He has made love to God and eaten the phallic eucharist of homosexual desire, and in so doing he has been given the courage to postpone no longer his acceptance of the homosexual self.

In the notebook "After all is said and done" Whitman had mused: "I see myself sweating in the fog with the linguists and learned men. —I look back upon that time in my own days. —I have no mockings or laughter; —I have only to be silent and patiently wait" (*NUPM* 1:183). The evocation of silence evokes unspoken texts as well. In *Calamus* the most powerful unspoken texts are those that describe how he and a lover sit in silence, that very silence being a sign of their homosexual desire. Throughout these opening sections, he has established silence in opposition to talking—to askers, talkers, and linguists—thus denying the validity of the very medium he employs—speech.

But in fact, the actions of these first lines deny not only the subjects of speech but the act itself, forcing the text toward its written rather than its spoken existence. Though he is surrounded by tempters—the "trippers and askers"—he is secure since he can look back—"backward"—on days when he contended with them. In each of his contentions with speech, he has taken a transgressive and violating action in order to liberate himself from the coils of empty talk that continually publish empty standards. He has rejected the houses and rooms of orthodox social intercourse in favor of breathing in and breathing out—speechless acts—and stripped himself naked as a symbolic and actual rejection of all the forms of custom. He has warned his student lover of the uselessness of speech and interpretation—getting at the meaning of poems—and brazenly invited him to have sex. He has rejected the great topics—the beginning and the end, procreation—and declared instead his passion not for talk but for the organs of himself and naked, clean and hearty men. He has accepted homosexual sex with a man whose casual departure at the peep of the day suggests the equal informality of the original meeting, and he has refused to accept the formal ciphering—another form of speech—that would invalidate and condemn the love. In each instance he commits a radical transgression against common morality.

In section 4 he once again confronts his talking adversaries and insists that the facts of biography do not define him. But these are not the "me myself." There may be comfort in the fact that he says here that even the "real or fancied indifference of some man or woman I love" cannot define him, having learned that sad lesson staring down the road after his departing lover. He distances himself from the struggles—from the pulling and hauling—of conventional and sexually orthodox society. The "what I am" stands aside and watches, witnesses and waits.

But if the pattern of transgressive action is sound, then he must also here act rather than talk. He does so in a bravura exercise in autoerotic sexual innuendo, an exercise that daringly and exhibitionistically mocks the society of trippers and conforming askers. Standing apart, he is "amused" by the interrogations of the learned linguists. As always, talk turns him in upon himself, and meditation followed by arousal results, for, I propose, he "looks down" and "is erect." Deriding the social act with sexual action, he bends an arm," placing it on a "certain rest." Then in a comedy of contemptuous masturbation, he too engages in pulling and hauling, wondering "what will come next" in "the game." What comes next in section 5 is ejaculation, orgasm, and revelation. Meanwhile as an apostle of love, "I witness and wait." These lines, of course, attest to that sense of distances said to be part of the spiritually ascended self as well as of the creating artist—what Thoreau had described as "a certain doubleness by which I can stand as remote from myself as from another."[28] Whitman is also, as R. W. B. Lewis says, the "new Adam" here standing erect in paradise.[29] But we give less than credit to Whitman if we ignore the very real comic impulse sex often prompts him to indulge, or if we forget how profound and complex are the many daring chances he takes in pursuit of his announced intention to drench his words with sex.

In section 5 the full measure of homoerotic imagery is displayed, and stunningly. This is the first major exploration in the poem of the possibilities of indirect, even coded, homoerotic discourse, a full scale engagement of homoerotic textual semiotics. The grammar of this passage should be heeded. It begins in the present with a doctrinal exhortation, a credo: "I believe in you my soul. . . . the other I am must not abase itself to you, / And you must not be abased to the other." It continues with another form of the opening invitation of the poem, this to the masculine soul: "Loafe with me on the grass." But the grammar changes, and rather than continue with the present-tense seduction, he recounts one from the past. Save for one or two other moments when he is recounting an example from history, this is the only moment in the poem—save for the immediately preceding lines—couched in the past tense, and the only moment in the poem when the speaker recalls rather than recounts a personal event. This electric moment has taken place before the poem was written. It is this past event that has brought him to a state of spiritual and sexual preparedness, to a moment of spiritual and aesthetic revelation wherein he is able to compose his poem — verbally and extempore — which he now does as he and the soul/student/lover/reader loafe on the grass. It is this past event that, as Miller says, has led to the "metamorphosis of a conventional timid hack writer into America's greatest and most courageous 'original.'"[30] Indeed it becomes clear that because the sexual event empowers the poetic voice the remembered homosexual event is the point at which Whitman places his "birth as a poet."[31]

The opening lines indicate a present seduction: "Loose the stop from your throat." This is a sexual invitation, suggestive of the unloosing of buttons and the loosening of clothes. In light of the act of fellatio to come, the loosening of the throat also has clear sexual as well as musical and vocal significance. But it is not words — logical discourse — nor music — emotional discourse — nor custom or lecture — social and intellectual discourse — that the poet wants. Once again he rejects speech. He rejects "even the best" of these things in favor of the hum of the valved voice, the sexual discourse, and the sexual usage of the mouth and throat. He does not want meaning, rather he seeks the meaningless hum and lull evoked by sexual pleasure. The relaxed machine-like purring of the throat, the "valved voice," produces this unmusical, meaningless, unrhymed, wordless humming that calms and soothes the poet, indeed hypnotizes him and sends him into the trance-like, yet sexually aroused state in which an ecstatic revelation will occur. It is this sexual lull and hum, the only possible sound that the voice can make when the penis has entered the mouth, that for Whitman is special music. Here then is the most potent denial of speech thus far, in which sex and the phallus have been figuratively and literally substituted for speech, the phallus entering the mouth there to jet the stuff of new words.

The speaker's seductive invitation anticipates and describes the pleasure he "wants." As if to arouse the soul/lover/reader, or perhaps even to teach him, he tells an erotic story of a past seduction, which makes even clearer what has been done and what he hopes will be done. He recalls that incandescent memory, its startling climax, and its resulting spiritual revelation: "I mind how we lay in June, such a transparent summer morning." Whitman and the masculine soul have been stretched on the summer grass before and have made love before. Then the soul turned over upon him, placing his head athwart his thighs. Certainly then the unstopped throat, its valve now fully opened, can no longer be the agency for talking but for sexual pleasure. Speech has been silenced by sex. These lines are a precise example of Whitman's dictum about the impossibility of getting "at the meaning of poems." Meaning is not assigned it is enacted. The medium of speech is empowered by sex. These lines are "about" and demonstrate the origin of poems, both as texts and, Whitman's point, as sexual acts.

Even while fellatio is suggested by the text, the poet reminds the soul of another act, more active and penetrative, how the soul plunged his tongue to the poet's "barestript heart." The bare, stripped, vulnerable heart, the heart of the poet's sexual and aesthetic consciousness, accepts the phallic tongue, here now an image not only of sexual mastery but of aesthetic inspiration, just as it was when the poet was powerfully penetrated in the Fierce Wrestler episode. The "barestript heart" awaits revelation; the vulnerable and lovelorn poet needs comradeship. He allows himself to be aroused, taken, mastered, just as he surely was — or in the fluid time scheme of the text, will be — by the loving bedfellow and by the Fierce Wrestler. At the moment of climax, with the reception of the seminal fluid no longer blocked by closed valves, then swiftly around him arises the peace that passes all understanding and the knowledge that he is one with god. Self-love leads to universal love, and the final symbol of this universal love is itself phallic: "limitless are leaves stiff or drooping." The phallic leaves of grass, the phallic mullein, pokeweed, and calamus leaves, cover the landscape, the masculine landscape as he will soon call it, with a forest of phallic suggestion.

This is the climax aesthetically, and for the speaker literally, of the five opening sections, which are in one sense a verbal accompaniment to a continuous masturbation that moves in great waves of both verbal and sexual arousal toward a climax. Yet at very nearly the moment of the possibility of a present ejaculation, he circles back to that first sexual encounter that had allowed the freeing of the spermatic words. The climax finally comes at the moment when the tense changes again: "I know the hand of God is the elderhand of my own." If in the beginning of the poem he celebrates himself only and holds himself in his own love grip of autoerotic arousal, he has now, in section 5, though still under the

aegis of singular autoerotic fantasy, turned away from the single
unitary self and invited a partner into his solitary world. He is the
solitary singer no longer, for he recognizes that the power of love
lies in its sharing.

This scene echoes and recalls the earlier lines when, disguised
and naked, he entered the sacred grove and received the few light
kisses and also those when he lay in the arms of the hugging and
loving bedfellow. But here the general has become explicit. The
wild trance has become transcendent. There is no question of
postponement. No cyphering is needed here to comprehend what
is manifestly true, that the kelson—the keel, the binding timber—
of the creation is love, expressed here as homosexual love. The
circular flow of exchanged inspiration for which semen is the
outward sign—for the drinking of semen is the most significant
event of this sequence—not only unifies the soul and the body but
also gives the power of new speech, and by stopping the mouth it
has deprived him of the possibility of speaking the old speech of
the trippers and askers. Whitman at last discovers as he drinks this
cup his only proper and now fulfilled procreant urge, and he knows
that God—the fierce divine wrestler without doubt—has reached
out his hand. This hand is indeed the elderhand of his own,
whether it grips his erect penis or guides his creating pen.

These lines, as Galway Kinnell says, "may be about the self and
the body and the soul, but to begin with it is about a man and his
lover."[32] This firm reminder is useful since not only to begin with
is it about that but to end with also. The phallic presence, and erect
behind it the presence of the Fierce Wrestler, makes it clear that
Whitman, in choosing here to relate his mystical and aesthetic
revelation in a homosexual idiom, has also chosen the most daring
of all aesthetic and philosophical transgressive positions—the equation of the soul with the phallus, of the spiritual with the homosexual—and that he sites the birth of the poem in the homosexual act.
The conclusion of this scene, like so many of Whitman's revelations, is and must be silence. Old and useless words have been
finally exorcised, the talkers and askers who since the beginning of
the poem have been constantly present have at last been banished,
rendered impotent and invisible by this powerful communion of
homosexual love. The peace that rose about him then allows him
now to "know" and to tell his listening reader/lover that homosexual love is the foundation of all "creation." And as the outward
token of that "limitless" phallic grace, around them rise stiff and

drooping leaves. With new voices, the speaker and his reader are now prepared to embark on the great business of the poem, the creation of themselves.[33]

Sections 1–5 are in a sense a circular introduction to the poem proper, the narrative of which I read as beginning at section 6. As I have suggested, because of its recollection of a time prior to the beginning of the poem, section 5 must at its conclusion effectually place the reader back at the beginning again. This return demands a rereading so that the celebration of self can be properly understood in the homoerotic context that has been fully ratified by section 5 and so that the reader-become-lover can fully participate in a homoerotic and homosexual context. After all, section 5 is the physical enactment (and the cause) of the announcement of the first line. If, revising Kinnell, section 5 is first about a man and his lover, it is finally about the self and soul and the sexual celebration of that unified self. Hence it properly both concludes and then begins again with "I celebrate myself," and the injunction to the reader has now been given double force because the speaker is now not only teacher but lover.

Section 5 has also given the speaker a new voice, and thus the lexical proprieties and clichés of trippers and askers have been banished to be replaced with the stunning simplicity of the opening of section 6, "What is the grass?" These are the first words he utters in his new tongue. But now, of course, given the intensity of the homoerotic contexts of the opening sections and the instant transition from the stiff leaves of the masculine landscape to the "grass," it is also clear that "grass" itself must have an irreducible homoerotic connotation, not only from its verbal contiguity and physical resemblance to the stiff leaves, but because nothing in the poem to come can be unaffected by the complex homoerotic textures that characterize the first five sections. Indeed, the exchange of semen that the mutual fellatio suggests mirrors the circularity of the verbal path that has lead from self celebration back to homosexual awareness and back again to self-celebration. If this is doubted he gives us a sign, literally waves a flag, the "flag of my disposition." This is a sweet flag he waves, for it bears the image of "Sweet Flag," the calamus root, sacramental symbol of homosexual love, the same flag that flies next to the guarded tents, and the sweet flag that grows next to the *Calamus* pond. That flag with its pole is described, we recall, in the notebook "Sweet Flag," one of his earliest notebooks: "Sweet Flag, sweet fern. . . . I am a mystic in a trance exaltation. . . . trickling sap flows from . . . the manly maple tooth." (*NUPM* 1:194). When that flag is flying there can be little doubt about the nature of that "disposition.

So it is that sections 6–19 display even more intensively Whitman's homosexual aesthetic while defining the central image of the poem. Grass, in section 6, is a sign of death since it is the "beautiful uncut hair of graves," but it is a sign of life as well, exemplified in a lengthy listing of animals, men, scenes, and occupations. But most of all, "it means." There is an unsettling disjunction between the expected continuation of that phrase, "it means *something or other,*" and the first presumption that what it "means" is "sprouting alike." Indeed it does "mean" that, that is, the equality of his audience. But because of the fractured grammar and that inserted separating comma, what he also actually says is that grass does not have a signified meaning, but is — if only for the space of a pause — the transcendental signifier. That pause between "means" and "sprouting" allows the reader to gather strength to leap across the expected and prosy clichés of equality directly to the first statement about grass, the startling and exquisite lines: "it seems to me the beautiful uncut hair of graves" that "transpires from the breasts of young men." Young men are his first thought and the most poignant for it invokes desire: "It may be if I had known them I would have loved them."

Of course no denial should be made of the universal context of these lines and their weaving of men, women, mothers — humanity — into "hopeful green stuff," nor of his program of transforming death from the worst fear to the greatest blessing, though his assertion that life and death unite and disappear in the grass has been the subject of extensive and conflicting commentary, which wavers between seeing the section as on the one hand triumphant and on the other tragic.[34] But I would like to emphasize an aspect suggested by Gelpi's comment that the "merge" is the central point of this section.[35] Whereas Gelpi urges that the merge confirms androgyny — "his consciousness must incorporate male and female" — in fact the speaker's focus is not androgynous but solely masculine. For he takes pains in section 7 to insist that "every kind" should be for "itself and its own." This seems to be a kind of separatism, and indeed it is. What he wants for himself are *boys* who have loved women, proud *men* who have been slighted, presumably in love, and the begetters of children. It should not be ignored that the young men are "all that have been boys," sexual

brothers to "all who are or have been young men" in the first
Calamus. He also wants sweethearts (who are sexually innocent),
old maids (who have no relations with men), and mothers (to
whom he is surely a son). None of these women are sexually
threatening. The men, however are sexually and emotionally
experienced, the boys because of their love of women, the men
because they have been slighted—a state not unknown to Whitman
if we believe *Calamus*. This is not an androgynous relationship as
Gelpi suggests—again that confusion of homosexuality with androgyny—it is a masculine relationship with men that sexually
excludes and cannot include sexually possible women.

Indeed it is the men who attract most of the poet's attention. In
sections 10–14, Whitman sees the trapper with "luxuriant beard
and curls." He follows the movements of the blacksmiths with
"hairy chests," admiring the "lithe sheer of their waists" that
"plays even with their massive arms." He witnesses and waits,
observing the "negro that drives the huge dray of the stoneyard"
and caressingly describing him: "His blue shirt exposes his ample
neck and breast and loosens over his hip band / . . . The sun falls
on his crispy hair and mustache, falls on the back of his polish'd and
perfect limbs." Like the anonymous "young giant" of the notebooks, whom he might have loved, "I behold the picturesque giant
and love him," so too the "young fellow who drives the express
wagon (I love him, though I do not know him)." Whitman's
description of the driver should be momentarily placed against
another scene from the Crockett almanacs I mentioned earlier.
There is no doubt that the sexual attraction of the black driver
energizes Whitman's passage. In contrast, one of the bravura
claims of that wild rough, Davy Crockett, is that "I can . . . make
love like a mad bull, and swallow a nigger whole without choking
if you butter his head and pin his ears back." The association
between making love and the transformation of the black man into
a smoothly entering phallus that Crockett can swallow without
choking may not be intended but is no accident in the veiled
homoeroticism of these texts. The black man as gigantic threatening phallus is a staple of white racism and an ironic theme in
black literature.[36] Whitman too transmutes the Fierce Wrestler
into a phallus, and the sexual power and phallic presence of the
black driver invites his caress. But the Crockett text is a racist text,
while Whitman's is not. Crockett's purpose is obviously sexual
humiliation, domination, and cannibalism with the intent to de-

stroy.[37] Whitman describes himself as the "caresser of life" and substitutes homoerotic desire for racist violence. Though eroticizing him, Whitman empowers rather than destroys the black driver. Throughout these lines it is the men who are most carefully caressed, whose descriptions are most sensually evocative, for he is "enamored " of these men, of "men that live among cattle . . . of builders and steerers of ships and the wielders of axes and mauls, and the drivers of horses." His eyes and his words caress these men into life.

Whitman's persistent focus on male physical beauty, it need hardly be said, is an index to homosexual desire, but it is also a convention in gay texts to dwell lovingly and longingly on the specific beauty of men. As I will show below, both Melville's picture of Marnoo in Typee, and Taylor's description of the handsome Hylas, whose "loins were moulded / As if some pulse of power began to waken," are erotic and very nearly suggestive pornographic depictions of the powerful sexual attractiveness of young men. The detailed description of men and youths as a very thinly veiled homoerotic exercise is employed not only in the specifically erotic and pornographic descriptions in the classical sources — such as those, found in Catullus or Martial or in some of the lyrics of the Greek Anthology, that celebrate specifically genital size and male attraction — but in more general catalogs detailing the attraction of hair, eyes, lips, cheeks, bodies, thighs, and buttocks, which can be found not only in Marlowe but in Shakespeare's "The Lovers Complaint," in Richard Barnfield's sonnets, even in Keat's picture of the sleeping Endymion, and in specific pornographic homosexual texts of the nineteenth-century such as the pseudo-Wildean Teleny. Whitman is the most accomplished and specific practitioner of the genre in American letters. Whitman's lists of men in the notebooks are little epiphanies of descriptive passion, and his pictures of voluptuous boys in the fiction, such as Nathan, show that he was engaged with and fascinated by the convention whether he knew that it was a convention or not. It need hardly be said that his own descriptions of himself as a sexual icon are among the most powerful; section 24 of "Song of Myself," portraying the "spread of my own body," is exemplary. His detailed description of the well-made man in "I Sing the Body Electric" is the best example of specific masculine description in his text, while the pictures quoted here are only among the first that fill "Song of Myself."

Women in the catalogs in "Song of Myself," like the women in the earlier works, are described most often not by their appearance but by their role. The trapper's bride, it is true, has "long eyelashes and voluptuous limbs," but this is no more imaginative than his description of the Inca's daughter or the temptress Mrs. Conway. Nowhere in this catalog does he bring to the description of women the stunning originality of the description of the "lithe sheer" of the blacksmith's waist. While the driver is described not in terms of what he does but in terms of his sensuous attraction, the women are rarely physically described, appearing instead in their familial roles or occupations—as a "spinning-girl," "the "young sister" and the "elder sister" who spin, the "one-year wife," the "clean-haired Yankee girl" working at her sewing machine, and the "bride" who "unrumples her white dress," thus accentuating her purity.

The only woman who is described at length is the woman whose persona Whitman assumes as the twenty-ninth bather. However the mask is all there is, and as Schyberg noted, Whitman is "in reality the lonely young women watching the young men bathing."[38] This observation, probably first made by Schyberg, is common to Whitman criticsm, just as common as the presumption that the twenty-ninth bather is in fact a woman who represents "misdirected sexuality" and is a representative of "the position of women, the restrictions of class . . . the demands of the sexual instinct upon the imagination."[39] In this sequence in section 11, the next homoerotic scene in the poem, twenty-eight young men, naked and floating belly up in the sea, are watched and desired by the woman, who peers at them from her window. Her desire, described by some as sexual voraciousness, by others as indiscrimination, and by still others as sexual frustration born of long denial, is recognized by the speaker: "Which of the young men does she like the best? / Ah the homeliest of them is beautiful to her."[40] Desire overcomes caution, though not physically, and in a separation of soul and body echoing the speaker's own experience in section 5, the woman stays "stock still" in her room yet goes off to "splash in the water" with the objects of her desire. The isolated and closeted woman, hidden "aft the blinds of the window," may accurately reflect Whitman's own need for sexual concealment, concealment not only behind the blinds but behind gender, just as it reflects the need for the concealment of homosexual desire. The assumption of the female persona is one of those very "costumes and plays" that Whitman is eager to shed in "The Sleepers" but that here allows him, at once safely yet still daringly, to make a statement about homosexual desire, just as he had done before in the notebook entry "Bridalnight." Killingsworth is surely accurate when he describes the section as showing the "transformative power of the 'hysterical' woman's fantasy," which "parallels that of the poet and the revolutionary," and implies that the scene can be inscribed among those in the poem that stress the "redemptive qualities that result from transgressing social boundaries."[41] But he does not stress enough that not only the boundaries of sexual action taken by a "hysterical" woman but sexual privacy through voyeurism, gender roles through gender misdirection, and sexual norms through homosexuality are transgressed. Once Whitman leaves the woman's body behind in her house, which is the same house that is full of the stale perfumes of sexual convention in the opening lines, he leaves women behind also, discarding what she stands for—the richly dressed morality of orthodox society. He is now spirit only, the pure masculine spirit that intoxicated him in the notebooks and in the beginning of the poem and that penetrated him in the person of the Fierce Wrestler, the loving bedfellow, and the soul. This spirit—the genital master—takes possession of him and, man alone, he dances down to the beach for his rendezvous with the erect gang of men, surely a forest of stiff, not drooping, leaves.

Released from sexual constraint, "dancing and laughing," rejoicing in sexual freedom, "along the beach came the twenty-ninth bather." This recalls the same response the speaker reported when describing how he danced, laughed, and sang after his night with the hugging and loving masculine bedfellow. This echo suggests that such verbal recollections are useful in determining homoerotic context. In section 6 he had announced his attraction to groups of young men in what will become formulaic: "It may be if I had known them I would have loved them." When this repeated formula occurs, it almost always encodes an eroticized description. Here the twenty-ninth bather also looked at the young men and "saw them and loved them." The scene is sharply etched and tactile. The twenty-ninth bather's hand runs "tremblingly" over their bodies, descending from their temples to their ribs and genitals. They respond, even to the unseen stimulus, for their bellies "swell" to the sun, just as the penis swells in arousal. In an ambitious act of multiple fellatio, the twenty-ninth bather satisfies each of the young men in turn.[42] As they float on their backs, the bather "seizes fast to them" and "puffs and declines with pendant and bending arch." The likelihood that the bather is engaging in coitus with them is practically and physically impossible since the men are not lying on the firm sand but are floating on their backs in the water. But it is certainly quite possible for the bather to bend over them as they float and satisfy them orally as "puffing" surely suggests, as the "pendent and bending arch" surely pictures. In an interestingly related notebook entry, Whitman creates this fantasy again: "Faith. Becalmed at sea, a man refreshes himself by swimming round the ship—a deaf and dumb boy, his younger brother, is looking over . . . and the swimmer floating easily on his back smiles and beckons with his head, Without waiting a moment, the young child laughing and clucking springs into the sea and as he rises to the surface feels no fear but laughs and though he sink and drown he feels it not for the man is with him there." [43]

Here, the floating swimmer, an image to be repeated later in the poem and again in "The Sleepers" and "I Sing the Body Electric," an image that in each instance has powerful homosexual associations, is very nearly a sea-changed Fierce Wrestler, whose sexual attraction is coupled with his power to protect. The child, laughing with the same joy that the twenty-ninth bather evinces, ecstatically leaps to possess the erotic swimmer, who like the twenty-eight bathers, floats on his back, his genitals unprotected and inviting. Water, the sacred pond, and the sea are, throughout the poem, baptismal locales for homoerotic experience.

We have seen Whitman fantasize fellatio when he is not imagining being penetrated by Fierce Wrestlers or plunging tongues, and the twenty-ninth bather sequence is another example of a particularly complex fantasy in which the poet, entering eagerly into the persona of the woman, becomes the disguised homosexual participant in what is ostensibly a heterosexual act. Nevertheless, it is all homosexual fantasy. Scenes of sexual possession are a staple of homoerotic literature, and scenes wherein this possession is enacted next to or in an enclosing world of water are as symbolically frequent. Hercules searches for Hylas next to the sacred water, Narcissus loves and admires his own beauty reflected in the water, and Baron Corvo desires the boys bathing in St. Andrews Bay. Forster has Maurice and Alec make love in the boat house and Reverend Beebe plunge into the comradely pool with the handsome Freddy. From the shores of his watery wonderworld, Mann's

Tadzio beckons Aschenbach to "an immensity of richest expectation." Vidal's gay heroes wrestle next to their Arcadian spring, and
Hopkins's bathers become espoused as they swim in their sacred
pond, while Whitman himself will repeat the trope again and again
next to the margins of pond waters arm in arm with his lover or his
troop of dear friends, as he goes to "the bank by the wood."

   This sequence also shares with other similar passages in gay
literature the presence of the voyeuristic poet watching naked men
or boys. Both Corvo and Hopkins, the former in "Ballad of Boys
Bathing" (1890) and the latter in "Epithalamion" (1888), watch
from a distance as handsome naked youths cavort in the water.
Eakin's painting "The Swimming Hole" in fact shows the artist as
observer of the scene.[44] S. S. Saale's "Sonnet" (1890) describes
erotic water sports as does Kains-Jackson's "Sonnet on a Picture by
Tuke" (1889). An American example of this voyeuristic convention
in gay texts, as I will show in the next chapter, is Thoreau's
fantasizing in his journals about the nudity of young men as he
watches them swimming. Thoreau was early taken by such sights,
thus depriving Whitman of the primacy in American letters of
recording such a scene from the perspective of desire, though not
depriving him of the greatest achievement in the genre, or the most
unusual, since no other poet watches his young men while he is in
drag, and no other poet defies the conventions of homoerotic
voyeurism by having sex with them. Surely as the young men
"spend" freely at the end of the sequence, showering Whitman
with seminal rain just as he will again be showered with it in the
climactic section 28, he is empowered by this baptismal sacrament
of virility.

   He will shortly attest that the prospect of eating and sleeping
week in and week out with men is a seductive attraction, and here
he realizes that desire, at least in fantasy. But I would caution
against the too easy assumption that the actor here *is* a woman.[45]
The speaker has abdicated the "I" position, thus somewhat and
deliberately confusing the source of the voice. It is the point of the
passage that these men "do not know" who puffs and declines over
them, "they do not think" whom they souse with the ejaculated
seminal spray, for anonymity—or transvestitial inversion—is the
essence of the delicious and daring masquerade in which the poet
here sexually engages with these heterosexual men—his roughs.
They are the young men of the preceding catalog here collected in
one place and swimming in the baptismal waters of the *Calamus*

pond. He secretly converts their heterosexual experience into his own homosexual delight.

This fantasy, a kind of retributive rape wherein straight men are secretly seduced by gay desire, is one of the more potent and exciting threads in the homosexual discourse. Gilbert describes the sequence as "an encoded fantasy of transsexualism" within which I would also include the frisson of transvestialism.[46] The woman is "richly drest," and shortly, in another but similar fantasy, Whitman will "adorn himself." Women in "Song of Myself," unlike men and unlike the speaker, are never naked—the bride rumples her white dress, another woman is "loose-gowned." They are always dressed, just as they are mostly described by their clothes in "I Sing the Body Electric." If indeed it is the masculine spirit that leaves the body of the woman in her social house, he leaves that body there fully dressed, casting aside the vestments as well as the flesh of woman he has momentarily donned to lure and deceive the young men and to obliterate gender boundaries. Cross-dressing is a radical act far more potently directed against straight male fantasies than it ever is against women themselves, especially when the cross-dresser is himself homosexual.[47] Gelpi feels that the "passage displays how divided Whitman himself is; he identifies as much with the lonely lady as with the robust young men she lusts for. . . . The understanding of both sides is rendered through the bisexuality, and so the homosexuality, of the poet's perspective." Gelpi's useful suggestion that bisexuality is in fact homosexuality ought not to pass unnoticed, but I do not think that Whitman is divided here. The assumption of roles is a deliberate strategy of the text; the assumption of female roles is a divisive strategy of the text, deliberately intended to emphasize homosexuality and to destroy the hitherto published standards of gender and gender roles. Gelpi's assumption of division encodes not only nineteenth-century theorizing about "inverts" being "women in men's bodies" but, unfortunately, twentieth-century uncritical attitudes that seem to imagine that gay people are "like women" or "want to be women."[48] It is precisely such assumptions about homosexuality that the text attempts to destroy. One does not have to identify with women in order to like and lust after men. Martin also underscores the radical sexuality of this passage—and its inscription as a counterdiscourse within nineteenth-century sexual theory—when he points out that Whitman's lines ought to be read "against nineteenth-century medical theories of the conservation of energy, through the withholding of sperm. To the 'capitalism' of heterosexual intercourse (with its implications of male domination and ownership) Whitman opposes the 'socialism' of non-directed sex."[49] I would agree with all that, except for the last. This sex is directed, radical, and deliberately transgressive.

But if we should doubt that his attentions to these men are meant to be anything other than homosexual, his peroration should make clear his implications. He has offered a series of pictures, which have been generated by the question "What is grass?" These pictures include the dead from whose graves the grass grows, further vignettes including the multiple crowds, the solitary Whitman, the marriage of the trapper, the runaway slave, and the twenty-eight bathers, and a series of careful descriptions of handsome sexually appealing men — a butcher boy, a blacksmith, a driver of a team. He comments on all of these pictures, including that of the twenty-eight bathers, with the observation "in me the caresser of life wherever moving. . . . backward as well as forward slueing, / To niches aside and junior bending." One cannot help but idly wonder about the "niches" and the "junior" to whom he bends. Does some of his caressing take place in hidden corners — niches — suggestive of quick and anonymous sexual adventure? Does he bend to juniors — to younger men — just as "with bending arch" he bends over the bodies of the bathing young men, and is the purpose of his bending the same?

The lines that follow the bathers sequence (sections 12–15) underscore the homoeroticizing of men, for the showered semen of the twenty-eight bathers scene plants new fantasies, not only about blacksmiths and butcher boys, but about the picturesque giant, who is another version of the Fierce Wrestler, and impels him to create further fantasies about being in close contact with groups of men — what he has just done spectacularly in the twenty-eight bathers sequence. In the last lines of section 14, he announces that "I am enamored of growing outdoors, / Of men that live among cattle or taste of the ocean or woods / . . . . I can eat and sleep with them week in and week out." Though the sequence has begun by asserting that "for me mine male and female," the previous demand that "every kind" be "for itself and its own" is his real project in sections 11–14. The only kind he seriously considers is men.

As Martin points out, Whitman's roughs are not traditional erotic figures, "not Greek shepherd boys, nor are they traditional pederastic figures at all. . . . they are men at work, ordinary and democratic."[50] That is, they are not figures out of an aristocratic homosexual tradition but new members of the democracy of homoerotic equality Whitman is cataloging here. However, the "rough"—from whence in homage to Whitman we no doubt derive our useful phrase "rough trade"—and attractive though socially and culturally unequal youths are certainly figures who populate the imaginations and homoerotic texts of writers as culturally disparate as Marlowe, Symonds, Wilde, and Forster. I do not think that Whitman's rough pose or his posing for roughs ought to conceal a slight though real contradiction in his project for homosexual freedom—namely, the middle-class (homo)sexual attitudes he evinces, which run parallel with those "Victorian male attitudes" Killingsworth and Gilbert have identified, when he praises not only the sexual freedom but the social and cultural lack of sophistication of these men and boys. The Walt Whitman who found delight in the uneducated Fred Vaughn, Peter Doyle, the farmer boy Harry Stafford, and the illiterate soldiers he nursed shares much with Oscar Wilde's predilection for telegraph boys and Symonds' passion for peasants and Venetian gondolieri, shares with them, indeed, the aristocratic passion that responds to its cultural and social though not sexual opposite, for though Whitman cannot be inscribed at all within the English aristocratic homosexual tradition, his origins within an American bourgeois lower middle class and his own acquired literacy separate him considerably from men he desires in the text and in life.

The fantasy of sleeping with men week in and week out, like the twenty-eight bathers, is a fantasy of sexual possession, not unlike the kind of thing recorded, for example in some of the texts Ellis transcribes in *Sexual Inversion,* in which one of the respondents imagines himself as the "servant of several adult naked sailors" upon whom "he performed services for their genitals," while another, also dreaming of men, imagines "a serried rank of congregated thighs across which I lay."[51] In "Song of Myself," the very mention of these men, and the elaboration of these fantasies prompt the speaker to offer in section 14 a curious assessment of himself and his method: "What is commonest, cheapest, nearest, easiest is Me, / Me going in for my chances, spending for vast returns, / Adorning myself to bestow myself on the first that will take me" (252–56). Not unlike the twenty-ninth bather, Whitman adorns himself as a sexual lure to attract anyone who "will take me," perhaps the very men with whom he wants to eat and sleep.

He walks the erotic streets of homosexual desire in yet another disguise, in the role of a prostitute or in the clothes of a female impersonator. He is easy, cheap, and common, available for any adventure. He seductively "adorns" himself, an act that in comparison with his other persona, the coarse, gross, and sensual masculine poet, is shocking and deliberately perverse, just as the suggested image of the cheap, easy, and common prostitute is shocking in comparison to the wholesome persona of the American poet.

In a notebook entry, "Truly What is Commonest" (*NUPM* 1:185), he points out that "what is commonest, readiest, cheapest is often the profoundest, the most curious–has its beginnings the farthest back and is the hardest problem for thought or science from the start." Indeed, the question of homosexual identity is profound. In this text, it is clearly the hardest problem for thought or science, and thus the contradictions of sexuality pose profound and curious problems. Sexual passivity is echoed in the admission that he is available to anyone who will take him, and as Martin suggests, this passivity points to an attempt to "eliminate pride and power"—traditional masculine heterosexual attributes—"from sexuality and . . . this is to be accomplished by a deliberate acceptance of the passive role."[52] Yet in this bewildering complex of sexual possibility, it should also be noted that just as the twenty-ninth bather is the active and aggressive partner, so the poet is easy, common, and cheap and adorns himself, like the prostitute, with the intention to seduce. He will take risks: "going in for my chances, spending for vast returns." It is risky business indeed to fantasize sexual reversal, even riskier to practice it, dangerous to masquerade as a woman in order to seduce men, most dangerous to admit of and engage in the disapproved rituals of homosexuality. But the rewards, the "vast returns" are worth the masquerade, the disguise, and also the spending—not only in emotional commitment but also in substance of soul and semen—that is demanded.[53] The multiple economies engaged here not only include the spiritual and the seminal but suggest the interesting possibility that unlike most prostitutes, the speaker may spend money in order to obtain a sexual object. Whether the returns are physically vast like the penetrating phallus of the Fierce Wrestler or spiritually vast like the penetrating tongue of the masculine soul, the rewards—sexual freedom, a new art,—are worth any danger (and any monetary expense as well), and show, as Killingsworth suggests, that "the sexual imagination . . . is potentially redemptive as well as a motive force in social revolution."[54]

In this passage Whitman flirts with several ideas about homosexual identity. Bychowski, commenting on these lines, insists on "feminine identification" as "one of the sources of Whitman's homoeroticism," though I would engage the same strictures here as I invoked above. If indeed Whitman is adopting the role of a female prostitute, then he may be asserting certain culture-bound presumptions: that homosexuals are effeminate, that homosexual sexuality is passive, that homosexuals are dedicated to seduction, especially the seduction of heterosexual men, who are the object of greatest desire, that a component of homosexual identity is necessarily a masquerade, and also that this identity is associated with sexual practices that are linked with the available sexuality of the prostitute. Indeed, contemporary accounts of gay life, for example the autobiography of a late contemporary of Whitman's, Ralph Lind (b. 1874), who called himself "Jennie June" when in drag seducing roughs, attest to the dangerous social milieu of the homosexual.[55] But unlike the more prosaic world of heterosexuality, this world, dangerous though it may be because of its excitement, its glamor, and the power of its sexual lure, is worth every risk. In his poem "The World Well Lost IV" (1886), another contemporary of Whitman, Marc-Andre Raffalovitch, would write: "Our lives are wired, like our gardenias." But unlike the wired and hothouse life of that English homosexual, Whitman pursues open sexuality, willing to "bestow myself on the first that will take me, . . . Scattering it freely forever." In "Spontaneous Me" he randomly casts the "bunch" of semen to "fall where it may." (*LG Var* 1:257). Here too, he spends freely, as freely as the twenty-eight bathers, scattering his seed "forever," across the entire text of his poem, and here too he adopts women's garments in order to liberate homosexual desire through the mockery and blurring of gender.

When Whitman informs his language with heterosexual imagery or metaphor, the sexuality is often transferred or "inverted," to use an antique term in a specific sense. Whitman either adopts a feminine persona and sexually passive role, becoming the object of sexual mastery by a powerfully masculine figure—he is the bride hurt by the bridegroom—or, brilliantly contradicting himself in this too, becomes, in his imagined female role, the aggressor, the female impersonator, even the whore. The aggressive twenty-ninth bather, the archetypal temptress, or the prostitute with whom he identifies himself are indeed the only women in the poem who have a sexual identity. He seems to identify only with women whose sexuality is at once available and, in the terms of orthodox society, morally questionable. But by inhabiting them himself, he effectively displaces their gender and their sexuality. But he also encodes them within the homosexual and homoerotic terms of his text. When he celebrates the sexual freedom of these women and encloses it within the parameters of his own unquestioned right as a male to be sexually free, he erases, for women and for homosexuality, the proscriptive moral text, and gives to homosexuality, both textual and actual, the right to be as sexually liberated.

When Whitman speaks metaphorically about sex the subtext is always homoerotic, and these texts and subtexts are stronger and more fully realized, richer and more complex, than those that confront heterosexuality. Sexual descriptions and fantasies about men, masculine/ homoerotic sexuality, and sexual possession are profound, penetrating, and inevitably productive of his most accomplished lines. When he writes about women he moves uneasily upon the surface of his diction. The description of the bride who "unrumples her white dress" and of the blacksmiths—the lithe sheer of their waits plays even with their massive arms"—exist on different levels of accomplishment. The Indian bride—"she had long eyelashes. . . . her head was bare. . . . her coarse straight locks descended upon her voluptuous limbs and reached her feet"—is far less effectively described than the "negro who drives the huge dray" of section 8, whose "blue shirt exposes his ample neck and breast and loosens over his hipband" and "who tosses the slouch of his hat away from his forehead." The former is a cliché; the latter employs an active and original diction: "loosens," and "the slouch of his hat." This latter description is finely observed and specific, couched in the language that Whitman described earlier as "living and buried speech . . . always vibrating here." Even the twenty-ninth bather in her fleshly form is described only as "handsome" and "richly dressed." She is static, stock still, whereas that freed masculine spirit is seen puffing and declining within that exquisite "pendant and bending arch." Even the descriptions of women's work does not rise to equal that of men (which of course may well be deliberate if their work is seen as repetitive and dehumanizing). The spinning-girl "retreats and advances" to the hum of her wheel, but the carpenter dresses his plank to incredible music: "the tongue of his foreplane whistles its wild and ascending lisp." Only the prostitute, to whom he so effectively responds is given an effective verbal identity: "The prostitute draggles her shawl, her bonnet bobs on her tipsy and pimpled neck." This is "living and buried speech," and one of the forces that keeps such speech buried is its relation to orthodox morality. The subtext of such speech is pain: "what howls restrained by decorum." Whitman attempts to assuage the pain and to include the prostitute in his liberated circle. He is all identifying sympathy: "I do not laugh at your oaths nor jeer you."

Throughout sections 15–18, Whitman gathers all the threads of immense diversity, cataloging all sorts and conditions of men and women who "all tend inward to me, and I tend outward to them." In section 16, Whitman sees himself as "maternal as well as paternal," the inseminator and the bearer of America's children as well as their bard. His own "diversity" is the subject of these sections, a diversity mirrored in the catalog of men and women he enfolds within himself. Men predominate here. The women are the soprano, the spinning-girl, the quadroon girl, the squaw, the elder and younger sisters, the new bride, the pregnant woman, the prostitute, and five friendly matrons. Though Whitman watches these women from a distance, he has no contact with them, whereas he consorts with the men. He is "comrade of Californians. . . . comrade of free northwesterners, loving their big proportions, / Comrade of raftsmen and coalmen—comrade of all who shake hands and welcome to drink and meat." These inhabitants of America, together with their occupations, thoughts, and complex feelings, are "the grass that grows wherever the land and water is" (358), and they become elements that make up the "meal pleasantly set . . . the meat . . . for natural hunger" (372), a meal that Whitman, ingesting his subject, eagerly devours.

In section 19 all these elements are focused into an intimate, sexually charged reverie, returning us to that moment on the grass, to that night with the loving bedfellow, to the orgiastic delight of the twenty-ninth bather, and finally, in repetition of the now familiar circularity of his tropes, to the beginning of the poem, when the poet experienced a "few light kisses, a few embraces, a reaching around of arms." After the catalogs of vast numbers of men and of multiple experience, after the daring moments of sexual and homosexual bravado, the sum of all these is finally and most meaningfully conflated in a moment of soft and reflective intimacy, a moment that, if it is like the other moments of sexuality we have discussed thus far, can only describe homosexual union: "This is the press of the bashful hand. . . . this the float and odor of hair, / This is the touch of my lips to yours. . . . this the murmur of yearning, / This the far off depth and height reflecting my own face, / This is the thoughtful merge of myself and the outlet again." All the elements that have hitherto been attendant upon homosexual love and that will appear in *Calamus* are there: the bashful hand and the "yearning" reminiscent of all the bashful yearnings of the earlier verse and prose that have been only for men and that in *Calamus* will be only for men; the mirror imagery of reflecting masculine faces "reflecting my own face." The "merge of myself" recalls the merging in section 5 of masculine body and soul. The "you" of section 1 is now intimately kissed—"my lips to yours." The entire passage echoes the lines in section 2 that describe a "few light kisses. . . . a few embraces." But most of all there is the silence. For as we will see, in *Calamus* especially, Whitman most often celebrates the intensity of homosexual love not in words but in silence, in the soft hum of a valved voice, or as in *Calamus* 29, in an image of a "youth who loves me and whom I love, silently approaching." He shows the two of them "content, happy in being together, speaking little, perhaps not a word." And in *Calamus* 11, the two men lie quietly together in the "stillness in the autumn moonbeams." Here too the tone is quiet, introspective, and intimate. Merged once more with his soul, he quietly concludes this symphonic passage with a soft and reflective coda, converting the extensive lists and vast expenditures into a poignant and specific single moment of confidence and love, talking no longer to the cosmos, or to men, but directly now to the soul, to the reader, to the lover, to us.

In that peaceful moment after the consummation of desire and after the testimony of love, Whitman confides, enfolding the reader ever more securely within the homoerotic text, "this hour I tell things in confidence, / I might not tell everybody but I will tell you." It may well be thought that the confidences already disclosed have been privileged enough, but their very disclosure has been the substance of the lesson he has taught. The pointed distinction made between the "you" and "everybody" singles out the reader from the mass of comrades as one who is now especially worthy of such confidences, one who has travelled with the poet through initiatory sexual experience and learned his lesson well. Whitman has consistently refused to speak to "talkers" and "trippers and askers," always keeping silent.

But now he will break that silence to his special listener, knowing that the "things" he has to disclose—homosexual experience and desire— have surely found a willing hearer. Martin, though discussing the loving bedfellow sequence, recalls that the Greek terms for the active and the passive male lover meant "breathing out" and "breathing in."[56] This "thoughtful" moment, which harks back to the beginning of the poem, recalls his invocation of "my inspiration and respiration" that creates a "few light kisses" and a "reaching around of arms," just as it echoes the inbreathing of loving fellatio and the puff and decline of the twenty-ninth bather. In the structure of "Song of Myself," the first great meditation—or section or movement—which had opened with the erotic proem of sections 1–5 and essentially begun with section 6, comes to an end in section 19. Now the poet and the lover/reader respire and inspire together, the poet breathing out confidences, the reader/lover breathing in the origin of poems and the redemptive power of homosexual love.

Though he has disclosed much he has more yet to tell. Assertions, questions, boasting, and revelation fill sections 20–30. "Hankering, gross, mystical, nude," sexually desirous, blunt, ecstatic, and unmasked in section 20, Whitman rejects all convention, all religion, and firmly places himself at the cosmic center, the still point to which "the converging objects of the universe perpetually flow." His task in section 21 is to "get what the writing means," "translate" the pains of hell into a new tongue, and "chant a new chant." Clearly, the focus is again on language and its functions. Though the great announcement he has to make is that he is the poet "of the Body" and "of the Soul," his further assertion that he is "the poet of woman the same as the man," and that "there is nothing greater than the mother of men," focuses attention on the reproductive body, skewing the description away from the simple but more profound assertion of equality made in the notebooks (*NUPM* 1:73), that is, that the woman is "never the same" as the man. This sentiment does not appear in the poem. Instead he asserts the maternal role, projecting her status as fecund mother rather than as socially equal woman. She is described only as mother of "men" without his usual addition "and woman." Having made a nod to maternity while canceling equality, he then turns to the real subject of the chant, the writing and the translation, the language of the erotic body, the language of unspeakable love wherein he will discover the "unfolding of words of ages . . . a word of the modern. . . . a word en masse" (483–84).

In section 21 and 22, he invokes one of his favorite scenes of sexual adventure out of doors in the "mad naked summer the night." He is nude and hankering, chanting his chant of dilation, and he calls "to the earth and sea half-held by the night." In the first sequence his lover is the voluptuous coolbreathed earth, which in his cosmogony in "The Analogy" is surely female, just as "voluptuous" is one of the favorite and few sexually suggestive terms he ever applies to women. To the earth he will give unspeakable passionate love. In the second, the lover is the sea, here clearly a masculine lover, reminiscent in its mastering passion of the Fierce Wrestler. He will "resign" himself to the sea, accepting the invitation to "have a turn together." The phrase "cushion me soft. . . . rock me in billowy drowse" suggests perhaps a more maternal impulse than homosexual at first reading, yet he demands that the sea give him the seminal "brine of life," flowing unchecked from the phallic "stretched ground swells." Though he may give love to the voluptuous female earth — "smile for your lover comes" — he is given love by the sea — "dash me with amorous wet" — dominator in one instance, dominated in the second.

In the encounter with the voluptuous earth there is only distanced passion; with the sea he is specific. He is invited by seductive "crooked inviting fingers." He knows the sea refuses "to go back without feeling me." He undresses. He promises repayment in kind of the seminal wet. He is overwhelmed by the ocean's masculine power and breathes in unison with the "convulsive breaths," eventually becoming, just as he had with the Fierce Wrestler and with the soul, "integral with you." The ocean is specific, personified, and the sexual encounter is rich in physical and sensual detail and results in an absolute spiritual as well as sexual union. But not so with the earth. Here the experience is scenic rather than sexual.

> Earth of the slumbering and liquid trees!
> Earth of the departed sunset! Earth of the mountains misty-topt!
> Earth of the vitreous pour of the full moon just tinged with blue!
> Earth of shine and dark mottling the tide of the river!
> Earth of the limpid grey clouds brighter and clearer for my sake!
> Far swooping elbowed earth! Rich apple-blossomed earth!
> Smile, for your lover comes!
>
> (SM 439–46)

Whitman is writing romantically not sexually. Though in his best style, he still distances this alleged description of metaphoric heterosexuality from any really felt sexual passion. This, in its subject though not its style, is the clichéd writing of heterosexual romance; his hymn to the sea is the felt admission of homosexual desire. How indeed does one explain the curiously interjected lines 449–50 that come between the earth and sea passages—lines rejected after 1855—other than as the signal of the real context: "Thruster holding me tight and that I hold tight! / We hurt each other as the bridegroom and the bride hurt each other." This thruster is the Fierce Wrestler, and he will shortly be the inviting sea. While his cosmogony may demand that the earth be his female lover, and indeed while the preceding logic of the poem demands that the poet of "woman the same as the man" offer a metaphoric sexual allegory of heterosexual experience, the homosexual desire of the poet overrules logic and doctrine with the demands of passion. The earth here may be in initial conception female, but there is no sexual passion in the description of the act. The love between earth and poet is characterized as "coolbreathed," placid, "slumbering," and "limpid." The invoked "prodigal" does not ring convincingly against these cool images, nor does the now introduced "thruster." Instead, both prodigal and thruster, rather than serving as a conclusion to the earth sequence, are more effectively seen as an introduction to the ocean sequence. He has had no difficulty in characterizing the voluptuous earth; the passage is rich in descriptive adjectives. But his evocation of prodigal, thrusting love tests his ability: it is "unspeakable," unsayable, part of the forbidden discourse of homoeroticism that he intends to newly utter. Unutterable love in his texts cannot rely on the conventions of romantic adjectival description. The earth was passively—hence conventionally—described, employing the old tongue of trippers and askers. Passion must be translated into the active new language of sexual act. The poet says, "I resign . . . guess . . . behold . . . believe . . . undress. The attentions of the sea are imperatively demanded: "hurry . . . cushion . . .rock . . . dash me."

The "unsuccessful" verses devoted to the earth/female imagery are displaced and replaced by the passionate thruster, whose violent passion will hurt him in the *same way* that the thrusting bridegroom hurts the bride and will thus inseminate him with the power to speak passionate homoerotic love. The sea will realize that love, just as the Fierce Wrestler realized it before. With the earth — with heterosexuality — he is a distant and a distancing lover, able to speak only in romantic clichés that have no significant sexual subtext. But once held in the thrusting grip of his dominating fantasy, he is able then to submit — resign himself — to the masculine sea, and become "integral" with homosexual desire.

Once having done so, the epiphany follows, for he realizes as he "moistens the roots of all that has grown" — an image in which he masturbates on the roots of things, ejaculating upon other phallic roots, fertilizing with his semen the phallic grass and the calamus root yet to luxuriantly bloom — that there is no better minute "than it and now" and that he has found "a word," the "word en masse," a "word of faith," a "word of reality," the "password primeval." His tongue has been freed to speak because he has been inseminated by the plunging tongue of his soul, by the thrusting penis of the Fierce Wrestler, and by the inseminating sea. He has also been awakened by the baptismal semen, which has become integral with him, and which he has ingested and imparted. He has found the language of his art. Indeed, he has found himself, for it is now, in section 24, that he reveals his name: "Walt Whitman, an American, one of the roughs, a kosmos." The word is now made flesh.

Assuming roles and putting on masks is one of the symbolic actions of the poem. Even though Whitman asserts that he is undisguised and naked, this too is a mask, for his nakedness has allowed him to assume the masks of all the characters he creates, both men and women. It is not until section 24 that he is able to strip away the masks that have hidden him and name himself. At this moment, his homosexual identity firmly established and accepted, Whitman rejects the strategy of feminine role playing in favor of his exclusive masculine persona, sole inhabitant of his masculine landscapes. After section 24 he will not again, in "Song of Myself," adopt or entertain any transformation of gender.

In the early works, a poetics of homoerotic desire begins to develop at the textual junction created by the unsettled tension between the use of, and the expectations created by, an uncomfortable and unconvincing language of heterosexual desire, and the nuances and implications of a partially veiled, perhaps partially understood, homoeroticism, which calls for the creation of a specific, passionate and precise language of homosexual desire. The notebooks and the sections of "Song of Myself" thus far discussed are the erotic laboratory for this language experiment. By the beginning of section 24, the experiments have been so successful that he can speak that language at last, for he has discovered the "password primeval," the ancient tongue of his true desires. Up until this point, however, there has been little, or at least rudimentary awareness of the social or political implications of homosexuality. At this moment in the poem, homosexual desire exists without a name, and it has not been fully involved with a political or social program. Instead it is primarily identified with, indeed even defined as, private autoeroticism. Whitman has not yet discovered, perhaps because he has not yet experienced, the homosocial need of comrades.

Rejecting any further references to heterosexual or feminine projections in the rest of "Song of Myself," in section 24 Whitman devotes himself exclusively to the shaping of masculine land-scapes. His great work in exploring those landscapes begins at the annunciation of his identity. If the poem is an essay in the develop-ment of fluency, fluency achieved through homosexuality, he has achieved that, for at that crucial juncture, his voice is freed to speak and he is able to utter words hitherto unspoken: "through me many long dumb voices." The dumb voices for whom he is spokesman are the voices of slaves, prostitutes, deformed persons, thieves, and dwarfs, and they are most of all "forbidden voices, / Voices of sexes and lusts. . . . voices veiled and I remove the veil, / Voices indecent by me clarified and transfigured." Though he makes no specific assertion as to the nature of these sexes and lusts nor about the message of the indecent voices, words for homosex-uality expressed only its presumed indecency, asserted its forbid-den nature, inscribed it within a sexual economy of lustful excess, and only described it in veiled terms.

Whitman would insist in 1856 that there was no word for the ardent friendships of young men, and J. A. Symonds echoed the sentiment, observing in 1891 that "the accomplished languages of Europe in the nineteenth century supply no terms for this persis-tent feature [homosexuality] of human psychology, without im-porting some implication of disgust, disgrace, vituperation."[57] Indeed Whitman himself in "The Sleepers" speaks of the "sick-grey faces of onanists." There is ample evidence to suggest that "onanism" was associated with homosexuality in the medical and in the popular mind in the late nineteenth-century, and this asso-ciation may be present in Whitman's formulation, though the presumption of sickness is based also upon the supposition that onanists are enervated, drained, and wasted, in fact "spent" — or "used up" like Davy Crockett — because of the presumed effect of excessive masturbation.[58] Though "sodomy" and "buggery" were commonly in use in criminal law and "pederasty" was also available in English, so far as I know Whitman never uses them. This is not remarkable, of course, since the acts to which these words refer were often, even in legal brief, described as "unnatural acts" and generally accompanied by a stated reticence even to name them. An anonymous eighteenth-century writer asks why "it" — sex between men — "is yet without a Name: What shall it then be called? There are not words in our Language expressive enough of the Horror of it."[59] Or a Maryland court in 1810, for example, seemingly unsure whether "it" should be named or not, finally described the attempt by one man on the body of another as "that most horrid and detestable crime (among Christians not to be named), called sodomy."[60] An 1825 broadside is equally loath to name its subject, saying that "the mere suggestion of this subject is so revolting that we should gladly omit further consideration of it." However, in order to move towards naming the "subject," the author paints a picture of boys in prison who had been prostituted by male prisoners. They are "among the most unnatural and deformed objects, which I ever saw. The peculiar skin, the strained and sunken eye, the distorted mouth and head, and the general expression of the countenance, as if God had impressed the mark of the beast upon them, for unnatural crime." The writer does not understand why this should be so until "I learned that the sin of Sodom is the vice of prisoners and Boys are the favorite prostitutes."[61]

At this moment in "Song of Myself" Whitman speaks as much for such diseased and despairing persons as for the ardent friendships of young men, and at this juncture a new awareness of a more potent and political role for the homoerotic voice is manifest. Just as the sexually suggestive litany in "Sweet Flag," a litany enumerating his homosexual icons, "illuminated" and "clarified" his sexual and poetic life, so here that clarifying and transfiguring power transforms indecent voices of sexes and lusts into the materials of a poetry of political and social action, creating the link between "the password primeval," that newly learned language that has given access to the guarded tents of homoerotic desire, and the newest political construction, "the sign of democracy."

In sections 24–29, the focus is exclusively on the now identified "Walt Whitman" and the ecstatic and aesthetic implications of masturbatory homoeroticism. The earlier scenes of homosexual fantasy have been a prelude for the orgiastic revels to come. While earlier he had explored several varieties of erotic encounter, here he puts aside not only all masks but all constraints as well. At last he is truly undisguised and naked. The broad dominating metaphor of the sequence shows the poet moving from an unrestrained and ecstatic exploration of the possibilities of homosexual masturbatory fantasy to that moment when he introduces the potent icon of the Fierce Wrestler who becomes lover, rapist, and muse. The wrestler's violent mastery leads the poet to the highest moment of ecstatic knowledge he has thus far achieved, allowing him to definitively identify and define the nature, purpose, and subject of his art.

Surrounding the creation of this icon is the most intense, suggestive, and direct homosexual imagery he has yet employed. In section 24, the "spread of my own body" is the symbol and the fact. His body, spread out and cruciform, lies hankering and naked upon the summer grass, just as he had done in section 5. Here he is an earthbound counterpart to the young men lying and floating upon the waves or another version of Whitman himself embraced by the ocean. He engages in an adoring fantasy about his own body. Sex becomes a ritual and an act of worship, invoking again the "trance exaltation," and the baptism of the seminal sea, but now he worships at the most sacred shrine, his "divine" body, the phallic temple. His body has become more than flesh in fact, for it has become "translucent"—a variation of clarification and illumination—glowing with divine light, and it takes many forms, changing from the specific translucent mould, to the "shaded ledges and rests" of a mountainous masculine landscape, dominated by the "firm masculine coulter," the erect and waiting phallus. These images, which foreshadow the following sequence on touch and echo the notebook genesis of those same lines, allow us to watch the poet as his hands wander erotically across the plains, crevices, and hillocks of his translucent body, filled with the pulsating light of sexual vigor, until they encounter the center of desire, the masculine coulter. It is erect and ready. It is indeed a plow, an instrument of cultivation, that tills the soil and violates the land, that penetrates and prepares the furrow for the inseminate seed: "whatever goes to the tilth of me it shall be you." The "tilth" is the furrow, and the masculine coulter creates it. The coulter/penis, literally in hand, by penetrating the ground, also penetrates the poet.

Masturbation leads to an instantaneous longing to be mastered, and the aroused passions anticipate the fountains of semen to come: "my rich blood, the milky stream pale strippings of my life." Longing creates momentary images of shared sexuality: "breast that presses against other breasts." But it is his own breast and body that is the focus still: "it shall be you." He is powerless to stray long from phallic domination: "Root of washed sweet-flag . . . nest of guarded duplicate eggs, it shall be you." The homoerotic notebook entry "Sweet Flag" finds its home here. In those notebook revelations, he reached out to grasp the calamus root and the testicular melons, and that phallic contact sent him into the "mystic trance exultation" translated here into the "occult convolutions" of his brain. That notebook trance was "wild, untamed, half-savage / coarse,"—the latter word we recall being a specific term of approbation for his young roughs—and here the masturbatory fantasy is clearly and specifically masculine: "mixed tussled hay of head and beard and brawn it shall be you." The head, beard, and brawn are his own—indeed, as Zweig says, "he describes himself as a . . . bearded erection"—but in the promiscuous manner of a masturbation fantasy, they are part not only of the fantasizer but of the fantasized—the golden lads whose hair he tussles, whose beards he strokes, whose brawn he admires and desires, Bill Guess, Peter, George, and a thousand others.[62] If there is doubt still about the homophallic nature of this idyll, then the phrase "trickling sap of maple, fibre of manly wheat" offers enough obvious phallicism, and the notebook source confirms the object of desire: "Trickling sap flows from the end of the manly maple tooth of delight . . . spend / spend" (*NUPM* 1:194)

When he made love to the ocean in the earlier lines, the poet specifically sexualized and "masculinized" that event, but as we saw, his apparent lovemaking to the presumably feminine earth was devoid of suggestive heterosexuality and instead was a hymn of natural description only. But here, homoerotic passion gives power to his images, and nature itself becomes another masculine lover. The "soft tickling genitals" of the wind—which could not strictly speaking tickle if they did not also, like a penis, extend—"rub against me." The "broad muscular fields" and the reaching branches of "liveoak,"—his alternate calamus symbol—excite him.

Nature becomes symbol and sexual metaphor, and the symbols and metaphors powerfully speak of homosexual love, just as nature becomes sex-object for Whitman's shadowing rough Davy Crockett, who finds masturbatory relief when he "commenced flapping an old oak tree . . . with my arms til the fire flew" and who found another "tree about two feet threw and not a limb on it for thirty feet," which he would climb and "slide down to the bottom again," thus making his "legs . . . feel mighty warm and good."[63] The phallicizing of nature, of course, is also wittily though provocatively noted by Thoreau's affair with "the shrub oak with its scanty garment of leaves rising above the snow . . . rigid as iron."[64]

In his fantasy once again walking the hills and fields, traversing now the masculine landscape, the wandering poet enters the Arcadian garden that he pictured at the beginning of the poem, and that he will sanctify in *Calamus*. He encounters there the loving lounger in his path. This figure is the central and primary archetype of the homosexual imagination and the dominating icon of homoerotic fantasy—the anonymous image of passionate sexual desire as well as the ideal friend, the archetypal comrade. He stands for the unexpected sexual encounter that is unfettered by the artificial demands of name, custom, or social status. We have met him before. He is every handsome young man in the stories. He is every rough detailed in the notebooks. He is the Fierce Wrestler, the loving and hugging bedfellow, and the masculine soul. He is desire, sex, lust, and love: "Hands I have taken, face I have kissed, mortal I have ever touched, it shall be you." This mortal is not the infantile regressive self as Kinnell implies, nor as Cavitch says, the mother. The pleasure taken here is neither the "infant's joys in the body" nor the "sexual response to the mother" but instead the erotic, phallicized response to the created presence of and delight in a male lover.[65] The loving lounger is the controlling and empowering image of the passage, for he is in fact one of those "strangers who seem to touch the fountains of our love and draw forth their swelling waters" (*EPF* 74).

And yet this is an autoerotic fantasy, and it is to that which he wittily returns: "I dote on myself. . . . there is a lot of me and all so luscious." But contemplation of sexual possibilities, recollection of the hands he has taken and the faces he has kissed, and desire for the loving lounger elevate him to another stage of awareness. He is now moving toward the trance of exaltation. Already he is deserted by waking rationality; he is unable to explain either physical or emotional experiences, and he enters a wonderland wherein the commonplace is miraculous: "I cannot tell how my ankles bend . . . nor the cause of the friendship I emit. . . . nor . . . the friendship I take. . . . to walk up my stoop is unaccountable." His friendship is not only emitted like sunlight but like semen, for what he "takes" is sex as well as affection. In the notebooks he demands that masculine touch "take drops of my life" and avers that touch "takes" all his sexual energy. In this eroticized state wherein natural facts offer rewards far greater than "the metaphysics of books," he experiences a foretaste of the ecstasy yet to come and compares the natural with the sexual fact, the sunrise—and emitted friendship—with ejaculation, the friendship he takes and the libidinous prongs with the overpowering phallus: "To behold the daybreak! . . . Something I cannot see puts upward libidinous prongs, / Seas of bright juice suffuse heaven." Just as the sunrise is explosive, so is his ejaculation as he lies looking up at the heavens in section 25. Enclosed in the stream of upward-jetting semen, he and his soul "also ascend," for they have "found our own," a reaffirmation of the revelation of section 5. But here, the poet advancing more deeply into the dreamworld of the sexual subconscious, achieves even more than "peace and knowledge." He is one with homo-eroticized nature, which has penetrated him with libidinous prongs and brought him to a brilliantly transgressive climax. He baptizes heaven with his semen, and he encloses and commands its power to create; he can "now and always send the sunrise out of me."

But the voyage is not yet complete, nor the fantasy fully realized. The experimentation with the delights of self-gratification that have led to one moment of informing orgasm will lead to another and enlarge the poet's awareness even more. In sections 25–27, the wonders achieved through ejaculation lead the poet into broad fantasies and meditations on the correlation between erotic arousal and language—"Speech is the twin of my vision"—since poetry is derived from the sexual trance—"with the twirl of my tongue I encompass worlds." But in section 26 language enfolds other eroticisms as well, namely the foundations of textuality in sound itself: "I will do nothing . . . but listen, / and accrue what I hear into myself." The sounds of human voices and of cities—living texts—stir him, but nothing so much as music: "a tenor large and fresh as creation fills me, the orbic flex of his mouth is pouring and filling me full. / I hear the trained soprano. . . . she convulses me like the climax of my love-grip." In the notebook from which these lines derive, the focus is different and telling. There "the orbed parting" of the tenor's "mouth shall lift over my head the sluices of . . . delight." But now, in the homoerotically charged atmosphere of these lines, the tenor, like his Fierce Wrestler, "fills him" and also recalls the mouth that drained him dry in the notebook. The soprano in the notebook convulses like the "love-grip of her in whose arms I lay last night." In the poem there is no other women; the love grip is his own masturbating hand—"the climax of my love-grip"—and the ecstasy induced is as exciting as the ardors aroused when he first confronted the phallic calamus. This ecstasy approaches and eroticizes death; his windpipe is "squeezed in the fakes of death." The image of the coil—the fake—around the throat, inducing asphyxiation, mirrors the gripping hand tightening around the penis. Did Whitman know also that a rope slowly tightened around the neck during masturbation unbearably heightens the orgasm? In the poem the pressure on his windpipe is "let up again" so that he can "feel the puzzle of puzzles" and "that we call Being." But in the notebook he is more precise about his state: "lulling me drowsily with honeyed morphine—tight'ning the fakes of death about my throat, and awakening me again" to discover "the most positive wonder in the world, and that's what we call life" (*NUPM* 1:127). This positive wonder, the ejaculating erect penis, is the act and image of life. It is the foremost among the "live parts" that are his "knowledge."

Voices and visions provide multiple counterpoint to the steady action of the caressing hand, the rapidly rising passion, and the ever-increasing and profound increment of knowledge. As he is whirled by music, "wider than Uranus flies," he confronts in section 27 "the puzzle of puzzles"—the question "To be in any form, what is it?" The answer is that the translucent body is no longer a "callous shell." Indeed, as in every moment of sexual arousal in the poem, he repeats the image of dissolution. He is neither shell nor body, but the conduit for the passage of sexual energy. He has left his body, ascended to the spiritual plain of incorporeal sexual feeling where he is pure spirit and ecstasy. He has become now so caught up in the inevitable and imperiously demanding movement toward his most powerful orgasm that all that is material has slipped away and he is conscious only of touch: "I have instant conductors all over me." Here again he becomes the phallus, his entire body responding to pressing and feeling fingers as the penis does. The conductors lead "every" object "harmlessly" through him, an assertion that resists those readings that urge either the dominance of homosexual guilt or primal sexual tragedy in these lines.[66] Instead, section 28 is a triumphant assertion in which he unequivocally banishes any latent homosexual guilt and asserts the primacy of his homosexual passion and the centrality of it in the creation of his poems. Section 28 is the definitive heart of Whitman's homoerotic poetics.

We have seen the genesis of these lines in the notebooks. The fulfilled ecstasy is realized in section 28. There, touch, always homoerotic in its implications, always the physical agent of fantasy now serves a new function, for it brings him "quivering . . . to a new identity." This is a thrilling revelation in a poem in which the achievement of identity has been the main business. He sought identity when he lay down with his soul, when he screamed after the departing bedfellow, when he became the twenty-ninth bather, when he accepted the kisses and embraces of men, and when he named himself Walt Whitman. In naming himself he found one identity. But now there is another, and this more electric than all the rest. Just as his body has become incorporeal and translucent, pure feeling, the blood that flows in his veins is transformed to "flames and ether." This ether is the atmosphere in which Platonic images reside and the same atmosphere Whitman will describe as he moves toward the guarded tents of interior love, but it is also as opiate and destructive of the rational senses as the "honeyed morphine" of music or the "trance exaltation.

Whitman is entirely focused now in one intense point, the erect phallus, "the treacherous tip of me." However, unlike the other scenes in which he is comfortably alone in his fantasy, companion to another facet of himself, or recollecting a departed and mythic lover, the introductory verse to this section gives a new context: "To touch my person to some one else's is about as much as I can stand." He is not alone now; the new identity is predicated upon the existence and the touch of someone else, and this predication creates the anticipation, not the fear, that informs the beginning of the sequence. He is surrounded by temptation and by "prurient provokers" who stiffen his limbs and who are "straining the udder of my heart for its withheld drip." The erect and stiffened limbs begin to respond to the pressing fingers as they caress the testicular udder into seminal response, trying to call up those earlier milky streams. As "touch" continues to arouse, it is clear to him that the person for whom he reaches with the erect phallus—the "treacherous tip"—is "hardly different from myself." It is this realization that quivers him into the new identity. He is not different because he is male. He is the Fierce Wrestler, named in the notebook, but here excitingly anonymous. The prurient provokers who behave licentiously toward him, who deprive him of his best—that is, of his potent ejaculated semen—and who unbutton his clothes and hold him by the bare waist, are not only the general temptations of homosexual desire but the fingers of the specific hand that masturbates. The provokers hold him, and fetch the rest of the herd—the enclosing fingers and fist—"around" to "enjoy" and "worry" him, as, "uniting" they enclose around "a headland." While the headland may well be a site of sexual encounter as Killingsworth suggests, it is also quite simply another term for the erect penis around which the hand has closed, the penis that the poet has become.[67] But this is a double fantasy, for unlike all the other masturbation fantasies of the poem, this one has introduced a distinct other—not the speaker but another who finds the speaker out of control of his own fantasy experience. The enclosing hand, which in Section 5 was pictured as God's elderhand and the poet's creating and designing hand, is now not only his own but a powerful other hand that master's him. The poet has lost control; he is being overpowered and raped. This is, though, an exclusively masculine rape, and there are no fantasies of gender-reversal, no longing, as Bychowski suggests, to be a woman. Nor is the passage simply or generally the "'quivering to a new identity' as a sexually aware adult." The new identity is homosexual and rejects the "opposite equals" of the heterosexual and procreative world. The fantasy imagines what it is like for a man to be raped by a man, by someone "hardly different from myself."[68]

Though there may be latent guilt engendered by succumbing to homosexual rape, suggested by "treacherous" and "prurient" and by his "anger" at what they are doing, this is instantly dissipated by the conductors who harmlessly conduct through him even that powerful object, the marauding penis, and allow him to realize that they are "depriving me of my best as for a purpose." Not only that, but even in the midst of the combination of anger, doubt, resistance, and sexual ecstasy, there is a clear assurance that even "confusion" itself will be deluded, that is, reversed and hence clarified in "the calm of the sunlight and pasture fields." This Arcadian vista comfortingly recalls the bower of sexual bliss into which he entered in the beginning of the poem and certainly

foreshadows the masculine landscapes he will shortly enter as well
as the secret *Calamus* world. As these vistas beckon, his fantasies
are dominated by the masculine imagery inscribed fully in the
notebooks but resonant here, and he succumbs to the final triumph
of irrational sexual homoerotic passion, the domination by the
"red marauder." His entry into the sexual headland is allowed
because the sentries of moral law and heterosexual custom have—
at last—deserted him, those same sentries whose posts he will pass
on his way to the guarded tents of interior masculine love.

Unable any longer to resist, he enters into the "Sweet Flag"
sexual trance: "I talk wildly. . . . I have lost my wits." Freed in the
trance from the constraints of reason or sexual orthodoxy, he is able
to recognize that, even though he is "given up by traitors," the
ultimate choice has been his own. He will not postpone his
"acceptation." He knows that he has sought out homosexual
fulfillment and has ratified the truth of his essential self: "I went
myself first to the headland. . . . my own hands carried me there."
He literally holds in his hands the responsibility for his passionate
desires. This is the same strategy he employed when he accepted
the plunging tongue, when he determined to postpone no longer
his acceptations at the departure of his hugging divine bedfellow,
and when he accepted the pain of the "thruster holding me tight."
He abandons himself to the "red marauder," the marauding,
demanding, thrusting red-tipped penis, at the head of which—the
headland—his worrying fingers have gathered and gripped, focusing the passion of homosexual desire. In an early manuscript
reading, this imagery of the gripping hand is made clear: "My
hand will not hurt what it holds and yet will devour it, / It must
remain perfect before me though I enclose and divide it" (Trigg
567). But unlike the other masturbatory fantasies, wherein the
other seems to be created by the speaker from within himself, this
red marauder, like a rapist coming in the night, is an external
force—a real presence in the text other than the speaker. And in the
shifting landscape of this dream vision, the assertion that "some
one else's" person/penis is dominating him "about as much as I can
stand" identifies the marauder as the Fierce Wrestler, who tested
him to see how much he could "endure.

But Whitman does not yet quite reject the imagery of criminality and banditry with which he has invested the act. He resists
yet a moment longer the final acquiescence to homosexual identity,
which is, of course, the new identity to which he has been

"thrilled" and which thrills him. Thus he demands: "Villain touch, what are you doing? . . . my breath is tight in its throat; / Unclench your floodgates! you are too much for me." Something shocking, perhaps even unfamiliar, certainly painful, is about to happen. The similar notebook entry records some deletions that I here introduce and conflate with the text Whitman did not cancel: "Unloose me touch, [I can stand it no longer] You are taking the breath from my throat. / Unbar your gates [can hold {would keep}] you [no longer for if I do you will kill me,] are too much for me. [Pass out of me. Pass as you will Gods! will]" (*NUPM* 1:76).

The breathless exclamation "Gods!" painfully defines the nature of the act; he is surely being raped. Though the breath taken from the throat could suggest oral intercourse, the exclamation and the assertion that he can hold him no longer coupled with the demand to "pass out of me" and the assertion that "you will kill me" suggest the initially painful yet overwhelmingly pleasurable experience of anal penetration. He wants his rapist to unbar his gates, ejaculate his semen, and fill him. In the poem the image is far more effective, for there the gates become floodgates, and they are unclenched like muscles, opened like valves.

Between sections 28 and 29 there is a sudden disjunction. He moves suddenly from being in the midst of the act—"you are too much for me"—to a moment of post-coital meditation: "Did it make you ache so leaving me." These lines are all that is left of the powerful rape scene of the notebooks. Though I have quoted that scene in Chapter 5, below I would like to conflate the deletions (in brackets) in order to establish another useful text that fills in the hiatus between the rape and the rumination, giving us the event itself.

> Fierce Wrestler, do you keep your heaviest [strike] grip for
>   the last?
> Gods![Wrestler] Will you sting me even at parting?
> Will you struggle even at the threshold with [gigantic]
>   [delicious] spasms more delicious than all before? [Will
>   you renew this and]
> Does [even as you fade and withdraw] it make you ache so
>   to leave me?
> Do you wish to show me that even what you did before was
>   nothing to what you can do?
> Or have you and all the rest combined to see how much I
>   can endure

Pass as you will; take drops of my life [only go, or is] if that
    is what you are after
Only pass to some one else, for I can contain you no longer.
I held more than I thought
I did not think I was big enough for so much ecstasy
Or that a touch could take it all out of me."

                                                        (*NUPM* 1:77)

The language deleted, the violent "strike" instead of "grip,"
the exclamation "Gods," and the verbs "sting" and "withdraw"
suggest anal penetration rather than fellatio, as does the general
tone of mastery, the almost helpless question "will you renew
this?", and the observation that he did not think he was big enough
to receive anally the rapist's penis. The introduction of "all the
rest" and the possibility that the rapist will "pass to some one else"
create a momentary hint of an orgiastic scene of multiple sexuality.
At the same time he urgently asks his partner to "take drops of my
life" hinting at oral pleasures, as do the "delicious" spasms. This
hint is enlarged in another manuscript version of this scene:

Grip'd wrestler! do you keep the heaviest pull for the last?
Must you bite with your teeth at parting?
Will you struggle worst?
I plunge you from the threshold.
Does it make you ache so leaving me!
Take what you like, I can resist you; Take the tears of my
    soul if that is what you are after.
Pass to some one else;
Little as your mouth, it has drained me dry of my strength.

                                                        (Trigg 568)

Here it is the wrestler who is "grip'd," apparently held orally
or anally by the speaker. Of course anal and oral sex are conflated
not only in the varying manuscript sources but in the 1855 text
itself, and specificity about an orifice is not entirely the point,
though it is a significant point since the mechanics of homosexual
sex allow a kind of mirroring participation and parallel exchange
not possible in heterosexual experience. Moon says in his comments about the twenty-eight bathers sequence, "homosexual acts
are symmetrically reversible," and with that he helps to answer
Killingsworth's question about the wrestler scene: "What is the

exact nature of the experience and the role of the speaker in it?"[69] The nature of the experience is homosexual; the role of the speaker is as the fantasizing partner/creator in an act of homosexual rape. The result is orgasm and impregnation, a triumphant ejaculation in which all the other orgasmic moments of the poem join, and in which the jets of life and the seas of bright juice, the milky stream pale strippings of life, and the spreading peace and knowledge of love are all jetted into the waiting and eagerly receptive poet. The floodgates are unclenched not now by a single hand only but through mutual sexuality. Masturbation, the solitary vice, has been superceded by a violent yet ecstatic union between the poet and his masculine muse.

In "Song of Myself" all that remains of the notebook entries is the invocation to "blind loving wrestling touch." It is a brilliant conflation, yet there can be no doubt that the rapist wrestler still anonymously dominates the imagery of the moment. Even though the person has disappeared, the vital organ of pleasure remains, the uncircumcised penis, sheathed, hooded, and sharptoothed. The withdrawing penis is personified, and the central image is now the jetting fountain of ejaculating sperm that descends like a fertilizing rain upon the body and spirt of the poet. His new identity, forcibly created by the thrusting penis and the realization of and acceptance of homosexual pleasure, is now nourished by the jetting ejaculations, which water the landscapes of his homoerotic art. The floodgates are indeed opened, and in a daring metaphor of mutual sexual satisfaction, he recognizes the aesthetically procreative nature of his homosexual union. The phrase "parting tracked by arriving" is curious and indirect. The ejaculation and withdrawal of the partner is followed or accompanied by the arrival of the poet's own orgasm. The rich showering rain of semen, released from the unclenched floodgates, repays sharptoothed touch for its ejaculatory gift. The poet's own ejaculation is payment to himself for the wonderfully intermixed combination of pleasure and pain caused by the thrusting phallus. Each of the partners is repaid by the mutual orgasm. The lines reflect even more specific possibilities of homosexual sex, for the one partner may have withdrawn before ejaculation in the mouth or anus and showered the poet's body with his rich gift of semen while the poet, masturbating, ejaculates in unison with him. The line "parting tracked by arriving" reflects this possibility of mutual masturbation, since "tracked" suggests making of tracks, or the making of the furrow by the masculine coulter, a furrow in which the drops of semen fall like seeds on flesh. If they participated in mutual fellatio, "the perpetual payment of the perpetual loan" suggests reciprocal oral pleasure, since the semen ejaculated simultaneously into the mouth of each partner accounts for the circulatory imagery of these lines as both of them ingest the sacramental semen, each partaking of the jets of life of the other. It may be urged that the curious financial images "payment," "loan," and "recompense" are inspired by and linked to the verb "spend," which Whitman has used in "Sweet Flag" to indicate ejaculation. The image recalls the revelatory lines 260–61 wherein he adorns himself "to bestow myself on the first that will take me." He announced at that juncture that he was "spending for vast returns," and presumably whoever takes him will give these vast returns. He has now been repaid in vast returns by the Fierce Wrestler and by sharptoothed touch, for the flood of ejaculated semen on which both of them seem now to float is part—but only a part—of the "recompense richer afterward."

As with section 5, the brilliance of the lines lies in the conflation of oral and anal sexuality, in the multiple suggestion of masturbation and mastery, in the nuanced presentation of several varieties of homosexual experience. The final lines in section 29 have no counterpart in the notebooks, and radically alter their sexual focus for they make the leap from the frenzied arena of passion to the profound theater of art, where wild passion becomes inspiration. Fertilized by the showering semen, now the mixed rain of the two men showering down on the geographically described body, and also on the landscape of the imagination, the new "sprouts take and accumulate." The seeds of art are planted and instantaneously grow, becoming "prolific and vital." This is the richest recompense. The harvest is stupendous and plentiful, and we have heard before what its vegetation is: sweet flag, flour-corn, manly maple tooth, life-lilies, aromatic calamus, fibre of manly wheat, and the leaves of grass themselves, all these growing in "broad muscular fields" in the "calm of sunlight and pasture fields." As he surveys these fields with their stalks of phallic life, he makes the leap of metaphor from sex to life to art. Here the literally seminal is converted to the metaphorically seminal, the sprouts will explode into poems, and his poetry will define and henceforth describe "landscapes . . . masculine full-sized and golden."

Here is no symbol of heterosexual fertility, and in this supreme moment of sexual and aesthetic union there is no place to add his afterthought phrase "and women," for women have no passionate place in this exclusive masculine and homosexual moment. Bloom says that Whitman achieves "orgasm and poetic release through a Sublime yet quite literal masturbation."[70] Bloom's American Sublime invests the homoeroticism of the lines with equal sublimity. But it is not the masturbation but the imagined consummation of homosexual desire that creates and defines the Sublime and translates the flesh into the word. And it is more than release, it is the assumption of new knowledge and identity.

The fertilized sprouts, soon to be calamus leaves, grow in the heartland of Whitman's homosexual imagination, and in the passionate center of this grove sacred to the love of men, on the banks of the *Calamus* pond, rises the phallus, the primary icon of worship, object and altar of desire. The poet is the great high priest and magus of this worship, having been purified and sanctified by his encounter with the phallic God and by his perilous passage through the dark land of sexual uncertainty, a passage he described profoundly in "The Sleepers." He can now lead other devotees to the masculine landscapes, and they are ready to follow: the lover/eleve, the thruster, the loving bedfellow, the twenty-eight young men and the twenty-ninth bather, the loving lounger, the Fierce Wrestler, all those whose "hands I have taken," whose "face I have kissed," all those mortals "I have ever touched," all those who have bashfully pressed his hand, all those men in whose face he has seen his own reflected. The sacramental union has taken place, and the eucharistic semen has been shared. The pleasures of this erotic text are those of sacred and magical texts. As we read, the recitation invokes, like transubstantiation, the beautiful bodies into life again, the sexual sacrifice is reenacted once more. In that constantly recreated garden, his Eden, the bank by the woods now consecrated solely to masculine desire, we too walk, astonished at the vision that is "projected," gazing in wonder at those masculine landscapes that have so miraculously appeared and that so richly surround and arouse us.

The landscapes that Whitman has "projected" while having sex are those he will now delineate in the poem. Not only is the homosexual ecstasy and orgasm that he describes in section 28 the theater for his inspiration, but it is also so powerful, profound, and convincing that he can have no doubt about the spiritual and emotional truth of his identity. He is justified not by faith but by sex, and he concludes that his homoerotic passion cannot, must not, should not be hidden or denied. Thus he "projects" his landscape, imagines, plans, conceives, and bequeaths it to the future. He uses the same verb in the *Calamus* poem "In Paths Untrodden" when he resolves that he will sing only songs of manly attachment, "projecting" and "bequeathing hence types of athletic love." Section 28 is a private revelation empowered by sexual discovery and announcing something yet to come. The *Calamus* poem celebrates a public epiphany. It announces a new intention empowered by his recognition that homosexual life is not only sexual but social, defined not only by sexuality but by sensibility—the "substantial life" that "contains all the rest." This life is a lifeline, connecting him to every other man, those living then, those who will read him, those who read him now. In section 28, the fusion of sexual and aesthetic experience allows him to foresee the masculine landscapes in which this radically new vision of homosexual life will grow.

In the quiet and meditative aftermath of this violent sexual experience, the third movement of the poem begins with section 30. Whitman announces a simple but profound revelation: "All truths wait in all things." All things include homosexuality, and in this experience he has found the truth that can never be discovered in "logic and sermons." The greatest truth is that "a leaf of grass is no less than the journeywork of the stars" (662). This recalls the opening question of the poem, "What is grass?", and he answers it, associating the grass with the homoerotic masculine sprouts and both with the journeywork of the stars, the labor of primal creation. In section 31, his new homoerotic identity has given him the knowledge to make this association and new powers to master all the materials of creation: "I incorporate gneiss and coal . . . am stucco'd with quadrupeds and birds all over." It has given him as well the ability to speedily accumulate the materials of his art: "Myself moving forward then and now and forever, / Gathering and showing more always and with velocity" (696–97). But the great achievement resulting from this communion with homoerotic touch is his newly discovered ability to do something he has not been able to do before with comfort or certainty, indeed something he has not even been able to speak of save by longing indirection. Now he can conceive not only of homosexual sex, but of homoerotic friendship, "Picking out here one that shall be my amie, / Choosing to go with him on brotherly terms" (700–701).

While there should be little doubt about the implied gender of the sexual partners he has imaginatively created in the poem thus far, there can be no doubt at all about the gender of the partner he is now prepared to seek. He will go with "him" when he is found. This is the first time he has used the masculine pronoun in such a context in "Song of Myself." When he hints at sexual experience in section 2—"a few light kisses. . . . a few embraces"—when he mentions the "loving bedfellow," and when he describes the passionate moment with his soul in section 5, there is no clear or specific indication (though surely there is adequate implied proof) of the gender of his desired object. His sexual involvement with the twenty-eight bathers is masked by his adoption of feminine identity, as is his momentary appearance as a prostitute adorning him/herself for those who will "take me." There is no direct indication of the gender of any of his fantasized sexual partners. Even section 28, unless the notebooks are consulted, is without specific gender reference. Thus it is significant that this new "velocity," his new understanding of the truth that "waits in all things," has allowed him now to clearly identify the partner he seeks. He has certainly discovered the difference between the exciting but solitary experience of masturbatory fantasy and the overwhelming passion, or at least the promise, of shared sexuality. But he has also realized that there is a more satisfying and more pertinent quest, and a more compelling need as well, the quest for the ideal friend, for someone "hardly different from myself" with whom too share his days and nights.

The need for an ideal friend is, in the last lines of section 32, placed in a tense and telling position against the tantalizing metaphor of the "gigantic beauty of a stallion" and in comparison to the animals with whom he might live. Though he may wish to live with the animals, it is not from their innocent ranks that he will choose an "amie." The stallion, symbol of power and lust and raw male energy is also a vehicle of unfocused homosexual desire. Martin points out that in Theodore Winthrop's early homoerotic novel *John Brent* (1862), the narrator Richard Wade has "an ecstatic . . . relationship . . . with his black stallion . . . which is consistently presented in terms of (male) friendship and sexuality."[71] An anonymous Boy Scout leader, though writing much later, engages the same trope when he celebrates his sexual relations with youths: "No one can take away the memory of . . . the mad abandon of those hours I gamboled with a naughty naked colt."[72] Davy Crockett, whose texts so often thinly hid homosexual desire, too rides stallions, one of whom "I grabbed by the scuff of the

mane and jerked him down and instantly mounted him slick . . . I
then locked my feet under him . . . and off we put . . . jest as we
cum to Mad Creek . . . the critter tried to brush me off, but I
pulled his head . . . after that he laid right down, and grunted the
perfect cart-horse submission."[73]

Whitman, too, has ridden the sexual stallion and experienced
the sexual passion of riding him: "My heels embrace him . . . his
well built limbs tremble with pleasure." Though the scoutmaster's
colt is a real boy, his identity though not his sex is concealed by
metaphor, and Wade and Crockett metaphorically substitute stallions for real men. Whitman's stallion stands in opposition to the
"brotherly" though sexual relation he envisages with his "amie,"
for the stallion represents not only male sexuality but untamed
autoeroticism, since it is as "responsive to my caresses" as is the
creating phallus, which he need only "press, feel with his fingers"
in order to be "happy" and to summon the ecstasy of touch.[74] But
now that he has discovered a new truth, the spiritual profundity of
homosexuality that until then he had only "guessed at," he can
now resign the stallion and reject autoerotic sexuality in favor of
the experience of homoerotic friendship and the full use of his
homoerotic identity. In doing so, not only does he find that he can
resign the passion symbolized by the stallion, but he realizes that
he has gained another new power: "I . . . do not need your paces,
and outgallop them, / And myself as I stand or sit pass faster than
you." The stallion is also, of course, Pegasus, possessor of Keats'
"viewless wings of poesy." Whitman no longer needs Pegasus or
his paces, those measured feet of formal poetry that enclose the
techniques and materials of an outmoded and no longer useful
aesthetic. In rejecting the poetry for which Pegasus is the symbol,
he rejects those poems that do not breathe with manly love. He
embraces now, instead of the quivering flanks of the sexual stallion, the image of the ideal friend, who "shall be my amie" and go
"with him on brotherly terms." In rejecting autoerotic fantasy as a
source of poetic power, he reintroduces into the poem the "you" of
the opening lines, now also possessed of a new identity, now the
amie/eleve.[75]

The opening lines of section 33—"Now I know it is true what I
guessed at"—recapitulate and attest to his recognition of the
meaning of the three sexual/spiritual experiences that mark the
great revelations of the text: his encounter with his soul on the
summer grass, his ecstasy when he lay worshiping the spread of his

own body, and when, as he "walked the beach"—the headland, the
phallic promontory—he realized the meaning of his experience
with "blind loving wrestling touch," the depersonified, liberating
Fierce Wrestler. Each of these recollections of homosexual awakening are also assertions that these moments have led to a still more
startling transformation. Convinced now of his homosexuality
and of the intimate connection between that sexuality and his art,
he leaps now from flesh to spirit. The wild trances and irrationality
are gone, burned away by the power of passion. His animal
passions—the stallion—have been purified and dismissed, his sexual madness cured. What remains now is sublime confidence and
the serenity of the risen bard, a new lord of life whose sensual
ecstasies are transformed now into the powers of the prophet. He
becomes disembodied and vast. He spans the continent, floating
above it like a giant balloon, his ballasts loosed, but also lying upon
it like a lover upon the supine body of his friend: "My elbows rest
in the sea-gaps . . . my palms cover continents." He transforms
America into the object of his desire. When he "guessed" at the
truths his sexual experiences implied, he then only dimly appre-
hended what he now knows. The transforming power of his
acceptance of homosexual identity has given him new insight and
brought him now "afoot with my vision." The poet, a bard at last,
indeed a giant who like the colossus bestrides his nation, takes to
the road to fulfill his destiny, become now his own muse. Self and
soul, art and ecstasy are at last combined. He has become his own
fondest fantasy, the Fierce Wrestler, an American comrade.

The vision of America he now proceeds to share in sections 33–
37 is one of the greatest and most detailed of his catalogs. It is a
gathering of American lives, scenes, cities, and places, a primer of
geography both physical and spiritual, and a detail map of the
masculine landscape. Singing it, listing it, and naming it, a process
of magical possession and creation, he also enfolds it all within
himself. The experience he celebrates is the raw multiplicity of the
American scene. He ascends from the earthbound realms of the
private and interior world—from the grass, from the beaches, and
from his room where he has been "alone in my bed"—and, like a
great eagle flying across the face of America, hovers over the vast
public domain. The catalog is incredibly rich, for it is created from
the materials of American life. The sequence is impressively
visual; the floral, vegetable, human, and animal inhabitants of the
land vitally and convincingly inhabit the text.

Though some readers find only random adventures here, suspecting "hidden currents" that "manipulate the surface drift" but not identifying them, it is the geography of the catalogue which unifies it.[76] It is an active catalog for it progresses from the country to the city, and, more importantly, from the material to the spiritual—from specific act and object through sensual and emotional events to another moment of spiritual awareness. He begins in line 715 "by the city's quadrangular houses," moves to "log huts or camping with lumbermen," continues his pilgrimage "along the ruts of the turnpike, and arrives via "the path worn in the grass" to the silent and holy spot that is found "wherever the human heart beats" (738). The brilliant leap from specific sites in the physical landscape, "where," for example, the "cattle stand" or the "trip-hammer's crash," to the emotional landscape of the beating human heart is the key to the structure of this passage, which moves from the physically specific to the spiritually general.

The passage is unified also by what Whitman sees and approves. Floating above the land in a "pear-shaped balloon" (739), he descends and goes on foot, joining the nation at play or in communal rituals: "Jigs or a good game of base-ball," "he-festivals with blackguard jibes and ironical license and bull-dances." (Are these "he-festivals" rituals of male bonding, baseball games, or something more akin to the midnight orgies of young men, with their very nearly mythic "bull-dances"?) "apple-peelings," "beach-parties and friendly bees and huskings and house-raisings." These wanderings please him; he is pleased with "the native and pleased with the foreign" (773). From the communal he moves to more intimate human associations: he is "pleased with women, the homely as well as the handsome," he will shortly be pleased with the two friends he encounters in the streets, and he is certainly pleased with the dark-cheeked bush boy he takes home with him. His journey has taken him across prairies, savannahs, and forests into the farmlands, through small towns and into the community life of rural America. However, these events offer no friendship nor intimacy, for they are the rituals of heterosexual life, of courtship and flirtation. Though he may be pleased with the women, he is not satisfied by them, and he soon returns to the "path worn in the grass," a sacred pilgrim road traced amidst the leaves of grass, which leads him into the more promising streets of the city.

Now he finds himself "looking in at the shop-windows in Broadway the whole forenoon . . . / Wandering the same after-

noon . . . / My right and left arms round the sides of two friends
and I in the middle" (780). Miller observes that few critics have
taken time to "enjoy the endless inventiveness of the I's associations and suggestiveness" But he misses the special homoerotic
pleasure of these last lines when he insists that when Whitman
looks into the shopwindows while wandering Broadway he merely "recreates his youth."[77] Whitman's idle wandering and pausing
on Broadway, in fact, is a sexual quest. In the reflecting windows,
and in the mirrors of eyes, he can see offerings of love. His window
shopping has—inventively and suggestively—procured him two
friends. But even that is not enough; desire must create a lover.

The longing and successful search for a friend in the city streets
impels Whitman to more complex fantasy. The city disappears.
Now he is in the wilderness far from the settlements, always the
site of his most intimate and sexually potent fantasies, coming
"home with the bearded and dark-cheeked bush-boy. . . . riding
behind him at the drape of the day" (781). While the 1855 edition
has the speaker "riding behind" the boy, in 1867 and in subsequent
editions the line reads: "behind me he rides." In 1855 the young
man is "bearded and dark-cheeked" while in 1867 he is "silent and
dark-cheek'd." This revision not only reverses the physical position of the two but changes the appearance of the young man. In
1855 the beard suggests manhood, and his position riding in front
not only suggests that he is leading the poet to his home but
signifies a position of sexual power, that he is in fact the seducer. In
the notebooks it is bearded young men whose masculinity so
powerfully attracts Whitman. In the later text the boy is not
bearded, is perhaps younger, and is silent and follows the older
speaker. In *Calamus* Whitman is often the lover of such silent young
men. Indeed "silence" is often indicative of a moment of profound
sexual attraction, as it is for example in *Calamus* 29 and 43. The
lines may hint at a reevaluation of the nature of psychological and
sexual power and suggest speculations concerning a change in
Whitman's attitude about the relationship of older and younger
men, not only psychologically and socially, but perhaps in the
arena of sexual activity as well. In 1855, the thirty-five year old
Whitman is attracted to the dark-cheeked boy, whose beard suggests maturity and power. But in 1867, he is bearded no longer and
is now, in the eyes of the forty-seven-year-old and more mature
Whitman, a seductively silent dark cheeked-boy only. In 1855,
Whitman was possessed by the Fierce Wrestler and admired the

bearded roughs. In 1867 he had become the fatherly lover of boys
like Peter Doyle. In 1855 in earlier lines he had commanded the
reader to "Undrape. . . . you are not guilty to me . . . I see through
the broadcloth . . . / And am around, tenacious . . . and can never be shaken away." Perhaps the "drape of the day" will be followed
by just such a command, given here by the bearded rough who the
poet has submissively followed home, anticipating perhaps another Fierce Wrestler. I dwell on this small point only in order to
demonstrate some of the special and subtle pleasures of a homoerotic text.

The dark-cheeked boy is of course a familiar icon. As an object
of desire he is the same boy Whitman has long loved and brought to
life in fantasy, whether as the Fierce Wrestler, Langton, Wild
Frank, or as the more compliant young men found in the fiction.
He will be the muse of *Calamus*, one of the two boys clinging
together, and the friend asleep in the speaker's arms on the beach,
the eternal comrade. It is surely apparent that one of the central
strategies of the fiction and of Whitman's poetry is repeated here.
The lonely wanderer encounters the image of love and together
they go "home" to inhabit that potent and ideal landscape of
homosexual literature, the sanctuary "far from the settlements" of
inhibiting heterosexual life. There they can join in wilderness
pursuits together. Though he has followed his vision across America and experimented with the pleasures of American common life,
even at the "apple-peelings, wanting kisses for all the red fruit I
find," and though he is "pleased with the women," as always it is
the sight of a masculine object of desire that moves him to the most
profound imagery, for the dark-cheeked boy inspires thoughts far
deeper than jigs and baseball games. These thoughts conjure
images prophetic of *Drum-Taps*. Emotions darkly understood are
implied, powers yet to be realized are hinted at, incredible visions
created: "By the cot in the hospital reaching lemonade to a feverish
patient . . . Hot toward one I hate, ready in my madness to knife
him . . . speeding through space . . . speeding through heaven
. . . appearing and disappearing / I tread day and night such roads.
/ I visit the orchards of God" (797). In these orchards, which he has
reached by that lonely path on which he has tarried to spend time
only with friends and the dark-cheeked boy, he will be able to pluck
the ripe "aromatic Calamus sweet-green bulb and melons," which
are no doubt as "grateful to the hand" there as they are in his
fantasies. Now he has transcended physicality and become pure

soul: "I fly the flight of the fluid and swallowing soul." In the oral
and seminal contexts that have thus far so often informed the
poem, the soul that swallows experience confirms the speaker's
omnivorous sexual appetite, an appetite that is manifest primarily
in scenes of homoerotic oral sexuality. In this prophecy of the text's
final lines of seminal dissolution, the fluidity of the soul conflates
the poet's sexual appetite—and the poet—at once with the semen
that it is and the semen that it swallows.

The passage in which the speaker boasts that he turns "the
bridegroom out of bed" to stay with the bride and "tighten her all
night to my thighs and lips" (814) is an incursion into the text not
only of a strong heterosexual libido but also of the brutality that
seems to be associated with heterosexuality at those few moments
when such sexual possibilities enter the poem. This is the first time
in the poem that a direct and specific depiction of heterosexual
intercourse in which he has situated himself as actor occurs. It is
also, save for his boast that he will start babes on women fit for
conception, the last. Though he refers to heterosexual union—the
trapper and his bride (178) and the boys who love women (131)—
and though he views "from the top" of the hill the "youngster and
the red-faced girl" as they go up the "bushy hill" presumably to
make love (142), yet when his prodigal lovers "hurt each other as
the bridegroom and the bride hurt each other," the scene is a
homoerotic transference. Indeed he presumes that brides and bride-
grooms do in fact "hurt each other," certainly a possibility, but
more likely in the kind of homosexual relationships he has imagined and already described in the notebook Fierce Wrestler sequence. In the paradigm of the male/active and female/passive
roles that sexual advice books constructed, if there is pain, it will
be inflicted by the bridegroom, not the bride. When he starts babes
on women, he will do so forcibly, also brutalizing the passive
receptacles of his seed. These passages, like the one above, are not
so notable for heterosexuality as for brutality, while the youngster
and the red-faced girl—she, not he, red-faced—identifies heterosexuality as shamefaced and furtive. The rape of the bride is at
considerable variance with the presumptive intent of the passage,
which is to catalog all the experiences that the soul can swallow—
"All this I swallow" (826). Heterosexual experience must necessarily be included as part of the catalog, but in these lines he inflicts
rather than ameliorates pain. As Miller reminds us, the opposition
between the bridegroom passage and the lines that follow, which

describe the reaction of the woman to her drowned husband, recalls that, as in section 8, where the picture of the red-faced girl and boy is followed by the sprawled suicide, "sexuality is followed, almost inevitably that it appears, by death."[78] It is heterosexuality, however, that is bound in that dreadful union.

Not only sexuality but the fierce tragedies of human life must be part of this swallowed fluid. Thus Whitman is the hounded slave, the fireman, the soldier, and the sailor on the ship of war. The need to swallow experience and ingest the jets of life impels him into a nearly uncontrollable desire to ingest sensation. "I did not think I was big enough for so much ecstasy," he had breathlessly observed as the Fierce Wrestler withdrew after the poet insisted that "I can contain you no longer." Like the moment of sexual abandon, he recognizes here too that he has lost control. "Oh Christ! My fit is mastering me," he interjects in the midst of the catalog. But he recovers and continues to list what he becomes: a prisoner, a mutineer, and a beggar. The strain of multiple identity overwhelms him, and as in each instance where he has been so strongly ravished by sensual experience, he converts the overwhelming sensations into spiritual ecstasy: "I rise extatic through all, and sweep with the true gravitation, / The whirling and whirling is elemental within me" (953–54). In the notebook entry "You Know How the One," he says I "shall uncage in my heart a thousand new strengths, and unknown ardors and terrible extasies—making me enter intrinsically into all passions—dilating me beyond time and space . . . stabbing me with myriads of forked distinctions." (*NUPM* 1:126). There, the "extasies" were induced by music, by the "tenor" whose "mouth shall lift over my head the sluices of all delight" and by the soprano whose music convulsed him like a "love-grip." I have shown above how the love-grip of the soprano was derived from the love-grip of the Fierce Wrestler, which in 1855 becomes his own masturbating hand. In these lines the elemental whirling describes his entry into all passions and his dilation into new consciousness. But like the ecstasy produced by music, this sensation is sexual too. It results from swallowing the intoxicating fluids of experience. The underlying metaphor is incredibly bold and powerfully oral. The soul, its elbows resting in sea gaps, its palms covering continents, lying across the body of America just as it lay across the poet's body in section 5, performs fellatio upon the supine nation, eagerly engorging its erect phallus. In a notebook he had cried to the Fierce

Wrestler, "little as your mouth, it has drained me dry of my strength." Here he is that fellating wrestler, hungrily swallowing and draining dry the ejaculated fluids of seminal American life: "All this I swallow and it tastes good. . . . I like it well, and it becomes mine.

Section 38, which begins the fourth movement, sounds, suddenly, a cautionary note. He has been stunned and finds himself on the verge of "the usual mistake." This mistake, in this context, must certainly refer to the events of the preceding lines, lines in which he details a sensual rather than spiritual life. He has swallowed life to its seminal dregs, greedily ingesting the life of the senses, the real rather than the ideal. He describes this feeding, or as I have suggested, this orgiastic sexual voraciousness, as a "fit" that has mastered him. He invokes Christ, and recalls images from the crucifixion. But it is not Christ's crucifixion he is recalling. He is clear about it; it is "my own crucifixion." His crucifixion was attended by mockery, pain, and insults. Now, suddenly aware that the ecstasies he has been describing are indeed a fit that has clouded the clarity of perception, he is appalled that he could look at this moment from the past with a "separate look," standing aside and viewing dispassionately what had so painfully happened to him. But what had happened to him? What does he remember that casts such a powerful and cautionary light on the significance of the "whirling and whirling" that is "elemental within me," and that, on the verge of the usual mistake, he had nearly forgotten? Here conflated into one image, the crucifixion and crowning represent the essential spiritual/sexual events that "Song of Myself" primarily recounts—namely, the gradual and often painful perception of his homosexual nature and the triumphant development of his vocation as a poet. His awareness of—though perhaps not entire acceptance of—the former was the catalyst for the latter. Yet, his crucifixion is inevitably followed by his own resurrection, wherein he is "replenished with supreme power." The crucifixion and bloody crowning, the "mockers and insults," and the transformation of resurrection that follows, must recall the other significant sacrificial moment that was also attended by pain and rebirth—his penetration by "sharptoothed touch," which quivered him to a "new identity." In the notebooks, touch brings the rest around, and they "all stand on the headland and mock me," in a sexual parallel to the mockery of Christ. There he is guarded by the sentries, given up by Judas-like "traitors" to his sacrificial punishment, and finally, in the notebook, penetrated by the Fierce Wrestler, in the poem, crucified upon the phallic cross of "blind loving wrestling touch." This sacrifice and his resurrected new identity as poet and as homosexual lover allow him to achieve at once the manner and the matter, the voice and the subject, of his art, which is represented by the masculine landscapes that surround him. In section 38, he recalls his aesthetic and sexual Golgotha and recognizes that he must not forget the new life into which he was born then, and that he must revel in the "replenished power" that has come to him now. This signifies a further transformation. Then he was reborn as man and poet. Now he is resurrected as teacher, prophet, and saviour, and now not only the lover/eleve but many disciples surround him: "Eleves, I salute you."

Students and disciples surround him because he has become an ascended sexual master. Having explored the intimate possibilities of both autoeroticism and shared homoeroticism, he moved from the private into the public world and engaged in sexual communion with humanity. In the lines that follow, he will explore the sexual implications of divinity. He will no longer occupy the persona of the individual poet. "Walt Whitman" will disappear, and in his place will be the teacher and saviour. The dramatic verbal evidence of this shift from the personal to the universal is the change in identification of himself from "I" to "we" when he identifies himself with his disciples: "I troop forth replenished with supreme power, one of an average unending procession, we walk the roads. . . . we pass the boundary lines. . . . our swift ordinances are on their way over the whole earth" (964–66). Thus, he can no longer look at his past or his future with a "separate look." Resurrection has multiplied what has been confined to the grave; resurrection has healed him. He resumes that overstaid fraction of himself that is the spirit, lost for a time in the orgy of sensual experience, so as to become again the essential, single, unitary self. The lessons of sexual experience have been learned, and the teacher is now ready to salute his "eleves." He surrounds himself with "numberless gangs" of them. These gangs are the gangs of "roughs" he celebrates in the notebooks and also the "troop," the "great crowd" of friends and lovers, who will accompany him in the *Calamus* poem "These I Singing in Spring." Just as he will give them tokens there, here too they wear a sign of comradeship—the "blossoms we wear in our hats."

Further self-identifications follow. In section 39 he is the friendly flowing savage who emanates "new forms" and who needs now neither the superficial light of the sun or indeed the superficial earth itself, for he has a deeper subjects to explore. In section 40 he might "tell how I like you, but cannot." He hints that he might "tell the pinings I have. . . . the pulse of my nights and days." *Calamus* language and *Calamus* imagery have begun to appear, for therein longing and pining characterize his desires. For example, in *Calamus* 6, adhesiveness is described as the "pulse of my life," and secrecy surrounds his disclosure concerning the love of comrades, which is "the secret of my nights and days." Martin observes that though Whitman is "less than totally frank," his "universal references serve at least in part to conceal the specifically homosexual source of his poetry. He 'cannot' tell what he feels because of the social pressure that weighs upon the homosexual. He can hint, he can indicate, but he must always withhold confirmation of his sexual nature."[79] Though he is not ready to reveal "how I like you," he can take direct sexual and exemplary action:

> I do not give lectures or a little charity,
> What I give I give out of myself.
> You there, impotent, loose in the knees, open your scarfed
>   chops till I blow grit within you,
> Spread your plams and lift the flaps of your pockets,
> I am not to be denied. . . . I compel. . . . I have stores
>   plenty and to spare,
> And anything I have I bestow.

In the notebook version of these lines he "infuses" the "ungrown brother" with the seminal "jets of life." Here the grit is blown, like the breath of life, into the new eleve, but the echo of the more precise sexual imagery of the notebook can still be heard. Most importantly, since his resurrection Whitman has assumed a new authority. He is no longer mastered, penetrated, or crucified. He is now the master, infusing his student with his seminal power, compelling their sexual homage, as "loose in the knees" they kneel before him to drink the jets of life and wisdom from his own supremely replenished and now inexhaustible stores. The exercise of jetting power creates even greater energies, and pausing to bestow a kiss on the drudge of the cotton fields, he asserts his intention to start babes on women, into whom he "jets the stuff of far more arrogant republics." Though he may do this, the republics in which he is most interested are far more arrogant than those created through heterosexual copulation, for they are certainly the republics and cities of lovers he will soon detail in *Calamus*.

In section 41, his powers have now magnified and become godlike. He raises the dead and takes on the dimensions of all the old gods, at once blessing and displacing them with a witty and sacramental "spirt of my seminal wet." After perusing the images of these toppled gods, he decides that he himself can best fill out the "rough deific sketches." He finds godhead in the common man and woman now. The sacred icons he catalogs are handsome working males. He puts forth "higher claims" for them. The "framer framing a house . . . with his rolled up sleeves" and the firemen, with their "brawny limbs," are no less to him than "gods of antique wars," just as are the "three lusty angels," who are, perhaps, harvesting the accumulated phallic sprouts with their whizzing scythes. Typically his icons are masculine; typically also he includes only one woman in his list. She is the "mechanic's wife with her babe at her nipples interceding for every person born," an image of divine motherhood, sacred but not sexual. The juxtaposition of the strong, witty, and subversive sexual image of the lusty angels, the very antithesis of cliché, against the solemn and hushed piety of his clichéd description of the mechanic's bride is a verbal mirror that reflects the notebook assertions of the weakness and invalidity of woman's love. However the language soon becomes active again, and the comic Dionysiac manner surfaces again as he phrenologically exclaims, "by my life-lumps . . . already a creator." The consciousness of his divinity is strong upon him, and he awaits "my time to be one of the supremes." He has come to the supreme moment of his life, "the day . . . when I shall do as much good as the best, and be as prodigious." Since he has been resurrected, ascension is at hand; transformation into divinity is imminent. Epiphany becomes apotheosis. The day when he shall do as much good as the best comes round at last, and he details it in the final sections of the poem. In section 42, he is called, but it his own voice summoning, a voice orotund sweeping and final, ready to announce the final words. His great symphony is nearing completion. The "performer" is ready now; he has "passed his prelude," and the "loose fingered chords" reach their "climax and close." He has become the Bard.

Having played the "reeds within," he is now ready to sound the public melody and to share with humanity the newly released hum of his valved voice, which sounds that most ancient and primal of sacred songs. His text is unity, divinity, happiness, and triumph over death through the agency of homosexual love. For this is his sermon to the multitude. In it he acknowledges his unity with all men, recognizing the "duplicates of myself under all the . . . concealments." In section 43, his faith is the "greatest of faiths and the least of faiths, / Enclosing all worship ancient and modern." And in section 44, his high purpose indeed, is to "launch all men and women forward with me into the unknown," for he is the "acme of things accomplished" the "encloser of things to be." He has become divine.

Section 44 begins the fifth and final movement and initiates the journey from immortal preexistence into life, into manhood, and finally into the "ineffable grace of dying days." But before approaching death he must explain life, and he announces that age to age has joined to culminate in him and that "all forces have been steadily employed to complete and delight" him. He stands on "this spot with my soul." The new identity to which he rises in section 45 is "manhood balanced and florid and full!" The operative word in the line is "manhood." In the notebooks he had observed that "the heart of man alone is the one unbalanced and restless thing in the world" (*NUPM* 1:106). Through sexual and spiritual initiation he has brought peace and balance to his heart. In a notebook, he noted that "the expression of a perfect made man appears not only in his face but in his limbs. . . . to see him walk conveys the impression of hearing a beautiful poem "(*NUPM* 1:151). In "Song of Myself," he is now that perfect made man who by apotheosis has become that beautiful poem. He would later say: "Camerado, this is no book, / Who touches this touches a man."

He is now prepared for death and transformation, a "rendezvous . . . fitly appointed. . . . God will be there and wait till we come." In 1867 he would add to this an audacious description of God: "the great Camerado, the lover true for whom I pine" The great Camerado is the force he will describe as the "genital master." He is the Fierce Wrestler transformed into spirit, the masculine "soul of the universe" with which he has achieved communion, thus satisfying the requirements of the restless and unbalanced manly soul for love. But the final scene is not yet to be enacted, for though his identity is fully realized, understood, and explained, in section 47 he announces his final and greatest role: "I am the teacher of athletes." Here the Fierce Wrestler, the swimmer, the hordes of loving comrades and attractive roughs, the firemen, and the builders are conflated into athletes, into the lovers who "suffocate" him. In 1860, describing his homosexual songs, he declares that he will bequeath to the world "types of athletic love." As the teacher of athletes his great task is to teach the lessons he has learned about homosexual love to men who love only "as he is capable of loving." To confirm his intention he now clearly identifies his athlete and eleve as "the boy I love."

This boy is the same boy we have encountered in all Whitman's previous writings. He most tantalizingly appears at the end of "Pictures" as "the young man of Manahatta, the celebrated rough, / (The one I love well . . . him I sing for a thousand years)." There he is prophecy; here he is the beneficiary of all Whitman's poetic power: "I act as the tongue of you." Just as Whitman was once inseminated by a plunging tongue, so here he becomes that tongue, and he will penetrate, plunging his tongue to the heart of this athlete/eleve/lover. But sadly, though the "you" has returned now as lover and student, he has learned his lessons, and all that remains for him is to learn the final lesson of independence and to be told that parting is near: "I will certainly kiss you with my goodbye kiss and open the gates for your egress hence. . . . He most honors my style who first learns under it to destroy the teacher" (1224, 1233). The condition of love is freedom and the boy the poet loves must now "become a man in his own right."

Yet such freedom only binds the lover closer, for "my words itch at your ears till you understand them." He asserts that he will "translate myself . . . only to him or her who privately stays with me in the open air" (1247), recalling his invitation in section 1 to "stop this day and night with me." The weight of the entire poem now gathers around "privately," and it is clear that in that privacy he will celebrate a loving communion. Those who understand him and to whom he will translate himself are the morally and sexually innocent: "Only the "roughs and little children" can "commune with me." In March 1854, Whitman recorded his communion with a trinity of these roughs, the three lusty angels Bill Guess, Peter, and George Fitch. These celebrated roughs began these comments, and I invoke their spirit again in remembrance here, just as Whitman enshrines them among those who share his special communion. His strongest affections are reserved for these roughs and the athletes: "The young mechanic is closest to me. . . . he knows me pretty well." Perhaps in a witty—or unconscious—reversal of earlier lines, he has taken the young mechanic from the mechanic's wife who remains suckling her infant while Whitman, turning her out of bed, now tightens the mechanic all night to his thighs and lips as he had once said he would do to the bridegroom's bride. He engages one last fantasy of masculine desire: "I go with fishermen and seamen, and love them, / My face rubs the hunter's face when he lies down alone on his blanket." Though Whitman may offer his translation to everyone— "to him or her"—it is clear that he knows to whom his special language is directed and who especially has the power to translate the subtler meanings of his texts into a privileged tongue. He knows too that translation is not only a matter of the transformation of language, but like sacred relics and the saints, his own body can be—will be—translated into incorporeality, indeed, into those spaces reserved for the divine.

But even desire, and concern with such questions, is beyond him now. In section 50, a moment of supreme and transcendent happiness very nearly renders him incoherent: "There is that in me. . . . I do not know what it is. . . . it is a word unsaid." The effort to explain sends him into a trance: "I sleep. . . . I sleep long." What is this unspoken word? In a few lines he will say that it "is not chaos or death. . . . it is form and union and plan. . . . it is eternal life. . . . it is happiness." But in fact the "word" itself is none of these because it is "without name," a "word unsaid" and perhaps unsayable. It is not in any dictionary. In his efforts to explain it he can resort to no "utterance or symbol," only to a simple but cosmic equation: "To it the creation is the friend whose embracing awakes me." Thus, just as the poet's friend awakes him with an embrace, so the creation awakes "it" in Whitman. What is awakened by the friend's embrace is the poet himself, love, and desire. What is awakened by the embrace of creation is the consciousness of the meaning and direction of that desire.

Throughout "Song of Myself," Whitman has described the achievement of spiritual and aesthetic awareness in terms of awakening. He has also made it very clear that he has been trying to create a new language that would adequately express the meaning and complexity of homosexual desire and of his awakening realization that this desire is the shaping and motive force of his own discourse. This has been a difficult, almost impossible task. He is

nearly speechless and seems to bow before the impossibility of
saying the "word unsaid." He is not able to say what he means, for
he concludes the poem without naming the love that, even here,
cannot speak its name. As Martin suggests, "Whitman was clearly
seeking to give the fullest possible explanation to the sexual origins
of both his mystic vision and his belief in a new democratic society.
He constantly sought honesty. But it was difficult to achieve when
the honest word, had it existed, would have been misunderstood as
sexual perversion and sin."[80] But that mysterious "it" is nevertheless clear, defined by the enfolding masculine embrace of his
friend—the reader/eleve/Fierce Wrestler. He has introduced into
the poem its indispensable second term—"the friend"—without
which the "self" is incomplete, the song unsung. The friend has
awakened him to the certain knowledge of his homosexuality, to
the recognition that "it" is the source of his inspiration, and to the
need to inscribe that knowledge and the discourses of that desire
into the written text.

In "The Primer of Words" (1855/56) he so inscribes it when he
speaks of the "tenacity of friendship and passionate fondness for
their friends" that characterizes the "young men of these states."
However they have "remarkably few words . . . for the friendly
sentiments"; such words "do not thrive here." The young men
"have an aversion for" them; they "never give words to their most
ardent friendships" (*DBN* 3:740). Inventing words, creating a
fertile soil in which they can thrive, overcoming that aversion, and
giving words to friendship are definitions of his language experiment, the intentions of his project, the achievements of his texts.
"Song of Myself," and all his poems, give speech to the speechless.
In a manuscript version of *Calamus* 2, he describes his own experience of that speechlessness, "I have stifled and choked too long
. . . I will sound myself and love—I will utter the cry of friends."
(Bowers 72). In *Calamus* 36 ("Live Oak with Moss XI"), wherein
his friend is the "athlete" who is enamored of him, he is equally
unable to speak coherently, asserting that "there is something
fierce and terrible in me eligible to burst forth. / I dare not tell it in
words, not even in these songs."

In "Song of Myself" the "terrible pressures" that prompted
him to write, and even his speechlessness, are relieved by the
embrace of his friend. In all his poetry, Whitman will never use
"friend" in any way other than to indicate that rare and masculine
creature of his most profound desires. I have described "friend" as

the "second term," but more correctly it is the complementary term of a balanced dyad, for "Song of Myself" is not only concerned with the "self" who identifies himself as "Walt Whitman"; it is about friends as well. The poem is a catalog of friends and a record of their awakening embraces. Enfolded within the friend who embraces and awakens him are all the collected friends who people this poem: the unnamed "you" whose assumptions Whitman imperiously commands, the unspecified and invisible lover who offers "a few light kisses," the loving bedfellow, and the soul whose plunging tongue awakened him to the profound knowledge of the unbreakable connection between masculine love and spiritual satisfaction. "The Friend" is the runaway slave, every one of the twenty-eight young men. He is the butcher boy, the blacksmith, and the picturesque black giant. He is every American working man named in the poem. He is the hurting thruster and the dominating masculine sea. He is "Walt Whitman" the eponymous rough and his deified and worshipped body. He is the Fierce Wrestler, that sharp-toothed touch. He is the one "that shall be my amie" and the "dark-cheeked bush boy," the saluted eleves, the impotent ungrown brother, the suffocating lovers, and the athletes he teaches. He is "the boy I love," who is the friend "whose embracing awakens me."

Awakened out of his deep trance by the embrace of his friend, his "wrenched and sweaty" body purified and "calm and cool," like a creature out of myth—a masculine sleeping princess—he has been embraced into new awareness. And in section 52, all mortal dross burned away, he is ready for immateriality: "I depart as air. . . . I effuse my flesh in eddies and drift it in lacy jags." I recall that notebook entry where he observed "the soul of the universe is the genital master, the impregnating and animating spirit. —Physical matter is Female and Mother, and waits barren and bloomless, the jets of life from the masculine vigor, the undermost first cause of all that is not what Death is" (*NUPM* 1:176). I recall it because it explains that here, in these last hushed lines, Whitman has achieved union with the masculine oversoul and attained balanced spiritual manhood. Sexual initiations and sacrificial moments have led him to this union with the genital master, which, surpassing the love of woman, can alone "satisfy the requirements of the manly soul for love and comradeship" (*NUPM* 1:341). He has chosen to let physical matter and the "Female" remain barren and bloomless. His "masculine vigor" has never directly intersected with the "Female" or the Mother in "Song of Myself." Instead, he has engaged in a remarkable variety of homosexual experimentation, receiving the jets of animating masculine vigor from fierce wrestlers, and jetting them into ungrown brothers and athletic eleves.

At the end of the poem there is no more sexual boast or display. Instead he settles the final responsibility for interpretation—for reading, for rereading, and for getting the meaning of poems—upon the now strong shoulders of the reader/lover: "What have you to confide to me?" It is in the act of confiding itself that the reader will discover the "origin of poems." The poem ends in the deep silence that always accompanies profound homoerotic emotional intimacy in Whitman's texts, the only sound being the departing echo of his wordless barbaric yawp, the final rejection of language itself. He is untranslatable and soon to be incorporeal. He now stands above the demands of both flesh and spirit, beyond gender, and beyond the needs of sex or comrades. The flesh falls away, the spirit effuses and he is absorbed into the oversoul. Departing as air, he abandons and rejects physical and female matter and instead embraces, absorbs, and is absorbed by the impregnating and animating spirit of the masculine universe. Whitman himself ceases to be matter, ceases to be physical, and becomes himself the impregnating masculine spirit. He is seminal in every sense. Because he promises to become "good health" to us and the "filter and fibre" of our blood, it is clear that we too must have swallowed and ingested him. Our reading has been a great and pleasurable surrender to this fierce poet who penetratingly possesses us, who with his embrace so profoundly awakens us, and whose final promise so comforts us. Should we seek him his fidelity is eternal: "I stop somewhere waiting for you." At the ultimate moment of the text, the final sentence, beginning as the poem does with "I," ending as the poem does with the nomination of his friend—"you"—explains the final meaning of all his many revelations. He resorts movingly and tellingly to the simplest language of love, uniting the "I" and the "You" by that faithful promise. Fiedler has also noticed that the poem "begins with . . . I' but ends with 'you,' a 'you' believed in though never possessed."[81] He is right about the language, but wrong about the love. The poem is a mutual act of possession. Writing it and speaking in it, the "I" creates and possesses not only himself but the "you." Reading it, the "you" creates and possesses the "I." The ending leads us to the beginning again; that final "you" now nestles hard against the initial celebrating "I."

In the world of Platonic archetypes, Urania, the Heavenly Goddess, is she whose power gives birth to and blesses homosexual love. Men who are inspired by this goddess are "attracted towards the male sex, and value it as being the naturally stronger and more intelligent. . . . they do not fall in love with mere boys, but wait until they begin to show some intelligence, that is to say, until they are near growing a beard. By choosing this moment to fall in love they show . . . that their intention is to form a lasting attachment and partnership for life."[82] This great mother's inspiration allows homosexual lovers to produce children of the spirit and not of the flesh. As Diotima explains it in the *Symposium,* there are "those whose creative desire is of the soul, and who long to beget spiritually, not physically, the progeny which it is the nature of the soul to create and bring to birth. If you ask what that progeny is, it is wisdom and virtue in general; of this all poets . . . may be said to be begetters." Diotima adds that "When a man finds in a beautiful body a "beautiful and noble and gracious soul, he welcomes the combination . . . and finds much to say to such a one about . . . the qualities . . . which mark a good man, and takes his education in hand. By intimate association with beauty embodied in his friend . . . he succeeds in bringing forth the children"—the spiritual progeny—"he has long desired to have." These children will "surpass human children by being immortal as well as more beautiful. Everyone would prefer such children as these to children after the flesh."[83] Having born these children, Diotima continues, the good man and the poet may, through the proper initiation, finally find themselves "gazing upon the vast ocean of beauty." But the mysteries of love and the contemplation of absolute beauty can only be attained by pursuing the "right way." This right way is followed by a man who makes "right use of his feeling of love for boys" and is hence "initiated into the mysteries of love" by beginning with "examples of beauty in this world, and using them as steps to ascend continually with that absolute beauty as" his aim. "This" she says, "is the region where a man's life should be spent, in contemplation of absolute beauty."[84]

In 1859/60, Whitman would write: "Primeval my love for the woman I love! / O bride! O wife! more resistless, more enduring than I can tell, the thought of you! / Then, separate as disembodied, ethereal, a further born reality, my consolation, I ascend to the regions of your love, O man, O friend" (Bowers 112). The regions of love are surely those where Whitman sought to spend his life. Having found, but found wanting, the primeval love of woman, he "then"—at that point—turns, as disembodied now and ethereal as he is at the end of "Song of Myself," to a new reality, the contemplation of absolute beauty with that apostrophized and consoling friend. In the "Preface" he describes the regions of love that he wants to inhabit with his friend: "Now there shall be a man cohered out of tumult and chaos and the elder encourages the younger and shows him how . . . they two shall launch off fearlessly together till the new world fits an orbit for itself and looks unabashed on the lesser orbits of the stars and sweeps through the ceaseless rings" (Cowley 22). Whitman began his long journey toward that Arcadia when he first plaintively hoped to find "one heart to love / As I would wish to love." In his journey across these masculine landscapes, he both discovered and created them as he passed. From the shadowy shores to the hidden bank by the woods—the verge of the *Calamus* pond—crossing hills and fields, tarrying on streets and beaches, and charting his sexual nations, he has embraced comrades and has now come to contemplate the sea of beauty from which he will soon draw forth the calamus. He is ready, at the end of "Song of Myself," to launch off fearlessly with his friend—the "boy I love"—and enter into the rich expectation of that potent, new, and masculine world.

7

Brethren and Lovers

I wonder if other men ever have the like, out of like feelings?

—*Calamus* 9

It seems to me there are men in other lands yearning and thought-ful . . . if I could know these men . . . I know we should be come brethren and lovers.

—*Calamus* 23

In one of the anonymous reviews he wrote of *Leaves of Grass* (1855), Whitman asked, "If this is poetry, where must its foregoers stand?"[1] In a notebook probably written in the early 1850s, Whitman gave one answer to his belated question when he rather anxiously resolved to "take no illustrations whatever from the ancients or classics, nor from the mythology, nor Egypt, Greece, or Rome—nor from the royal and aristocratic institutions and forms of Europe. —make no mention or allusion to them whatever, except as they relate to the New, present things—to our country—to American character or interests. —Of specific mention of them, even for these purposes, as little as possible" (*NUPM* 1:101). The manuscript shows that "Greece" was circled in this list of things to be avoided. It is almost as if the inevitable association with the substantial homoerotic literature of Greece had even then come to mind, not perhaps as if it were unsavory, but rather as if he wanted to assure that his interest in manly affection would even be uninfluenced by ancient texts that were undoubtedly instinct with the breath of manly friendship. The evidence of a penciled circle is surely slight. However, he will allow mention of these things—perhaps not only homoerotic Greece but the aristocratic homosexuality of Europe—if they relate to the "new, present things—to our country." In his 1856 letter to Emerson, he associates his intended promulgation of manly friendship with the new things this country needs.

Taking illustrations from Greece and the classics was often construed to be a sign for homoerotic content in literature, and "Greece" was already as much a signifier as "Oscar Wilde" or "Whitman" would become. Sometime after 1859, in fact, he did look into Plato—Volume 1 of the Bohn Plato, containing both *Phaedrus* and *Symposium,* had been available since 1854—and apparently he read the *Phaedrus.*[2] His allusion indicates that he absorbed with some attention the homosexual implications of that text. Plato, he says, "makes Socrates the defender and eulogist of the platonic love Phaedrus, —and Lysis—advocates it plainly, but carries it into higher & purer regions." His use of "plainly" indicates that it is a topic not always plainly discussed, and the word "advocates" clearly suggests Whitman was aware that "platonic love" might need advocacy, if not then, then in his own time, and that its earthly imputations of sexuality needed, even in his notebook, the affirmation that this love could enter higher and purer realms. Whitman continues his comments about the dialogue: "By love he evidently means the passion inspired in one man by another man, more particularly a beautiful youth." This is, he says "astounding to modern ideas" (*NUPM* 5:1882–83). However, he was neither unaware of nor perhaps that astounded by homosexuality in Classical times, as he affirms in a commentary on Shakespeare's sonnets written about the same time. He suspected that "the ancient Greek friendship seems to have existed" between Shakespeare and "the beautiful young man so passionately treated," who was "so subtly the thread of the sonnets" (*NUPM* 5:1742). Here, aside from the recognition of "Greek friendship" as a textual sign for male-male love, there is a typical hallmark of Whitman's homoerotic style—the phrase "beautiful young man." The linkage of that phrase with the description of Shakespeare's treatment as "passionate" recalls that earlier relation between "manliness" and "passionate fondness." But "subtly" is the crucial word. It is a critical term—a definition of the place of indirection in homosexual texts and a recognition of homosexual love as the thread that binds the poems together. It is of course not Whitman who is astounded. His observation identifies in "modern ideas" the existence of homophobic attitudes concerning male-male love, attitudes he had by then already confronted in his own fiction. In the conclusion of the entry, he quotes Lysis: "I . . . have a fond desire for the possession of friends—& I had rather have a good friend . . . an intimate, than the gold of Darius . . . so fond am I of intimate friends." Whitman comments, almost wistfully, using the verb he will later employ when talking of his own desire for the love of friends: "Lysis is a beautiful youth whom [Hippothales] loves & pines for" (*NUPM* 5:1883).

When reading Plato, Whitman made a note to "see indeed as very significant [Sections] 80–81–82–83–84." These sections of the *Phaedrus* (253c–256e) are those in which Plato talks about "Love and Counter-love" and pictures the effects of love upon the ideal male lovers. When two such are together,

that flowing stream which Zeus, as the lover of Ganymede, called the "flood of passion" pours in upon the lover. . . . when the other is beside him he shares his respite from anguish; and when he is absent he likewise shares his longing . . . though he supposes it to be friendship rather than love. . . . he feels a desire, like the lover's . . . to behold, to touch, to kiss him, to share his couch: and now ere long the desire, as one might guess, leads to the act so when they lie side by side . . . swelling with desire for he knows not what embraces and kisses the lover . . . and when they lie by one another, he is minded not to refuse to do his part in gratifying his lover's entreaties."[3]

The intimation that when apart the lovers desperately long for one another and when together, lying side by side, they share respite from anguish recalls Whitman's mixed ecstasy and anguish in the presence and at the departure of the loving bedfellow in "Song of Myself" and is very nearly a prose translation of the sentiments of the third of the "Live-Oak" cluster (*Calamus* 11) "When I Heard At The Close of Day." If he was astounded when he read the *Phaedrus,* he translated that astonishment into the sublime. In "The Child's Champion," the "fountains of love" are set swelling by "strangers" he encounters in the streets. They flow here too, and when the child and his champion sleep together, it may well be Platonic angels who bless them. Though Whitman certainly intended his anonymous question about foregoers to pointedly exclude any contenders for the new laurels he was claiming and to situate himself splendidly alone, his inclusion of these remarks in his musings—together with that potent verb "pine"—suggests that he recognized some "foregoers" who had strongly breathed the subtle chloroform of manly love, and that though he would make no allusion to them, he was ready to take some illustrations from them, inscribing these within his vision of that "new and present thing" he most passionately and urgently discerned in the American character.

In a notebook comment on Tennyson some years later, he revives his early complaint about the unmanliness of American literature but observes that "Tennyson's poems are certainly not Democracy's poems . . . yet to me [they] are important for their profoundest Democratic help. . . . Tennyson . . . has express'd certain characteristic colorings of our century—certain glistening lights and shades, (our age while moral and manly at the marrow is largely . . . love-sick with elegance) not alone among artists, perhaps better than any other" (*NUPM* 5:1760). In an 1860s notebook he censured an unnamed poet in whose writings "the lesson of Democracy . . . the amplitude of Democracy" was absent, the same charge he would level in 1878. However, this poet did offer one thing: "Much is in his writings, and the young men of America are probably . . . debtors to them more, far more than to those . . . authors" (*NUPM* 5:1757). Whitman's use of the formula "young men of America" should suggest the same homoerotic shading as it does in the letter to Emerson, and the mysterious and unspecific hints about "certain" characteristics, "certain" lights and shades, recall his similar response to the subtle thread of homoeroticism in Shakespeare's sonnets. Whitman reviewed *Maud and Other Poems* in 1855 and mentions *In Memoriam* in a late notebook. His indirection suggests that he may have recognized in Tennyson's description of his relationship with Hallam, couched in matrimonial terms and described in a language not at all dissimilar to Whitman's own "secret signs," a text woven of equally subtle threads. Dellamora has identified the homoerotic threads of Tennyson's poem and sited it within a nineteenth-century English homoerotic discourse. He interestingly reverses the direction of my comments here when he points out that in England, beginning in 1856, and certainly during the last two decades of the century, the name Whitman had become a "Whitman signifier," indicating by the presence of that name a reference to homosexuality or homoerotic texts.[4] Whitman's discussions of Plato, Shakespeare, and Tennyson signify in the same fashion, and indicate an awareness of a larger homoerotic discourse.

On most subjects Whitman was quite willing to be blunt and brash. In a review of his own poems written at the same time as the 1855 article about Tennyson, he proclaimed, "An American Bard at last!" Tennyson had pointed out that "words, like Nature, half reveal / And half conceal the Soul within." Whitman's response to these writings employs a critical language that half reveals the homoeroticism of such texts by using the same half concealed indirections that the texts themselves employ in their presentation of homoerotic discourse. His discussions of homoerotic texts demonstrate an awareness of the homoerotic discourse and a purposive, even though initially hesitant, attempt to establish a positive and constructive critical commentary about it, which he may have felt was as absent in American literature as manly love itself.

There are also American companion texts that contribute to the American homoerotic discourse and illuminate Whitman's participation in the conventions of homoerotic textuality. Emerson himself had not ignored friendship, and what better father for Whitman to cheekily misread to his face than Emerson. In his journals in 1820, Emerson had written about an inexplicable passion for the young Marvin Gay, whose talk of the turning eyeballs so unnerved and fascinated him that Emerson was finally prompted to helplessly demand: "Why do you look after me? I cannot help looking out as you pass." So powerful was the fascination that Gay inspired and yet so distant remained the friendship that Emerson transposed the scant reality into a more satisfying fiction. He created an author and invented a play. The author is "Froedmer," his play "The Friends." In it the imagined Malcolm is no doubt the richly fantasized but very real Marvin Gay, of whom Emerson drew a little sketch, underneath which he penned a prayer to his icon: "grant me still in joy or sorrow / In grief or hope to claim thy heart." The mythical Froedmer's lines are equally to the point: "Malcolm I love thee more than women love."[5] The love that passes that of woman is the obvious reference, just as David and Jonathon is the obvious analog in Emerson's fantasy.

Some years later, in 1834, Emerson meditated upon his disturbed response to Gay: "The disturbance, the self-discord which young men feel is a most important crisis."[6] In the same entry, he speculates on Shakespeare's "unknown self" and notes "how remarkable in every way are Shakespeare's sonnets. Those addressed to a beautiful young man seem to show some singular friendship

amounting to a passion." Whitman makes nearly that same observation in 1856 when he recognizes "ancient Greek friendship"
between Shakespeare and "the beautiful young man so passionately treated." In that single entry, Emerson linked his own "self-
discord" with the passion of Shakespeare's text.

Like Whitman, Emerson chose to transform his self-discord
into a fiction. Though Emerson's is of infinitely briefer compass,
he translated his unknown self into the double fiction of his
youthful drama, while Whitman would describe that self-discord
in a *Calamus* poem as the self "which I have stifled and choked too
long" (Bowers 71). Emerson's early texts spotlight a deeper memory that lies behind the urbane prose of his essay on "Friendship"
written in 1841, the same year as Whitman's fiction on the same
subject, "The Child's Champion." In the poem that precedes the
essay, Emerson asserts that friendship is inspired by a "ruddy drop
of manly blood." The friend also inspires "daily sunrise" and a
"sun-path." Emerson fears that "he was fled," but when his friend
returns "my careful heart was free again." Most strikingly, Emerson says, "through thy friendship fair" surge "the fountains of my
hidden life." This is a subtle prophecy of the unexhibited and
"substantial life" that Whitman also found in friendship. Emerson,
too, is responsive to strangers: "How many we see in the street
. . . whom, though silently, we warmly rejoice to be with! Read
the language of these wandering eye-beams." The sentiment, if
not the adventure, is precisely parallel to Whitman's own street
cruisings and to the "talk of those turning eyeballs" that he invokes
in *Calamus*. It is allied to the crucial observation in "The Child's
Champion" that it is "wondrous" how "in the hurried walks of
life" we meet with "young beings who "touch the fountains of our
love." Like these fountains, too, is Emerson's description of the
friendship as "jets of affection," invoking Whitman's often repeated image of the seminal "jets of life." Friendship, Emerson
says, is like a law of nature, "the soul puts forth friends as the tree
puts forth leaves," in the same way perhaps, as Whitman's live-oak
put forth "joyous leaves" that made him "think of manly love."
Emerson describes friendship in terms that are pronouncedly
sexual: it is a "delicious torment," for "we seek our friend . . .
with an adulterous passion which would appropriate him to
ourselves." He would not "treat friendship daintily, but with
roughest courage." Perhaps facetiously, Emerson says, "I much
prefer the company of ploughboys and tin-peddlers to . . . silken

and perfumed amity."[7] Emerson was urbanely witty here; Whitman did seriously prefer the company of ploughboys and peddlers for they were the strangers who spoke his special language.

In the same year that Whitman wrote to Emerson, Thoreau wrote to a friend that "Walt Whitman . . . is the most interesting fact to me at present. I have just read his 2d edition (which he gave me) and it has done me more good than any reading for a long time."[8] Perhaps the good it did him was to spark the shock of recognition that leaps between Whitman's text and Thoreau's speculations about the relationship between love and friendship, which he had entered in a journal written late in 1839: "Then first I conceive of true friendship when some rare specimen of manhood presents itself." The equation he makes between friendship and manhood is the same Whitman draws. A month or so later he would describe such specimens, in curiously botanical terms, as "these young buds of manhood," recalling Whitman's own inseminating male symbol, the budding calamus root. He asks about them: "By what degrees of consanguinity is this succulent and rank growing slip of manhood related to me?" This is a curious choice of phrase, for the degrees of consanguinity are those very limits within which marriage is allowed or disallowed. Like Whitman, who later ingests whole worlds, he seems to see these rank growing slips of manhood as something succulently edible, young buds perhaps to be plucked and ravenously devoured. In the presence of this rare specimen of manhood he may "then worship moral beauty" manifest in that manly flesh. Such worship inspires him to transcendental ecstasy: "They"—these specimens of manhood—"are some fresher wind that blows, some new fragrance that breathes." Thoreau's "new fragrance" is a companion, though perhaps less dangerous, perfume to Whitman's "subtle chloroform." These men are creators, nature gods, for "they make the landscape"—certainly masculine landscapes—"and sky for us," expanding Thoreau's horizons just as Whitman's blood was expanded by the sunlight of Paradise when certain men were with him.[9]

Thoreau engages in a speculative exercise in which definitions of friendship become freighted with metaphors that extend beyond the language of the friendship tradition and engage with the more passionate declarations of homoerotic love. For one who would be perceived as even icier and more distant from human affection than Emerson, Thoreau fills his journals with remarkable effusions about love and friendship. These two things, separated in heterosexual literature and generally dichotomized in the friendship tradition wherein the object of love is a woman and the object of friendship a man, are comfortably united by Thoreau, who protests that "commonly we degrade Love and Friendship by presenting them under a trivial dualism."[10]

Thoreau, like Whitman, separates manly love from heterosexual passion: "The rules of other intercourse are all inapplicable to this." What a weight of implication and significance lies on "this" intercourse that has its own special rules and laws and is set apart from "other" intercourse. The love of man for man exists in a divine realm far beyond the sway of Venus Pandemos. Friendship, embodied in that rare specimen of manhood, is a "parcel of heaven," the divine region of manly love to which Whitman too ascends. When we are separated from that "parcel of heaven we call our friend," that separation is "source enough for all the elegies that ever were written,"[11] one of which Whitman will write when he describes in *Calamus* 10 how he "knew too well the sick sick dread lest the one he loved might secretly be indifferent to him."

Like Emerson, Thoreau apostrophized friendship in a poem called "Friendship" (1838), which in fact is about love. The poem, an imitation of Donne, is infused with Platonism: love is the "connecting link between heaven and earth," and lovers are "kindred shapes" and possess a "kindred nature" and are intended "to be mates, / Exposed to equal fates / Eternally." But what is most striking about this poem is his use of Whitman's own live-oak image, for the lovers are also "two sturdy oaks" whose "roots are intertwined insep'rably." Wittily—and tellingly—Thoreau announces that this "love cannot speak," though it will be apparent "without the help of Greek, / or any other tongue."[12] The Platonic imagery, the reference to Greek as a tongue in which love might not be secret, and the very secrecy of the love itself infer a complex of associations that place even this minor text firmly within a context of homosexual literary conventions.

Thoreau's references here refer to classical locations of homoerotic mythology. Thus, in a journal entry in January 1840, he expatiates on Whitman's theme of a city of lovers, indicating clearly the sex and the passionate relationship of his imagined inhabitants by offering exemplary types: "History tells us of Orestes and Pylades, Damon and Pythias, but why should not we put to shame those old reserved worthies by a community of such." Of "such" what? Of such lovers, he means. Whitman in

Calamus 28 speaks of such when he hears "of the brotherhood of lovers . . . how affectionate and faithful they were." Like Whitman, who dreamed of a city of new friends, Thoreau too has an Arcadian vision: "Constantly, as it were through a remote skylight, I have glimpses of a serene friendship land." Whitman glimpsed that land, a land where his "happiest days were those, far away through fields, in woods . . . he and another wandering hand in hand . . . apart from other men." Thoreau also populates his land with one other only: "I would live henceforth with some gentle soul such a life as may be conceived, double for variety, single for harmony, — two, only that we might admire at our oneness, — one, because indivisible. Such a community to be a pledge of holy living. How could aught unworthy be admitted into our society?" Whitman's communities of friends will make the continent "indissoluble"; there friendship is "invincible." In Thoreau's society there cannot be anything "unworthy," just as Whitman's "new moral American continent" will represent the "just . . . passionate friendliness" of the States. Like Whitman, Thoreau also looks for manly friendship in literature, asserting that "it once certainly existed but now almost seems to have gone out of the experience of the race." Thoreau is concerned that "the nearest approach to a community of love in these days" — note that the earlier vague "community of such" has been pointedly identified — "is like the distant breaking of waves on the seashore."[13]

Throughout his journals, Thoreau returns to the theme of that love he seems to see as existing most perfectly between men. Like Whitman, who knew that masculine love inspires special language, Thoreau affirms that this love invents "poetical life." It lifts him into Platonic and Whitmanesque "higher walks of being," what Whitman called in *Calamus* 38, "the regions of your love, O man, / O sharer of my roving life." In another allusive passage in 1840, he recalls "the other day I rowed in my boat a free, even lovely young lady." Aside from his curious observation that she is "even" lovely, he compares the easy social intercourse between them with other relationships in which "mean relations and prejudices intervene to shut out the sky and we never see a man as simple and distinct."[14] Does this suggest that the accepted relationship between men and women is easy when compared with those relationships between men that are affected by prejudice?

In other passages, Thoreau echoes Whitman's desire to meet some one to love as he is capable of loving: "For many years have I striven to meet one even on common manly ground and have not succeeded." If he could meet such a one, it would be that parcel of heaven, for a friend is "as holy a shrine as any God's." His friend dwells in the "distant horizon as rich as an eastern city." He "seems to move in a burnished atmosphere . . . his house is incandescent to my eye." He is an "apology for my life. In him are the spaces which my orbit traverses."[15] This language is surely far more than the language of mere friendship, or the conventional language of a desexualized friendship tradition. Thoreau employs the style to celebrate his fixed orbit about a male friend. In his presence "I am ashamed of my fingers and toes. I have no feature so fair as my love for him. There is more than maiden modesty between us." Whitman sees "perhaps more" than poetry in the body of a wellmade man and violently destroys any maiden modesty that might exist between him and his lover when he demands that his lover hurt him like the bridegroom hurts the bride. But what is that "more" between Thoreau and his friend? An extravagant metaphor ripe with suggestive sexuality hints if not at consummation then at fantasy: "He sails all lonely under the edge of the sky, but thoughts go out silently from me and belay him, till at length he rides in my roadsted." Perhaps this friendship was not unlike that which obtained between Emerson and Marvin Gay or those about which Whitman often lamented, for Thoreau extends his metaphor further, and it consorts with Emerson's painful cry, "why do I look out at you as I pass," or Whitman's own "sick, sick dread." Thoreau says: "But never does he fairly anchor in my harbor. Perhaps I afford no good anchorage . . . his house is incandescent to my eye, while I have no house, but only a neighborhood to his."

On Sunday 18 October, the day before he wrote the lines above, Thoreau confided to his journal: "I cannot make a disclosure—you should see my secret.—Let me open my doors never so wide, still within and behind them, where it is unopened, does the sun rise and set." His friend, of course, is his secret, that friend who dwells in the distant horizon. Indeed, secrecy seems to be much a part of this friendship—"does he forget that new mines of secrecy are constantly opening in me?"[16] Thoreau's love "cannot speak," nor does he seem willing to utter it in any place but his presumably private journals, where the secret of his friendship can be safely revealed. The secrecy attendant upon homosexual relationships or simply upon the "unmanly" construction that may be imputed to a passion between men needs no elaboration here as a theme in homosexual literature. When Emerson most pointedly confesses his love for Marvin, he translates his avowal into fictitious drama. Whitman determines to "shade down and hide my thoughts" in *Calamus* 44, and when he describes, just as Thoreau does, an infatuation with "an athlete who loves me" in *Calamus* 36, he "dare not tell it in words."

Thoreau's text homoeroticizes friendship, an involvement of text and concept that is precisely parallel to such involvement in Whitman's own far vaster text. One brief passage echoes resonantly against the scene of the twenty-eight erotic bathers in section 11 of "Song of Myself": "Boys bathing at Hubbard's bend, playing with a boat (I at the willows). The color of their bodies in the sun at a distance is pleasing, the not often seen flesh-color. I hear the sound of their sport borne over the water. . . . What a singular fact that . . . men were forbidden to expose their bodies under severest penalty."[17] Perhaps that "at a distance" tells us about Thoreau's own sexual bravery and curiosity, just as the wistful desire can be heard in the plaintive observation that the color of flesh is "not often seen." Hiding in the willows by the banks of the stream watching these young buds of manhood at their naked sport, Thoreau, a watcher only, at a distance and voyeuristically, absorbs a scene in which Whitman would later unhesitatingly and triumphantly participate. Though he may not have wanted to, Thoreau could only, like Whitman's twenty-ninth bather, "stay aft the blinds of the window." Perhaps desire did not impel him enough to proceed, "dancing and laughing" like Whitman's spiritual and sexual avatar, to the shores of his own *Calamus* pond populated with boys and bathers. Instead he sought the safe solitude and the chastity of Walden.

I do not know if Thoreau heard his own obscured subtext when he commented in that letter to a friend that Whitman "does not celebrate love at all" yet "even on this side . . . has spoken more truth than any American or modern that I know." We know enough to realize that for Thoreau "love" could well be the idealized homoerotic yet presumably chaste passion that had been a subject of his journals. "This side" is the side upon which Whitman places "men like me." Perhaps however, Thoreau is quite aware of subtexts: "Walt Whitman can communicate to us no experience, and if we are shocked, whose experience are we reminded of?"[18] The confessional hint here fascinates, but for my purposes it is sufficient to observe that some of the experiences of which he is reminded are those inscribed within the homoerotic conventions that interpenetrate Emerson's, Whitman's, and Thoreau's texts: indirect but powerful sexual imagery often couched in matrimonial terms, the invocation of classical locations illustrating faithful male-male love, the fantasizing of safe friendship lands and cities of friends, the search for and creation of the icon of the ideal friend, the special nature of homosexual love that passes the love of women, and even specific scene and image—boys bathing, and the signifying live-oak.

Whitman responded to two other American writers whose texts are also inspired with a distinct atmosphere of manly friendship, Bayard Taylor and Herman Melville—the one never to be, the other not yet "strong," to use Bloom's useful term. Whitman reviewed *Typee* in 1846 and *Omoo* in 1847, and he mentions Taylor in a notebook entry in 1854. To Melville's thinly encoded tale of two friends' adventures in the South Seas—as representative of a generic convention in the homosexual novel as is Charles Warren Stoddard's more pronouncedly homoerotic *South Sea Idyls* (1873), which Whitman would also read and heartily approve—he responded that it was a "strange, graceful" book, one to "hold in one's hand and pore dreamily over of a summer day."[19] Dreams are the stuff of which sexual fantasy is made in Whitman's texts, and such terms as "strange," "graceful," and "dreamily" consort with "subtle" and "certain glistening lights and shades," which he respectively applied to Shakespeare's and Tennyson's texts. What did he find in *Typee* that was "strange"? The Arcadian South Sea paradise is a geographic mirror of the strange and inexplicable sexual locale he describes in "Song of Myself" as perfumed by "subtle chloroform" and as brightened by the "sunlight of Paradise," a place wherein his blood is expanded by "certain men" he meets. This landscape may well have appealed to the "dreamy" nature, the very nature that seems to be so characteristic of some of the young men who inhabit his early poetry and fiction, and the state that is so often the prelude to homoerotic and masturbatory fantasy in "Song of Myself." "Reverie," so nineteenth-century medical theory warned, "was commonly held to lead to masturbation."[20] His review connects these dreamy reveries with an equally dreamy summer day. In both "Song of Myself" and *Calamus*, it is during such erotically charged summer days and "mad naked summer" nights that some of his most homoerotically adventurous fantasies occur. In his discussion of *Typee*, Martin reminds us that the book,

for most of its contemporary readers a travel narrative, could serve as
the kind of allusive text about which I have spoken above: "For
nineteenth-century homosexuals, in search of both a justification for
themselves and a possible realization for their desires, the journey to
an exotic landscape offered the possibility of locating a place where
there might be others like them, a place where friendship might play
its legitimate part in social life." Martin includes *Typee* within a genre
he calls "the quest for the Golden land," which I have elsewhere
identified as a version of homoerotic pastoral."[21] When reading
Typee, therefore, Whitman, fascinated by the idea of a world of male
friendship and sexuality, might very well have found that it inspired
reveries—dreamy reveries—of friendship and desire, reveries that
touched special chords in his own "psychology," a term he will use in
describing Taylor's homoerotic verse. Whitman is given to sexual
indirection even in his reviews. The hand that "held" the book also
holds the penis, which is of course, in that phallic metonymy in
"Spontaneous Me," the book itself.

Melville engages in psychological play and verbal indirection
in *Typee* and *Omoo,* and in reading these perhaps Whitman asked
Thoreau's question: "Whose experiences are we reminded of?"
Tom, the narrator of *Typee,* first encounters Toby "leaning over the
bulwarks, apparently plunged in a profound reverie." Reverie is
dangerous to sexual balance, and Toby is for Tom one of those men
who, for Whitman, expand the blood: "He was a young fellow of
my own age, for whom I had all along entertained a great regard. . . . he was active, ready, and obliging, of dauntless courage, and singularly open and fearless in the expression of his
feelings. I had on more than one occasion gotten him out of scrapes
into which this had led him; I know not whether it was from this
cause, or a certain congeniality of sentiment between us, that he
had always shown a partiality for my society." Toby's fearlessness
about expressing his feelings and yet his intentional isolation from
the common run of men place him in the company of Whitman's
roughs and comrades. The "certain" congeniality between them is
another verbal indirection, the same "certain" Whitman employs
to indicate certain erotic shadings in a text. Tom responds to Toby
in other, more physical ways as well: "There was much even in the
appearance of Toby calculated to draw me toward him . . . Toby
was endowed with a remarkably prepossessing exterior. Arrayed
in his blue smock and duck trowsers, he was as smart a looking
sailor as ever stepped upon a deck."[22]

In one of his poems, Bayard Taylor also will express fascination with a sunburnt sailor:"

> I pine for something human,
> Man, woman, young or old, —
> Something to meet and welcome,
> Something to clasp and hold."

He confesses: "I have a mouth for kisses. . . . I have a heart in my bosom / Beating for nobody's sake. . . . O warmth of love that is wasted!" So powerful is his desire—he too "pines" for love—that "I could take the sunburnt sailor, / Like a brother, to my breast."[23] The sailor is an icon of immense power and popularity in homosexual literature, life, and fantasy, and is, of course, Melville's central erotic image. Though Whitman will personify his sailors in his water-born swimmers, in a poem proposal in a notebook entry made in the early 1850s, he conflates young men, the south seas, sailors, and manly attraction, putting them all together on one curiously named vessel: "Poem of Young Men / The Sumatra young man, curious, handsome, manly, gentle, that came aboard 'the flirt'" (*NUPM* 4:1332). What curious psychology connects this young Sumatra man and the name of the ship can be left to the speculation of deeper probers, though surely it is material with which Melville would have amusingly flirted.

In *Typee,* Tom elaborates further on Toby's isolation: "He was a strange wayward being, moody, fitful, and melancholy—at times almost morose." Social and emotional reticence is a characteristic common to homosexual fictional characters in nineteenth-century literature, at least it is so in Whitman's mythology wherein his young men are so often notable for their silence, and the most passionate moments are those where no words are said.[24] Toby is a singular young man, just as curious as the "singular young man" in one of Whitman's notebooks of the mid-forties who "remained much by himself. . . . most of the time he remained silent. . . . he loved . . . to sit or lean on the rails of the fence. . . . He was rather less than the good size of a man: his figure and face were full, his complexion without much color, his eyes, large, clear, and black." (*NUPM* 1:150). Toby also is "singularly small and slightly made, with great flexibility of limb. . . . his naturally dark complexion had been deepened by exposure to the tropical sun, and a mass of jetty locks clustered about his temples, and threw a darker shade into his black eyes." The mixture of sexual power and boyish beauty is the same in which Whitman delights in his early fictions as well as in such iconic couples as the two boys clinging together and the two lusty apprentice wrestlers. Toby combines reticence with the erotic attributes of the rough, the precise combination of sexual attributes that Whitman finds in men who inspire his lank pennants to rise. As Martin says, "travel books should also be thought of as a possible Victorian form of genteel pornography" permitting the "exploration of alternate sexuality."[25]

Tom recognizes their bond, and while planning to jump ship, he enunciates the comradely concept when he realizes that Toby is the "very one of all my shipmates whom I would choose for the partner of my adventure." He is the ideal "comrade . . . to divide its dangers." This, of course, is a primary fantasy in Whitman's fiction and poetry: the two comrades in *Calamus* 26 who "one the other never leaving . . . up and down the road going" enter into adventures in *Calamus* 10 "far away through fields, in woods, on hills . . . apart from other men." Toby and Tom make their escape and enter into just such a paradise. As Tom describes it: "I looked straight down into the bosom of a valley, which swept away in long undulations to the blue waters of the distance. . . . Over all the landscape there reigned the most hushed repose, which I almost feared to break, lest, like the enchanted gardens in the fairy tale, a single syllable might dissolve the spell." Tom suggests to Toby that this enchanted garden might provide a "capacious and un-tenanted valley, abounding in all manner of delicious fruit" and urges that "we should at once take refuge in it and remain there as long as we pleased."[26] This is the happy valley, Thoreau's friend-ship land, the same hidden Arcadia into which Whitman goes in order to walk away from other men hand in hand with his ideal friend. It is a potent image, this safe haven from the homophobic oppression of civilized law and moral judgment, and it occupies a central place not only in Whitman's mythology but in the homo-sexual imagination as well.

Readers of *Typee* know that Tom is soon provided with the services of Kory-Kory, whose purpose is to solely minister to Tom's comfort. Kory-Kory is "twenty-five years of age, about six feet in height, robust and well made." An interesting feature of his aspect, which is tattooed and painted, is his beard, "plucked out by the root from every other part of his face" save for "hairy pen-dants . . . which garnished his under lip . . . and . . . chin." The curious detail of the plucked beard suggests an association with the Berdache, American Indian cross-dressers who also devoted themselves to men with the devotion socially expected of women.[27] Kory-Kory is devoted to Tom, and serves him with jealous efficiency, bathing him, feeding him, carrying him, lighting his pipe, sleeping next to him, and offering, in short, all the intimate services that might be provided by a nineteenth-century wife—or a devoted lover. In *Two Years Before the Mast,* Richard Henry Dana describes the devotion of a Kanaka, Hope, who is to him as Kory-Kory is to Tom, and outlines the principles of intimate male friendship in this Marquesan society: "Every Kanaka has one particular friend, whom he considers himself bound to do everything for, and with whom he has a sort of contract,—an alliance offensive and defensive,—and for whom he will often make the greatest sacrifices. This friend they call the aikane; and for such did Hope adopt me, I do not believe I could have wanted anything which he had, that he would not have given me."[28]

So too Kory-Kory serves Tom, an intimate picture of devoted male friendship. Whitman had observed that the male friendship of the *Phaedrus* was "astounding" to modern ideas and that *Typee* was "strange." I do not think that the male friendship in this book was either strange or astounding to Whitman, but instead appealing. Appealing too may have been the interesting promiscuity, or at least intimacy, of Tom's sleeping arrangements—"the next morning I found Kory-Kory stretched out on one side of me, while my companion lay upon the other."[29] Both Melville and Whitman describe scenes of men sleeping together. Melville places Tom between the devoted innocence of Kory-Kory and the sexually charged presence of Toby, symbolically placing him between love and desire. Melville foreshadows the matrimonial intimacy of Queequeg and Ishmael, and the scene looks ahead to Whitman's own exciting nights with the "loving and hugging bedfellow" and with his friend in *Calamus* 11 "sleeping by me under the same cover."

If Whitman was captivated and plunged into dreamy reverie by themes and images with which he was even then experimenting in his own fiction—his Toby is Wild Frank, his Kory-Kory is Windfoot, his Tom is Langton—he could well have been taken by the nearly divine image of the handsome youth Melville introduces in the person of Marnoo, the ideal friend, a homoerotic Adam in this sexual paradise. Marnoo is "taboo," sacred and not to be harmed, a condition similar to that enjoyed by the Berdache mentioned above. Marnoo is indeed a figure from myth and legend, and he is a stranger too, that exciting embodiment of sexual promise and homoerotic fantasy Whitman encounters on the streets and invites to the guarded tents of homosexual love:

> The stranger could not have been more than twenty-five years of age, and was a little above the ordinary height; had he been a single hair's breadth taller, the matchless symmetry of his form would have been destroyed. His unclad limbs were beautifully formed; whilst the elegant outline of his figure, together with his beardless cheeks, might have entitled him to the distinction of the Polynesian Apollo; and indeed the oval of his countenance and the regularity of every feature reminded me of an antique bust. . . . The hair of Marnoo was a rich curling brown, and twined about his temples and neck in little close curling ringlets, which danced up and down continually when he was animated in conversation. His cheek was of a feminine softness, and his face was free from the least blemish of tattooing. . . . a slight girdle of tappa, scarcely two inches in width, but hanging before and behind in spreading tassels, composed the entire costume of the stranger.[30]

This description is filled with the "sunlight of Paradise," and Melville's blood seemed to be remarkably expanded by a passionate attention to what he describes. All of the elements of such descriptions are here: sensuously curling hair; feminine cheeks or face, yet a masculine and perfect bodily form, an inevitable comparison to classical—hence homoerotic—beauty; and of course nakedness, here tantalizingly presented. What Whitman would later describe as "the masculine muscle" is covered only by a scant two inches of the sacred veil, the same veil—a cunning cover—that hides the sweet phallic douceurs in Whitman's text.[31] Whitman had already engaged in luxuriant descriptions of males in his fiction and notebooks and in "I Sing the Body Electric." His precise and erotic self-descriptions in "Song of Myself" share common ground with Melville's equally eroticized males, as Melville's invocation of the Arcadian fastness invokes the Calamus grove. Melville elevates the taboo Marnoo—the archetypal beautiful boy, the truly ideal friend, and the very image of Apollo—to near divinity. Thus he invokes another convention of gay texts that Whitman engages when, in the bardic and sexual ecstasy of the last lines of "Song of Myself," he assumes the role of prophet and priest—a role Carpenter describes when he speaks about the "unusual powers of divination and prophecy . . . to be found in homosexual folk . . . a conviction . . . so rooted and persistent that it spread over the greater part of the world." It is in fact Apollo who Carpenter invokes as the classical exemplar of this homoerotic priestly state.[32] By raising Marnoo to such sacred status and Toby to the position of desired sexual icon, Melville creates as potent a living icon as that Emerson desired when he wished that his "friend . . . be different from any individual I had seen. I invested him with a solemn cast of mind, full of poetic feeling, & an idolater of friendship."[33] Whitman's own Fierce Wrestler is as passionate a conflation of priest, poet, rough, and idol.

In a notebook entry in 1854, Whitman said that Bayard Taylor's poems "have as attributes what might be called their psychology— You cannot see very plainly at times what they mean although the poet indirectly has a meaning" (*NUPM* 5:1771). "Indirectly" indicates a special literary tongue, and this term is a definition of the constantly engaged and experimental discourse concerning the theories, practice, and implications of living a homosexual life that is part of Whitman's special tongue. Taylor's indirect meanings and his "psychology" deal with that same manly friendship Whitman hoped to see mentioned in print. Taylor's *Poems of the Orient* (1854) implies homosexuality and engages tropes and imagery that conventionally define homosexual literature. Robert K. Martin has shown how Taylor's poetry and later fiction responds to generalized homosexual textual conventions.[34] Taylor's early poetry— written before 1854—hints at a broad conception of homosexuality, one far more consonant with Whitman's feeling that love, friendship, sex, and masculine attraction could indeed be conflated into one complex of feeling and desire. Taylor's meanings are not too opaque, and in the poems that Whitman emphasizes, the oriental lyrics, his meaning is quite clear. Whitman's hints about their "psychology" suggest that Whitman did breath their recognizable air. His comment that Taylor only "indirectly" signifies seems to demonstrate an impatience with the genteel misdirection of their language and to imply that he finds them inadequate representatives of the program and project he intends to undertake and the discourse he intends to found.

The "psychology" Whitman discerned in Taylor's *Poems of the Orient* is almost immediately evident in Taylor's dedication to

Richard Henry Stoddard. Stoddard had dedicated his *Poems* to Taylor in 1852, and in his dedication he asked Taylor to "join our hands, / And knit our souls in Friendship's holy bands." As Martin points out, "holy bands" inevitably recalls "holy bonds" of wedlock, which suggests that "Stoddard is establishing a model for friendship (which he Platonically capitalizes) that will be parallel to, and perhaps even superior to, the love of man for woman."[35] Taylor's "Proem Dedicatory" to Stoddard wishes that his friend "were with me" and "couched on [Mount] Tmolus side / In the warm Myrtles, in the golden air." Here again is the pastoral Arcadia, and the implications of "couched" suggest as much as Whitman's more obvious encirclement by the arms of his friend in *Calamus* 11. Taylor avers that if Stoddard were with him, "little were the need of this imperfect artifice of rhyme" since, presumably their companionship—or their love—would provide music enough. But, "I am solitary"—a complaint familiar in Whitman's texts—and thus, Taylor says, "I cannot choose but sing," Whitman's own response to loneliness.[36] His songs, employing Whitman's favorite wrestling trope, are sternly bent

> On wresting from her hand the cup, whence flow
> The flavors of her ruddiest life . . . the unshackled range
> Of all experience . . . that my songs may show
> The warm red blood that beats in hearts of men.

Whitman's own version of this had already been entered in "Live-Oak XII" (Bowers 118) where the "blood of friendship hot and red" that flowed in the veins of the eleve "silently selected by lovers" coursed in unison with Emerson's "ruddy drop of manly blood."

Taylor's book introduces some thirty poems on oriental themes. The Orient was exotic, pagan, and presumably tolerant of homosexuality. As Crompton points out, what repelled orthodox writers about this culture was what "inevitably drew homosexual or bisexual writers to it."[37] Taylor and his friend arrive in Greece, for him an Oriental land, where, as Whitman knew, the "ancient Greek friendship" had been practiced and approved. In "A Paean to the Dawn" Taylor praises the freedom of Greece where "love was free, and free as air / The utterance of Passion." In this Arcadia love and passion could speak freely: "the heart in every fold lay bare, / Nor shamed its true expression." This "free air" is the same that love requires in Whitman's notebooks, the same "atmosphere" that

loosens his tongue in "Song of Myself" and eventually allows the
free and unashamed expression of homoerotic desires. Taylor's
folded and unashamed heart curiously foretells Whitman's similar
context in *Calamus* 2, centering around the revelation and release of
his homosexual feelings: "Do not fold yourself so in your pink
tinged roots timid leaves! / Do not remain down there so ashamed,
herbage of my breast." Because Greece was the historic locale for
the expression of manly love, and since the "expression" of heterosexual love was the subject of most poetry, Taylor seems certainly
to mean that it is homosexual love that, since the Greeks, has been
"shamed in its true expression."[38]

In Greece, Taylor not only finds inspiration but discovers that
love can be uttered in "true expression" and is embodied in ideal
figures who possess a "perfect limb and perfect face" that "sur-
passed our best ideal . . . the Beautiful was real." Taylor joined
beauty, physical perfection, and Greece with the "true expression"
of love to say that in his own poems as well as in that idyllic time
"men acknowledged true desires." Such desire was not denied:
"Impulse and Deed went hand in hand." Taylor's acknowledgment
of what he presumes to have been Greek sexual freedom, though
indirectly stated, is nevertheless precise in its meaning. Taylor
announces that he will "seek the fountain head / Whence flowed
their inspiration, / And lead the unshackled life they led."[39]
Taylor's "fountainhead" suggests of course not only the fountains
set flowing in "The Child's Champion," sources of unshackled
life, but the *Calamus* pond, source of Whitman's inspiration. In this
friendship land, Taylor can renounce "the World's false life," just as
Whitman would come to renounce standards hitherto published,
so that he too could be free to "utter the cry of friends."

Strengthened by the example of Greek friendship, the poet and
his friend continue on their journey, and in "The Poet in the East,"
they find another land where the poet feels instant identification,
for "his native soul was there." Here he sees "the familiar visions
that mocked his quest / Beside the Western streams." These
western streams flow through lands in which passion, especially
homoerotic passion, cannot be truly and freely uttered. The visions, "visible forms of early and precious dreams," those Platonic
forms of idealized homosexual love that Taylor spoke about in " A
Paean to the Dawn," are now made real. In a line curiously
prescient of Whitman's *Calamus* 20, Taylor observes that "a brother
to him was the princely Palm / For he cannot live alone." He

determines to abide "on the lost Arcadian shore: here is the light on sea and land, / And the dream deceives no more." Taylor enters into his Arcadia, just as Whitman will enter into his garden, to become "undisguised." On the Arcadian shore Taylor is released from the deceiving visions that "mocked" him "beside the repressive Western Streams," just as Whitman, when next to the *Calamus* pond, has also escaped from the conforming life. The western streams in "The Nilotic Drinking Song" are the Schuykill or the Croton. The free eastern waters are those in which "Ganymede dipped for Jupiter," and they remind Taylor of Anacreon's stave and the "honeyed lips of Hylas."[40]

In "Hylas" (1850), a poem included among Taylor's "Romances and Lyrics" in the collected poems, Taylor takes the opportunity to create a fully eroticized male portait. Hylas, Hercules' favorite, is drowned when the water nymphs, taken by his beauty, pull him into their sacred pond. Hercules, mad with grief, leaves the argonauts to search for him, repeatedly calling his name in vain. Theocritus had told the story, and Taylor uses it as his most extended "literary exercise" in homoerotic poetry. Martin suggests that Taylor's "use of the Hylas myth as a poetic subject is part of an attempt at self-definition and also part of an attempt to situate himself in a poetic tradition which will justify his emotional life."[41] Taylor's description of Hylas is more detailed than Whitman's descriptions of handsome youths in his fiction, though no more telling than the erotic vignettes of such youths that Whitman sharply penned in "Song of Myself." Hylas is introduced in a passionate aura of male eroticism, as Taylor describes his slow disrobing: "Unfilleting his purple chalmys . . . Then, stooping lightly, loosened he his buskins." He soon stands

> Naked, save for one light robe that from his shoulder
> Hung to his knee, the youthful flush revealing
> Of warm, white limbs, half nerved with coming manhood,
> Yet fair and smooth with tenderness of beauty."

Hylas "dropped the robe, and raised his head exulting." Taylor dwells on the details of his beauty:

> the thick, brown locks, tossed backward from his forehead,
> Fell about his temples; manhood's blossom
> Not yet sprouted from his chin, but freshly

Curved the fair cheek, and full the red lips, parting,
Like a loose bow, that has just launched its arrow.
His large blue eyes, with joy dilate and beamy,
Were clear as the unshadowed Grecian heaven;
Dewy and sleek his dimpled shoulders rounded
To the white arms and whiter breast between them.
Downward, the supple line had less of softness:
His back was like a god's; his loins were moulded
As if some pulse of power began to waken;
The springy fulness of his thighs, outswerving,
Sloped to his knee, and lightly dropping downward,
Drew the curved lines that breathe, in rest, of motion."[42]

Taylor's high Romantic diction may not be precisely the kind of manly love that Whitman hoped to find in print, but it surely shows that Taylor had read the homoerotic lyrics of *The Greek Anthology*, and it is certainly an intensely erotic description, indeed daringly so, as desirous as Melville's description of Marnoo, as specifically sexual as any description by Whitman. At that intimated point where "downward the supple lines had less of softness," Whitman's frank "masculine muscle" is also answeringly ready to waken. Here is the "hard stuff of nature" indeed, Whitman's "well-hung" rough. Taylor's gaze is fixed upon Hylas' loins and thighs just as Whitman's gaze is fixed in equal fascination upon the tight fitting trousers of his firemen in "I Sing the Body Electric." Taylor is fascinated—almost to the point of incomprehensiblity—not only by the decreasing softness but also by the rising "pulse of power" that awakens to "springy fulness" and soon becomes "outswerving," dropping, quite amazingly, to his knee.

Taylor concludes his oriental poems with a final intriguing comment. In the East, he says, "I found, among those Children of the sun, / The cipher of my nature,—the release / Of baffled powers, which else had never won / That free fulfillment."[43] "Song of Myself" is precisely about the release of such baffled homoerotic powers. When Whitman says in *Calamus* 2, "I have stifled and choked too long / I will escape from the costume, the play which was proposed to me / I will sound myself and love—I will utter the cry of friends," he records such a release. Perhaps Taylor recognized that, for in a letter to Whitman dated 2 December 1866, he says: "I may say frankly that there are two things in [*Leaves of Grass*] which I find nowhere else in literature, though I find them in my own nature. I mean the awe and wonder and reverence and beauty of Life, as expressed in the human body, with the physical attraction and delight of mere contact which it inspires, and that tender and noble love of man for man which once certainly existed, but now almost seems to have gone out of the experience of the race" (*Corr* 1:295). How curiously similar this is to Whitman's complaint and to Thoreau's. When we hear Taylor's confession — "I find them in my own nature" — Whitman's observation about Taylor's "psychology" seems startlingly perceptive, especially so when that "nature" is ranged beside Whitman's own speculations about "men like me."[44] When such texts as Taylor's are read together with those of Emerson, Thoreau, Melville, and Whitman, it seems clear, despite Whitman's self-conscious perception that the air was still, that the breath of manly friendship was at the least a stiff breeze riding with the transcendental wind.[45]

In "Song of Myself" Whitman says that the word he is looking for, the word that in 1856 he hopes to find to express manly friendship, is "the unfolding word of the ages . . . a word of the modern . . . a word en masse . . . a word of faith that never balks." It is also, like that other word that gave him access to the tents of interior love, a password. It is the "password primeval" and allows him to speak here in "forbidden voices." Though the tents may veil interior love, it is now his task to remove the veil and to reveal, clarify, and transfigure that love, by finding and uttering the word of pure power. This is pure sexual power translated into a language that strips away veils and transgresses boundaries established by power, engaging as Foucault says "in the intensification of pleasures connected to the production of the truth about sex."[46] In this sense then, his search for words becomes that dominant confession Foucault sees as the primary voice of nineteenth-century sexuality.

The erotic need to express himself is affirmed in *Leaves of Grass* (1856). In "By Blue Ontario's Shore" he affirms that "after this day I take my own modes of expressing love for men and women" (*LG Var* 1:206, line 265). The primary mode is finally defined in "Song of the Open Road," where he utters the word at last: "Here is adhesiveness, it is not previously fashioned, it is apropos." (*LG Var* 1:230, line 91). Though "adhesiveness" is used in phrenology, as has been constantly pointed out, it is clear that Whitman uses it differently. His use is not in fact a borrowing; it is "not previously fashioned." It is a new word with a new meaning, and all his poetry to this point has offered

manifold illustration of that meaning. It means manly love. The word
"is apropos," and appropriate to it is the appearance of loving
strangers: "Do you know what it is as you pass to be loved by
strangers? / Do you know the talk of those turning eye-balls?" The
"talk" is a special language—allusive and masculine only—and only
men like him are fluent in its subtleties. After he announces that
adhesiveness is apropos to the talk of the turning eye-balls, he once
again asks: "These yearnings why are they? These thoughts in
darkness why are they?"[47] The first question contains that key word,
"yearning," which with its companion "pining" nearly always indicates homosexual desire in Whitman's erotic vocabulary.

In *Calamus* in *Leaves of Grass* (1860), when Whitman begins his
specific exploration of what it means to be homosexual, he again
considers the "word unsaid" and tries to "unloose" it. That word is
a song in "Proto-leaf," which introduced the third edition, and
there it is the "song of companionship . . . a new ideal of manly
friendship" to be enunciated in the "new evangel-poem of lovers
and comrades" (Bowers 13). The 1860 edition contains an apostrophe to "adhesiveness," which he describes to his "comrade" as a
"pensive aching to be together" though "you know not why and I
know not why" (Bowers 34–35). This aching to be together is
explained not only in "The Child's Champion" but in the attraction that calls him to the guarded tents of his desired comrades and
in every longing reference to the attraction of the "young men of
these states." "Adhesiveness" is a password here as well. It is the
"word to clear one's path ahead endlessly." It is the word that could
clear from the path the "obstacles" Langton saw as standing
between him and his love for Charles, the word that opened the
path to the guarded tents. "Adhesiveness," as Whitman will make
clear in the first of the *Calamus* poems, is the word that will permit
him to walk untrodden paths in search of a world that sanctions the
love of comrades and in search of the power to change the world
that does not sanction that love. As he enters the *Calamus* garden,
he makes ready to celebrate the new found word. He can "talk" at
last; the word is unloosed. He is "no longer abashed"; he has
escaped from the "usual adjustments and pleasures" and now has
found the strength to "unbare my breast," "sound myself and
love," and "utter the cry of friends" (*Calamus* 2). He is able to ask
the most important homosexual questions: "I wonder if other men
ever have the like, out of the like feelings?" "Is there even one other
like me?" He wonders too if there are "other men in other lands,

yearning and thoughtful," dreaming his dreams. The texts of Thoreau, and Emerson, Melville, and Taylor, through their use of some of the conventions of homosexual literature, imply some of those dreams. I would like to turn now to another version of the sexual discourse in which Whitman also signifies, and which, like his, participates in those pleasures associated with the production of the truth about sex.

Whitman's question in 1860—"Are there other men who have the like out of the like feelings?"—had already been answered in his own notebooks and in the 1856 letter to Emerson wherein he affirmed the "tenacity" and "passionate fondness," the "manly readiness to make friends," displayed by American young men. Captured in little epiphanies in Havelock Ellis' and John Addington Symonds' *Sexual Inversion* (1897), the eventual first volume of *Studies in the Psychology of Sex,* are the sexual biographies of some of the young men whose affection Whitman recognized as being so tenacious and passionate.[48] Their commentary, constructed into text by Ellis and Symonds, is a fascinating voice in that eager confessional Foucault has identified as so communicative a part of the nineteenth-century sexual discourse. Of course what they tell is subject not only to the degree of their own desire to reveal the secrets of their nights and days and to the degree of pleasure they may have derived from the construction of their discourse but to their perception of what Ellis or Symonds hoped to hear. Whitman's text operates within the same framework of the textual inspiration and erotic pleasure derived from confession, and from the seductive lure of a potential reader's expectation. In "Song of Myself," he says, "I might tell how I like you, but cannot, / And might tell what it is in me and what it is in you but cannot." Note the teasing and mysterious "it." He continues: "and might tell that pining I have, that pulse of my nights and days." That coy "might" is intended as profound seduction. "Might" is the pivotal word that first creates and then empowers an audience that will induce (seduce) him into telling his secrets. He "cannot" tell them, not because he is not able—his words prove his undoubted ability—but because he has not yet been sexually aroused enough to receive power and because he has not yet been empowered, either by his audience or by himself, to reveal the secret.

Yearning and pining, the pulse of nights and days, and seduction, are both the subjects and the effects of the Ellis and Symonds biographies, all of them predicated on the revelation of a secret. Foucault says that the exploitation of sexual silence is indigenous to sexual texts and that "modern societies . . . dedicated themselves to speaking of [sex] *ad infinitum* while exploiting it as the secret."[49] This is Whitman's strategy and the function of the Ellis and Symonds texts. The audience Whitman addresses is given the chance to impose upon him the necessary conditions of dominance—sexual, verbal, and social—so that he will have no choice but to tell his secrets. However he will also tell them theirs. He will become not only the respondent to the questions of the listener but the listener's oracle as well. Foucault says that because of the efficacy of the process, "this discourse of truth finally takes effect, not in the one who receives it, but in the one from whom it is wrested."[50] Thus the weak questioner—"are there men like me"—becomes the "strong" poet; the sexually seduced becomes the seducer and sage, for in instant reversal he reveals to the listener "what it is in you." The Ellis and Symonds texts make that same revelation. So when their anonymous words are read against Whitman's own confessional revelations, we can inscribe each of them within the textual system of the other. They are all Whitman.

These texts are the written records supplied by "self-confessed" (in Foucault's sense), homosexual men, who describe the growth of their homosexual feeling and the details of their physical homosexuality. They were all contemporaries of Whitman, some English, some American. Some were younger, some older; some were writers, others workers. But all of them were comrades, and like Whitman, they all asked, "what is this adhesiveness?" Here, just as in 1855, the authentic confessional voice is heard, and just as in "Song of Myself," so in these lives the songs are drenched in sex and resound with the mirthshouting music of manly love. Whitman wrote at the same time, and in some instances in the same country, in which these men lived the lives on which they offer reports. They tell us what it was like to need the love of comrades at the precise moment in chronological, sexual, and emotional history when Whitman expressed that same need. I would like to situate Whitman among them as one among the multitudes he claimed to contain, as one among the many young men whose midnight orgies he claimed to have joined, midnight orgies that, both in fact and fantasy, are as richly described in this confessional prose as they are in Whitman's passionate text.

The texts are given in their subjects' own words or in Ellis' or Symonds' paraphrase. They sometimes identify the respondents by initials and age—C. M. aged 32, R. S. aged 31, T. D. aged 20. The youngest is 20, the oldest in his seventies. Most were in the middle years when the book was published in 1897, though Ellis and Symonds had been collecting material for it for some years before that. An occasional geographical or ancestral point of origin is offered—"Highlander," "Of lowland Scotch parentage," "American of French descent," "Englishman, born in Paris." Sometimes an identifying profession is supplied—"Physician," "Engaged in business," "Now at University," "Artist," "Government official," "Employed in a workshop," "An actor," "Without profession," "Of Independent means," "a brain worker," a "clerk," all sorts and conditions of men.

The lives are remarkably detailed. The subjects describe themselves in youth, tell when they first discovered an attraction to their own sex—it is usually very early—candidly detail their relationship with masturbation and with other boys, and reveal the time, place, details, and often the partner of their first homosexual experience. They detail also their fantasies and report their erotic dreams, paint pictures of ideal friends and describe real ones. They report their sexual prejudices and their sexual preferences, reveal their attitude toward women, and make powerful assertions about the morality and the nature of homosexuality. Along the way they speculate about the relationship of homosexuality to art, music, or literature, about the possibility of long-term homosexual relationships, and about the problem of social attitudes toward the lives they lead and the passions they embrace. The cumulative effect of these voices is to describe the categories, customs, myths, and fantasies of one who we could well fantasize to be a composite comrade, one whose eye might have offered love to a passing poet.

The lives in this book span the century. The oldest, discovering sexuality at about the time Whitman was born, claims that when he was between 6 and 8, sometime in the late 1820s, "the sight of the naked body of young men in a rowing match on the river caused great commotion" (case 27). We can recall a similar commotion that affected Thoreau in similar circumstances, and perhaps the same feeling prompted Whitman to become the twenty-ninth bather. One of the youngest respondents rather proudly lets us know that by the time he was 19, just about the time of Whitman's death, he had "had relationships with about one hundred boys." He names none of them, but that is no where near as many as Whitman names in his notebooks or in the catalogs in his poetry. Another man in his thirties, probably born at about the time Whitman published *Leaves of Grass,* discloses that at the age of twenty-four, "I began to understand the relationship of the physical phenomena of sex to its intellectual and imaginative manifestation. . . . it was the study of Walt Whitman's *Leaves of Grass* that first brought me light upon this question" (13). That "question" of course is the homosexual question.In his own case study, John Addington Symonds reveals that this was the same question that began to incomprehensibly torment him in his earliest years and that became clear to him in an intellectual revelation at 18 when he read Plato to discover that "his own nature had been revealed." Long before his death, he came to a settled and comfortable position concerning the question, when he too read Whitman and found in "Whitman" the sexual signifier that allowed him to conclude "that his sexual dealings with men have been thoroughly wholesome to himself, largely increasing his physical, moral, and intellectual energy, and not injurious to others" (25).

In the cases that Symonds and Ellis collected and that Ellis finally included in his book in 1897 — Symonds died in 1893 and his literary executor insisted that the first edition bearing Symonds' name be suppressed and his name deleted from later editions — we can see that men's passion for homosexual attachments and attraction to their own sex is neither a late nor an artificial occurrence. It is present early, and most of them feel it is congenital. In one case "homosexual desires began at puberty" (4), and another notes that "at the age of 8 or 9 . . . I felt a friendly attraction toward my own sex and this developed after the age of puberty into a passionate sense of love" (7). One young man recalled that "at the age of five I recollect having a sexual dream connected with a railway porter. It afforded me great pleasure to recall this dream, and about that time I discovered a method of self-gratification (there is not much teaching required in these matters!)" (8). A university student explains that "when I was 10 . . . I first began to form attachments with other boys of my own age, in which I always had great regard to physical beauty" (11). The young man who had relations with a hundred boys by the time he was 19 quite precociously "at the age of 4 first became conscious of an attraction for older males" (12), while a 38-year-old Scotchman began pastoral duties so early that "soon after 5 he became so enamored of a young shepherd that the boy had to be sent away" (17). An Englishmen was "attracted to men as far back as he could remember" (18). Another confesses that his "homosexual desires began so early that it is impossible to trace them" (21), and for an Englishman, tellingly "born in Paris," his "earliest recollections show an attraction for males" (23). Symonds himself is quite specific. At about the age of 8, "he became subject to curious half-waking dreams. In these he imagined himself the servant of several adult naked sailors: he crouched between their thighs and called himself their dirty pig, and by their orders he performed services for their genitals and buttocks which he contemplated with relish" (25). I need hardly point out the place that adult sailors have in the mythology of Melville, and I have shown Taylor's desire to "take the sunburnt sailor" to his breast. Whitman, of course, instead of sailors, enshrined street roughs and drivers as his fantasized icons, but for the Fierce Wrestler he surely performs at least textual services that surpass even those of Symonds' both in imagination and detail.

In *Specimen Days* Whitman reports that in his teens, when wandering the beaches of Long Island, "I . . . met the strange, unkempt, half-barbarous herdsmen, at that time living there entirely aloof from society or civilization." He also "spent intervals many years, all seasons . . . absorbing characters, the bay men, farmers, pilots — always had a plentiful acquaintance with the latter, and with fishermen — went every summer on sailing trips" (*PW* 10–12). The implication is not that association with older men is necessarily any sign of nascent homosexuality, but Whitman did find the company of such men fascinating early on, and they appear shortly afterward in his fiction, either as roughs and ready heroes or as the protectors — and sometimes the persecutors — of younger boys. Allen describes Whitman's boyhood: "His companions were outdoor men, especially uneducated herdsmen, farmers and fishermen. . . . he always felt at home with them and they took readily to him, willingly feeding and sheltering him."[51] One of Ellis' respondents, a mysterious "man of letters" who offers the longest, the most eloquent, and the most detailed description of himself, reports: "At the age of 14 I went . . . to a farm house where I was allowed to mingle familiarly with the farm laborers, a set of muscular young men. I became a great favorite, and having childish caressing manners . . . I was allowed to take many liberties with them . . . I used to sit on their knees and caress them and hug them to my heart's content. One of them used to return my caresses and squeezes and once allowed me to put my hand under his shirt" (26).

Compare this episode and Symonds' dream of being a servant to sailors to some of Whitman's early encounters with men. Whitman invokes such erotic adventures when he writes in section 1 of "The Sleepers" about that "gay gang of blackguards" who "make me a pet besides, and surround me, and lead me and run ahead when I walk, / and lift their cunning covers and signify me with outstretched arms." In what may be an earlier notebook version of these last lines, he adds: "They undress delight." In section 17 of "Poem of Joys" (Bowers 203), Whitman also translates these feelings into a reversal of the situation in which he becomes to boys what men had been to him: "Behold me well clothed going gayly or returning in the afternoon, my brood of tough boys accompanying me, / My brood of grown and part grown boys, who love to be with no one else so well as they love to be with me, / By day to work with me, and by night to sleep with me."

In *Specimen Days* Whitman describes how he enjoyed "wandering the solitary crossroads" of Long Island and the "long, bare unfrequented shore, which I had all to myself" (*PW* 10–12). Meditations about solitude and records of solitary moments comprise a good deal of the texture of Whitman's writing; he is after all the "solitary singer," a lonely dreamer. For Ellis' respondents, loneliness and youthful solitude is a major text, and similar temperaments seem to be possessed by different men. One man describes himself as having a "strongly nervous temperament . . . and sensitive." An "American, of French descent, aged 31," reports that "I was a dreamy indolent boy. . . . I was passionately fond of flowers, loved to be in the woods and alone" (9). An Englishmen was "a delicate, effeminate boy," while another was "always delicate and averse to rough games." Symonds was "a weakly and highly nervous child, subject to night terrors and somnambulism, excessive shyness and religious disquietude" (25). An Englishman in his seventies says that at school he was "shy and reserved, and had no particular intimacy with anyone, though he desired it" (27). Case 10 says that "as a child . . . I lived too much alone and spent most of my time in reading. I was very sensitive to ridicule . . . so that I shrank from the other boys, while at the same time I longed for their friendship. I withdrew into myself and indulged my imagination." Allen says of Whitman, "we hear of no special friends or boon companions," and he reports that Whitman felt that his childhood was unhappy.[52] These fragments from Ellis' text, if nothing else, support the received clichés of homosexual boyhood—lonely boys, self-obsessed and inward turning, idolizing and vaguely eroticizing older heroes, caught up in worlds of private imagining, already embarking on strange seas of thought, and happiest when alone in a solitary fastness yet always obsessed by the seemingly unobtainable ideal friend. The American, who loved to be in the "woods and alone," was "constantly falling in love with handsome boys whom I never knew; nor did I try to mix in their company, for I was abashed before them . . . sometimes I played with girls . . . but I cared for them little or not at all" (9).

In Whitman's early poetry and fiction, his characters are young men and boys between the ages of 12 and 17. They are generally orphans or sons of widowed mothers. They can mostly be described by gathering adjectives from the tales. Tim is "slight, fair-looking," too "unearthly fair for health." Reuben is "naturally delicate." Quincy is quiet and "gentle." An older boy is described as "beautiful in his manly proportions," another as a "beautiful youth." They are temperamentally similar—quiet, shy, gentle, dreamy, indolent, and withdrawn. Of course there are also the roughs, like Wild Frank, who expand Whitman's soul. In the poetry one youth looks for one heart to love, while another, in "Each Has His Grief," is a "wearied child." The "obscure youth" of "Ambition" is lonely and "sick at heart." The telling notebook fragment about the "Singular Young Man" could well be included in Ellis, for this young man who "remained much by himself. . . . most of the time he remained silent" is temperamentally a brother to Ellis' other lonely youths. This solitary lounger will become the poet of "Proto-Leaf" (1860), who Whitman describes in sections 1–2 as one who has "withdrawn to muse and meditate in some deep recess." He identifies with the hermit thrush, "solitary, singing in the West," for he has learned the meaning of "what has come to the surface after so many throes and convulsions."

In nearly every case Ellis records, there is one common thread, and that is, at the strongest, repugnance toward, and at the least disinterest in, women. While most of these men seem appalled by the prospect of sexual relations with women, many of these accounts throw some disabusing light on the notion that homosexual men dislike women as social or intellectual companions. They are not women haters, even though they are lovers of men. Many express sentiments similar to those in case 5: "He is very good

friends with women, but has strong repulsion from sexual relations with them, or any approach to it." Case 4 is similar: "While
very friendly and intimate with women of all ages, he is instantly
repelled by any display of sexual affection on their side." An
Englishmen, who describes himself as "high bred, refined, and
sensitive," says that "I am capable of a great regard and liking for
women when I deem them worthy of it; otherwise I have a strong
repulsion to them, and have never touched a woman" (15). Another
Englishman "intellectually likes women very much," though sexually they "do not attract him" (18). The Parisian born Englishman
feels "absolute indifference" to women. "He admires them in the
same way as one admires beautiful scenery" (23). Edward Carpenter reports that "my feeling toward the female sex was one of
indifference and later . . . one of absolute repulsion" (7). One man
has had dreams about women, though "the latter have usually
partaken somewhat of the nature of nightmares" (8), while Symonds, though he dreamed of naked sailors, and as we shall see later
on, of beautiful young men, "never dreamed of women, never
sought their society, never felt the slightest sexual excitement in
their presence, never idealized them" (25). The emphatic American
can have the last word:

> I never in my life had any sexual feeling for a woman, nor
> any sexual connection with any woman whatsoever. The very
> thought of such a thing is excessively repugnant and disgusting
> to me. . . . I am not attracted by young women in any way.
> Even their physical beauty has little or no charm for me, and I
> often wonder how men can be affected by it. On the other hand
> I am not a woman hater, and have several strong friends of the
> opposite sex. They are however, women older than myself, and
> our friendship is based solely on certain intellectual or aesthetic
> tastes we have in common. (9)

Whitman had several strong friends of the opposite sex, and he
was not a woman hater. These women were mostly older women or
mothers, intellectuals or other men's wives, and his social relations
with them were similar to those described by the American
respondent. But search his texts for any lengthy descriptions of the
"physical beauty" of women, and the search will turn up very
little; such beauty does not affect his texts. In a notebook entry, he
wondered how men could be affected by the "invalid" and "tran-

sient" love of women (*NUPM* 1:341). He did, of course idealize one woman, and he might well have identified with the 25-year-old man "employed in an ordinary workshop," who "lives in the back alley of a large town in which he was born and bred. . . . His mother is a big masculine woman and he is much attracted to her. Father is slight and weakly. He has seven brothers and one sister. . . . He declares he never cared for any woman except his mother, and that he could not endure to sleep with a woman" (20). In a late notebook, Whitman wrote about his mother: "She was . . . of splendid physique"—an odd phrase with which to describe a woman—"and health, a hard worker, and had eight children . . . no tenderer and more invariable tie was ever between mother and son than the love between her and W. W." (*NUPM* 1:28). If texts can inseminate one another, then these two texts can have useful congress together.

For many of these men erotic dreams were confusing, though not confused, indicators of desire, and once desire was clear, physical gratification was not far to seek, nor was much teaching needed to learn its methods. Thus, masturbation plays as important a part in the accounts these young men tell of their early triumphs over self-discord as it plays in Whitman's notebooks and poetry. Masturbation, received medical and moral opinion preached, was immoral, sinful, and dangerous, injurious to health and sanity, a secret sin and a terrible curse, an incurable addiction, and a pathway to hell, and even worse, a probable indicator and cause of homosexuality.[53] Yet according to Ellis' studies, despite the prohibitions of priests and parents, these men did it and persevered in it not only as a solitary vice but as a shared activity between strangers, friends, and lovers and as a communal delight in groups. While it is perfectly clear from these studies that all the other forms of sexual activity in which men can engage were engaged in, masturbation seems to have been the most common and the most widely preferred, there being attendant upon it neither the occasional repugnance connected to what they all call "paedicatio" nor the rarer unwillingness to engage in fellatio. Whitman describes both anal and oral sex in his poetry and notebooks, yet masturbatory autoeroticism is as central to his sexual practices as it is to those of the men on Ellis' pages, who as eagerly as Whitman set the fountains of love flowing.

It is not that they were not warned, however. The father of a 34 year old artist tells him that "if you do this, you will never be able to use your penis with a woman." While this may have been a stronger argument to continue rather than to desist, the young man's doctor genially assured him that "masturbation is death. A number of young men come to me with the same story. I tell them they are killing themselves, and you will kill yourself too" (13). But despite the vast amount of advice and medical literature, which is essentially summarized by these two comments, masturbation was the one thing few of these men could resist, Indeed it seemed to be a spontaneous discovery: "I discovered—entirely by myself—the act of masturbation" (13). Or it was happened upon "apparently by instinct" or "quite naturally" or was "spontaneously acquired" (11). All of these testimonies suggest doubt as to its unnatural origins. "In early youth," one man "masturbated to excess, sometimes three times daily" (3). Some were more careful, practicing "onanism to a limited extent" (4) or "only occasionally, partly from fear of ill effects, partly because the practice gives him no real satisfaction" (3). Others embraced it eagerly. The American declared: "Once while bathing I found that a pleasant feeling came with touching the sexual organs. It was not long before I was confirmed in the habit. At first I practiced it seldom, but afterward much more frequently" (9). The university student may have been influenced by a father's stern advice, for "at 12 [I] learned masturbation, apparently by instinct, and I regret to say, practiced it to excess for the next seven years, always secretly and with shame. . . . masturbation was often practiced daily" (11). A 27-year-old Scotchman seems to be more comfortable with it: "I am satisfied with the pleasure of the hand, and indeed prefer it. The utter abandon of the person with me is necessary to any degree of pleasure and the acts must be mutual," (22) The Scotchman who loved the shepherd boy "practiced masturbation many years before puberty and attaches importance to this as a factor in the evolution of his homosexual life" (17). Perhaps while the Scotchman dreamed of his shepherd, an Englishman of about the same age masturbated "in a sort of dreamy state between sleeping and waking." His masturbation was "accompanied by lascivious thoughts and dreams of men" (28). Dreams of men and of "full sized," "masculine landscapes" enrich Whitman's poetry. When he dreams of men, the floodgates are unclenched, and "rich showering rain" and "seas of bright juice" powerfully jet themselves, suffusing even heaven.

What Whitman may have specifically done during the midnight orgies of young men is forever hidden from us, but an

Irishman is not reticent about his orgies: "At about the age of 14 he practiced masturbation with other boys of the same age and also had much pleasure in bed with an uncle with whom the same thing was practiced. Later he practiced masturbation with every boy or man with whom he was on terms of intimacy; to have been in bed with anyone without anything of the sort taking place would have been impossible" (19). It might occur to the perceptive reader familiar with the extent and obsessiveness of Whitman's masturbation imagery that perhaps those young men with whom Whitman "slept" may have encountered some such similar preoccupation. One of Ellis' subjects writes: "Inverts are, I think, naturally more liable to indulge in self-gratification than normal people, partly because of the perpetual suppression and disappointment of their desires, and also because of the fact that they actually possess in themselves the desired form of the male."[54] As a gloss on this I refer to section 28 of "Song of Myself": "Is this then a touch? . . . quivering me to a new identity. . . . Treacherous tip of me reaching and crowding to help them, / My flesh and my blood playing out lightning, to strike *what is hardly different from myself*" (my italics).

Masturbation provided the physical occasion for erotic fantasy. Whitman was able to translate these fantasies into poetry, though for many—most—of Ellis' subjects, these pages are the only repository for descriptions of that "dreamy state between sleeping and waking" in which thoughts and dreams of men were so lasciviously entertained, the same dreamy state, by the way, that Whitman said that Melville's *Typee* induced. A half-waking dream that C. M. recounts occurred on a boat called, wonderfully, *The Friends,* perhaps one of the same fleet as "The Flirt" on which Whitman encountered the "handsome" and "manly" Sumatra boy. On this amorous bark the up and down motion of the waves would "suggest to him that a young man lover was lying supine, and that he was himself sitting astride and masturbating him" (3). The man who discovered masturbation while "having a sexual dream about a railway porter" is joined by another, also responding to a costume, who has fantasies about circus performers: "I longed to see them naked, without their tights, and used to lie awake at night thinking of them and longing to be loved and embraced by them. A certain bareback rider, a sort of jockey, used especially to please me on account of his handsome legs, which were clothed in fleshlings to his waist, leaving his beautiful loins uncovered by a breech clout." He also "used to tell myself endless stories of a visionary castle inhabited by beautiful boys." Like Thoreau and Whitman, he "used to take great pleasure in watching men and boys in swimming" (9). An Englishman in his fifties who is a government official "finds that uniform or livery (soldiers, sailors, grooms and footmen) are a temptation" (16) in dreams as well as life. Symonds, who we have already discovered dreaming of naked adult sailors, also "enjoyed visions of beautiful young men," more specifically of "the large erect naked organs of grooms or peasants" (25). In Whitman's texts the phallic image is such an icon. "Sheathed hooded sharp-toothed touch" is the large naked and erect organ of the Fierce Wrestler.

Case 26—how very much would we like to know who these men were—seems to have spent his life in an erotic dreamland. He desired in his dreams to "nestle between the thighs or have my face pressed against the hinder parts of my object of [male] worship." One of his earliest dreams was to "imagine myself in a tank with three lovers floating in the water above me. From this position I visited their limbs in turn; the attraction rested in thighs and buttocks only." Other recurrent fantasies often took place in church, where "the clergyman, whose sermon I did not listen to, supplied me with an occasion for reverie on the charms his person would have for me under other circumstances." One vivid imagined circumstance was the notion "of a serried rank of congregated thighs across which I lay and was dragged. . . . I was able in my imagination to lie in the thick and stress of conglomerated deliciousness of thighs struggling to hold me; I was able to imagine at least six bodies encircling me with passionate contact." We can conflate figures from Ellis' pages—footmen, grooms, peasants, sailors, and policemen—with icons from Whitman's poetry— roughs, strangers, loving loungers, bush boys, fierce wrestlers, giant swimmers—and they become interchangeable but equally desired. Symonds' naked sailors and Whitman's twenty-eight bathers consort together, just as the sexual mastery that the dreamer I have just mentioned so much desires echoes Whitman's own longing for the powerful discipline of naked sharptoothed touch. This dreamer who imagined his lovers floating in the water above him bathes in the same erotic waters as Whitman's "beautiful gigantic swimmer swimming naked" in "The Sleepers," and swims with the swimmer of "I Sing the Body Electric" who in the "salt transparent greenshine . . . lies on his back and rolls silently with the heave of the waters." Whitman's own "congregated deliciousness of thighs" are young men who "float on their backs, their white bellies bulge to the sun, they do not ask who seizes fast to them." We of course want to ask. In the dreams and fantasies Ellis records, there is a parallel world in which an answer can be found. The twilight world of erotic fantasy provided a fertile ground out of which could grow what Thoreau called the "young buds of manhood," buds Whitman imagined as "masculine full sized and golden." In these histories, the subjects describe their ideal friends and tell what about other men attracts them. Whitman is very clear about what attracts him; he lists pages of examples in his notebooks and offers catalogs of men in his poems. A perfect man is "like a beautiful poem," he says, conflating his two most powerful passions into a single image. The descriptions of unknown lovers in Ellis' text are also eloquent. The remarkable R. S., the American, confesses almost breathlessly that

the chief characteristic of my tendency is an overpowering admiration for male beauty. . . .I have absolutely no words to tell you how powerfully such beauty affects me. Moral and intellectual worth is, I know, of greater value, but physical beauty I see more clearly and it appears to me to be the most vivid (if not the most perfect) manifestation of the divine. . . .It may be that my rage for male loveliness is only another outbreaking of the old Platonic mania, for as time goes on I find that I long less for the actual youth before me, and more and more for some ideal, perfect being whose bodily splendor and loving heart are the realities whose reflections only we see in this cave of shadows. (9)

If the initials belonging to this literate man were not R. S., one might almost suspect that they were E. T., R. W. E., or H. D. T.

Near the end of *Calamus*, Whitman reveals that an athlete is enamored of him. Athletes are fixed stars in the cosmos of homosexual desire. Ellis says of one man that "his male ideal has . . . for some years tended toward a healthy, well-developed, athletic or out of door working type, intelligent and sympathetic, but not especially intellectual" (4). Whitman's description of his omnibus drivers (who "entered into the gestation of *Leaves of Grass*") as having "immense qualities . . . in their simple good will and honor . . . not only for comradeship and sometimes affection. . . ." echoes here. Edward Carpenter, who went to America to see

Whitman and was somewhat taken it appears by the working class
Harry Stafford, says that "now, at the age of 37 — my ideal love is a
powerful strongly built man of my own age or rather younger,
preferably of the working class. Though having solid sense and
character, he need not be specially intellectual. If endowed in the
latter way, he must not be too glib or refined. Anything effeminate
in a man, or anything of the cheap intellectual style repels me very
decisively" (7). Whitman was also suspicious of intellect in men he
loved. An ideal friend is pictured in *Calamus* 29. He is the "youth
who loves me and whom I love." The two sit together "speaking
little, perhaps not a word." Whitman's lovers are rarely verbal.
They pick him out by "signs"; they "silently" approach; they
demonstrate rather than declare their love. And as he shows in
section 47 of "Song of Myself," they are never effeminate, these
athletes, these tough boys, these roughs:

> I am the teacher of athletes. . . .
> . . . .
> The young mechanic is closest to me. . . .he knows me
>   pretty well,
> The woodman that takes his axe and jug with him shall take
>   me with him all day,
> The farm boy ploughing in the field feels good at the sound
>   of my voice. . . .
> . . . .
> My face rubs to the hunter's face when he lies down alone in
>   his blanket.

Athletes are not the only objects of desire, just as they have not
always solely been so for Whitman. Case 18 is attracted to "youths
from 18 to 24, slightly built, and pretty rather than handsome. Big
muscular men have little attraction for him." For the Irishman,
youths between the ages of 18 and 25 must have "an intelligent eye,
a voluptuous mouth" (19). An English actor is "attracted to individuals who are slightly effeminate, especially boys between the
ages of 14 and 18" (20), and a 27-year-old Scotchman prefers "boys
about 17 to 20 years of age. . . . I like the smooth hairless face and
body of a boy: a slight feminine trait adds to the attraction, but it
must not be too developed. I prefer dark boys to fair" (22). The
Parisian born Englishman, no doubt corrupted by perfidious Gaul,
prefers boys who are "fair, smooth-skinned, gentle, rather girlish

and effeminate with the effeminacy of the ingenue not the cocotte. His favorite must be submissive and womanly; he likes to be the man and the master" (23). It would do no harm here to recall the final scene of "The Child's Champion," wherein young Charles, aged 14, rests securely in the embrace of his handsome protector Langton who "folded his arms around him, and while he slept, the boy's cheek rested on his bosom" (*EPF* 76 n. 38).

Symonds, like Whitman, liked roughs (which is of course one reason why he liked Whitman), sailors, grooms, and peasants. He consorted in later life with his own version of an omnibus driver, the strikingly handsome gondolier Angelo Fusato. Symonds "has always loved men younger than himself . . . the men he sought are invariably persons of a lower social rank than his own. . . . he is not attracted by uniforms but seeks some uncontaminated child of Nature." Symonds surely found Whitman's poetry filled with children of nature—two boys together clinging and that dark-cheeked bush boy—for they appealed to Whitman as much as they did to the woeful Victorian, who first read Whitman in 1866. From reading Whitman, Symonds says, "I imbibed a strong democratic enthusiasm, a sense of the dignity and beauty and glory of simple healthy men."[55] Simple healthy men are Whitman's ideals too. The men in the notebooks, three-hundred or more of them in an 1857 notebook, are all simple and healthy. There are Tom Riley, a "handsome Irish fighter," Arthur, "big round sandy hair coarse, open," Jack "with beautiful beard," and Bill, "big dark complexioned." There are Johnny with "full eyes and liquid," Jack, a "big young fellow," and Tom Egbert, "sailor open neck" (did Whitman know about that telltale open neck, which Ellis' earlier reported as a presumed sign of the invert?). There are boys too: Justin, 17, Mike Butler, 18, Jay, 19, and August, 16. The descriptions sometimes speak to masculine power"—"coarse" or "strong"—and other times to other kinds of sensuality—"liquid eyes," "full eyes," "goodlooking." There are curiosities: Bob the "hermaphrodite" or the actor Ansel Jenning's "old boy friend." Among the three hundred capsule descriptions in this notebook alone, we never find estimates of "moral and intellectual worth." Like his fellow American (Case 9), Whitman looks instead for physical beauty, perhaps also seeing it as "the most vivid manifestation of the divine," perhaps as nothing so metaphysical. In the poems, these men all in some way or another appear, flesh made words. There they have no flaws; they are perfect men, like poems.

Ideal friends seem to be the creations of desire, and communion with the ideal is most often achieved, so these stories say,
through rather direct physical expression. Masturbation and the
imagined ideal friend go, as it were, hand in hand. But upon
gaining a sexual majority, few of these men were content to
languish in the dream world. They sought real life instead, sometimes obsessively choosing paths untrodden, hoping that their
dreams would become real flesh, their fantasies real men. Most of
them seem to be, as case 3 elegantly puts it, "tormented by the
great wish." This vague formula precisely points to sex. It is as
vague a formulation as Whitman used when he described his great
wish as something "that is in me. . . .I do not know what it
is. . . .but I know it is in me. . . . it is a word unsaid. . . . to it the
creation is the friend whose embracing awakes me." To be embraced by a friend was the great wish of case 3, more explicitly, to
have sex with a man. His preferential activity was limited to
mutual masturbation. When case 3 was 20, he and another young
man "went through a portion of those ceremonies which, unlike
fellatio or *paedicatio* are not repellant to my more esthetic nature.
Neither is mutual masturbation (with the right person) at all
disagreeable to me." A 33-year-old "manual worker" uses his
hands only for work and resists putting himself in anyone else's.
Though his "homosexual feeling is clear and defined," he seems to
avoid actual sex. He has a relationship with a man, however "so far
as the physical act is concerned this relationship is definitely not
sexual, but it is of the most intimately possible kind, and the
absence of the physical act is probably due largely to circumstances. There is no conscious desire for the physical act for its own
sake, and the existing harmony and satisfaction is described as very
complete. There is, however, no repulsion to the physical side, and
he regards the whole relationship as quite natural" (1).

The vital information in this description of a non-sexual
homosexual relationship is the observation that the subject's homosexuality is clearly defined, defined without physical manifestation, and self-defined by the subject. This young man, who is
"mentally bright, though not highly educated, a keen sportsman,
and in general a good example of an all-round healthy Englishman," just the kind of man Whitman liked to picture, stands at one
end of a homoerotic spectrum, a spectrum that extends from his
contented abstinence to examples of others' obsessive pursuits of
the pleasures of the great wish, from undefined longings to specific

and precise descriptions of homosexual experience. The elements of this spectrum, and the men whose lives construct it, may cast some light on Whitman's own attempt to answer the question "What is the meaning anyhow of my [love] [attachment] adhesiveness [for] toward others?" It may also intimate what he hoped to find in the "guarded tents of each other's most interior love." Just as in the case of the all-round Englishman, where sex was not the defining element in his homosexual relationships, to try and find such evidence as a sole confirmation of Whitman's sexuality asks the wrong homosexual question, just as the location of any firm evidence to prove the existence of his mythical children or to identify that equally mythical and mysterious woman in New Orleans would shed no light at all on the real direction of his desires. It may well be that Whitman's sexual life mirrors that of this young Englishman. Or perhaps in the confidences of one of his English disciples there can be found another reflective image and echo. Edward Carpenter, that English Whitman, who we recall liked working class men and indeed lived with one in a happy relationship, has "never had to do with actual pederasty, so called," by which I presume he means anal intercourse. He continues, "my chief desire in love is bodily nearness or contact, as to sleep naked with a naked friend; the specially sexual, though urgent enough, seems a secondary matter. Pederasty, either active or passive, might seem in place to me with one I loved very devotedly and who also loved me to that degree, but I think not otherwise. . .and I think that the actual sex gratifications (whatever they may be) probably hold a less important place in this love than in the other [heterosexual love]" (7).

Indeed, a large number of men seem to be uninterested in those acts by which homosexuality is usually defined: "We never attempted, nor had any inclination to attempt to penetrate the anus, from this practice I used to invariably find that we shrank as unnatural and beastly" (14). Another Englishman does not "practice *paedicatio* and very rarely *fellatio*. I like embracements, spooning, and real kissing, followed by mutual masturbation" (15). This man was a boy of responding kisses surely, while another, having a young officer get into bed with him and have "him inter-femora several times . . . always desired that done to him with some violence, or to take himself the active part. . . . he abhors *paedicatio*" (16). The literate young university student thinks that "naked contact would suffice, in any case intercrurral connection. *Paedica-*

tio and *fellatio* I abhor" (11). So too does another Englishman, aged 35, who "finds that mere contact of body to body is sufficient to produce the physical effects and pleasure of coition. *Paedicatio* disgusts him, unless he is passionately devoted to a person who insists upon it, and even then he feels it to be debasing and bestial. *Fellatio* excites him intensely" (18).

Fellatio enters into the experience of several men. One man has "been an active participant in *paedicatio* and has tried the passive role out of curiosity, but prefers *fellatio*" (27). A 70-year-old Englishman "is exclusively passive; also likes mutual fellatio." A 34-year-old Englishman "likes *paedicatio* to be practiced on him, but he does not care to practice it." Fellatio, however, he likes either actively or passively, and he is also able to satisfy himself by intercrurral connection" (29). For the Parisian born Englishman, as for many of these respondents, "*paedicatio* is the satisfaction he prefers, provided he takes the active part, never the passive role" (23). While preferring educated men, a thirty-four-year-old Englishman says, "I like soldiers and policemen for the actual sensuality of the moment. . . . I like tall, handsome men, (the larger they are in stature the better), very strong and as sensual as I can get them to be, and I like them to practice paedicatio on me and I prefer it done roughly, and I rather prefer men who are carried away by their lust and bite my flesh at the supreme moment and I rather like the pain inflicted by their teeth and elsewhere" (29).

In a variant manuscript version of section 28 of "Song of Myself," Whitman exclaims: "Grip'd wrestler! do you keep the heaviest pull for the last? / Must you bite with your teeth at parting? (Trigg 568). As a nineteenth-century sex researcher of more prudish sentiments than Ellis' might have said, we must draw a veil over any further revelation of such facts as these and close the flap on the guarded tents of interior love. But before doing so, let men of letters have some last words about sex. Symonds seems to be the most usefully representative because of the variety of his sexual experiences:

The methods of satisfaction have varied with the phases of his passion. At first they were romantic and Platonic, when a hand touch, a rare kiss or mere presence sufficed. In the second period sleeping side by side, inspection of the naked body of the loved man, embracements, and occasional emissions after prolonged contact. In the third period the gratification became more frank-

ly sensual. It took every shape: mutual masturbation, intercrurral coitus, fellatio, irrumatio, occasionally paedicatio. . . .he
himself always plays the masculine active part. (25)

That "man of letters"—Case 26—shares with Whitman an
obsessive desire to precisely enumerate the landmarks in these
masculine landscapes: "I developed a liking for imagining myself
between two lovers. . . . it was my habit to analyze as minutely as
possible those who attracted me. I studied with attention their
hands, the wrists . . . I estimated the comparative size of the
generative organs, the formation of the thighs and buttocks, and
thus constructed a presentiment of the whole man." He describes
himself as lost, though he did not wander alone, in a "perfect maze
of promiscuity," a maze in which Whitman too may have wandered when he traversed the inviting streets of Brooklyn and
Manhattan, cataloged the eyes offering love, and listed and carefully described the young men who also wandered there, taking
from liquid eyes or a beautiful dark beard a presentiment of the
whole man.

This last writer also has other affinities with Whitman. He is a
master of a luxuriant and erotic style in which he describes how,
from the age of 14 until his twenties, he had been in a kind of sexual
bondage to "a schoolfellow, a few years my senior . . . who took a
particular delight in inflicting pain on me." A few years later, when
he again encountered the person, "now a man having reached
majority," their relationship was resumed. He describes this first
of many encounters: "He put me into his bed while he undressed
himself and came toward me in perfect nudity. In a moment we
were in each other's arms and the deliciousness of that moment
intoxicated me." But apparently he had not achieved orgasm until
"at another meeting . . . I had been allowed to prolong my embrace and to act, indeed upon my full instincts. . . . I felt the
coming of something acutely impending; I took courage in my
hands and went boldly forward, In another moment I had hold of
the mysterious secret of masculine energy, to which all my years of
delirious imaginings had been but as a waiting at the threshold, the
knocking on a closed door." At last, and at the last meeting
between them,

he proposed to attempt an act which I had not previously considered possible, far less had I heard that it was considered the

worst criminal connection that could take place. I had a slight
fear of pain but was willing to gratify him, and for the first time
found in my submission a union of the two amative instincts
which had before undisputed sway in me: the instinct for tenderness and the instinct for cruelty. . . . My delight was enormous;
I was filled with emotions. I have no words to describe the extraordinary charm of the warm smooth flesh upon mine and the
rougher contact of the hairy parts. Yet I was conscious, even at
the time, that this was but the physical side of pleasure, and that
he was not and never could be one whom I might truly be said
to love.

This eloquent description of first ejaculations and of the overpowering effects of penetration can be comparatively placed next to
Whitman's own supremely celebratory account of what I am sure is
a similar event—engaged in with a sexual opponent quite as fierce
as that respondent's cruel though irresistible lover—which begins:
"Fierce Wrestler! do you keep your heaviest grip for the last?"
Whitman revels in tenderness and cruelty in these lines, and like his
anonymous comrade in Ellis, he too is filled with enormous
delight: "I did not think I was big enough for such ecstasy"
(*NUPM* 1: 77).

Before departing from these fascinating men who generously
revealed their homosexual feelings and sexual experiences, it is
worth asking what they felt about homosexuality itself. This is the
inevitable homosexual question, addressing not only propriety or
morality but the nagging queries of self-doubt and self-esteem that
are inspired in anyone whose deepest desires embrace what the
world rejects with scorn or disgust. From what sources, outside of
their own private needs and sexual experiments, in history, literature, or life, did they derive explanation of and justification for
their desire? What convictions support the fact that few of these
men reject or desist from their hopeful pursuit of the great wish,
from their attempt to answer their own homosexual question?

These men whose sexual journeys so interestingly parallel
Whitman's own sexual pilgrimage, all of them walking the same
untrodden path together, mostly lived their active sexual lives in
the years shortly after Whitman had offered, to a largely uncom-
prehending world, the charts and maps he had drawn of his special
masculine landscapes. His gospel could well have been preached to
all of them. But if not Whitman's poetry, then homosexual litera-

ture does seem to play some part in these records, raising concious-
ness, as we say, that a city of lovers might exist, offering to these
men, as we have seen it offered to others, a foundation and even a
justification for what they all describe as the overwhelming and
inevitable impulses of desire. I have mentioned case 13 whose
"study of Walt Whitman's *Leaves of Grass* first brought me light
upon this question." We know that Symonds too found Whitman a
revelation. Unhappily, that wonderfully literate American of French
descent, aged 31, who like Whitman loved to be in the woods
alone, does not mention his countryman, though in his entry he
does use "manly love," Whitman's phrase. Instead, in "some
writings of Mr. John Addington Symonds," he discovered "certain
allusions" that coupled with "recent experiences . . . stirred me to
a full consciousness of my inverted nature." Certain paintings and
sculptures affected him — "some Praxitilean demi-god, or Flan-
drin's naked brooding boy." For him the "old Platonic mania" was
as powerful as the great wish (9). The university student finds
confirmation in art and literature too: "Male Greek statuary, and
the Phaedrus of Plato have a great, though only confirmatory
influence on my feelings. My ideal is that of Theocritus XIII,
wherein Hercules was bringing Hylas to the perfect measure of a
man" (11). For Symonds, "all art which represented handsome
males deeply stirred him," and when he read Plato, "a new world
opened, and he felt that his own nature had been revealed." So too
the Englishman, born at about the same time as Whitman, added
an aesthetic dimension to his sexual emancipation when he "became familiar with pictures, admired male figures of Italian mar-
tyrs, and the full rich forms of Antinous" (27). We may remember
that when Bronson Alcott and Thoreau visited Whitman they
noticed that he had pasted on the wall prints of Hercules, and
Bacchus and a satyr, masculine and sexual subjects certainly,
homosexual subjects as well.[56]

The Englishman mentioned above also read with avidity "the
Arabian Nights and other Oriental tales, translations from the
classics, Suetonius, Petronius," finding in them what Whitman
seemed to find in Taylor's oriental tales. The literary man whose
sexual bondage was so spectacular, engaged in sado-masochistic
fantasies not only while masturbating but while reading. He says:
"I was so possessed by masculine attraction that I became a lover of
all the heroes I read of in books. Some became as vivid to me as
those with whom I was living in daily contact. For a time I became

an ardent lover of Napoleon (the incident of his anticipation of the
nuptials with a second wife attracting me by its impetuous brutality), of Edward I, and of Julius Caesar, Charles II I remember by a
caressing cruelty with which my imagination gifted him." Thoreau admired the ancient worthies who were also ancient exemplars
of devoted homosexual love, and Whitman loved heroes too,
reading in the literature of manly attraction, and saying so in
Calamus 28 when he describes "the brotherhood of lovers," that
other homoerotic icon, the devoted lovers of the Theban Sacred
Band.

"Long was I held by the life that exhibits itself—the usual
pleasures and aims—the intercourse to which all conform, and
which the writers celebrate / But I escape and celebrate the untold
and carefully concealed life, / I celebrate the need of the love of
Comrades." These lines, appearing in a notebook written perhaps
in 1858 (*NUPM* 1:406), are among the earliest drafts of the first
Calamus. Reworking it he added, "But now I know a life which
does not exhibit itself yet contains all the rest." Such a sentiment
would not be lost on the men who appear in Symonds' and Ellis'
text, least of all on Symonds himself. The concealed and substantial
life of homosexuality was hedged by fascination. It colored all
other concerns of life. Its presence was exciting and yet threatening, casting a stalking shadow against the moral prohibitions of the
exhibited life. To be homosexual was at once tantalizing and
impossible, the need of comrades and the need for concealment
creating a painful tension between the desire and the act. Surely
young men who were told that "a naked man is the most disgusting
spectacle on earth" or who were warned that masturbation was
"death," as were two of Ellis' respondents, might have some
questions about homosexuality. As one rather offhandedly says,
"It seems to me in this country to be forbidden that one man should
care very much about another. In fact I have heard people say that
they can't understand how one man may feel any affection for
another." Troubled by the fact that he did, the respondent went to
the doctors. Upon hearing his confession, one doctor "walked out
without a word. He would not see me again." The second doctor
"would hardly listen. He at once said that such inclinations were
unnatural, and evidently made up his mind that I was insane." The
young man concludes, "it is really a matter of psychology, not of
medicine"—recall Whitman's comment about Taylor's psychology—"and poets know more about such matters than doctors" (10).

Though English schoolboys were often presumed to be per-petually engaged in steamy homosexual adventures, and one re-spondent does describe the dormitory servant who introduced him to masturbation, it is probably just as true, as T. D. the university student says, that "at school the idea was held in abhorrence by an enormous majority, and public opinion is a strong factor" (11). Case 13 agrees: "All these things were treated by masters and boys alike as more or less unholy . . . a kiss was as unclean as *fellatio.*" Case 14 sensibly insists that "it is better to spread abroad the spirit of open comradeship which is natural to men and boys," but "against this stands the law, which is a relic of the ages gone by. It is a farce, where every public school boy knows, and in most cases practices, homosexual habits, to attach a penalty to this practice." The effects of social condemnation can be severe. Symonds, de-scribing himself, pointedly says:

He has suffered extremely throughout life owning to his senses of the difference between himself and normal human be-ings. No pleasure he has enjoyed, he declares, can equal a thou-sandth part of the pain caused by the internal consciousness of pariahdom. . . . although he has always before him the terror of discovery he is convinced his sexual dealings with men have been thoroughly wholesome to himself, largely increasing his moral, physical, and intellectual energy, and not injurious to others. He has no sense whatever of moral wrong in his actions and he regards the attitude of society toward those in his posi-tion as utterly unjust and founded upon false principles." (25)

What a relief it must have been to reject all that and openly be, as Whitman determined to be, "an example to lovers." In an early version of *Calamus* 1, Whitman at first determined only to escape and "celebrate that concealed but substantial life." But in the revision of the poem, his horizons widen, and he makes a new and more radical decision. Now he will escape entirely from the heterosexual world, reject its conformities, and sing no songs but those of manly attachment. And indeed, one after another, these men also affirm themselves as Whitman had already done. C. M., "although he has suffered so much from unsatisfied homosexual desires . . . says that he would not be prevented from being an invert by any consideration." This firm assertion is as powerful as Whitman's own when he insists that he will "never again" utter any call but the call of friends. As Carpenter asserted: "I cannot regard my sexual feelings as unnatural or abnormal, since they have disclosed themselves so perfectly naturally and spontaneously within me" (7). Whitman too spoke about natural and spontaneous disclosure and the unfolding of phallic and homoerotic roots that represent "hungering desires." He calls upon the phallic "blossoms of my breast" to remain hidden no longer since he is "determined to unbare" his breast (Bowers 72). Whitman's countryman, R. S., the young American who was stirred to consciousness by reading Symonds, is not sure of the origins but is without doubt as to the validity of his homosexuality: "I am certain that, even if it were possible, I would not exchange my inverted nature for a normal one. I suspect that the sexual emotions and even the inverted ones have a more subtle significance than is generally attributed to them; but modern moralists fight shy of transcendental interpretations or see none, and I am ignorant and unable to solve the mystery which these feelings seem to imply" (9).

Not so ignorant at all is this appealing and introspective young man, for it is precisely the transcendental nature of these feelings, their implications and not their facts, that infuses Whitman's art. "To me," T. W. (case 10) concludes, "what other people call unnatural is the most natural of all conditions." This theme is repeated: "I am an absolute believer in the naturalness of my inclinations" (15). "He sees no harm in homosexual passions" (17); "He does not consider he is doing anything wrong and considers his acts quite natural" (19). An English actor insists, "This love is right, and capable of being made noble, far more so than the love of woman, and to call it unnatural is grossly unjust and untrue" (21). The Parisian born Englishman, inventing social constructionism with a verbal Gallic shrug, disdains judgment: "he has no moral feelings on these matter; he regards them as outside ethics; mere matters of temperament and social feeling" (23). Another says, "I believe that "affection between persons of the same sex, even when it includes the sexual passion and its indulgence, may lead to results as splendid as human nature can ever attain to" (4). Whitman said of his city of friends in "Live-Oak IX" that "nothing was greater there than manly love—it led the rest" (Bowers 114). Perhaps such splendid results could be seen there in the "actions of the men of that city, and in all their looks and words."

Homosexual love produces splendid results for some of these men. The eloquent case 26, who languished so long in sexual bondage, found at last an ideal friend: "I believed I was a rebel from the law, natural and divine, of which no instinct had been implanted in me. . . . I was 30 however, before I found a companion to love me in the way my nature required. Under sexual freedom I have become stronger." Stronger too became the young man who discovered his homosexuality in Whitman's pages, for he found a comrade, "a young man some years younger than himself and of lower social class, whose development he was able to assist." Just as young Charles transforms Langton, this eleve transformed him too: "his love lighted up the gold of affection that was within me and consumed the dross. It was from this that I first learned that there was no hard and fast line between the physical and spiritual in friendship . . . everything in life began to sing with joy, and what little of real creative work I have done I attribute largely to the power of work that was born in me during those years " (13).

Triumphing over the trivial dualism that both Emerson and Thoreau could not surmount and that seemed to be problematic for Taylor, this young hero discovered what Whitman had already found, that his life had begun to sing with joy when he sung of himself and his need of the love of comrades. In that early version of *Calamus* 1, Whitman asked:

> "Was it I who walked the earth disclaiming all except what I
>   had in myself."
> Was it I boasting how complete I was in myself?
> O how little I counted the comrade indispensable to me!
> O how my soul — How the soul of the man feeds, rejoices in
>   its lovers, its dear friends!
> And now I do not care to walk the earth unless a lover, a
>   dear friend, walk by my side.
>
> (Bowers 68)

Those who speak in Ellis' text seem to feel that homosexuality is unique to themselves, and like Whitman they declare it the central question of their lives, feeling also a profound alienation from their own sex. Like Whitman too, almost all of them come to determine that it is natural and worthy of the triumphant song. As Carpenter says, "My own sexual nature was a mystery to me. I found myself cut off from the understanding of others, felt myself an outcast. . . . I was . . . on the brink of despair and madness with repressed passion and torment" (7). Another respondent shares this: "I felt much perplexed and depressed by my views on sexual desire and was convinced they were peculiar to myself" (8). For yet another, so solitary were these cognitions of vice that "I had an idea at that time that the whole thing was so much an original invention of his and mine that there was no likelihood of it being practiced by anyone else in the world" (26). As Whitman says in *Calamus* 16: "As if I were not puzzled at myself! / . . . O conscience struck! O self convicted! / Or as if I do not secretly love strangers." The great wish is fulfilled in these texts when it is discovered that these passions are not unique: "Later on . . . though slowly, I came to find that there were others like myself" (7). Or as another learns: "My next discovery was that my case, so far from being peculiar, was a common one, and I was quickly initiated into the mysteries of inversion, with its freemasonry and argot" (8).

Those midnight orgies of which Whitman speaks may have been his initiation into the sexual freemasonry of the states. Manly love was everywhere, as one correspondent observed: "Of its extraordinary prevalence I am assured, for I have found it every-where—I have travelled much—and in all stations of life." In 1856 Whitman too was finally sure that manly friendship—the "real quality of friendship"—is "always freely to be found" among the "muscular classes" (*DBN* 3:741). In the 1856 letter to Emerson he insists that manly friendship "is "to be everywhere observed in The States" (Bradley 739). If the lists in his notebooks are not adequate to demonstrate that he was not alone in this fraternity of desire, then the pages of his poetry make clear that what may have been solitary fantasy in "Song of Myself" had by the time he wrote *Calamus* become not only the textual invention of a sexual free-masonry but a manifesto of its creed, a dictionary of its signs. As he said in *Calamus* 41, "I perceive one picking me out by secret and divine signs . . . / Some are baffled, but that one is not—that one knows me." What these signs signify—a semiotics of recognition, attested to in gay life and recorded in gay texts—is what he inscribes in his texts and is in part the subject of this book. He answers his own question about the existence of men like himself with a prophecy: "Ah lover perfect and equal, / I meant that you should discover me so by faint indirections, / And when I meet you mean to discover you by the like in you."

The men who share their homosexual lives and feelings in Ellis' pages are in composite "the homosexual" Foucault describes as a species. In that sense they produce a homosexual text. The intertextualities that connect Ellis' text with Whitman's suggest in what sense Whitman's text is a homosexual text as well (and perhaps also in what sense he may be classified within that species). The respondents seemed to be attracted to men early in life, and they engaged generally with eagerness in masturbation, which was often an obsession, and—sometimes willing, sometimes reluctantly, sometimes not at all—in the other possibilities of homosexual play. Many of them confessed to being dreamy or indolent in youth, and these dreams became rich fantasy lives inhabited by handsome, available, and muscular young men—roughs, shepherds, working men, soldiers, and sailors—or by more passive and effeminate youths. In life as well as fantasy, they ardently pursued friendship, love, and sex, some of them sharing quite incredibly active and adventurous sexual experiences. They responded to women as social, but rarely as sexual, beings, expressing often a positive abhorrence of the notion of heterosexual union and an equally positive conviction that homosexual love was nobler, more passionate, and more profound than heterosexual love. Almost none of them expressed any desire to be anything other than what they were, even though many of them keenly felt that they were outcasts or pariahs in a world that condemned what to them seemed natural and imperative emotions. With remarkable unanimity, they celebrated homosexuality and considered it natural, elevating, and the source of creative power. Many of them suspected that they were a discrete and physiologically unique species. The language of their texts is heavily freighted with the common imagery of homoerotic literary and imaginative conventions. They subscribe to Arcadian ideals, appeal to classical examples, translate tutors, teachers, and older men into erotic fantasies, celebrate mythic and real lovers, fantasize sexual dominance and submission by conjuring up wrestlers and youthful Ganymedes, create wishful fantasies of bands of devoted lovers and cities of friends and speak specifically about sexual dreams and fears, and utter sometimes adversarial, sometimes victimized and anxious, sentiments about their relationship with society. Nearly all of them express a deep sense of isolation and alienation from the common expectations of male sexual conduct, generally represented to them by stern fathers, teachers, doctors, or priests. All of them, without exception, looked for the ideal friend. Together they shared in the production of a defining discourse about sexuality—about what Ellis finally decided to call homosexuality.

Whitman's texts are inscribed within this discourse and participate in its categories and conventions, its imagery and tropes. That discourse communicates what Foucault described—that in common these men seemed to be convinced that they possessed a past, shared a mysterious physiology, and were personages, life forms, a species. Foucault designates Carl Friedrich Westphal's use of the term "contrary sexual feeling" as the moment when the "homosexual" was born and when act was displaced by "feeling." Westphal describes this as "the feeling of being alienated, with one's entire being, from one's own sex."[57] Whitman recognized that the "sex" from which he was alienated was that which habitually traversed the busy walks of life, walks he identifies as the habitation of the pleasures, profits, and conformities of received and published sexual standards concerning the nature of gender roles and their conflation with "masculine" or "feminine" style.[58] He reclaims those streets for a more transgressive sexuality that rejected the old business of sexual barter and politics transacted there. He attempts to redress that alienation by recasting the definition of masculinity, inscribing within it the necessity for creating what he called "organic equality" among men.

The production of the sexual discourse that led to Westphal's formula and that allowed Ellis' respondents to offer such remarkably interpenetrative readings of themselves as a sexual species and to call upon a context that might well be thought of as employing and even creating a conventional language of homosexual literary discourse, a language evident everywhere in Whitman's own texts, can certainly claim Whitman as an early, original, and definitive contributor. Whitman's interest is to assess within himself and for himself, and eventually for all who are young men, what it means to be touched in a same-sex sexual context: "Is this then touch?" However touch is only the beginning, inspiring him as he says to a library of instant knowledge. He knows that the possession and affirmation of the truth about sex is power. That knowledge and erotic power are demonstrated at every turn in the erotic fabric of his texts and in his conflation of the sexual with the political and the aesthetic. Therefore, of course, the immateriality of argument about his sexual actions is obvious. Like the discourses that constructed sexuality, Whitman is his own constructing text, in which he creates, defines, and engages in the textual realization of homosexual desire. The text is sexuality; the text is sex.

By 1856, when Whitman wrote to Emerson, "manliness" had come to mean a certain way of being sexual that included not only the constructed modalities that prescribed the presumed "natural" sexual, economic, political, and power relationships between men and women—with women always being in a subsumed position vis-à-vis men—but the proscriptions against variance from these modalities. Manliness had also definitively begun to exclude affectional, and had rarely included the possibilities of sexual, relations between men. Such things were defined increasingly in the case of affectional, and definitively in the case of sexual relations, as unmanly. Views about male-male sex had traversed a spectrum Cohen defines as moving from "sodomy to gross indecency," from sin to crime, displacing transgression against God's law by a transgression against the "natural" (that is, the "heterosexual") uses of the body, and criminalizing that transgression since it was also by legal extension a transgression against the "purity" of the body politic itself.[59]

Whitman's texts transgress these very transgressions, asserting the value to the body politic of male-male sexual love and insisting that manly affection and "organic equality" among men is itself the very definition of manliness and the best hope of democracy. Whitman was situated at the point when these prohibitions began to be additionally interpenetrated by the proscriptive and prescriptive discourse of science, medicine, and psychiatry, which moved the discussion of same-sex practices into the realm of emotional response as well as act and further toward defining what would shortly be called "homosexuality" as a physiological defect and mental aberration, indeed as a species of insanity. By siting manliness and manly affection within the discourses of male purity, within the nascent discourse of feminism, and within the scientific discourse that included phrenology, and by creating within his own texts a "psychiatric" model—before psychiatry— for the exploration of the place of masculine desire within the purviews of the conscious and subconscious, even unconscious, "self," Whitman allied his project with the "new" movements in science and social analysis. By doing so he transgressed against the constructions that sought to medically proscribe same-sex relations, for by encoding same-sex love within his texts not only in the surface manifestations of ideology but as tropes in the very fabric of the text, he made it impossible for a criticism—a homophobic criticism—which invalidated a text only because it dealt with the "sin to heinous to be named" to be a meaningful criticism, and he indeed forced a confrontation not only with homosexuality but more importantly with the sexuality of texts as well as with the different subject of textuality as sexuality.

Sedgwick suggests that the nineteenth-century sexual discourse was in many ways incoherent, positing that "a deadlock or incoherence of definition prevails" between what she describes as "separatist" and "integrative" conceptions of homosexuality—that is, on the one hand a definition of homosexuality as a "trait of a distinct and fixed minority" and on the other—the integrative—homosexuality read as "a universal human potential," the debate that I mention in my introduction and that Sedgwick also identifies with the current discussion about constructionism and essentialism.[60] In these terms, though Whitman certainly recognizes the spectrum of possible choice within sexualities, he seems to advocate a separatist position, most profoundly within the *Calamus* poems, but in fact from the very beginning of his textual explorations. He speculates about "men in other lands" and recalls the "brotherhood of lovers," constructs cities of lovers and defines comradely love as "a substantial life," perhaps a definition that predicts the current construction of gay life and "lifestyle" and certainly a prophecy of Foucault's "singular nature." When read with his notebook observations about the "psychology" and subtlety of Plato, Shakespeare, Tennyson, Melville, and Taylor, these speculations and recollections and his insistence on the necessity that "blood like mine" flow in the veins of any young man who would be "selected by lovers" suggests that Whitman made a firm distinction between "young men" and those "others" who continue to advocate hitherto published standards.

Employing Rubin's assertion that "although sex and gender are related, they are not the same thing," Sedgwick draws distinctions between "two quite opposite possibilities for defining" same-sex desire that have "prevailed often at the same time."[61] These are "the gender-integrative," which is best exemplified by Ulrich's concept of the third sex, the "woman's soul trapped in a man's body," which "points to an essential femininity in gay men" and valorizes androgyny, and the concept of "gender-separatism," which valorizes "manhood-initiation models" and the "man-loving man," who is, in Benedict Friedlander's paraphrased formulation, "the highest stage of gender differentiation." Men who need women were "seen as less manly than those who transcended the procreational imperative in favor of this higher masculinity."[62] In one argument, Whitman's text could be defined as a representation of varieties of initiation into the male sexual world. I have argued that it is in fact a depiction of initiation into homosexual manhood and a demonstration of the textual and aesthetic consequences of that initiation. Further, whatever he might have said in his formulae advocating the procreative imperative, and despite what he said to Symonds in his disclaiming reply, Whitman did transcend that imperative in his real and fictive life. He is a man-loving man in the fullest sense, rejecting what he described as the intransience of women's love, and advocating the sole validity of men's. Though manliness for him was manifest as an absolute contrary sensibility and mode of action to the models of effeminacy that he rejects in the letter to Emerson, his manliness is also defined by the literal unnecessariness of women in the deep structures of the male-love advocating project of his texts. Woman's sexual liberation is vital to his program, but it is a liberation that enables women to produce well-made men and heroes, whose realization of "organic equality" is the ultimate object of Whitman's ideology.

When he does cross gender boundaries, Whitman primarily invokes androgyny, and his role is inevitably the voracious "manly" woman—the twenty-ninth bather or the seductive woman who adorns herself—or it is inscribed within the transvestiture of his own adorning in order to achieve vast sexual returns in which he becomes an object of sexual commerce. These roles, strictly speaking, are not androgynous at all in the deepest sense of sexual identification with women. These characters are not even "men in the bodies of women." Instead they are men who for the moment have appropriated women's bodies, though in the case of the prostitute the traditional order is subverted and inverted, since Whitman "spends" instead of getting, bestows himself instead of being purchased. These "women" are, like men, possessors and independent—the twenty-ninth bather owns "her" house and is sexually agressive. Also like men they can "wrestle" and "resist," words he uses of women in "A Woman Waits for Me"—the same terms he employs in "I Sing the Body Electric" when he describes the wrestling "embrace of love and resistance." They are in fact manly counter examples set up against those effeminate men who cannot "fight, work, shoot, ride, run or command." In his texts his sexual object-choices define his identity, for he equates himself with "young men," these with manly friendship, and this with the "phallic choice of America." That choice inspires Democracy, which inspires, and which he equates with, his poems. These poems are of course his own phallus. These equations circularly return to the self who "selects lovers," ideally "Western Boys" who inhabit the western Arcadia "where all men are comrades," special men-loving men, who are or have been "young men." He rejects unmanliness, effeminacy, the intransience of women's love and its threatening demasculinizing projection toward himself, and the proscriptive strategies of the pre-poetic "speech" of the talkers and askers, all in the service of the production of sexual knowledge and truth. He desires that passionate sexual silence in which ecstasy cancels speech, and in which the only true embrace, and the most valid, is that of the Fierce Wrestler.

I do not intend to reduce the irreducible, or to fix Whitman within any single discourse. He resists reduction and fixing the most and participates in the incoherence and contradiction of sexual discourse as powerfully as he participates in its construction. But if he did anything, and he did much more, he did separate, blur, sometimes even erase sex from gender. Perhaps more accurately, he made it possible to wrest sexual identity from the grip of prescribed gender roles and inscribed it within a transgressive spectrum of alternative erotic choices and locales. He called into question the ideological and political foundations of gender and sexual identity. In his fiction and definitively in his poems, he radically altered the textual possibilities surrounding the perception, discussion, and expression of object-choice and sexual identity. Discerning no breath of manly friendship in print, he infused the jets of that special life into his texts, founding and forecasting, in short, the very discourse in which we are now all so richly engaged.

8

Epilogue

The Path Ahead

What is it I interchange with strangers?

— "Song of the Open Road," 1856

"First be yourself what you would show in your poem," Whitman wrote in an unsigned review of *Leaves of Grass* in September 1855.[1] The self he intends to be is described in this review and placed securely within the masculine and homoerotic contexts he had so carefully constructed. Absent from this review, as he is from the title page of *Leaves of Grass*, Whitman is free to engage indirection, hint at subtle "psychology," and erect signposts to direct both those readers who had already perhaps distinguished "certain lights and shades" in those lines and those who might be "eligible"—to borrow his word from *Calamus 36*—to read them properly.

The first signpost is clearly marked. The author of these poems is "masculine, affectionate . . . sensual." He is no "dilettante democrat" but "loves the streets—love the docks . . . the free rasping voices of men . . . the ungenteel ways of laborers . . . likes to make one at the crowded tables among sailors and work people . . . would . . . go with tumultuous men, roughs, receive their caresses and welcome, listen to their noise, oaths, smut, fluency, laughter, repartee." He likes to go "down in the bay with the pilots . . . cruise with the fishers" or ride "side by side with the driver" on a Broadway omnibus (Bradley 777). This catalog is charged with homoerotic intimation: the electric promise of the streets and docks, close and erotic physical intimacy with men, their bodies close and inviting at the table, and their thighs intimately touching side by side on the narrow driver's seat of the Broadway omnibus, or necessarily close in the cramped confines of a fishing boat—as close as they must surely be in that other image of male sexual intimacy, the erotic "guarded tents" of "interior love." The caresses of roughs and tumultuous men reveal at last the unspecified inhabitants and explain the suggestive mystery of the opening erotic lines in "Song of Myself": a few light kisses. . . .a few embraces. . . . a reaching around of arms."

The second sign is more indirect. This poet "celebrates natural propensities in himself." "Propensities" is linked to that same powerful verb—"celebrate"—which is the sign pointing toward all the eroticisms in "Song of Myself." Celebrating is both a festive and a sacramental act; celebrations suspend the ordinary business of life and sanctify, extoll, and ratify its special creeds and most deeply felt desires. "Propensities" also stands at the same charged point as "myself" does in the poem. Propensities are specific, not general. They indicate particular dispositions of mind, point to a bent in a certain direction. These propensities are never defined in this review. But just as Whitman took the time to note that Plato's "astounding" text "advocates" the "ancient Greek Friendship," so here too he glancingly indicates with a seemingly nonchalant word that these propensities are "natural." If "propensities" did not also carry the weight of specific imputations, if the phrase "certain propensities" was not also inscribed as part of its unspoken text, if the utterance of "natural" did not invoke unnatural and imply an ancient proscriptive discourse, if there were no question, there would be no need for such advocacy here any more than there would have been in his comment about Plato.

But with this there is a further qualification: these propensities are "in himself." This is indirection too and points to his veiled references to "certain" psychologies and "certain lights and shades" he found in other "subtle" texts. These "propensities in himself" might not be shared by all men but only by certain men—and the sign points ahead—who are capable of loving like he is, in whose veins "flows blood like mine." The hidden voice in the text is here clearly identified for those who can hear it, and a further context is also clearly established. Such natural propensities are associated with "the taste of the Paradisiac tree of knowledge of good and evil." In "Song of Myself," Whitman calls himself "not the poet of goodness only," asserts "I do not decline to be the poet of wickedness also," and invokes "forbidden voices . . . voices of sexes and lusts . . . voices veiled . . . voices indecent by me clarified and transfigured." When he wrote to Emerson, he had no doubt that the voice of homosexual desire—the breath of manly love—had been surely the most carefully veiled, and of all the voices of sexes and lusts, the one most often presumed to be the most indecent. The insertion of that innocent "natural" and its association with the fruit of the tree of knowledge of good and evil, which he so willingly plucks, invokes the notebook *Calamus* garden in which he picks and eats the phallic fruit that inspires him with homoerotic paradisiac ecstasy—the same ecstasy he experiences in the close erotic company of certain men, when the sunlight of paradise warms his blood.

About the propensities, as about the lusts and forbidden voices, Whitman "comes to no conclusions, and does not satisfy the reader." Many readers of these poems remained unsatisfied, disturbed, or appalled like Higginson. But there are certain readers who will be satisfied, those for whom these poems are written. He is clear about who they are: "His whole work" has as an "evident purpose to stamp a new type of character . . . and publish it not as a model but an illustration for the present and future of American letters and American young men." As he will say in *Calamus* 1, in a transfiguration of this sentiment: "I proceed for all who are or have been young men." As he will say to Emerson, when he writes him in a few months time: "Such character is the brain and spine to all, including literature, including poems. Such character [is] strong, limber . . . full of ease, of passionate friendliness." In the review, he adds one more telling phrase in which advocacy presides: "Whatever is needed toward this achievement he puts his hand to, and lets imputations take their time to die." The imputations that may arise concerning passionate friendliness, concerning the caresses of roughs and the closeness of men—the imputations Higginson could only make in Latin—are translated, transfigured, and finally, destroyed by a stroke of the triumphant pen, by a caress of the affectionate hand.

By the time Whitman wrote Emerson, he had not only infused American literature with the "breath of manly love" he had also come to conclusions about it, enough to satisfy any doubting reader. In the 1856 edition, in section 6 of "Song of the Open Road," he announced "here is adhesiveness" and translated into that poem those same notebook images of men who expanded his blood and aroused his lank pennants of joy. He also employed "adhesiveness" to answer the question posed by the very lines he had taken from the 1855 review and translated in "Song of the Open Road" (1856) into poetry: "What is it I interchange so suddenly with strangers? / What with some driver as I ride on the seat by his side? / What with some fisherman drawing his seine by the shore as I walk by and pause?" By then, he had probably also written in his notebooks the specific assertion he would soon make in "Proto-Leaf" (1860), in which adhesiveness—that curious and awkward word for manly love, that binding, merging, together clinging, tightly embracing word—is transfigured into and identified as a word "to clear one's path ahead endlessly," a signpost definitively pointing toward masculine landscapes.

Notes
Works Cited
Index

Notes

1. Introduction: Before Homosexuality

1.   Foucault's choice of 1870 and his definition of homosexuals as a "species" is explained in his *The History of Sexuality,* Vol.1, *An Introduction* (New York: Random House, 1978), 43. Though this may be old news to many readers, the terms *homosexual* and *homosexuality* first appeared in print in 1869 in two anonymous pamphlets written by Karl Maria Kertbeny, an Austro-Hungarian translator. I am uncomfortable with them and also aware of their decay in the present gay discourse, but I will use them in the body of my text because their shorthand value in both common and critical use is more convenient than any terms that, though perhaps more accurate, are certainly more awkward. As Eve Kosofsky Sedgwick points out, in *Epistemology of the Closet* (Berkeley and Los Angeles: University of California Press, 1990), 83, the category of "the homosexual" has "failed to disintegrate" not only because it is useful to homophobes but because for both lesbians and gay men it "does have a real power to organize and describe" our experience of "sexuality and identity."

2.   See Jacob Stockinger, "Homotextuality: A Proposal," in *The Gay Academic,* ed. Louie Crew (Palm Springs: ETC Publications, 1978), 135–52. Stockinger's term did not then partake of the broader notions of what he might have called interhomotextual.

3.   David M. Halperin, *One Hundred Years of Homosexuality* (London: Routledge, 1990), 29.

4.   J. Hillis Miller, *Thomas Hardy: Distance and Desire* (Cambridge, Mass.: Harvard University Press, 1970), 36. Again addressing this point, Whitman said that the "process of reading is not a half-sleep, but in [the] highest sense an exercise, a gymnast's

struggle . . . the reader . . . must himself or herself construct
. . . the poem." (The source of this citation from Whitman, so
apropos here, seems to have deconstructed itself out of existence in
my notes. I would take it as an act of signal kindness—and as a
lesson in scrupulous scholarship—if any reader who might come
across the source could help me (re)construct my text by recalling
it to my attention.)

    5.   Foucault 1:27.

    6.   As Halperin, (156 n. 3) points out, the introduction of
homosexual and its distinction from the more general *inversion,*
which implies gender-deviance, mark "a sharp break with traditional ways of thinking." Kertbeny's use of the term was legal; it
soon began to be used in a medical/psychiatric context.

    7.   Whitman, far more than, let us say, Marlowe or William
Beckford, might well recognize in our contemporary gay modalities the inherited though much reinterpreted products of his own
since, as some recent scholarship suggests, what we now call
"homosexuality" and the "modern homosexual" is "a unique
creation of the late nineteenth century." Martin Bauml Duberman,
Martha Vicinus, and George Chauncey, Jr. eds., *Hidden From
History: Reclaiming the Gay and Lesbian Past* (New York: New
American Library, 1989), 5.

    8.   The discussion of the meaning or even the value of
homosexual/homosexuality has entered a rich and provocative phase,
thanks surely to Michel Foucault, to whom, obviously, I here
indicate my debt—shared with every scholar who approaches the
subject. Gay scholars now powerfully confront the questions of
homosexual textuality as well as the questions of the use and
meaning of the terms themselves. Halperin (45), gives the best
summary of the current discourse and carries the dissolution of
homosexuality to its radical and perhaps even logical conclusion by
claiming that "there is no such thing" as "homosexuality itself" or
"heterosexuality itself." Those words "do not name independent
modes of sexual being, leading some sort of ideal existence apart
from particular human societies, outside of history or culture."
My borrowing from Julia Kristeva comes from "The Novel as
Polylogue," in *Desire in Language: A Semiotic Approach to Literature
and Art,* ed. Leon S. Roudiez (New York: Columbia University
Press, 1980), 159. For useful summaries of the history of the
changing legal view of homosexuality see Ed Cohen, "Legislating
the Norm: From Sodomy to Gross Indecency" in *Displacing Homophobia Gay Male Perspectives in Literature and Culture,* ed. Ronald R.

Butters, John M. Clum, and Michael Moon (Durham: Duke University Press, 1989), 169–206. For an exciting discussion of gender and sexual identity see Eve Kosofsky Sedgwick, "Across Gender, Across Sexuality: Willa Cather and Others" in the same volume (53–73).

9.   See Sedgwick (*Epistemology*, 16) for an illuminating discussion of the use of *gay* and *homosexual*.

10.   On otherness see Halperin 54.

11.   Sedgwick, *Epistemology*, 40.

12.   While I would like to believe the former, the evidence for the latter position is powerful and convincing, though recent essays by Saslow and Trumbach, for example, seem to make the chronological boundaries as susceptible to flux and instability as the terms of the discourse itself have been.

13.   Sedgwick (*Epistemology*, 40) does not see the argument between essentialists and social constructionists any longer as a debate but as a deadlock.

14.   Havelock Ellis, *Studies in The Psychology of Sex: Sexual Inversion* (Philadelphia, 1901), 1.

15.   As with almost any term employed in the study of gay origins, life, or literature, the usefulness of distinguishing between *homosexual* and *homoerotic* has been questioned. Some scholars — Robert K. Martin, *The Homosexual Tradition in American Poetry* (Austin and London: University of Texas Press, 1979) for example — asserts that there is no difference; others banish the words altogether; and still others find them, as I do, useful if somewhat delicate, terms. These words are more appropriate than *gay*, which though it may currently describe the kind of history in which I participate and identify this writer, is bound too firmly by chronology and politics to be useful when talking about Whitman.

16.   Whitman anticipates Foucault's demonstration in the *The History of Sexuality*, Vol. 1, that "knowledge" and "sex" had become, as Sedgwick (*Epistemology*, 73) says, "conceptually inseparable from one another." He anticipates also the association of secrecy with sexual secrecy, specifically secrecy about homosexuality. A word also about my use of "Whitman" in the preceding line. I will not, in fact, set Whitman apart in inverted commas to indicate special allegiance to concepts of text or intertextuality, to insist on some denial or assertion of his originary place, or in circumlocution to avoid invoking his name. But while it is easier to believe that Walt Whitman imagined, intended, and wrote his poetry in a limited and originary sense, or to read him only as an

actor and not an agent in it, yet neither of these positions account for the complexity of the questions concerning voice, presence, author and intention, as well as considerations of speech and writing, which are raised by this text.

17. Harold Bloom, *Wallace Stevens: The Poems of Our Climate* (Ithaca: Cornell University Press, 1977), 387. I also heed him carefully when he urges, in *Agon: Toward a Theory of Revisionism* (New York: Oxford University Press, 1982), 335, that "the American critic . . . needs to keep faith with American poetry and the American negative which means that one must not yield either to the school of Deconstruction or to the perpetual British school of Common Sense."

18. In a useful echo, Geoffrey Hartman, in *The Fate of Reading and Other Essays* (Chicago: University of Chicago Press, 1975), 19, observes about texts: "The book begins to question the questioner." He continues with a little drama: "*Interpreter:* Who's there? *Book:* Nay, answer me; stand, and unfold yourself."

2. Words Unsaid

1. Carroll Smith-Rosenberg, *Disorderly Conduct: Visions of Gender in Victorian America* (New York: Oxford University Press, 1985), 91. See Michael Moon, *Disseminating Whitman: Revision and Corporeality in "Leaves of Grass"* (Cambridge, Mass.: Harvard University Press, 1991), 20–25, for a discussion of the anti-onanist discourse, which Moon sees also as hompohobic discourse. Moon's book concerns itself precisely and cogently with the process of Whitman's revisions not only in response to, but as a counter-discourse within, the spectrum of sexual discourse.

2. See Martin (*Homosexual Tradition,* 4) on Holloway's willingness to deduce heterosexuality from the later published version of an earlier manuscript that clearly suggests homosexuality.

3. Eduard Bertz to W.C. Rivers, quoted in Martin Duberman, *About Time: Exploring the Gay Past* (New York: Gay Presses of New York, 1986), 92.

4. Duberman 87.

5. Martin, *Homosexual Tradition,* 6. See Moon, *Disseminating Whitman,* 4–25, for commentary on the early origins of American homophobia.

6. The sad story of Newton Arvin is too familiar, and academic homophobia still sits smugly on promotions committees. After a surface coverage of several gay studies programs, a

recent article in *The New York Times* (12/30/90) entitled "Out of the Closet, Into the University," by Felicity Barringer, concludes with a comment by Roger Chace, president of Wesleyan Methodist University, who observes that the study of "particularisms, i.e. gender or ethnic or gay studies will be one of the "driving energies" of higher education. Chace then wonders whether the intellectual questions posed by these studies are "inherently interesting" and ends the piece saying that "some gay studies programs will be founded and fail. At other places they will be founded and succeed. My guess is, that number will be small." The homophobic logic of Professor Chace's opinion, ill-concealed beneath the appearance of evenhanded scrutiny, leads inevitably to the conclusion that they will fail because they are not inherently interesting. This exemplifies a general academic attitude that willingly and uncritically trivializes gay studies in the same way that gay people are often trivialized by pejorative social constructions. The instruments are not blunt here. See Sedgwick (*Epistemology*, 52–53) for a witty and very useful schematization of the kinds of objections routinely raised against the legitimacy of homosexual texts.

7.   Gay Wilson Allen, *The Solitary Singer: A Critical Biography of Walt Whitman* (New York: Macmillan, 1955), 222.

8.   William White, "Walt Whitman in The Eighties: A Bibliographical Essay," in *Walt Whitman Here and Now*, ed. Joann P. Krieg (Westport: Greenwood Press, 1985), 223. He makes what is I hope an unintended comparison between apparently serious heterosexual contributors in serious scholarly journals as opposed to frivolous gay "writers" in even more frivolous gay magazines. One of the "other subjects" he mentions is an article on an unknown Whitman letter recommending an Army Doctor, which addition to primary texts I do not denigrate nor mock when I wonder if this physician while taking a pulse could have detected that more primary pulse as well.

9.   David S. Reynolds, *Beneath the American Renaissance: The Subversive Imagination in the Age of Emerson and Melville* (Cambridge, Mass.: Harvard University Press, 1988), 328. Reynolds' important book has no indexed entry on homosexuality, and the entry for Whitman's "sexual orientation" leads us only to Reynolds' unwillingness to come to any conclusion.

10.   See Martin (*Homosexual Tradition,* 33) on "adhesiveness."

11.   Martin, *Homosexual Tradition,* 6. Martin's book itself sustains that kind of attack in the pages of Edwin H. Miller's *Walt*

Whitman's "Song of Myself": A Mosaic of Interpretations (Iowa City: University of Iowa Press, 1989), wherein Miller dismisses some of Martin's comments. For example see notes 37 and 138 in Miller's text.

12.   John Snyder, *The Dear Love of Man: Tragic and Lyric Communion in Walt Whitman* (Boston, 1975). David S. Leverenz, *Manhood in The American Renaissance* (New York, 1989), 30. Robert K. Martin draws attention to this passage also, in his review of the Leverenz book in *Walt Whitman Quarterly Review* 7 (Winter 1990): 143–46. As Martin says, "no one can possibly talk about manhood in the American Renaissance without Whitman or his young men." In fact, Leverenz devotes only a few pages to Whitman.

13.   Milton Hindus, ed., *Walt Whitman: The Critical Heritage* (London: Routledge, 1971), 33.

14.   Quoted in Jonathon Ned Katz, *Gay American History,* (New York: Thomas Y. Crowell, 1976) 26.

15.   See M. Jimmie Killingsworth, *Whitman's Poetry of the Body: Sexuality, Politics, and the Text* (Chapel Hill: University of North Carolina Press, 1989), 36, 164, 97. This is not to accuse Killingsworth of homophobia. His book amply demonstrates the absence of that. It only suggests that even the most wary scholar must tread delicately through the thorny lexical thickets that still surround definition with judgment.

16.   Eve Kosofsky Sedgwick, *Between Men: English Literature and Male Homosocial Desire* (New York: Columbia University Press, 1985), intro., 83.

17.   Duberman 94.

18.   Justin Kaplan, "The Biographer's Problem," in *Walt Whitman, Sex and Gender, The Mickle Street Review* 11 (1989), 87–88.

19.   Kaplan, "Biographer's Problem," 88.

20.   Duberman 92.

21.   See Frederik Schyberg, *Walt Whitman,* trans. Evie Allison Allen (New York: Columbia University Press, 1951); Martin, *Homosexual Tradition;* David Cavitch, *My Soul and I: The Inner Life of Walt Whitman* (Boston: Beacon, 1985); Betsy Erkilla, *Whitman: The Political Poet* (New York: Oxford University Press, 1989); Killingsworth; and Michael Moon (1991). The history of the critical response to Whitman's homosexuality and/or his homoerotic texts and the history of the homosexual response to Whitman's homosexuality and his texts, two somewhat different subjects, have not yet been adequately written. The first subject is indirectly handled in such books as Harold Blodgett's *Walt Whit-*

man in England (Ithaca: Cornell University Press, 1934), wherein Blodgett discusses Whitman's English reception. But Blodgett did not recognize, nor could he have recognized in 1934, the questions about gay textuality that have now only lately arisen. Similar strictures may be applied to Betsy Erkilla's *Walt Whitman Among the French* (New Haven: Princeton University Press, 1980) and to a lesser extent, Gay Wilson Allen's *The New Walt Whitman Handbook* (New York: New York University Press, 1985), which does make an attempt to indicate whether critics have dealt with the homosexuality of poet and text. However, in speaking of Symonds' reactions for example, he says that Symonds "recognized symptoms of emotional abnormality in the poet" (12), and he goes on to say that Whitman's incredible letter denying the homosexual content of *Calamus* "allayed Symonds' worst suspicions about the origin of the Calamus emotions" (19). Symonds' suspicions were certainly there, but he was disappointed not mollified by Whitman's letter, and by the time he wrote to Whitman, he certainly held no opinions about homosexuality that described it as an emotional abnormality. Allen's interpretation offers another example of the discomfort that critics seem to feel when confronted with gay people and our texts.

As to the homosexual response to Whitman, that is a book in itself or at least a major article. Obviously, an important chapter in such a book would include the response to Whitman by American gay writers like Taylor and Stoddard. Symonds' interrogations of Whitman and Whitman's response have been so often dealt with that I have not discussed them here. However, those who have discussed this, and this includes every important biographer, have not really looked carefully at Symonds' questions, which are not questions about "sexual orientation" but about the sexual context of texts, precisely my subject here.

Such a discussion both of the critical response to Whitman's homosexuality and the homosexual response to Whitman's "homotextuality" will show that in the former category such comments as White's, Leverenz', and Reynolds' have not changed much in kind from Emory Holloway's sadly duplicitous attempt to rewrite the history of the pronouns of "Once I pass'd through a populous city," in *Whitman: An Interpretation In Narrative* (New York: Knopf, 1926) or even in vehemence from Mark Van Doren's comment in "Walt Whitman, Stranger," in *The Private Reader* (New York, 1942), that Whitman's "manly love is neither more nor less than an abnormal and deficient love" (82). Even Justin Kaplan,

Walt Whitman — A Life (New York: Simon and Schuster, 1980), who offers a fairly full account of Whitman's relationships with Doyle and Stafford, sees the *Calamus* poems as growing out of self-doubt and renunciation, and one cannot help feeling that Whitman's homosexuality is only partially perceived and perhaps somewhat pitied. Both the myth of a New Orleans romance, created perhaps to disguise the possibility that there were no women at all, and the myth of six children, which Whitman fostered to allay the supposed suspicions of Symonds, have been proven to be folly, yet Paul Zweig in *Walt Whitman — The Making of a Poet* (New York: Basic Books, 1984) can observe: "A century later, Whitman's sexual life is still a a mystery. Was he homosexual? Did he become openly homosexual in the 1850's, his new poetry a celebration of erotic freedom?" Zweig's answers to these questions are offered in an elegant essay, yet at the end of it all, we realize that his question, like so many others, has been aimed at what Whitman did, not at what conception of a homosexual identity his texts supply.

Some sort of comment on the question of homosexuality and Whitman is made by the Whitman contents of one of the most recent major anthologies of American literature, the vast *The American Tradition in Literature,* 6th ed., ed. George Perkins, et. al. (New York: W. W. Norton, 1985). Therein Whitman is represented by a fair number of poems, including "Song of Myself." But for *Calamus* there are only three, "For You O Democracy," "I Saw in Louisiana a Live Oak Growing," and "I Hear It Was Charged Against Me," three poems that are perhaps the most "innocent" of the group. In fact, the central and significant *Calamus* 1 has not been published in any anthologies I possess. In this anthology, a footnote describes the Calamus root as being a symbol of male comradeship, but in the critical and biographical preface to the selections, there is not the first breath of manly love, and no mention of homosexuality at all.

The critical suspicions about Whitman's homosexuality begin early enough with Griswold's sibylline Latin warning in 1855 that Whitman's poetry contained material instinct with that terrible crime that cannot be named among Christians and continue with Thomas Wentworth Higginson's observation in the *Nation* in 1892 that the object of "anything like personal or romantic love" always "turns out to be a man not a woman." The battle moved back and forth between those critics who saw or suspected homosexuality, (Symonds, Carpenter, Donaldson — though he insisted that the *Calamus* emotions were not based on any real experience — Bertz,

Schyberg, Canby, Arvin, Asselineau, Cowley) and those who
denied it (Bucke, O'Conner, Kennedy, Traubel, Binns, Perry,
Bazalgette, De Selincourt, Allen) or didn't mention it at all or
considered it to be the product of an unhealthy mood or while
admitting it characterized it as morbid or pathological. Later
critics, and the number is too vast to summarize in this note,
essentially continued to fight the "is he or isn't he?" battle, while
some, like White, think it is not an issue. Others have more
collateral trouble with the homosexuality than with the person or
the text, and many seem to want to separate sexuality and text,
subscribing to Havelock Ellis' assertion that Whitman's homosexuality had nothing to do with his work at all: "However important
inversion may be as a psychological key to Whitman's personality,
it plays but a small part in Whitman's work, and for many who care
for that work a negligible part" (Havelock Ellis, *Sexual Inversion*
[1901], 19.) Richard Chase presumed Whitman's sexuality to be
troubled, yet felt that this discord impelled Whitman to write his
poem. E. H. Miller, in *Walt Whitman's Poetry: A Psychological Journey*
(Boston: Beacon, 1968), took a thoroughly Freudian approach,
arriving at conclusions involving emotional immaturity, troubled
family relations, and a concept of homosexuality as deficient and
deviant. For so many critics, the subtext seemed and seems still to
be whether or not they recoil, like Leverenz, from homosexuality
and homosexuals.

Symonds, Carpenter, and Xavier Mayne are the earliest critics
to espouse, however partially, a theory of homosexual textuality in
Whitman's writings; Symonds' readings are very profound and go
beyond the question of personal sexuality to questions of textuality. Recent reevaluations of Whitman's homoerotic texts have
begun to be written. See Martin, *Homosexual Tradition* (1979);
Byrne R. S. Fone, "This Other Eden: Arcadia and The Homosexual Imagination," in *Literary Visions of Homosexuality*, ed. Stuart
Kellogg (New York: Haworth Press, 1983), 13–35; Joseph Cady in
various articles, among them "Drum-Taps and Nineteenth-Century Male Homosexual Literature," in Krieg 49–61; Sedgwick,
Between Men, 201; Sandra Gilbert, "The American Sexual Poetics
of Walt Whitman and Emily Dickinson," in *Reconstructing American
Literary History*, ed. Sacvan Bercovitch (Cambridge, Mass.: Harvard University Press, 1986), 123–54; Charley Shively, *Calamus
Lovers* (San Francisco: Gay Sunshine Press, 1987); Erkilla, *Political
Poet;* Killingsworth, *Poetry of the Body;* Michael Moon, *Disseminating Whitman*. Martin's book is of such seminal importance that it

holds a place in Whitman and gay criticism comparable in some respects to Foucault's work. I am more than happy to be in his debt, and I believe that I have been able to extend in directions of which I hope he would approve. Many of his conclusions so often anticipate and helped me to arrive at many of my own. As Martin describes this task in a review in *WWQR* 5 (Spring 1988), "we must see Whitman . . . in the context of an emerging sense of homosexual identity. . . . we must move from looking at what the text says to how it says it, recognizing that . . . meaning inheres in the text's shape, tensions, and rhythms. . . . we must look at the sexuality of the poems" (47).

22.   Killingsworth, xvi (Sedgwick, *Between Men,* 204).

23.   The introduction here of *sensibility* placed perilously close to *homosexual* inevitably suggests the phrase "homosexual sensibility" and its companion "homosexual imagination." The literature and the debate on whether there are such things is also rich, and a bibliography is too long to include here, but it probably can be said that there are conventions of homosexual texts that can be identified. Whether those conventions mean the same thing to those who interpret them now as they meant to those who engaged them is one of the questions of homosexual literary study. For early discussions of the concept of a gay sensibility and imagination see Xavier Mayne, *The Intersexes* (Naples, 1908) and John Addington Symonds, *A Problem in Greek Ethics* (Bristol: Ballantyne and Hansen, 1883). For an early collection of essays that presumes there is such a sensibility see Louie Crew and Rictor Norton, eds., *The Homosexual Imagination,* Vol. 36, no. 3 of *College English* (1974), especially the essays by the editors and by Jacob Stockinger. See also Louie Crew, ed., *The Gay Academic* (Palm Springs: ETC Publications, 1978), especially the essays by Byrne R. S. Fone, James W. F. Somerville, and Jacob Stockinger, the source for the term *homotextuality.* A later collection is Stuart Kellogg, ed., *Literary Visions of Homosexuality* (New York: Haworth, 1983), especially the editor's introductions and the essays by Louie Crompton, Byrne R. S. Fone and Robert K. Martin. Katz makes important observations on the topic, and Byrne R. S. Fone, *Hidden Heritage: History and the Gay Imagination* (New York: Avocation, 1979), Robert K. Martin, *Homosexual Tradition,* and Louie Crompton, *Byron and Greek Love: Homophobia in 19th-Century England* (Berkeley and Los Angeles: University of California Press, 1985) all engage in the discussion.

24.   See Moon, "Disseminating Whitman," (in Butters, Clum, and Moon, 238), who has also drawn attention to Whitman's formulation.

25.   Justin Kaplan, "Whitman and the Biographers," in Krieg 14.

3. Man's Words

1.   Foucault 1:43. Foucault chooses 1870 because Carl Westphal's article on "contrary sexual feeling" appeared then. However, Bentham's discussion of similar material (See Crompton 251) as well as the pseudonymous *Don Leon* (Crompton 343–62) could provide equally useful and earlier dates.

2.   Quoted in Gilbert 149. Gilbert's article speaks to the question of Whitman as a poet who had to "certify his poetic identity through covert repetitions of the aesthetic maneuvers which characterize the old world's male tradition of poetic representation" (148). But in his best poetry—that is, the poetry inspired by homoerotic fantasy—he radically transgressed against those same forms, indeed destroyed them, not only structurally, metrically, formally, but contextually. The *Calamus* poems are "traditional" in their repetition of modified genres.

3.   Sedgwick, *Between men,* 206, 173.

4.   The question of effeminacy as an indicator of homosexuality is addressed in articles by Trumbach and Weeks in Duberman, Vicinus, and Chauncey 129, 195. See Katz for a collection of interesting documents illustrating the late nineteenth-century American world of homosexual clubs and bars in which such effeminate roles indicated homosexuality. See also Ralph Lind, *The Autobiography of an Androgyne* (1918; reprint, New York: Arno, 1975) and *The Female Impersonator* (1922; reprint, New York: Arno, 1975). See also Xavier Mayne (221) for a record of a homosexual military subculture in San Francisco at the end of the century. His chapter on homosexual prostitution and homosexual baths and clubs (409) indicates the presence of such institutions in American cities.

5.   Michel Foucault, *The History of Sexuality,* Vol.2, *The Uses of Pleasure:* (New York, Pantheon, 1985), 12.

6.   Sedgwick, *Between men,* 206.

7.   Smith-Rosenberg 90–108. See also Reynolds (309) for a discussion of other such texts that Whitman resisted.

8.   Benedict Friedlander, quoted in Donald Mager, "Gay Theories of Gender Role Deviance," *SubStance* 46 (1985), 35–36, as quoted in Elaine Showalter, *Sexual Anarchy: Gender and Culture at the Fin de Siecle* (New York: Viking, 1990), 173.

9.   Sedgwick, "Across Gender," 56.

10.   Regenia Gagnier, *Idyls of the Marketplace,* quoted in Showalter 174.

11.   Cohen 177–193.

12.   Foucault 1:121.

13.   Crompton, chap. 1.

14.   Katz 26, 28, 33.

15.   Duberman 43–45.

16.   Moon, "Disseminating Whitman," 250. Lord Alfred Douglas was not the first writer to assume that homosexuality was the love that dared not speak its name. By the time Whitman was writing, homophobia in one guise or another was a powerful presence in American society. For examples of and commentary on American homophobia see Katz 11–127, and for England see Crompton 12, 251, 284.

17.   Foucault 1:43.

18.   See Siegfried Sassoon, quoted in Peter Parker, *Ackerley* (New York, 1989), 91, on the subject of fascination with homosexuality and, incidentally, for a useful location of the Arcadian myth of a safe gay homeland: "I so seldom read anything remotely connected with the subject nearest my heart that almost any work of that kind causes a peculiar emotional disturbance in me. . . . I have carried about with me an inward sense of home-sickness for that land where I would be—that Elysium, forever deluding me with its mirages in the desert of my frustrated and distorted desires." The presumed outlaw status of homosexuality and the erotic fascination with it have historically led gay writers to search for justification and for historical validity and continuity so as to demonstrate that in history and in literature there could be found, as Whitman put it in *Calamus* 8, "the examples of old and new heroes." This search suggested and revealed the existence of such desires, as Whitman said in *Calamus* 23, in "other men in other lands." But the search like the subject was shadowed with disapprobation and opprobrium, and such research texts were often as outlaw as the practices they chronicled or defended. For example, in 1785 Jeremy Bentham wrote but feared to publish his remarkable essay on "Paederasty." Nearly a hundred years later, John Addington Symonds circulated privately, in editions of 100 only, his seminal essays *A Problem in Greek Ethics* (1883) and *A Problem in Modern Ethics* (1891). Both were anonymously published. It was inaccurate for Whitman to say that there was no breath of manly love in literature, but it was accurate to observe that in American letters the presence of such material was minimal. Whitman's

remark may be imprecise as literary history, but it is not imperceptive as homosocial and even literary criticism and can be judged a brief and valuable document in the history of a homosexual consciousness.

19. The dating of this passage is apparently open to question. White does not try to date it. But in the same notebook with it, Whitman mentions that his brother is practicing the piano. He had bought Jeff a piano in January 1852, and the lines I quote, of course, appear in "The Sleepers" (ll.32–41) in much modified form. This could suggest, though it does not prove, that this notebook is pre-1855.

20. Gilbert and Gubar, chap. 3.

21. Killingsworth 64.

22. Lipking suggests that "women's poetics . . . begin . . . with . . . the possibility of never having been empowered to speak." See "Aristotle's Sister: A Poetics of Abandonment," *Critical Inquiry* 10 (September 1983), 67.

23. Ellis 177.

24. Foucault 1:42–43.

4. The Fountains of Love: Poetry and Fiction, 1838-1850

1. Allen, *Solitary Singer,* 35–37.

2. Kaplan, *Walt Whitman — A Life,* 86–87.

3. *EPF,* xviii.

4. Allen, *Solitary Singer,* 49.

5. Allen, *Solitary Singer,* 33.

6. Allen, *Solitary Singer,* 33–35.

7. Allen, *Solitary Singer,* 38.

8. Allen, *Solitary Singer,* 39.

9. Katz 655.

10. Melville, *Moby-Dick* (New York: Reinhardt, 1958), chap. 35, p. 157.

11. Smith-Rosenberg 91.

12. Kaplan, *Walt Whitman — A Life,* 62.

13. For the west see Robert K. Martin, "Knights Errant and Gothic Seducers: The Representation of Male Friendship in Mid-Nineteenth-Century American Literature," in Duberman, Vicinus, and Chauncey 173. On Arcadia see Fone,"This Other Eden."

14. Smith-Rosenberg 90–108.

15. Smith-Rosenberg 105–6.

16.   Smith-Rosenberg (93) identifies a central Jacksonian anxiety and theme as that of father-son conflict, which is of course central to these fictions as well.

17.   EPF 68 n. 1.

18.   The consecutive texts are identified as *NW, C, E,* and *Collect.* The copy text in my remarks is *Collect.*

19.   Moon, *Disseminating Whitman,* 29. Moon also speculates that Whitman's censorship arose from his awareness that "public attitudes toward male-male love . . . had changed substantially between 1841 and 1844" (33). Erkilla, (*Political Poet,* 30) sees the story as a "protest against the enslavement of the worker" and as a fable of "social transformation." It is certainly that, but it is also a more profound protest against an even deeper slavery. Whitman certainly had political projects, and Erkilla's focus on his political life is profound and convincing. But to read this story as a fable about the uses of public power only, rather than also about the interpenetration of power by desire and desire by power, limits rather than enhances this story.

20.   Killingsworth 84–85.

21.   Martin,"Knights Errant," 181.

5. Fierce Wrestler: Notebooks, 1845–1854

1.   Walt Whitman to Edward Carpenter, in *Days With Walt Whitman* (1886).

2.   For this literature see Martin, "Knights Errant," 169, and Roger Austen, *Playing the Game: The Homosexual Novel in America* (New York: Bobbs Merrill, 1977). See Moon, "Disseminating Whitman," for a discussion of the literature of solitary vice and its connection with Whitman.

3.   See Harold Bloom, *Agon,* 138.

4.   I am indebted to my student Gabriel de la Portilla for pointing out the kineticism, the felt sense of material energy, that this passage creates.

5.   My quote is from Derrida, *Of Grammatology,* trans. Gayatri Chakravorty Spivak. (Baltimore, Md.: Johns Hopkins, 1977), 43. The day after I wrote these lines in December 1990, I was speaking about them at The University of Paris to a colleague who hoped that my usage did not align me with that "camp." I gave assurances that I am not a camp follower. Though I do prefer to investigate and inhabit the guarded tents wherein only Whitman's uncertainty about the nature of language is quartered, I do think

that Derrida's extraordinary meditations have made the path and access to those tents, if neither easier nor clearer, at least infinitely more provocative.

6. As does Harold Bloom in *A Map of Misreading* (New York: Oxford University Press, 1975, 1980), 13.

7. Bloom, *Agon,* 189.

8. Smith-Rosenberg 108.

9. Smith-Rosenberg 106.

10. E. H. Miller, *Walt Whitman's Poetry: A Psychological Journey* (Boston: Beacon), 145.

11. Moon, "Disseminating Whitman," 239. Moon implies that the phallus in question, which in terms of contemporary American politics and male domination he wittily describes as a "heat seeking missile," is a straight and not a gay one.

12. Frances Wright, *A Few Days in Athens* (1822), 46. Erkilla (*Political Poet,* 18) also notes this parallel and states how it "intersects with and affirms a utopian republican discourse of self-mastery and 'divine friendship'."

13. See Shively for the suggestion that Vaughan was Whitman's first lover and may be the object of the "Live-Oak" core sequence in *Calamus.*

14. Quoted in Killingsworth 66.

15. As Richard Chase insisted that Whitman generally does. See *Walt Whitman Reconsidered* (New York: William Sloane Associates, 1955).

16. Elizabeth Cady Stanton, quoted in Killingsworth 69. See Madeleine B. Stern, "Some Radical Concepts of Sex and Marriage in Nineteenth-Century America," *Prospects* 2 (1973), 332–56, and Gilbert and Gubar.

17. Erkilla, *Political Poet,* 138.

18. Smith-Rosenberg 24, 29.

19. See Erkilla, *Political Poet,* 137; Killingsworth 73.

20. Harold Aspiz, "Walt Whitman: Feminist," in Krieg 79 and Erkilla, *Political Poet,* 137.

21. See Gilbert 153.

22. Killingsworth 66–67.

23. Killingsworth 67.

24. See the parody of Whitman, "The Counter-Jumper," quoted in Killingsworth 100.

25. For the "Sun-Down Papers" see Allen, *Solitary Singer,* 38.

26. Theodore Winthrop, *Cecil Dreeme,* 347, 348, quoted in Martin, "Knights Errant," 179. For Emerson, Thoreau, and Mel-

ville see Chapter 6 below. For the Uranian poets see Timothy d'Arch Smith, *Love in Earnest: Some Notes on the Lives and Writings of English Uranian Poets from 1889–1930* (London: Routledge, 1970). For American Uranian verse see "Edwin Edwinson," *Men and Boys: An Anthology* (New York, 1924).

27.   Thomas Wentworth Higginson, "Recent Poetry," *Nation* 55 (1892), 12, quoted in Killingsworth 102.

28.   Zweig 41.

29.   The quotation is from "I Sit and Look Out." On Whitman's editorials see Erkilla, *Political Poet,* chaps. 1, 2. On Whitman's view of the sexuality of women see Killingsworth 32–36.

30.   Killingsworth 33.

31.   Moon, "Disseminating Whitman," 246, 251.

32.   Foucault 1:104, 146–47.

33.   The question of fear is discussed by E. H. Miller, *Walt Whitman's Poetry,* Sandra Gilbert, and Gilbert and Gubar. However several readers have asserted just the opposite. Adrienne Rich for example says, "Whitman really does accept women's lust as a good and natural part of her being, rather than as a devouring force or self destructive drive." E. H. Miller, *Whitman's "Song of Myself",* 55.

34.   Martin, "Knights Errant," 175.

35.   Gilbert 136.

36.   Horace Traubel, *With Walt Whitman in Camden* (Boston, 1906), 2:370–71. Whitman claimed in "Song of Myself" that "my words are words of questioning and to indicate reality" (1082). His words indicate that the reality of comradeship was more vivid than his perception of women. He describes women either as inhabitants of roles or in their relationship to men, and rarely, in "Song of Myself" at least, in sexual contexts. Adjectives describing women are limited: cleanhaired, young, pure, handsome, red-faced, loose-gowned, and once, voluptuous. The most extensively described woman in "Song of Myself" is the trapper's Indian bride, who has "long eyelashes," "coarse straight locks," and "voluptuous" limbs. The reality of his response to women is equally distancing. He "turns outward" to groups of women; he "invites" a kept woman to his feast; he "favors" fully equipped women and is "pleased" with women and with a quakeress. The nearest he comes to a declaration of passion is when he is "convulsed" by the soprano's voice as he is convulsed by his own "love grip." Though he boasts that he *will* "tighten" a bride to his "lips and thighs" and *will* "start bigger and nimbler babes," on "women fit for conception," he

does not do it nor does he kiss them, love them, or as he does with men, dance, laugh, or sing in their presence. They are never "friends," even though he claims that women "accept," "desire," and "comprehend" him. Though women are "fully equipped," they are not fully described genitally in "Song of Myself" and rarely in later poems (the brilliant image of the "cleave of the clasping and sweetfleshed day" in "The Sleepers" for example).

Men on the other hand are identified not only by the rich variety of their activities but by an extensive decriptive vocabulary and a substantial lexicon rich with sexual implication. Words for men are man, bedfellow, male, driver, boatman, trapper, clamdigger, butcher boy, blacksmith, fireman, carpenter, pilot, mate, farmer, printer, young fellow, boy, young men, old men, friend, negro, giant, marksman, gentlemen, drover, canal-boy, mechanic, artist, sailor, lover, prisoner, fancy-man, rowdy, rough, hero, bridegroom, savage, farmboy, woodman, seaman, hunter, and comrade. They are described as masculine, picturesque, lithe, ample, hearty, clean, massive, lusty, friendly, crisp, strong, flowing, hairy, luxuriant, heavy, interrogating, upright, large, fresh, manly, disorderly, fleshy, sensual, a kosmos, loving, calm, commanding, steady, tall, and perfect. Whitman responds to men (and/or they to him) with kisses, jostling, bussing, dilating, seizing, wrestling, compelling, bestowing, raising, embracing, teaching, dancing, laughing, singing, gazing, plunging, reaching, loving, loitering, caressing, eating, sleeping, adorning, resigning, undressing, and unbuttoning. He blows them full of the jets of life, turns over upon them, "goes" with fishermen and seamen, and "loves" them. Phallic words abound: loveroot, crotch, plunging tongues, stiff and drooping leaves, swelling baskets, crooked inviting fingers, firm masculine coulter, fibres of manly wheat, soft tickling genitals, branches of live-oak, libidinous prongs, sprouts treacherous tips, red marauders, headlands, and the sheathed hooded sharptoothed touch. Only men enjoy orgasm; they souse with spray, dash with amorous wet, express trickling sap of maple, ejaculate milky stream pale strippings, send out seas of bright juice, unclench floodgates, restrain udders dripping with semen, and jet the father stuff. They finally, in fact, become semen, effusing in lacy jags and eddies.

37.   Killingsworth 8. See Erkilla, *Political Poet*, 125. Erkilla stresses, as does Killingsworth, the anti-racist thrust of the poem, especially in the section on men and women at auction.

38.   Killingsworth 6.

39.   Quoted in Aspiz 83, from Henry C. Wright, *Marriage and Parentage: or, The Reproductive Element in Man* (1855), 271.

40.   Showalter 170.

41.   Quited in Aspiz 82.

42.   Erkilla (*Political Poet,* 125) convincingly discusses the inscription of anti-slavery sentiments in these lines, and Killingsworth (8) suggests that the poems also registers opposition to prostitution. However, the limbs of the man at auction are described as "red, black, or white," suggesting that it is not so much a slave as a stud who is for sale, and the woman is sold not as a prostitute but as a breeder.

43.   Killingsworth 11.

44.   Killingsworth 10; D. H. Lawrence, "Whitman," from *Nation and Athenaeum,* 24 (23 July 1921), 616–618.

45.   Killingsworth 65.

6. Masculine Landscapes: "The Sleepers" and "Song of Myself," 1855

1.   See Killingsworth 15; Martin (*Homosexual Tradition,* 9) describes "The Sleepers" as a dream vision.

2.   Erkilla, *Political Poet,* 118. Erkilla primarily focuses on the political rather than the sexual resonances of the poem.

3.   Killingsworth 16.

4.   Kaplan, *Walt Whitman—A Life,* 183.

5.   Kaplan, *Walt Whitman—A Life,* 183.

6.   E. H. Miller, *Walt Whitman's Poetry,* 72.

7.   Killingsworth 18.

8.   In gay slang the prominent penis bulging beneath tight pants is a "basket."

9.   Sedgwick, *Between Men,* 205.

10.   Martin supports this reading (*Homosexual Tradition,* 11–12), while other critics prefer more heterosexual interpretations. Killingsworth is content to assert that "what we cannot doubt is that the lines are highly charged sexually" (21).

11.   Martin, *Homosexual Tradition,* 11; James E. Miller, *A Critical Guide to Leaves of Grass* (Chicago: University of Chicago Press, 1957), 133–134. A "vaginal" or perhaps more accurately "heterosexualized" critical reading of this sequence needs to account for the threatening "white teeth" that add to the lines the disturbing image of the *vagina dentata,* something hardly enticing even for the most resolutely heterosexual critic, so I am told.

12.   On the dehomosexualization process see Killingsworth, chap. 4, and Moon *Disseminating Whitman,* 50–51.

13.   Killingsworth 23. Moon (*Disseminating Whitman,* 86) discusses the passage in which the mother loses her Indian friend and suggests that it is "the most significant instance of . . . genuine feminine utterance in *Leaves of Grass.*

14.   Martin, *Homosexual Tradition,* 12.

15.   E. H. Miller's *Walt Whitman's "Song of Myself"; A Mosaic of Interpretations* (1989) is a remarkable and invaluable book, representing as he says "excerpts from the commentary of almost 300 readers who have brought various skills and insights to the poem during the last 130 years" (xxviii).

16.   Martin, *Homosexual Tradition,* 16.

17.   E. H. Miller, *Whitman's "Song of Myself,"* 47.

18.   For further discussion of this image and for additional references see Fone, "This Other Eden," and Robert K. Martin, *Hero, Captain and Stranger: Male Friendship, Social Critique, and Literary Form in the Sea Novels of Herman Melville* (Chapel Hill: University of North Carolina Press, 1986).

19.   See Plato, *Symposium* and *Phaedrus;* J. A. Symonds, *A Problem in Modern Ethics* (1891); and Edward Carpenter, *Homogenic Love, and its Place in a Free Society* (1895). Greek pedagogic pederasty is extensively discussed in K. J. Dover, *Greek Homosexuality* (Cambridge, Mass.: Harvard University Press, 1978) and Halperin. Martin (*Homosexual Tradition* and *Hero, Captain*) touches upon the convention as does Fone, (*Hidden Heritage* and *"This Other Eden"*). See Oscar Wilde's invocation of the theme in his definition of the love that dare not speaks its name and Charles Kains-Jackson's theoretical discussion in "The New Chivalry" (1894). Because gay people are obviously not taught to be gay by heterosexual parents, the role of teacher/lover is a particularly potent one in the gay literary imagination as well as in the experience of gay life.

20.   Killingsworth 28.

21.   Robert Duncan, "Changing Perspectives in Reading Whitman," 96–97, and Ernest Lee Tuveson, *The Avatars of the Thrice Great Hermes,* 233, quoted in E. H. Miller, *Whitman's "Song of Myself,"* 55.

22.   E. H. Miller, *Whitman's "Song of Myself,"* 56.

23.   See Plato's *Symposium.*

24.   E. H. Miller, *Whitman's "Song of Myself,"* 55–56.

25.   Martin, *Homosexual Tradition,* 16.

26.   Martin (*Homosexual Tradition,* 25) correctly insists that Edwin Miller makes a mistake in *Walt Whitman's Poetry,* 90, in asserting that the episode indicates the bisexual nature of the poet. But since to God all things are possible, Martin's insistence that the impregnation "need not take place through the vagina; there may be penetration of the anus . . . or through the ear" seems to demand too much literality and is truly a work of supererogation.

27.   See E. H. Miller, *Whitman's "Song of Myself,"* 56–57.

28.   E. H. Miller, *Whitman's "Song of Myself,"* 59.

29.   E. H. Miller, *Whitman's "Song of Myself,"* 58.

30.   E. H. Miller, *Whitman's Poetry,* 20.

31.   James Cox, quoted in Miller, *Whitman's "Song of Myself,"* 65.

32.   E. H. Miller, *Whitman's "Song of Myself,"* 63.

33.   John Berryman, in *The Freedom of the Poet* (New York: Farrar, Straus & Giroux, 1976), 235, also makes the suggestion that the poem really begins with section 6.

34.   See E. H. Miller, *Whitman's "Song of Myself,"* 68–70.

35.   Gelpi, quoted in E. H. Miller, *Whitman's "Song of Myself,"* 70.

36.   See, for example, Langston Hughes' "Slave on the Block" (1933) or chapter 1 of Ralph Ellison's *Invisible Man* (1953).

37.   The Crockett almanac (1837) is quoted in Smith-Rosenberg 97, where Smith-Rosenberg also makes the point about cannibalism and sexual violence. This is not to say that Whitman was without racism, which his occasional use of stereotyping and racial epithets denies. See Newton Arvin, *Whitman* (1938), 38.

38.   Frederik Schyberg 119–20.

39.   E. H. Miller, *Whitman's "Song of Myself,"* 77. Killingsworth 32.

40.   For the former position see Killingsworth (34) and for the latter E. H. Miller, *Walt Whitman's Poetry,* 94.

41.   Killingsworth 34.

42.   Martin, *Homosexual Tradition,* 21 also makes this point. Moon (*Disseminating Whitman,* 41–43) feels that "Whitman might have opposed such a literally 'sexual' reading . . . because limiting the determinate grounds for the exchanges which are represented . . . to specifically sexual ones is inevitably to produce a hermeneutic dead-end in a text which was designed to retain its fluidity and mobility of meaning(s)." Moon feels that other "economies" are also represented here—economies of gender, age, and class. But it could be argued that these economies are represented

in one form or another in most writings. Male homosexuality is not represented in most writings, and that is Whitman's point. Moon suggests that one reading might include "the speaker's appropriation of the woman's position for his own." He further suggests that the speaker passes into the water "along with the young woman" and that she could also be considered "as a feminine figure" with whom the speaker has "merged" though "without necessarily having merged her into himself." This creates the interesting possibility that there are not twenty-nine, but thirty bathers.

43.   Zweig 187.

44.   E. H. Miller (*Whitman's "Song of Myself,"* 77) points this out.

45.   An assumption made by many critics from De Selincourt to Snyder. See E. H. Miller, *Whitman's "Song of Myself,"* 74–77.

46.   Gilbert 130.

47.   See the remarkable book *Autobiography of an Androgyne* by "Jennie June" (Ralph Lind), upon which I comment below.

48.   Gelpi, in E. H. Miller, *Whitman's "Song of Myself,"* 76. For nineteenth-century theories see J. A. Symonds, *A Problem in Modern Ethics* (1891). Though Gelpi's comments are now 15 years old, I still discover similar attitudes about gay roles in the comments my students make during discussions of gay texts and gay people.

49.   Martin, *Homosexual Tradition,* 21. Miller includes this passage in his "Mosaic" and, curiously, when introducing another critic, observes that this critic like Martin "also dilutes the affect of the poetry." Martin's comment hardly dilutes—it vibrantly illuminates, just as the material that follows those remarks and concerns Whitman's radical siting of homosexuality as a force for "a major change" in society is the best summary of that position. I cannot help but feel that this insinuation of dilution is an example of the kind of critical homophobia that Martin points out in Miller's 1968 text and that in small ways also mars Miller's excellent current volume.

50.   Martin, *Homosexual Tradition,* 22.

51.   The reference is to case 26, Ellis and Symonds. Case 25 is Symonds himself.

52.   Martin, *Homosexual Tradition,* 23.

53.   M. Wynn Thomas, in "*Song of Myself* and Possessive Individualism," *Delta* 16 (May 1983): 3–17, points out the usage of spend.

54.   Killingsworth 35.

55.   Ralph Lind's two books, *The Autobiography of an Androgyne* (1918) and *The Female Impersonator* (1922) recount his fascinating life adorning himself for men in the streets of late nineteenth-century New York.

56.   Martin, *Homosexual Tradition,* 17.

57.   Symonds, *A Problem in Modern Ethics,* 4. However during that time, words, some of them kinds words, had begun to appear. Edward Prime-Stevenson (1868–1942) as "Xavier Mayne" in *The Intersexes* (1908), the first full-length study of homosexuality written by a self-identified homosexual in America, lists in his preface those words that do not suggest disgrace or disgust— "homosexualism, similisexualism, urningism, inverted sexuality, uranianism,"—though he does not mention Whitman's adhesiveness. Havelock Ellis (*Sexual Inversion* [1897]) notes the triumph of "homosexual" and "homosexuality" in a footnote: "Homosexual is a barbarously hybrid word. . . . It is however, convenient, and now widely used" (1). Symonds' comment appeared in *A Problem in Modern Ethics* (1891) and was, curiously, not quite accurate, since "homosexual" and "homosexuality" had in fact been used—indeed coined—in 1869. Symonds knew that Karl Heinrich Ulrichs, in a series of pamphlets written between 1864 and 1870, had used the word "Urning"—deriving it from the *Symposium,* wherein Plato nominates Aphrodite, daughter of Uranus, as the titulary goddess of male-male love—to denominate what Symonds knew himself to be and suspected Whitman of being.

58.   Vern Bullough, "Homosexuality and Its Confusion with the 'Secret Sin' in Pre-Freudian America," in *Sex, Society and History* (New York: Science History Publications, 1976), 112–24; Michael Moon, "Disseminating Whitman," 235–53.

59.   G. S. Rousseau, "The Pursuit of Homosexuality in the Eighteenth Century," in Robert P. Maccubbin ed., *Eighteenth Century Life,* n.s., 3, vol. 9 (May 1985), 136.

60.   Katz 26.

61.   Katz 27.

62.   Zweig 258–59.

63.   Quoted in Smith-Rosenberg 105.

64.   Quoted in Katz 493.

65.   Galway Kinnell, quoted in E. H. Miller, *Whitman's "Song of Myself,"* 94 and Cavitch 57.

66.   Snyder 74.

67.   Killingsworth 36.

68.   See Gustav Bychowski, "Walt Whitman: A Study in Sublimation," in *Homosexuality and Creative Genius,* ed. Hendrik Ruitenbeck (New York, 1967), 157–59; Killingsworth 37. Many critics fail to recognize that gay men have sex with men not because they want to be a woman but because men offer precisely what women do not. Gore Vidal suggested that the homosexual (he said "homosexualist") does not "enjoy a satisfactory sexual relationship with a woman because he himself is so entirely masculine that the woman presents no challenge, no masculine hardness, no exciting *agon*." *The Second American Revolution* (New York: Random House 1982), 45. This may be somewhat suspect now, but it is the point of section 28.

69.   Killingsworth 36. Moon, *Disseminating Whitman,* 42.

70.   Bloom, "Whitman's Image of Voice: To the Tally of My Soul" (1982), in *Modern Critical Views — Walt Whitman* (New York: Chelsea, 1985), 133.

71.   Martin, "Knights Errant," 172.

72.   Duberman 143.

73.   Smith-Rosenberg 106.

74.   E. H. Miller (*Whitman's "Song of Myself,"* 108) insists that the stallion is the brother, while Martin (*Homosexual Tradition,* 29) feels it is the "male lover." Miller (155) observes that Martin "notes, gratuitously, that Whitman makes vivid the banal sexual metaphor of 'riding' someone." Martin's observation, of course, is precisely to the point, as Crockett's and Wade's metaphors show.

75.   Martin (*Homosexual Tradition,* 223) points out that Whitman's faulty French, not "sexual ambiguity," accounts for the *e* in "amie." the exclusively male context leaves no doubt of this.

76.   See Tanner in E. H. Miller *Whitman's "Song of Myself,"* 109.

77.   E. H. Miller, *Whitman's "Song of Myself,"* 110, 111.

78.   E. H. Miller, *Whitman's "Song of Myself,"* 112.

79.   Martin, *Homosexual Tradition,* 30.

80.   Martin, *Homosexual Tradition,* 31.

81.   E. H. Miller, *Whitman's "Song of Myself,"* 138.

82.   Plato, *Symposium,* trans. Walter Hamilton (London: Penguin, 1951), 180e.

83.   Plato, *Symposium,* 208c–209e.

84.   Plato, *Symposium,* 209e–211a.

7. Brethren and Lovers

1.   Milton Hindus, *Leaves of Grass One Hundred Years After,* (Stanford: Stanford University Press, 1955), 44.

2.   Martin believes that he also read the *Symposium* in the Burges translation and points out that this translation often described men who loved men as "manly."

3.   Plato, *Phaedrus,* trans. R. Hackforth (Cambridge: Cambridge University Press, 1952), 104.

4.   Richard Dellamora, *Masculine Desire The Sexual Politics of Victorian Aestheticism* (Chapel Hill: University of North Carolina Press, 1990), 86.

5.   Katz 458–59.

6.   Katz 460–61.

7.   Emerson, "Friendship," in *Essays,* 1st Series (1841), (New York: A. S. Barnes, n.d.), 65.

8.   Katz 493.

9.   Katz 484. The question of Thoreau's homosexuality is rasied by Katz (650 n. 73).

10.   Katz 485. The friendship tradition, as practiced by the vast majority of orthodox, that is, heterosexual writers, participated in that dualism by imposing upon friendship a misread Platonism, and by firmly separating it from the presumed sole legitimate arena of sexual experience, the heterosexual. Such texts expressed capitalized Friendship in terms of male relationships only, as Emerson clearly does in his essay on the subject. This of course could also be a complicit action, for it thus allowed writers the chance to engage in extravagant protestations of male-male friendship, which could pass without any imputation of impropriety—either physically or emotionally—though such impropriety may indeed have been implied, intended, or even desired.

11.   Katz 485.

12.   Katz 482.

13.   Katz 486–87.

14.   Katz 486.

15.   Katz 487.

16.   Katz 488.

17.   Katz 490–91.

18.   Katz 493.

19.   Jay Leyda, *The Melville Log: A Documentary Life of Herman Melville* (New York, 1951), 211. On the conventions of homoerotic novels see Fone, "This Other Eden," 13–35. For a convincing discussion of the homosexual valance of Melville's texts see Martin, *Hero, Captain.* For Stoddard see Martin, "Knights Errant," 169–82, and Austen.

20.   See Martin, *Hero, Captain,* 16.

21.   Martin, *Hero, Captain,* 19. Martin's comments enlarge my own discussion (1983) of Arcadia as a gay literary image.

22.   Herman Melville, *Typee* (Garden City: Doubleday, 1961), 52–53.

23.   "The Poet's Journal" in Bayard Taylor, *Poetical Works,* Household Edition (1862), 11.

24.   On the nineteenth-century homosexual novel see Austen, chap. 1, and Martin, "Knights Errant," 169.

25.   Martin, *Hero, Captain,* 19.

26.   Melville, *Typee,* 73–75.

27.   Melville, *Typee,* 109–10. See Katz 281, and Carpenter, *Intermediate Types Among Primitive Folk* (London: George Allen, 1914) for discussions of this fascinating subject.

28.   Richard Henry Dana, Two Years Before The Mast (1840), 153.

29.   Melville, *Typee,* 116.

30.   Melville, *Typee,* 169.

31.   In *Omoo* (1847), which he had also read and reviewed, Whitman would have encountered Melville's further expiations on male friendship among the Polynesians, where, as he says, "in the annals of the island are examples of extravagant friendships, unsurpassed by the story of Damon and Pythias, in truth much more wonderful; for, notwithstanding the devotion — even of life in some cases — to which they led, they were frequently entertained at first sight for some stranger from another island." This passage has everything: male friendship itself, a justifying classical allusion to Greek lovers, and an intimation of the possibility of a lifelong relationship between male friends, together with the added frisson of promiscuous attachments to strangers. The narrator later describes his own friendships, one with the "handsome youth" Poky, who "could never do enough for me"; another with a "comely youth," who was "quite a buck in his way" (Did Melville too admire men we would call studs and Whitman called roughs?); and another with the fickle Kooloo, who assured the narrator that "the love he bore me was nuee, nuee, nuee, or infinitesimally extensive," but who "played the part of a retrograde lover; informing me one morning that his affections had undergone a change; he had fallen in love at first sight with a smart sailor." Toby too, it should be recalled, was "as smart a looking sailor as ever stepped upon a deck." Perhaps in "smart" he is using a sexually suggestive term. Certainly Whitman could hardly have avoided noticing that in Omoo the intimations of friendship have merged quite quickly and

quite obviously into a more perilous kingdom where the allure and temptation of homosexuality is rather more than implied.

32.   Edward Carpenter, *Intermediate Types,* 35, 27. For nineteenth-century examples see such stories as Bloxam's "The Priest and The Acolyte," in which the priest also stands for similar divinity, or the shamanistic contexts in the homosexual poetry of Alistair Crowley.

33.   Katz 458.

34.   Martin, *Homosexual Tradition,* 97–106.

35.   R. H. Stoddard, *Poems* (Boston, 1852), 121. Quoted in Martin, *Homosexual Tradition,* 106.

36.   Taylor, *Poems of the Orient,* 35–37.

37.   Crompton 118.

38.   Taylor 37–38. Some years later, Lord Alfred Douglas, speaking of homosexual passion in his poem "Two Loves" published in *The Chameleon* (1894), used a word that had by then become a coded synonym for homosexual love: "His name is Shame." He called it, of course, "the love that dare not speak its name," which love, in the same year, he celebrated in a verse called "In Praise of Shame." The word appears in "The World Well Lost IV" in the volume of poems *In Fancy Dress* (1886) by Marc Andre Raffalovich, who describes homosexual love as "sorrow; but men call him Shame." In "Preface" (*Poetical Works,* 1862), Taylor says that poetry can transform emotions: If the lover feels "shame for love unworthily bestowed, / That shame shall melt with pride." Whether the word had come to have its subtextual meaning in 1862, years before its firm definition by Douglas, is not sure. Nor is it sure that Taylor's use can be directly associated with a word that probably had not, in this precise form, penetrated to America. But there can be no doubt that he does unite "shame" and Greek love in this text, and this may be an early use, if not of the term, then of the association.

39.   Taylor 38.

40.   Taylor 38, 56–57.

41.   Martin, *Homosexual Tradition,* 101.

42.   Taylor 73.

43.   Taylor 66.

44.   If Whitman had any doubt about the discourse in which both he and Taylor participated, it would eventually be satisfied by Taylor's other poetry and his novel *Joseph and his Friend* (1870), a novel in which "Friend" is capitalized and with intended effect, making it one of the first of American homoerotic novels.

45.   Sedgwick (*Epistemology*, 58–59) talking about the gay contexts of literature points out that "we can't possibly know in advance about the Harlem Renaissance, any more than we can about the New England Renaissance . . . where the limits of revelatory inquiry are to be set, once we begin to ask . . . where and how the power in them of gay desires, people, discourses, prohibitions and energies were manifest. We know enough already, however, to know with certainty that in each of these Renaissances they were central. (No doubt that's how we will learn to recognize a renaissance when we see one.)"

46.   Foucault 1:71.

47.   Whitman's "thoughts in darkness" echo profoundly in Foucault's "dark shimmer of sex" that he says has "lifted up from deep within us a sort of mirage in which we think we see ourselves reflected." (1:157). That "we think" may have useful implications for Whitman's own repeated assertions about sexual doubt and puzzlement.

48.   Havelock Ellis and John Addington Symonds, *Sexual Inversion* (London, 1897). There have been so many editions of this work that I refer to case numbers only, these from the text I employ (1901), and place them in the body of my text.

49.   Foucault 1:35.

50.   Foucault 1:62.

51.   Allen, *Solitary Singer*, 16.

52.   Allen, *Solitary Singer*, 11.

53.   Bullough 112.

54.   Ellis 162.

55.   John Addington Symonds, *The Memoirs of John Addington Symonds*, ed. Phyllis Grosskurth (New York: Random House, 1984), 189.

56.   See Kaplan, *Walt Whitman—A Life*, 219.

57.   C. Westphal, "Die contrare Sexualempfindung, Symptom eines neuropathischen (psychopathischen) Zustandes," *Archiv fur Psychiatrie und Nervenkrankheiten*, 2 (1870), 73–108. Quoted in Halperin 162–63 n. 52.

58.   See Halperin 15.

59.   Ed Cohen 169. Sedgwick ("Across Gender," 59) provides a useful corrective to the notion of absolute displacement of one discourse with another, when she observes that "the two understandings, contradictory though they are, have coexisted, creating in the space of their contradiction enormous potentials of discursive power."

60.   Sedgwick, *Epistemology*, 67.

61.   Gayle Rubin, "Thinking Sex," quoted in Sedgwick, "Across Gender," 54; Sedgwick, "Across Gender," 58.

62.   Donald Mager, quoted in Sedgwick, "Across Gender," 59.

8. Epilogue: The Path Ahead

1.   *"Leaves of Grass*: A Volume of Poems Just Published," *Brooklyn Daily Times,* 29 September 1855. Quoted in Bradley, et al., *Leaves of Grass,* 777–79. Whitman's style clearly indicates the author, and Traubel and the other literary executors included the review as by Whitman in *In Re Walt Whitman* (1893).

Works Cited

Allen, Gay Wilson. *The New Walt Whitman Handbook*. New York: New York University Press, 1985.

———. *The Solitary Singer: A Critical Biography of Walt Whitman*. New York: Macmillan, 1955.

Aspiz, Harold. "Walt Whitman, Feminist." In *Walt Whitman Here and Now,* edited by Joann Krieg, 79–88. Westport: Greenwood Press, 1985.

Austen, Roger. *Playing the Game: The Homosexual Novel in America*. New York: Bobbs Merrill, 1977.

Berringer, Felicity. "Out of the Closet, Into the Universities." *New York Times,* 30 December 1990.

Berryman, John. *The Freedom of the Poet*. New York: Farrar, Straus & Giroux, 1976.

Blodgett, Harold. *Walt Whitman in England*. Ithaca: Cornell University Press, 1934.

Bloom, Harold. *Agon: Towards a Theory of Revisionism*. New York: Oxford University Press, 1982.

———. *A Map of Misreading*. New York: Oxford University Press, 1975, 1980.

———. *Wallace Stevens: The Poems of Our Climate*. Ithaca: Cornell University Press, 1977.

———. "Whitman's Image of Voice: To the Tally of My Soul." 1982. Reprint. *Modern Critical Views — Walt Whitman*. New York: Chelsea, 1985.

Bullough, Vern. "Homosexuality and Its Confusion with the 'Secret Sin' in Pre-Freudian America." In *Sex, Society and History.* New York: Science History Publications, 1976.

Butters, Ronald R., John M. Clum, and Michael Moon, eds. *Displacing Homophobia: Gay Male Perspectives in Literature and Culture*. Durham: Duke University Press, 1989.

Bychowski, Gustav. "Walt Whitman: A Study in Sublimation." In *Homosexuality and Creative Genius,* edited by Hendrik Ruitenbeck. New York, 1967.

Cady, Joseph. "Drum-Taps and Nineteenth-Century Male Homosexual Literature." In *Walt Whitman Here and Now,* edited by Joann P. Krieg, 49–59. Westport: Greenwood Press, 1985.

Carpenter, Edward. *Days With Walt Whitman*. 1886.

————. *Homogenic Love, and its Place in a Free Society.* Manchester: The Labour Press, 1894.

————. *Intermediate Types Among Primitive Folk.* London: George Allen, 1914.

Cavitch, David. *My Soul and I: The Inner Life of Walt Whitman.* Boston: Beacon, 1985.

Chase, Richard. *Walt Whitman Reconsidered.* New York: William Sloane Associates, 1955.

Cohen, Ed. "Legislating the Norm: From Sodomy to Gross Indecency." In *Displacing Homophobia: Gay Male Perspectives in Literature and Culture,* edited by Ronald R. Butters, John M. Clum, and Michael Moon, 169–205. Durham: Duke University Press, 1989.

Crew, Louie, and Rictor Norton, eds. *The Homosexual Imagination.* Vol. 36, no. 3 of *College English* (1974).

Crompton, Louis. *Byron and Greek Love: Homophobia in 19th Century England.* Berkeley and Los Angeles: University of California Press, 1985.

Dana, Richard Henry. *Two Years Before the Mast.* 1840.

Dellamora, Richard. *Masculine Desire: The Sexual Politics of Victorian Aestheticism.* Chapel Hill: University of North Carolina Press, 1990.

Derrida, Jacques. *Of Grammatology.* Trans. Gayatri Chakravorty Spivak. Baltimore, Md.: Johns Hopkins University Press, 1977.

Douglas, Lord Alfred. "Two Loves." *The Chameleon* (1894).

Dover, K. J. *Greek Homosexuality.* Cambridge, Mass.: Harvard University Press, 1978.

Duberman, Martin. *About Time: Exploring the Gay Past.* New York: Gay Presses of New York, 1986.

Duberman, Martin Bauml, Martha Vicinus, and George Chauncey, eds. *Hidden From History: Reclaiming the Gay and Lesbian Past.* New York: New American Library, 1989.

Duncan, Robert. "Changing Perspectives in Reading Whitman." In *The Artistic Legacy of Walt Whitman,* edited by E. H. Miller, 73–102. New York: New York University Press, 1970.

Edwinson, Edwin. *Men and Boys: An Anthology.* New York, 1924.

Ellis Havelock. *Studies in The Psychology of Sex: Sexual Inversion.* Philadelphia, 1901.

Ellis, Havelock, and John Addington Symonds. *Sexual Inversion.* London, 1987.

Emerson, R. W. "Friendship." In *Essays.* 1st ser. 1841.

Erkilla, Betsy. *Walt Whitman Among the French*. New Haven: Princeton University Press, 1980.

———. *Whitman: The Political Poet*. New York: Oxford University Press, 1989.

Fern, Fanny. *Fern Leaves from Fanny's Portfolio*. 2d ser. 1854.

Fone, Byrne R. S. *Hidden Heritage: History and the Gay Imagination*. New York: Avocation, 1979.

———. "This Other Eden: Arcadia and the Homosexual Imagination." In *Literary Visions of Homosexuality*, edited by Stuart Kellogg, 13–34. New York: Haworth, 1983.

Foucault, Michel. *The History of Sexuality*. Vol. 1, *An Introduction*. New York: Random House, 1978. Vol. 2, *The Use of Pleasure*. New York: Pantheon, 1985.

Gilbert, Sandra. "The American Sexual Poetics of Walt Whitman and Emily Dickinson." In *Reconstructing American Literary History*, edited by Sacvan Bercovitch, 123–54. Cambridge, Mass.: Harvard University Press, 1986.

Gilbert, Sandra, and Susan Gubar. *The Madwoman in The Attic: The Woman Writer and the Nineteenth-Century Literary Imagination*. New Haven: Yale University Press, 1979.

Halperin, David M. *One Hundred Years of Homosexuality*. London: Routledge, 1990.

Hartman, Geoffrey. *The Fate of Reading and Other Essays*. Chicago: University of Chicago Press, 1975.

Higginson, Thomas Wentworth. "Recent Poetry." *Nation* 55 (1892), 12.

Hindus, Milton. *Leaves of Grass One Hundred Years After*. Stanford: Stanford University Press, 1955.

———. *Walt Whitman: The Critical Heritage*. London: Routledge, 1971.

Holloway, Emory. *Whitman: An Interpretation in Narrative*. New York: Knopf, 1926.

Kaplan, Justin. "The Biographer's Problem." In *Walt Whitman. Sex and Gender. Mickle Street Review* 11 (1989): 87–88.

———. *Walt Whitman—a Life*. New York: Simon and Schuster, 1980.

Katz, Jonathon Ned. *Gay American History*. New York: Thomas Y. Crowell. 1976

Kellogg, Stuart, ed. *Literary Visions of Homosexuality*. New York: Haworth, 1983.

Killingsworth, M. Jimmie. *Whitman's Poetry of the Body: Sexuality, Politics, and the Text*. Chapel Hill: University of North Carolina Press, 1989.

Krieg, Joann, ed. *Walt Whitman Here and Now.* Westport: Green-wood Press, 1985.

Kristeva, Julia. "The Novel as Polylogue." In *Desire in Language: A Semiotic Approach to Literature,* edited by Leon S. Roudiez. New York: Columbia University Press, 1980.

Lawrence, D. H. "Whitman." *Nation and Atheneum* 24 (23 July 1921).

Leverenz, David. *Manhood in The American Renaissance.* New York, 1989.

Leyda, Jay. *The Melville Log: A Documentary Life of Herman Melville.* New York, 1951.

Lind, Ralph. *Autobiography of An Androgyne.* 1918. Reprint. New York: Arno, 1975.

———. *The Female Impersonator.* 1922. Reprint. New York: Arno, 1975.

Lipking, Lawrence. "Aristotle's Sister: A Poetics of Abandonment." *Critical Inquiry* 10 (September 1983).

Maccubbin, Robert P., ed. *Eighteenth Century Life: Unauthorized Sexual Behavior During the Enlightenment.* n.s., 3, vol. 9. (May 1985).

Mager, Donald. "Gay Theories of Gender Role Deviance." *Sub-Stance* 46 (1985), 35–36.

Martin, Robert K. *Hero, Captain and Stranger: Male Friendship, Social Critique, and Literary Form in the Sea Novels of Herman Melville.* Chapel Hill: University of North Carolina Press, 1986.

———. *The Homosexual Tradition in American Poetry.* Austin and London: University of Texas Press, 1979.

———. "Knights Errant and Gothic Seducers: The Representation of Male Friendship in Mid-Nineteenth-Century American Literature." In *Hidden From History: Reclaiming the Gay and Lesbian Past,* edited by Martin Bauml Duberman et al., 169–82. New York: New American Library, 1989.

———. Review of *Manhood in the American Renaissance,* by David Leverenz. *Walt Whitman Quarterly Review* 7 (Winter 1990): 143–146.

Mayne, Xavier [Edward Prime-Stevenson]. *The Intersexes.* Naples, 1908.

Melville, Herman. *Moby Dick.* 1850.

———. *Omoo.* 1847.

———. *Typee.* Garden City: Doubleday, 1961.

Miller, Edwin H. *Walt Whitman's Poetry: A Psychological Journey.* Boston: Beacon, 1968.

———. *Walt Whitman's "Song of Myself": A Mosaic of Interpretations.* Iowa City: University of Iowa Press, 1989.

Miller, J. Hillis. *Thomas Hardy: Distance and Desire.* Cambridge, Mass.: Harvard University Press, 1970.

Moon, Michael. "Disseminating Whitman." In *Displacing Homophobia: Gay Male Perspectives in Literature and Culture,* edited by Ronald R. Butters, John M. Clum, and Michael Moon, 235–53. Durham: Duke University Press, 1989.

———. *Disseminating Whitman: Revision and Corporeality in Leaves of Grass.* Cambridge, Mass.: Harvard University Press, 1991.

Parker, Peter. *Ackerley.* New York, 1989.

Plato, *Phaedrus.* Translated by R. Hackforth. Cambridge: Cambridge University Press, 1952.

———. *Symposium.* Translated by Walter Hamilton. London: Penguin, 1951.

Raffalovich, Marc Andre. "The World Well Lost IV." *In Fancy Dress.* 1886.

Reynolds, David S. *Beneath the American Renaissance: The Subversive Imagination in the Age of Emerson and Melville.* Cambridge, Mass.: Harvard University Press, 1988.

Rousseau, G. S. "The Pursuit of Homosexuality in the *Eighteenth Century." In Eighteenth Century Life: Unauthorized Sexual Behavior During the Enlightenment,* edited by Robert P. Maccubbin, n.s., 3, vol. 9 (May 1985): 132–68.

Schyberg, Frederick. *Walt Whitman.* New York: Columbia University Press, 1951.

Sedgwick, Eve Kosofsky. "Across Gender, Across Sexuality: Willa Cather and Others." In *Displacing Homophobia: Gay Male Perspectives in Literature and Culture,* edited by Ronald R. Butters, John M. Clum, and Michael Moon, 53–73. Durham: Duke University Press, 1989.

———. *Between Men: English Literature and Male Homosocial Desire.* New York: Columbia University Press, 1985.

———. *Epistemology of the Closet.* Berkeley and Los Angeles: University of California Press. 1990.

Shively, Charley. *Calamus Lovers.* San Francisco: Gay Sunshine Press, 1987.

Showalter, Elaine. *Sexual Anarchy: Gender and Culture at the Fin de Siecle.* New York: Viking, 1990.

Smith, Timothy D'Arch. *Love in Earnest: Some Notes on the Lives and Writings of English Uranian Poets from 1889–1930.* London: Routledge, 1970.

Smith-Rosenberg, Carroll. *Disorderly Conduct: Visions of Gender in Victorian America.* New York: Oxford University Press, 1985.

Snyder, John. *The Dear Love of Man: Tragic and Lyric Communion in Walt Whitman.* Boston, 1975.

Stern, Madeleine B. "Some Radical Concepts of Sex and Marriage in Nineteenth-Century America." *Prospects* 2 (1973).

Stockinger, Jacob. "Homotextuality: A Proposal." In *The Gay Academic,* edited by Louie Crew, 303–10. Palm Springs, Calif.: ETC Publications, 1978.

Stoddard, Richard Henry. *Poems.* Boston, 1852.

Symonds, John Addington. *The Memoirs of John Addington Symonds.* Edited by Phyllis Grosskurth. New York: Random House, 1984.

———. *A Problem in Greek Ethics.* Bristol: Ballantyne and Hansen, 1883.

———. *A Problem in Modern Ethics.* Davos, 1891.

Taylor, Bayard. *Joseph and His Friend.* 1870.

———. *Poems of the Orient.* 1854.

———. *The Poetical Works of Bayard Taylor.* Boston: Houghton Mifflin, 1862.

Thomas, M. Wynn. "'Song of Myself' and Possessive Individualism." *Delta* 16 (May 1983): 3–17.

Traubel, Horace. *With Walt Whitman in Camden.* Boston, 1906.

Van Doren, Mark. "Walt Whitman, Stranger." In *The Private Reader.* New York, 1924.

Vidal, Gore. *The Second American Revolution.* New York: Random House, 1982.

White, William. "Walt Whitman in the Eighties: A Bibliographical Essay." In *Walt Whitman Here and Now,* edited by Joann P. Krieg, 217–24. Westport: Greenwood Press, 1985.

Wright, Frances. *A Few Days in Athens.* 1822.

———. *Views of Society and Manners in America.* 1821.

Wright, Henry C. *Marriage and Parentage: or, The Reproductive Element in Man.* 1855.

Zweig, Paul. *Walt Whitman — The Making of a Poet.* New York: Basic Books, 1984.

Index

Adhesiveness, 4, 13, 30, 33, 42, 263–64
Alcott, Bronson, 249
Alcott, William, 45
Alger, Horatio, 28
Allen, Gay Wilson 12, 16, 42, 233, 273
American Tradition in Literature, The (Perkins et al.), 274
Anti-feminism, 23
Antihomophobic narrative, 6
Anti-onanist texts, 65
Arcadia, 217, 278n.18
Arvin, Newton, 17, 270n.6
Aspiz, Harold, 90
Asselineau, Roger, 17
"Athlete" as sign of homoerotic desire, 25, 26, 34
Aurora, 39, 40

"Ballad of Boys Bathing" (Corvo), 156
Barnfield, Richard, 152
"Baron Corvo" (Rolfe), 155, 156
Beckford, William, 218n.9
Bentham, Jeremy, 277n.1, 278n.18
Bertz, Eduard, 12, 16
Blodgett, Harold, 272n.21
Bloom, Harold, 8, 27, 72, 77, 183
Bloxam, John Francis, 292n.32
Bohn Plato, 206
Brasher, Thomas, 38

Brinton, Daniel, 40
Bucke, Richard Maurice, 12, 84
Buggery, 28
Burroughs, John, 12
Bychowski, Gustav, 161, 177

Carpenter, Edward, 17, 63, 138, 222, 236, 242, 245, 252, 253
Catullus, 152
Cauldwell, William, 40
Cavitch, David, 173
Cecil Dreeme (Winthrop), 95
Chace, Roger, 271n.6
Chase, Richard, 275
City and The Pillar, The (Vidal), 105, 137
Cohen, Ed, 257
Columbian Magazine, 53
Comradeship, 4, 24, 95, 101
"Counter-jumper," 21, 42, 91
Cowley, Malcolm, 17
Crompton, Louis, 28, 223

Dana, Richard Henry, 220
Davy Crockett Almanacs, 23, 52, 78–80, 151, 173, 185–86
Days With Walt Whitman (Carpenter), 17
Death in Venice (Mann), 136
Dellamora, Richard, 208
Democratic Review, 63
Derrida, Jacques, 7, 73, 280n.5

301

Disseminating Whitman (Moon), 18
Don Leon (anon.), 95, 277n.1
Douglas, Alfred, 278n.16, 292n.38
Doyle, Peter, 12, 16, 99, 159, 190
Duberman, Martin, 28
Duncan, Robert, 139

Eagle (Brooklyn), 38, 105, 154
Eakins, Thomas, 156
Effeminacy, 21–22, 41, 277n.4
Ellis, Havelock, 6, 34, 159, 229–61, 275
Emerson, Ralph Waldo, 4, 20, 23, 26, 27, 31, 209–11, 215, 222, 227, 229, 253, 254, 257, 263
"Epithalamion" (Hopkins), 136, 156
Erkilla, Betsy, 17, 90, 91, 106, 117, 273, 280n.19, 281n.12

Fern, Fanny, 101
Few Days in Athens, A (Wright), 88
Fiedler, Leslie, 202
Fierce Wrestler, 3, 6–9, 25, 36–37, 43, 48, 56, 58, 63–114, 120, 126, 129, 131, 134, 135, 141, 148, 151, 157, 158, 166–68, 173, 175–78, 180, 182, 187–88, 190, 192, 197–98, 200–210, 222, 240, 260
Forster, E. M., 136, 155, 159
Foucault, Michel, 4, 10, 11, 17, 19, 20, 22, 26, 29, 30, 35, 38, 100, 227, 229–30, 258, 267n.1, 293n.47
Freeman (Brooklyn), 38
Friedlander, Benedict, 23, 258
"Friendship" (Emerson), 210
"Friendship" (Thoreau), 212
Friendship tradition, 212, 290n.10

Gagnier, Regenia, 23
Gay, 269n.15
Gelpi, Albert, 142, 150, 157
Gilbert, Sandra, 91, 101, 157, 277n.2

Graham, Sylvester, 45
Greek Anthology, The, 152
Grier, Edward F., 53

Hallam, Arthur, 208
Halperin, David, 2, 5, 268nn. 6, 8
Harmodios and Aristogeition, 45
Higginson, Thomas Wentworth, 98, 263, 274
Holloway, Emory, 11, 273
Homoeroticism, 6, 20–62, 65, 255, 269n.15; textual conventions of, 45–46, 49–50, 67, 105, 131, 136–37, 152, 212, 216, 219, 221, 222
Homophobia, 14–16, 23, 28, 65, 270nn. 1, 5, 6
Homosexual: attitudes toward, 14; as category, 5; construction of, 4–6; definition, 6, 229–60, 267n.1, 268n.8; desire in texts, 20–35, 45–46; imagination, 18, 276n.23; justification of, 278n.18; sensibility, 18, 30, 276n.23; textual conventions. *See* Adhesiveness; Comradeship; Homoeroticism; Manly love
Homosexual Tradition in American Poetry, The (Martin), 121, 276–77
Homotextual, 267n.2. *See* Stockinger, Jacob
Hopkins, Gerard Manley, 136, 142, 156

Imre ("Mayne"), 136
In Memoriam (Tennyson), 208
Intersexes, The ("Mayne"), 288n.57

John Brent (Winthrop), 185
Joseph and His Friend (Taylor), 50, 95, 136

Kains-Jackson, Charles, 156
Kaplan, Justin, 16, 19, 273–74
Keats, John, 152, 186
Kertbeny, Karl Maria, 267n.1
Killingsworth, M. Jimmie, 15, 17, 61, 90, 91, 99, 100, 106, 109, 113, 119, 127, 139, 154, 159, 160, 177, 180, 272n.15
Kinnell, Galway, 148, 173
Kristeva, Julia, 4

Lawrence, D. H., 4, 113
Lecture to Young Men on Chastity (Graham), 45
Leverenz, David, 14, 15, 272n.12, 273
Lewis, R. W. B., 145
Lind, Ralph, 161, 288n.55
Lipking, Lawrence, 33
Long Island Democrat, 39
Long Islander, 40
Lovers Complaint, The (Shakespeare), 152

Manly love, 4
Mann, Thomas, 137, 155
Man's words, definition, 20–45
Marlowe, Christopher, 136, 152, 159
Marriage and Parentage (Wright), 111
Martial, 152
Martin, Robert K., 12, 14, 17, 51, 62, 100, 125, 130, 141, 157, 158, 160, 165, 185, 195, 200, 216, 222, 223, 225, 271n.11, 272n.12, 276, 286n.24, 287n.49, 289nn. 74, 75
Masturbation, 45–46, 65
Maud and Other Poems (Tennyson), 208
Maurice (Forster), 136
Mayne, Xavier (Prime-Stevenson), 136, 277n.4, 288n.57
Melville, Herman, 8, 56, 93, 136, 152, 216–22, 227, 229, 233, 258

Miller, E. H., 14, 119, 129–30, 140, 146, 189, 191, 275, 287n.49, 289n.74
Miller, James, 125
Miller, J. Hillis, 3
Moon, Michael, 17, 29, 56, 65, 83, 99, 180, 280n.19, 281n.11, 286n.42

New World, 53
New York Criterion, 14

Omoo (Melville), 216, 291n.31

Paederasty (Bentham), 278n.18
Perry, Biss, 12, 13
Phaedrus (Plato), 206–7
Pierre (Melville), 93
Plato, 138, 141, 258, 262
Poe, Edgar, 45
Poems of the Orient (Taylor), 222–27
Problem in Greek Ethics, A (Symonds), 278n.18
Problem in Modern Ethics, A (Symonds), 278n.18

Raffalovitch, Marc-Andre, 292n.38
Redburn (Melville), 56
Reynolds, David S., 13, 271n.9, 273
Rich, Adrienne, 282n.33
Richter, Jean Paul, 33
Rivers, W. C., 16
Roe, Charles, 37, 40
Rubin, Gayle, 258

Saale, S. S., 156
Saslow, James, 269n.12
Sassoon, Siegfried, 278n.18
Schyberg, Frederick, 17, 153
Sedgwick, Eve Kosofsky, 5, 15, 18, 22, 23, 124, 258, 267n.1, 270n.6, 293nn. 45, 59
Sexual Inversion (Ellis), 34, 159, 229–60
Shakespeare, 152, 206, 208, 258

Showalter, Elaine, 23, 110

Smith-Rosenberg, Carroll, 10, 11, 15, 23, 45, 52, 53, 78, 90, 280n.16

Snyder, John, 14

Sodomy, 28

Some Friends of Walt Whitman (Carpenter), 17

"Sonnet on a Picture by Tuke" (Kains-Jackson), 156

South Sea Idyls (Stoddard), 216

Stafford, Harry, 159, 242

Stanton, Elizabeth Cady, 89, 92, 101, 141

Stevenson, Edward Prime, 136. *See* Mayne, Xavier

Stockinger, Jacob, 2

Stoddard, Charles Warren, 216

Stoddard, Richard Henry, 223

Studies in the Psychology of Sex (Ellis), 229

"Swimming Hole, The" (Eakins), 156

Symonds, John Addington, 11, 16, 138, 159, 229–61, 273, 278n.18

Symposium, 76, 203, 206, 290n.2

Taylor, Bayard, 50, 95, 136, 152, 216, 218, 222–27, 229, 233, 249, 253, 258, 292nn. 38, 44

Teleny (anon.), 152

Tennyson, Alfred, 208, 258

Theocritus, 225

Thoreau, Henry David, 136, 145, 156, 173, 211–16, 227, 229, 231, 241, 249, 250, 253

Traubel, Horace, 7, 12, 40, 43, 65, 101, 132

Trumbach, Randolph, 269n.12

Tuveson, Ernest Lee, 139

Two Years Before the Mast (Dana), 220

Typee (Melville), 136, 152, 216–22, 239

Ulrichs, Karl Heinrich, 288n.57

Van Doren, Mark, 14, 273

Vaughan, Fred, 159

Vergil, 136

Vidal, Gore, 105, 137, 156, 289n.68

Views of Society and Manners in America (Frances Wright), 89

Walt Whitman, A Life (Kaplan), 274

Walt Whitman: The Making of a Poet (Zweig), 274

Walt Whitman Among the French (Erkilla), 273

Walt Whitman's Poetry (E. H. Miller), 275

White, William, 12, 15, 271n.8, 273

Whitejacket (Melville), 56

Whitman, Andrew (brother), 37

Whitman, Eddy (brother), 37

Whitman, George (brother), 37, 40

Whitman, Hannah (sister), 37

Whitman, Jeff (brother), 37

Whitman, Louisa (mother), 37

Whitman, Mary (sister), 37

Whitman: The Political Poet (Erkilla), 17

Whitman, Walt: accusations of homosexuality against, 11–14, 272n.21; anti-feminism in texts of, 89–114; authorial voice of, 7, 269n.16; creation of texts, 6–9; dehomosexualization of texts, 54; early poetry of, 36–46; feminism of, 23; fictional character of, 23; fiction of, 46–62; homosexual identity of, 2, 10–19, 272n.21; homosexual texts of, 1–36, 272n.21; notebooks of, 63–114; on "masculine" language, 20–35; picture of, 7; presence in texts of, 6–9, 269n.16; racism of, 286n.37;

women in texts of, 89–114
—Editions: *Leaves of Grass*
(1855), 2, 3, 10, 11, 20, 33,
34, 68, 90–91, 115–204; Preface, 98, 103, 128, 133, 204;
reviews of, 205, 261; *Leaves of
Grass* (1856), 20, 227; *Leaves
of Grass* (1860), 4, 228
—Early Poems, 36–46: "Ambition," 43, 235; "Angel of
Tears, The," 92; "Death of
the Nature-Lover," 43; "Each
Has his Grief," 42, 89;
"Fame's Vanity," 43; "House
of Friends, The," 45; "Leg-
end of Life and Love, A," 50,
68, 93; "Love That is Hereaf-
ter, The," 41; "Mississippi at
Midnight, The," 44; "Our
Future Lot," 39; "Play
Ground, The," 44;
"Resurgemus," 45; "Young
Grimes," 40
—Fiction, 46–62: "Bervance,"
49, 92; "Child and The Pro-
fligate, The," 53; "Child's
Champion, The," 6, 16, 53–
66, 70, 99, 138, 207, 210,
224, 228, 243; "Death in The
Schoolroom," 38, 47–48;
"Dumb Kate," 93; *Franklin
Evans,* 38, 50, 92; "Half-
Breed, A Tale of the Western
Frontier, The," 51, 93; "Last
Loyalist, The," 47, 92; "Last
of the Sacred Army, The,"
92; "Little Sleighers, The,"
93; "Madman, The," 50;
"My Boys and Girls," 47, 93;
"Reuben's Last Wish," 48,
92; "Shirval: A Tale of Jeru-
salem," 93; "Tomb Blos-
soms, The," 92; "Wild
Frank's Return," 48
—Notebooks, 63–114: "After
All is Said and Done" 144;

"Albot Wilson," 68–80, 87,
96, 134; "Analogy, The," 97,
123, 166; "Bridalnight," 107,
154; *Day Books and Notebooks,*
20–35; "Distinctness Every
Syllable," 67; "Do you Know
What Music Does," 97;
"Lect[ure] To Women," 94–
95, 132; "Loveblows. Loveblossoms," 83–87; "Memo-
rials," 96–97, 102, 107, 135;
"Of a Summer Evening," 64,
66–67; "Poem Incarnating
the Mind," 96, 141; "Song of
the Wrestler," 72; "Sweet
Flag," 83–87, 108, 118, 120,
125, 132, 134–35, 137, 149,
170, 172, 182; "This Singular
Young Man," 64–66, 235;
"Truly What is Common-
est," 160; "Understand That
You can Have," 100; "You
Know How the One," 80–83
—Poetic Works: "Bunch
Poem," 60; "By Blue
Ontario's Shore," 364; *Calamus* Poems, 1, 6, 24, 32, 38,
39, 41, 42, 44, 45, 70, 95,
115, 134, 136, 138, 144, 164,
173, 178, 189–90, 195–96,
210, 228, 241; "Calamus 1,"
137, 138, 151, 184, 250–51,
253, 258; "Calamus 2," 58,
63, 200, 224, 226, 228; "Calamus 4," 15, 27; "Calamus
5," 119; "Calamus 6," 30,
195; "Calamus 8," 278n.18;
"Calamus 10," 212, 216;
"Calamus 11," 60, 164, 207,
220, 223; "Calamus 14," 58;
"Calamus 16," 254; "Cal-
amus 17," 43; "Calamus 18,"
50; "Calamus 20," 224; "Calamus 22," 42; "Calamus 23,"
278n.18; "Calamus 26," 105,
219; "Calamus 28," 213, 250;

"Calamus 29," 164, 189, 242; "Calamus 36," 58, 200, 215, 261; "Calamus 38," 34, 215; "Calamus 41," 254; "Calamus 42," 20, 223; "Calamus 43," 189; "Calamus 44," 215; "Drum-Taps" poems, 32, 43, 45, 190; "Hours Continuing Long" ("Calamus 9"), 42; "I Saw in Louisiana a Live-Oak Growing" ("Calamus 20"), 42; "I Sing the Body Electric," 50, 101–14, 123, 152, 155, 157, 221, 226, 240, 259; "Live-Oak IX" ("Calamus 34"), 252; "Live-Oak XII" ("Calamus 42"), 223; "Native Moments," 121, 138; "Once I Pass'd through a Populous City," 75; "Pictures," 87, 98; "Poem of Joys," 234; "Poem of Procreation," 89–90; "Proto-leaf," 23, 228, 235, 264; "Sleepers, The," 60, 105, 107, 115, 117–29, 133, 154, 155, 169, 183, 234, 240; "Song of Myself," 129–204; sections 1–5, 129–49; sections 6–19, 150–65; sections 20–29, 165–84; sections 30–37, 184–93; sections 38–43, 193–97; sections 44–52, 4, 6, 7, 9, 19, 26, 28, 30, 43, 44, 47, 48, 56, 57, 61, 80, 82, 86, 94, 95, 98, 103, 107–9, 115, 128, 129, 197–204, 216, 221, 224, 225, 229, 230, 254, 262, 282n.36;

"Song of the Open Road," 13, 30, 227, 263, 264; "Spontaneous Me," 60, 123, 161, 217; "Starting From Paumanok," 35, 70; "These I Singing in Spring" ("Calamus 2"), 194; "Vigil Strange I Kept on the Field One Night," 15; "We Two Boys Clinging Together" ("Calamus 26"), 52; "When I Heard At The Close of Day" ("Calamus 11"), 52; "Woman Waits for Me, A," 259

—Prose Works: *An American Primer,* 25; "Backward Glance O'er Travel'd Roads, A," 19; *Democratic Vistas,* 13, 24, 27; "Primer of Words, The," 25; *Specimen Days,* 119, 132, 233–34; "Sun-Down Papers," 7, 41, 91

Whitman, Walter, Sr. (father), 81

Whitman's Poetry of the Body (Killingsworth), 15

Wilde, Oscar, 68, 159, 206, 285n.19

Winthrop, Theodore, 95, 185

"World Well Lost IV, The" (Raffalovitch), 161

Wright, Frances, 88–89

Wright, H. C., 109, 111

Young Man's Guide, The (Alcott), 45–46

Zweig, Paul, 172, 274